Baltic Souls

Jan Brokken is a writer of fiction, travel, and literary nonfiction. He gained international fame with *The Rainbird*, *The Blind Passengers*, *My Little Madness*, *In the House of the Poet*, *The Reprisal*, *The Cossack Garden*, and *Baltic Souls*, and his books have been translated into twenty languages. Brokken has won numerous prizes for his work, including the Golden Quill 2023 (a prize for his significant contribution to Dutch writing and culture) and the Bruce Chatwin Lifetime Achievement Award 2023 for his entire oeuvre. Four of his books have been made into movies; two are in production.

David Doherty is based in Amsterdam, where he has been working as a Dutch-to-English translator for over twenty years. His literary work includes novels by award-winning authors Marente de Moor, Peter Terrin, and Alfred Birney. *Summer Brother*, his translation of Jaap Robben's *Zomervacht*, won the 2021 Vondel Translation Prize and was longlisted for the 2021 International Booker Prize.

Baltic Souls

Remarkable Life Stories from
Estonia, Latvia, and Lithuania

Jan Brokken

translated by David Doherty

SCRIBE

Melbourne | London | Minneapolis

Scribe Publications
18–20 Edward St, Brunswick, Victoria 3056, Australia
2 John St, Clerkenwell, London, WC1N 2ES, United Kingdom
3754 Pleasant Ave, Suite 100, Minneapolis, Minnesota 55409, USA

First published in Dutch as *Baltische zielen* by
Uitgeverij Atlas Contact in 2010
Published in English by Scribe 2024

Typeset in Bembo by the publishers

Printed and bound in the UK by CPI Group (UK) Ltd, Croydon CR0 4YY

Scribe is committed to the sustainable use of natural resources and the use of paper
products made responsibly from those resources.

978 1 922585 83 7 (Australian edition)
978 1 957363 94 3 (US edition)
978 1 761385 88 9 (ebook)

Catalogue records for this book are available from the
National Library of Australia.

The publisher gratefully acknowledges the support of the
Dutch Foundation for Literature.

**N ederlands
letterenfonds
dutch foundation
for literature**

scribepublications.com.au
scribepublications.co.uk
scribepublications.com

Anyway, a son doesn't sit in judgement on his father.

Ivan Turgenev, *Fathers and Sons*

Curiously enough, much is said these days about history. But unless we can relate it to ourselves personally, history will always be more or less an abstraction, and its content the clash of impersonal forces and ideas. Although generalisations are necessary to order its vast, chaotic material, they kill the individual detail that tends to stray from the schema.

Czesław Miłosz, *Native Realm*

It is a curse to live in interesting times.

Ancient Chinese proverb quoted by Hannah Arendt

Contents

1

Pride

Estonia, September 1999
At sea, the sailors were fine company. From Dollard Bay to Øresund, I savoured the tales of storms and disasters that spiced up my mealtimes with Huig, Melle, and Aristides. But with dry land beneath our feet, they suddenly struck me as rough customers.

We had originally been bound for Oulu, one of Finland's northernmost ports, shipping salt on the outward leg and wood pulp on the way back. I was along as a passenger. But before we could even set sail, the charterer rejected our cargo as unfit for use as table salt.

After a day's wait in the port of Emden, the coaster was assigned another destination: Pärnu in Estonia. A country I knew only as one of a trio that we had learned by heart as schoolkids: Estonia, Latvia, Lithuania. It had the ring of a verse reeled off in the classroom, never to be forgotten.

Aristides, the Cabo Verdean cook, had sailed northern routes for Dutch shipping companies as long as he cared to remember and had been to Estonia back when it was still part of the Soviet empire. In those days, police officers were posted at the gangplank and the mooring lines, fore and aft: three strapping Russian women who each demanded a chair and called out, 'Cooky, chow.' Words they had mastered in every language. Aristides made sure the ladies ate their fill. After which they shouted, 'Cooky, fucky.' This was part of their repertoire in every language too.

Four days later, the coast of Courland appeared in the distance. Dunes so white, I mistook them for chalk cliffs. Further east lay a broad, dazzling strip of beach. Due south of the island of Saaremaa, the ship entered the narrows that grant access to the Gulf of Riga. Coniferous forests appeared on the horizon, smouldering in the last of the light.

The captain, wizened and wary, ordered Huig, Melle, and me to keep watch. Huig was convinced the old man was losing the plot; it had been an age since any captain had ordered him to scan the waves with the naked eye. Ever since the discovery of radio waves, the man at the helm has had radar to rely on. But on consulting the nautical chart, the captain had seen so many exclamation marks that he lost his nerve. The Gulf of Riga was awash with mines, set out by the Soviets when the Gulf was still off limits to foreign ships. Mines that had never been swept.

I leaned over the rail with Huig.

'Like we've a hope in hell of spotting mines at twilight,' he muttered, rollie wagging at the corner of his mouth.

'What does a mine look like?' I asked.

'Round and black.'

The water was one black expanse. There was another warning on the map: chemical pollution, no swimming. The Russians had left their mark here and no mistake.

The captain had powered down the engines. No vibration, no juddering; we were gliding yacht-like through the water. The smell of land, of pine forests, was on the air. The coast continued to exist as two strips: the light of the beach beneath the dark of the forest. Not a lighthouse in sight, no source of illumination. We seemed to be sailing into a secret world.

Huig had visited Riga some twelve years previously. A time when every foreign ship soon had two Soviet Navy patrol vessels for company. They tracked each ship from less than a mile away, keeping it constantly in their spotlights.

'Up at the rail, you couldn't so much as scratch your arse in case they thought you were pulling a gun. No telling what they might do.'

Since the dissolution of the Soviet Union, the Gulf of Riga has been open to ships of all nationalities. But Huig swore he saw a boat approaching. 'Either that or there's shit in my eye.' Sure enough, a Latvian coastguard patrol vessel emerged from the evening haze.

The Latvians' suspicions had been roused by what our helmsman had relayed over the radio: a ship bound for Estonia with no cargo? But the sight of the *Grachtborg* high in the water was all the reassurance they needed. They signalled that we were okay to proceed.

The Gulf of Riga, as seen from the *Grachtborg*.

The moon had just begun its ascent as the pilot boat turned alongside. Huig and I were done for the night, the pilot's knowledge of local minefields being far superior to ours. Our ship entered the port of Pärnu shortly after midnight and moored at a narrow quay directly opposite the town. We were the only vessel in port.

In the dead of night, I was dragged out of bed by the first mate. The border police wanted to see if my face matched the photo in my passport. I got dressed and headed for the captain's cabin. Three ill-tempered faces stared back at me. The guards had asked the captain for a few cartons of cigarettes and had been given a dressing down instead. 'Tight bastard,' muttered the first mate. 'If it wasn't for his holier-than-thou routine, we could all have stayed in bed.'

One by one, the nine of us had to stand before the border guards. As I was the only passenger on board, most of the questions were reserved for me.

'Why are you hanging around on this ship?'

'I wanted to see the Baltic,' I replied, still half-asleep.

'What's so special about the Baltic?'

'Mariners say it's the most beautiful of all the seas.'

'Can't say we've noticed.'

'The light is special. Soft and warm.'

'The light?' The men looked at each other.

'In autumn, it seems to smoulder.'
'What do you do for a living?'
'I'm a writer.'
'Ah …'
This meant I was crazy, not dangerous.
I detected a hint of scorn in the way they stamped my passport.

The next morning, a Monday, I went ashore. The houses of Pärnu were either girded in scaffolding or sporting a fresh coat of paint: yellow, red, blue, or a smart shade of grey. A whiff of cheerful diligence lingered in the streets. The various neighbourhoods were interspersed with parks, the largest of which led down to the beach. I marvelled at the women I saw — all snub-nosed, with legs up to the rafters.

The houses looked Finnish; the most eye-catching church was Russian Orthodox. The women in the vestibule, there to collect the entrance fee, wore headscarves, woollen cardigans, and thick woollen socks. Farming folk. When I bought three postcards, the eldest fished a little calculator from her cardigan pocket, wielding it as skilfully as a schoolboy would his smartphone.

The spa, right on the beach, transported me to Germany. It had the same air of distinction as the late nineteenth-century hotels of Baden-Baden. Steeped in the glory of days gone by, though they hadn't been gone that long. As late as the 1980s, Soviet bigwigs had still been coming here to revive their flagging spirits, chain-smokers who swore by the fresh air of the Baltic coast.

After strolling around town for hours, I asked a taxi driver to take me for a spin. I left the destination up to him and soon we were heading east, through vast forests. Not a village, not a building in sight.

As we set out, the Estonian said all of two words: 'Welcome' and 'Jakobson'. Forty kilometres later, he turned off the main road and headed up a track. At a water mill, we got out of the car and walked onto an estate. The silence had me wondering if the sky was lined with velvet. Estonia is similar in size to the Netherlands, but home to ten times fewer people. Perhaps that explained why the birds were singing so softly.

The driver rang the bell of a large wooden farmhouse. A young woman opened the door. She led me past rooms that, during the

A house in Pärnu, Estonia.

tsarist era of the mid-nineteenth century, had been home to one Carl Robert Jakobson. From what I could glean, he was a kind of Tolstoy. A gentleman farmer who owned eighty-five hectares of land and was determined to ease the plight of poor farmers. A polemicist who called for sweeping land reforms, in addition to being a writer, philosopher, politician, nationalist, and founder of the first daily newspaper in the Estonian language. He died of typhoid fever in 1882, aged forty-one.

He had three daughters, none of whom married, and they left the house to the state. A photo of the sisters — sourpusses all — conjured up visions of snow-covered fields and the sound of water bubbling in the samovar. The boredom was palpable. A father with an unkempt beard and an iron will, understanding eyes that peered through small round spectacles at the misery of the world, and his three daughters who were shunned by every man — a novel in the making. Yet Andra, my guide, spoke of Jakobson as if he were her own father.

'He led us into the future. Estonia's independence began with him.'

I returned to the ship, which by this time was being loaded with peat. Back in the Netherlands, the peat would be mixed with earth to

Carl Robert Jakobson's farmhouse.

make potting soil. The first mate reckoned it would take at least a full day for 3,500 tonnes of the stuff to tumble off the end of the narrow conveyor belt and into the ship's holds.

At our meal that evening, the seamen asked me for an appraisal of 'the Estonian women'. I told them about Jakobson's farmhouse. They glazed over as if I were a schoolteacher intent on boring the pants off them.

The next morning, the captain gave Huig, Melle, and Aristides the day off. It was their first shore leave in months. Huig suggested visiting 'that bloke's house'.

'Jakobson?'

Yep, on condition that I came along.

There I sat, wedged on the back seat between the broad, sagging bodies of bosun and seaman. Huig gazed out at the landscape as if it were a calm sea, while up front Aristides tried to explain the phrase 'cooky, fucky' to the taxi driver. I could feel my cheeks burning.

At the farmhouse, I contemplated taking a solitary walk in the woods. Andra's skirt was much shorter than it had been the day before, and to make matters worse, she showed no inclination to tailor the tone, length, and detail of her explanations to any audience.

The crew of the *Grachtborg* on the high seas.
On the right: Huig, in conversation with the author.

In deadly earnest, she steered the sailors through Jakobson's quarters. They waddled behind her on their crooked legs, Aristides unable to resist the occasional leery glance at her bare thighs. Huig and Melle, meanwhile, appeared to hang on her every word.

The tour of the library was followed by an exposition in the barn, surrounded by agricultural machinery that Jakobson himself had designed. Huig was already rolling himself a ciggie, but when Andra inquired whether we were still interested in viewing the water mill's drive mechanism, he slid it resolutely behind his ear. No innuendos, no nudges or winks, though I was still convinced all three were play-acting.

On the drive back to the coast, I sat there waiting for the banter to begin. The sailors stared out of the window, overcome by the silence of the woods and the soft autumn light. After a while, Huig said, 'You know what impressed me about that girl? The pride she has in her country.' In his accent, it sounded more like 'prayed'. 'That's something we've lost, don't you reckon?' The rest of us nodded, and I thought: no, not so much lost as jettisoned, when we decided our nation was a job well done and there was nothing meaningful left to achieve.

'Ready for a drink?' I asked, as the harbour came into view. The previous evening, I had passed a bar just as a group of young women were going in, slits in their skirts revealing a flash of thigh.

'You know,' Melle said, 'I can't say as I'm fussed.' I looked into his booze-fogged eyes. 'I'd like to hold onto this peace a bit longer,' he said.

Huig was hungry. We chose a decent restaurant, tables neatly decked. Inside, everything was blue, from the wooden ceiling and satin wallpaper to the velvet armchairs and the table linen. Before we tucked into our cod, the owner, his wife, both their sons, and their daughter came and sat with us at the table. Language was no barrier; Huig was happy to sketch the mechanism of the water mill on a napkin.

One year later, I received a postcard. From Tallinn. 'Great city. But not a patch on Jakobson. That place was ours alone, know what I mean? All the best to you, Mr Wordsmith. Seaman's greetings, Huig.'

The forests of Estonia lingered in my memory, a twilight zone between east and west, between northern and central Europe. To say nothing of the church towers of Pärnu, the Lutheran spikes alongside the onion domes of Russian Orthodoxy. The wooden country houses with so much history hidden behind their shutters and skirting boards.

That one, chance trip to the small port on the Gulf of Riga had sparked my curiosity about a corner of Europe that was thick with shadows. I wanted to know more about those countries, about the Baltic calm and the Baltic pride that Huig had homed in on so unerringly with his seaman's eye.

Pride is a different beast to nationalism, chauvinism, or conceit; pride is the belief in everything that makes you special, distinctive, and unique. Pride is faith in your own language, your own culture, your own ability and originality. The only true response to violence and oppression.

I made four, five, six journeys to Estonia, Latvia, and Lithuania. I travelled through Courland and to the region once known as East Prussia, now part of Russia's Kaliningrad territory. In Riga, Daugavpils, Vilnius, Tallinn, Tartu, Rakvere, and so many other towns and cities, I hoped to find some remnant of what had once been the strength and vitality of my own little patch of Europe. In the knowledge that travel, reading, and listening offer the shortest and most telling detours to yourself.

2

The Bookseller of Riga

JĀNIS ROZE AND SONS

Latvia, January 2007

Political assassination and unrequited love paved the way for the founding of Jānis Roze's bookshop in Riga. Nothing too traumatic, given Latvia's fateful place in the world.

The Latvia in which Jānis grew up was part of tsarist Russia. He was eighteen when Nicholas II of Russia ascended to the throne. Jānis never knew his biological father; his mother was unmarried when she gave birth to him in 1878. The boy had his stepfather, a poor man from the Latvian countryside, to thank for his surname.

At a tender age, Jānis entered the service of printer, publisher, and bookseller Jānis Ozols in Cēsis, a provincial town 100 kilometres east of Riga. Ozols taught him the trade. Jānis became an apprentice type-setter, printer, binder, book-cover designer, bookseller, and skilled in the craft of engraving copper stamps.

Cēsis, surrounded by wooded slopes, attracted writers and poets, not least because they knew Riga was only a train ride away when the days grew too short, too cold, too dark, and too lonely. Ozols published their novels, poems, and essays in beautifully crafted volumes infused with the spirit of Art Nouveau. He ran a flourishing business with thirty people on the payroll. The most promising of whom, in his eyes, was Jānis Roze. Shortly after the turn of the century, he promoted his young protégé to manager.

Jānis would undoubtedly have lived out his days in Cēsis, had it not been for the first mass uprising against the tsar. On Sunday 9 January 1905, a crowd of 150,000 men and women marched on the Winter Palace in St Petersburg. They were led by Georgy Gapon, a priest intent on presenting the tsar with a humble and loyal petition asking for justice and protection for the poor and the oppressed. He had no hope of speaking to the tsar himself, who was ensconced in his palace

Jānis Roze at home in Riga, 1932.

at Tsarskoye Selo, playing dominoes. As the marchers approached the palace, the cavalry opened fire. Forty people were killed, hundreds more injured. Father Gapon was trampled underfoot. His last words were, 'There is no more God, there is no tsar.' That same afternoon, massacres took place throughout the city, and 9 January would go down in history as Bloody Sunday.

Four days later, the uprising reached Riga. On 13 January, 15,000 workers demonstrated against the ruthlessness of the tsarist regime. The Russian governor-general ordered his soldiers to fire on the crowd: seventy were killed and 200 wounded. From Riga, the rebellion spread to all corners of the territory. Tenant farmers attacked Baltic German landowners and set fire to their houses; workers stormed the prisons. With hindsight, as Lenin later observed, this was where the revolution of 1917 began.

Nicholas II dispatched a punitive expeditionary force to Latvia. It took Russian troops a full year to restore order. An estimated 1,000 peasants, workers, and intellectuals sympathetic to the uprising lost their lives in summary executions. Printer and publisher Jānis Ozols was among them.

Under his own name, Ozols had written and published a diatribe against archaic oppression and degrading poverty in the Latvian countryside. He was arrested one evening and executed early the next morning. Jānis Roze faced the same fate. As manager of Ozols's print shop, he too was arrested; he too was sentenced to death. But the following morning, he was released without explanation. He would later tell his children that, locked in that prison cell in 1905, every hair on his head turned grey overnight. He was twenty-seven at the time.

Silver-haired though he was, Jānis still cut a dash. He was tall, broad-shouldered, and few women were indifferent to his air of quiet assurance and the engaging glint that rarely faded from his clear, grey-blue eyes. Six or seven years went by, years in which Jānis succeeded in keeping Ozols's firm up and running. At which point, Ozols's widow asked him to marry her.

Judging from a photo, she was a fine figure of a woman. But, as another picture proves, Emma Henriete Silarāja was more beautiful still. She was younger too, ten years younger than Jānis. It was Emma he fell for and Emma he married. And it was with her that he moved to Riga to escape the wrath of his former employer's widow.

In 1914, Jānis founded a publishing house of his own, followed in 1918 by a bookshop in a grand building on Krišjāņa Barona iela, a wide shopping street. The building had been completed three years after the turn of the century, and there was a hint of Art Nouveau

Emma Henriete Roze.

about the details. Above the shop, Jānis established the office of his publishing house, and he and Emma moved into the floor above that. He also took ownership of the other floors, and proceeded to rent them out.

It's the end of January 2007. The first snow has fallen at last, and the temperature has finally dipped below minus ten. Sunlight brightens the facades of Riga's newly restored buildings. I take a taxi to Krišjāņa Barona iela, and the driver drops me off outside the bookshop at number 5: Jānis Roze & Sons. A bronze effigy of the founder takes pride of place at the entrance. The cash register is manned by a gruff saleswoman with a mess of blonde hair. I ask to speak to the manager. She asks which firm I represent and calls her boss, who, one floor up, explains to me that Jānis Roze's head office is located elsewhere, at Miera iela 15/3. I hop in another taxi, which stops two kilometres away.

It takes me the best part of twenty minutes to find Jānis Roze's headquarters. Concealed behind blackened flats from the Soviet era, it turns out to be a warehouse. The front door refuses to budge; then I hear someone shout. A large man approaches. He is tall and broad-shouldered, with short silver-grey hair and clear blue eyes: Professor Ainars Roze, Jānis's grandson.

In cheerful English, with a strong Northern European accent, he asks me if I want to take the visitors' route or the book route. Unsure what he's getting at, I plump for the latter. We enter the warehouse, climb a flight of stairs, and head along a steadily shrinking corridor. At first, it's just a matter of keeping our heads down, but soon we have to hunch our shoulders. 'Once you know my family's history,' he explains, 'you'll understand why I've come to appreciate a building with a hidden passageway.' If it hadn't been for an emergency exit, Ainars later reveals, he would never have been born.

Ainars is now sixty years old. He combines his professorship in economics at the University of Latvia with the day-to-day running of Jānis Roze Ltd. In the little office, I meet the firm's other director, Ināra Beļinkaja, an elegant, diminutive figure. I take her to be in her fifties, but she later admits to being born 'in the last year of the war', which in her case is 1944. I will incur her wrath only once, the following afternoon, when I ask her when she's planning to retire. What kind of question is that? She has yet to turn sixty-three!

The office Ainars and Ināra share measures four by three metres. From this cramped space under the skylight, they manage the firm's 200 employees.

'Apologies for the misunderstanding,' Ināra says, nudging her

Ainars Roze in front of the photo wall in his office: 'It keeps me
connected to my forebears.'

glasses higher up her nose — I catch the name Givenchy on the
frame. 'I should have emailed to let you know that our offices are no
longer on Barona iela.'

'Yes,' Ainars interrupts, 'it's the same with bookshops the world
over. There are years when sales are sky high and years when you
struggle to flog a single calendar. We moved to this humble abode
in 2001, when business was ...' His hand traces a curve that plunges
sharply below the desk.

'A disaster,' Ināra sighs. 'We used to have that wonderful old office
above the shop: leather sofas galore, photographs and reproductions
of book covers on the walls. "The museum," we called it. Once a
month, the managers of our fifteen branches in Riga and the wider
provinces would gather at the museum. Looking around at the luxury,
they couldn't bring themselves to tell us sales were plummeting. This
was before our computer system was up and running. Now I can track
our sales on a daily basis. Back then, we relied on verbal reports from
our store managers. And they still had the old Soviet mentality: insist

that all is well, and never mention a problem unless there's no hiding
it. By the time we cottoned on, it was too late, and a major recession
had set in: 2001 was a tough year for every business in Latvia. The
investments made after independence had yet to pay off, and interest
rates shot up. Many a company went under. For us, it was touch and
go. Moving here allowed us to rent out the office on Barona iela. We
managed to get our costs right down. And we started automating like
billy-o.'

'We were almost toast,' Ainars chuckles. 'It's only now that I can
laugh about it. We survived by the skin of our teeth, but over the
past year, business has been ...' His hand climbs above the desk and
hovers high above the computer screen. 'Last year, turnover was up
30 per cent, to seven million lats. Things are almost going too well
nowadays. Our staff think so too. Their salaries were far too low. This
year we plan to raise them by 25 per cent.'

'Why don't we start at the beginning?' I hear myself say, two hours
later. Hours during which Ainars and Ināra have been chatting away
incessantly, often at the same time, shoving books, spreadsheets, annual
reports, and prospectuses under my nose, or answering the phone
while keeping one eye on the computer screen — when they are
not firing off urgent emails, that is, or dashing out of the room only
to return in the company of a department manager, a secretary, or a
young man called Jānis, who turns out to be Ainars's son, named after
the founder of the business. It's all go in the tiny office, controlled
pandemonium. To cap it all, Ainars goes in search of a pot of fresh
coffee and returns with wodges of chocolate cake. The warmth of
the north: a guest is someone to be spoiled, especially when they hail
from Western Europe.

The beginning! Ainars steers me towards five small photographs
on the wall. 'Here ...' He points to a clone of Friedrich Nietzsche:
the same unruly quiff, the same shaggy brush of a moustache, the
same brooding stare. 'Meet Jānis Ozols. The man who taught my
grandfather the trade. The man whose ideals he shared. Until 1905.
After his night in the house of death, my grandfather became more
cautious. That's him there.' Ainars's finger rests on the face of a man
who could be his twin. 'He had a quiet nature. No one ever heard
him shout or so much as raise his voice, not even when he had to take

the decision that makes every bookseller miserable and dismiss a sales assistant who was caught with their hand in the till. This is Emma Henriete, my grandmother — elegance personified. You'd never know she was a country girl. By faith, she was Russian Orthodox. My grandfather was Lutheran, like most Latvians, but religion carried little weight in my family. I couldn't even tell you which church they were married in. And here you have the children: Ilmārs, the eldest son; Jānis, my father; and Aina, the late arrival — she was nine years younger than my father.'

In the course of twenty years, Jānis Roze published 820 books, which sold a total of two million copies. In addition to buying published works, people came to his shops to purchase notebooks, cahiers, binders, pens, and other items of stationery. Jānis Roze was both a literary and an academic bookseller, with a shop in the old town centre, behind the university. Roze also had a branch at Riga Central Station. His was an upmarket bookshop, yet he had no qualms about selling calendars and almanacs. Latvians loved their almanacs. Those produced by Roze told readers when and in which villages annual fairs were held, ensuring that farmers and country folk were also among his customers.

The firm rode the wave of history. After the October Revolution of 1917, Lenin granted independence to the Baltic countries, assuming that they would join the Soviet Union. After all, the Latvians had outshone all other peoples in their support for the Bolsheviks. Lenin distrusted his own countrymen and, immediately before and after the Revolution, surrounded himself with Latvian bodyguards. The fact that the Latvian appetite for revolt stemmed from an ardent nationalism had eluded the great strategist, convinced as he was that the proletariat of all countries would unite. Latvians had fallen over one another in their eagerness to support revolution, but once freed from the tsarist yoke, they went their own way. In 1918, the Republic of Latvia was declared; after seven centuries of rule by German Crusaders, Prussian feudal lords, and Swedish, Polish, Lithuanian, and Russian nobles, the country had at last gained its independence. The mood of burgeoning national consciousness bordered on euphoria. Latvians began speaking Latvian and reading Latvian. The presses of Jānis Roze's publishing house were working round the clock. The

Seated, left to right: Jānis, Aina, and Emma Roze. Standing, left to right: Ilmārs and Jānis Jr.

bookshop sold stacks of folk legends and stacks of plays. Latvians adore the theatre, and for the first time they had the opportunity to stage plays in their own language.

Economically, Latvia prospered like never before. The old

merchant port of Riga grew into a centre of industry and high-end manufacturing. The Minox camera was a Latvian invention, and serial production of electric trains and trams began on the banks of the Daugava. To revitalise technology and trade, an educated class was needed: in 1935, Latvia boasted 30.4 university students for every 10,000 inhabitants, compared with 20.8 in France and 16 in Britain. And those students bought their books from Jānis Roze.

Global recession eventually gnawed away at company profits in Latvia, but compared to conditions in Western Europe, the 1930s were not exactly crisis years. Politically, however, the young republic did change. In 1934, Kārlis Ulmanis staged a coup and seized power. From then on, the country was ruled by an authoritarian regime: political parties were banned and newspapers censored. But after his ordeal in 1905, Jānis Roze had no desire to burn his fingers on political tracts or pamphlets, instead publishing lyrical poetry, novels, and stories steeped in folklore. His showpiece was the literary journal *Piesaule*, published monthly for seven years. Jānis Roze had become a fervent advocate of Latvian literature and scholarship; the authorities left him alone.

A modest man, Jānis steered clear of worldly circles and centres of wealth and power; he rarely showed his face outside his bookshop. Yet he did enjoy the company of writers, publishing academics, and graphic designers, and frequently invited them to his home in Riga or his summer retreat on the coast. Publishing was and would remain his passion, and he liked to keep his artistic hand in by regularly designing a book cover in the Art Nouveau style that to him was second nature, replete with curlicues and floral motifs.

His daughter, Aina, maintained that her father's retiring nature had robbed the world of an artist. For his part, Jānis set little store by his own artistic gifts, concentrating instead on building a collection of paintings. He was a perfectionist with an eye for quality; his books were printed on the finest, thickest paper, while he scribbled his notes on the back of used envelopes.

In 1939, everything changed, though at first no one was any the wiser. The non-aggression pact signed by Molotov and von Ribbentrop on 23 August 1939 included a secret protocol that carved up Europe into vast spheres of influence: the Baltic countries were to be subsumed

Jānis (front left) and Emma (second row right) celebrating St John's Day
with the bookshop staff in 1931. Jānis is crowned with the traditional
floral garland.

into the Soviet Union. This devil's pact between Stalin and Hitler
had far-reaching consequences: in October 1939, the Soviet People's
Commissar for State Security issued a secret order regarding the
'deportation procedure of anti-Soviet elements in Lithuania, Latvia,
and Estonia'. The number of Latvians to be deported was 100,000,
their names printed on lists that an army of Moscow bureaucrats had
spent all winter compiling.

On 17 June 1940, Soviet forces invaded Latvia, and on 5 August
1940, Latvia became the fourteenth republic in the Union of Soviet
Socialist Republics. That same summer, the booksellers of Riga
mourned their first fatality. From 1920 onwards, Jānis Roze's main
rival had been Valters & Rapa. Their business, a fine three-storey
bookshop, was directly opposite Riga's opera house, a plum spot on a
grand square that gave access to the historic city centre. Arturs Valters
was an older businessman, Jānis Rapa a young, idealistic poet. The

A street plan of Riga published and designed in Art Nouveau
style by Jānis Roze.

day Latvia lost its independence, Rapa threw himself out of a window and was found dead on the square in front of the bookshop. In one hand, he clutched a scrap of paper. On entering the boardroom, his employees noticed that the map of north-east Europe on the wall had been damaged. Before he jumped to his death, Rapa had torn Latvia from the map.

The year that followed Russia's occupation of Latvia passed without incident, but there was an unsettling edge to the calm, the kind that precedes a crushing offensive. Even so, the people of Riga had no idea what awaited them. Jānis Roze was among those who thought things might not be so bad: Latvia had no choice but to become part of Russia again, as it had been in previous centuries, only this time with the advantage that the Red Army offered protection against another aggressor: Nazi Germany.

In the small hours of 14 June 1941, Jānis and Emma's apartment was raided. Fourteen-year-old Aina was not at home. The summer holidays had just begun, and she had been at a party. The festivities had gone on well into the evening, and she had slept over at a friend's house in a Riga suburb.

Jānis and Emma were so confident there was nothing to worry about that they gave the agents the address where Aina was staying. The agents worked for the Cheka, the Soviet secret police, a forerunner to the KGB. The Rozes would be imprisoned, that much was clear, but at least they would be together, as a family. It can't have been long before Jānis began to doubt the wisdom of that decision. When Aina was brought home, she found her father sitting in an armchair, head bowed.

It is also possible that Jānis had consulted his wife and made a gut-wrenching decision: that by not resisting and perhaps even cooperating with Aina's arrest, he hoped to save his other children.

Grandson Ainars shows me a book. It is a book of names, each one the name of a deportee. Many such books have been published in Latvia in recent years, to offer bereaved families a memorial in the absence of a grave or a final resting place. The book in Ainars's hands comes with a street map of Riga, a copy of the one used by the Cheka in 1941. The addresses where Latvians were arrested are coloured red. As the map shows, not a single street, not a single block of houses, was passed over.

It was the Cheka's systematic approach that let part of the Roze family off the hook. Jānis and Emma lived with Aina on the second floor. On the third floor, eldest son Ilmārs had taken up residence with his wife and their son, born in 1940. The fourth floor was occupied by Jānis Jr and his young bride. But the form issued to the Cheka agents only said *Roze family, Barona iela 3/5.*

The brothers on the third and fourth floors heard the commotion downstairs as Jānis and Emma were arrested. Through a slit in the curtains, they also saw Aina being led in by two men in black suits. Aina, with her blonde plaits; the little sister they had always called 'Princess'. The third- and fourth-floor residents kept quiet until the agents had left and everyday life resumed in Riga. Then they took the emergency exit.

After a long exodus, Ilmārs reached London with his wife and child. He would never see Latvia again; he died in 1963. Jānis Jr and his wife crossed Latvia, Lithuania, and Poland, finally reaching Germany in an open goods wagon. There they were arrested and sent back to Latvia. But luck was on their side. Jānis's wife, who spoke fluent Russian, was a doctor, and the Soviet army was in dire need of medical personnel. The couple were assigned to a garrison in northeast Latvia, where Ivars came into the world in 1945, followed by Ainars in 1946.

For Jānis, Emma, and Aina, the parting of the ways came at Torņakalns railway station, three kilometres west of Riga, just across the river. From the same platform, Jānis was ordered onto a goods wagon to the right, Emma and Aina to the left, onto a wagon that bore the number nineteen. In the rush, Emma managed to slip her husband a bag. An hour later, she discovered it had been the wrong one and contained only bed linen and women's underwear.

On a bitterly cold morning, I take the train to Torņakalns. An old goods wagon stands outside the little wooden station. In memory of 14 June 1941, I suspect, when 15,424 Latvians were deported. Or 25 March 1949, when the improbable number of 43,231 people were crammed into goods wagons in a single night. It is not hard to understand why the Soviets selected Torņakalns as their point of departure: the playing fields around the station provided ample space to assemble the deportees. The Latvians were driven to the grassy

Jānis with his daughter, Aina, in the 1930s.

fields in trucks before being led to the trains in rows of two.

I pull open the door of the freight wagon. It is a short, tall model, built to run on Russian broad-gauge tracks. I walk the length: seven paces. Wooden bunks, one above the other. Impossible to survive for long, crammed in with forty or fifty other people.

The trains left for Siberia on 14 June 1941, in sweltering heat. The first stretch was slow going: some 3,000 wagons had to leave Latvia on this, the only track. Most did not reach the border until 17 June. Between the border and Moscow, progress was faster but beyond the capital, the wagons were shunted onto sidings every few kilometres. At the stations, the Latvians learned the reason: on 22 June 1941, Nazi Germany had launched a surprise attack on the Soviet Union, and troops had to be rushed to Moscow to protect the capital from the rapid German advance. These military transports were given priority. The trains carrying the Latvians could be stranded for up to three days at a time. In the end, the deportation took three weeks.

People were not allowed out of the wagons and had to squat above a hole sawn in the corner to relieve themselves. There was no way to wash the corner clean. Only two buckets of water per wagon were supplied each day: less than a quarter of a litre of drinking water per person. Once a day, the deportees were given a bowl of soup from kitchens hastily set up at the stations.

These details come from *With Dance Shoes in Siberian Snows* by Sandra Kalniete, whose mother, father, maternal grandparents, and paternal grandfather were deported in 1941. Sandra was born in Siberia in 1952; in 1991, she would become the first minister for foreign affairs of the newly independent state of Latvia. Sandra's grandmother and mother endured the same conditions as Emma and Aina Roze.

Aina drew pictures on the journey. Amid the haste of their departure, she had managed to grab a notebook, a nice one from her father's shop, decorated with a rose flanked by the letters *J* and *R*. She drew her mother, who was so warm that she had removed her stockings and her dress, and was wearing only a slip and a petticoat. She drew women and children piled on top of each other on the bare planks. She drew a baby in a cradle, one of the few infants to survive deportation and the lack of water for days on end.

All we know of Jānis's journey is an exchange he had with one of his fellow deportees. Through a crack between the planks of the wagon, he pointed out the sky, the beautiful clouds on the horizon.

Eventually, he reached Solikamsk in Siberia.

Jānis had been arrested as a class enemy: a man at the helm of a capitalist enterprise that employed sixty workers. Any Latvian who owned a piece of land, a house, a shop, or a business was deported, along with his entire family. It was an act of ethnic cleansing with a class component: the better-off had to pay.

Hardly surprising then, that when the Nazis marched into Riga on 1 July 1941, they were welcomed as liberators and showered with flowers. But once again, the Latvians were in for a shock. Cleverly capitalising on this short-lived outpouring of sympathy, Hitler was quick to set up the Latvian Legion, which he placed under the command of the Waffen-SS. Membership was anything but voluntary: boys and men were rounded up during raids and forced to join. In this campaign, some 100,000 Latvians were sent into battle against the Red Army as cannon fodder, a fate that befell several of Jānis Roze's employees.

Almost all of Riga's 80,000 Jewish residents died at the Rumbula killing site and in the camp at Salaspils. Again, a number of Jānis Roze's employees were among them. Half a million Latvians lost their lives during World War II, a third of the country's population. They came to be replaced by Russians and Ukrainians.

In 1997, Ainars obtained a copy of the verdict handed down to his grandfather. The records in Moscow show that a Soviet tribunal sentenced him to five years' hard labour on 13 February 1943. By then, Jānis had been dead for eight months. He perished from starvation and exhaustion in May 1942.

Emma and Aina also endured hunger, such terrible hunger that it often kept Aina awake at night. In a village a few kilometres from the penal colony, she was given a handful of books by Pushkin, Turgenev, and Lermontov in exchange for slippers she had knitted herself. After eighteen months in Siberia, she spoke enough Russian to memorise dozens of Pushkin's poems, reciting them in whispers at night until she no longer felt the gnawing in her stomach or the biting cold. Emma and Aina spent six years in the Ust'-Port penal camp, 350 kilometres above the Arctic Circle, where the Yenisey river flows into the Arctic Ocean.

Aina, like all Latvian minors, was released in 1947 and sent back to her homeland. At the time, she was seriously ill with tuberculosis.

Emma, like all the Latvian mothers, had to stay behind in Siberia. After six years of forced labour in the fields together, often in temperatures close to minus forty, having endured hunger, exhaustion, disease, frostbite, violence, and sexual harassment, having scratched and shaved each other's heads to alleviate the suffering of one of Siberia's worst torments — fleas — mothers and daughters were forced to part.

Emma refused. With no papers and next to no money, she embarked on a journey that was virtually tantamount to suicide: she escaped from the Siberian penal colony to travel with her daughter, who was coughing blood and unable to manage on her own. It took mother and daughter the best part of four weeks to make the journey to Latvia, travelling part of the way by road. Of all the inspectors, stationmasters, policemen, soldiers, and truck drivers they encountered, none had the gall to ask Emma for proof that she was entitled to travel freely. For thousands of kilometres, from the Yenisey to Riga, the determined glint of defiance in her eyes saved her from arrest.

On returning to Latvia, she had to lay low. To go into hiding with her son Jānis or any other member of her family would have been too big a risk. Instead, she found refuge with a friend of her husband's, a philosophy professor, who employed her as his housekeeper.

Ainars tells his story calmly: 'One day — I must have been about four years old — I was introduced to a lady who had come to visit us. I was told she was an aunt, a distant relation who had returned from abroad. I can't say I was bothered one way or the other. Every last detail was kept from me; my parents were terrified I might speak out of turn. Stalin died in 1953, and even then, Emma didn't dare report to the authorities. In 1956, Nikita Khrushchev denounced Stalinist repression at the 20th Congress of the Communist Party — and still Emma held back. At last, in 1958, she reported to Riga City Hall. I was twelve years old when she took me in her arms and said, "Ainars, be kind to me, won't you. I am your grandmother."'

Ināra Beļinkaja started work at Bookshop Number Three, formerly Jānis Roze's bookshop, in 1962. She was eighteen at the time, still just a girl. She came from a middle-class family and would certainly have been entitled to a scholarship, had it not been for the fact that she wanted to study English. There was no changing her mind, and so her only option was to study in the evening and work during the day. It was a friend who suggested that she work in a bookshop. 'There's practically nothing to do, and you can spend all day reading.' It wasn't quite that simple.

For starters, a communist bookseller was expected to know the title of every chapter and section of Lenin's collected works off by heart — all thirty-four volumes — so that if someone came into the shop and asked what Lenin had written on the efficiency of steam boilers in 1916, she could pluck the correct volume from the shelf without hesitation. She also had to know her way around the works of Marx and Engels. In other words, she was permitted to read and browse during her working hours, but not in the books that were close to her heart.

Moreover, working at a communist bookshop involved masses of administration, especially at a time of purges. Bookshop Number Three did not sell much in the way of literature; compelling novels such as Pasternak's *Doctor Zhivago* were banned. The shop mostly sold textbooks, and the professors who wrote them inevitably fell out of favour sooner or later. When this occurred, a bookshop employee was expected to respond in two stages. Following an order from the authorities, they had to tear out the title page and remove the book from the shelf. It then disappeared into the basement. Sometimes a professor would be rehabilitated, in which case their work ascended to the shop again. Any book that had languished in the basement for a year had to be destroyed. Inãra would drill holes through the cover and the pages within, before depositing the book in a bin.

The nice thing about the job was that interesting, open-minded characters were drawn to a bookshop like moths to a flame: students, writers, poets, philosophers, right-minded journalists from radio and TV, freedom-loving professors and teachers. Some were dissidents. Every other day, they visited the bookshop. If a book was banned, booksellers had two days to remove it from the shelves. Inãra would then tip-off whoever she thought might be most interested in reading it. For instance, she was able to make sure that Solzhenitsyn's last published novel in the Soviet Union found its way into the hands of a young writer. Not all booksellers dared to take such risks, but Inãra did. When she studied English in the evening, her radio was tuned to Radio Free Europe or the Voice of America.

Ināra Beļinkaja behind the counter of Bookstore Number Three in
Riga, in the summer of 1964.

Books were cheaper than newspapers in the Soviet Union. You
could pick up three or four for next to nothing. Works in translation
led to the most wonderful discoveries: Jean-Paul Sartre, Simone de
Beauvoir ... It was no accident that Riga's first group of dissidents
were known as the French Group. Inspired by the existentialists, the
group included writers, poets, and philosophers, as well as painters

and photographers. Most were regular visitors to Bookshop Number Three, until they were arrested and exiled. They ended up in Siberia too.

Booksellers earned a pittance, and so, in 1970, Ināra took a job on the side — as a revue dancer. As soon as she shut up shop, she would dash off to catch the bus that took the performers out to the coastal resort of Bulduri on the Gulf of Riga, a journey of about twenty kilometres. At a hotel called Pearl of the Sea, they did two shows a night: the first at ten, the second at midnight. There were queues around the block. In those days, entertainment was thin on the ground. Besides, restaurants were few and far between, and supper was served during the show.

Ināra had always loved to dance — the tango and the rumba in particular — but the revue performances were a racier affair altogether. The dancers had to decide down to fractions of a centimetre how short their skirts and how deep their décolletés could be. Communist bigwigs were not exactly known for their frivolity, yet among the audiences she recognised more than a smattering of party hardliners. Ultimately, the threat to Ināra's stage career came from a different quarter. When she quit in 1975, it was to appease her jealous husband.

As a dancer, she made three times what she earned at the bookshop. The extra income meant that her daughter, an only child, never wanted for anything. But the schedule was punishing; she was lucky if she got to bed by three in the morning. Even without a jealous spouse, something had to give or she risked jeopardising her career.

From junior sales assistant, Ināra had risen to the position of deputy manager, mastering the finer points of how to run the business along the way. She was entering her fifteenth year at Bookshop Number Three and was the most experienced member of staff by far. So, when a clueless colleague who had been working at the shop all of eighteen months was appointed manager in her stead, Ināra contacted the culture ministry and asked for an explanation. 'Why would we promote you?' the people's commissioner for book distribution asked her. 'After all, your expertise will be lost to us within months when you move abroad.'

'Abroad?'

'Your husband.'

This was the kind of twisted reasoning bureaucrats came up with when they had nothing better to do. Ināra was married to a Russian, a Russian who had come to Latvia after his entire family had disappeared in the late 1940s. A Russian Jew. In the mid-1970s, the Soviet authorities began allowing Russian Jews to emigrate to Israel for the first time. Many, under varying degrees of pressure, exercised that right. There was a veritable exodus going on. But Ināra was not Jewish, and her husband, a set designer, was too busy making the most of the opportunities offered by Riga, a city with a rich operatic and theatrical tradition. Emigrate? The thought had never occurred to them.

'Fine,' Ināra told the commissioner, 'I'll see you in six months.'

'Why might that be?' he asked.

'Oh, by then the bookshop will be on its last legs.'

And sure enough, six months later, she was appointed manager.

In 1981, the bookshop was renamed Amber. Not exactly original — seven out of ten shops in Riga were named after the golden-brown fossilised resin often found along the nearby coastline. Barona iela alone had three Ambers: one that actually sold amber, a women's fashion outlet, and a lingerie boutique. Boxes of dresses were delivered to the bookshop one day, boxes of bras the next. Ināra put up with this for a year or two and then applied for a name change. Did she have a suggestion of her own? Most certainly, she told the people at the culture ministry: 'Roze.'

'Rose, rose,' lamented the people's commissioner for book distribution. 'Why not birch? Or willow?'

His own surname was Latvian for willow.

'Simple,' Ināra replied. 'Unfortunately, we've never had a Willow who published 820 books in Latvian in the course of twenty years. But we did have a Roze. I think the bookshop deserves to bear the name of its founder, Jānis Roze, with his portrait in bronze by the entrance.'

By this time, Gorbachev was installed in the Kremlin and had been preaching perestroika for months. The Soviet Union's new party leaders were allowing more freedom of speech and attempting to trickle a little oil into the rusted workings of the planned economy. But this didn't make them any less keen to dispatch flagrant nationalists to the gulag. Ināra was risking her own skin.

Not that she had acted rashly. Before launching her crusade, she had secured the support of one of the shop's loyal customers: a critical journalist who hosted a popular early-evening chat show on Latvian television. He devoted several items to Ināra's efforts to have the name changed.

In her fifteen years at the bookshop, Ināra had immersed herself in the firm's history. In the basement and the first-floor office, she had found photographs and correspondence with authors, along with books published in 1923, 1928, 1935, 1940. She had learned the names of Roze's children. She had come to love Jānis like a writer who had long since passed, someone whose hand she had never shaken, yet who she had come to know through his books and letters. The journalist understood the depth of this connection and lent her his support.

Ināra had always assumed that every member of the Roze family had either perished in Siberia or fled to the West. One day, a frail sparrow of a woman came into the bookshop. Having heard about Ināra's campaign on TV, she enquired about the plans to change the name of the business. Ināra was wary. A few days earlier, she had received a visit from another woman asking questions, a well-known TV journalist. Something about the woman's manner had rubbed Ināra up the wrong way: her questions had been too precise, her clothes too chic. She wore too much perfume; sometimes you could smell the KGB on someone's skin. Ināra's instinct served her well; when the state archives were opened up in the 1990s, documents revealed that the journalist had been on the KGB payroll for years. But this frail sparrow was different. 'Jānis Roze, Jānis Roze,' she kept asking. 'Why Jānis Roze?' To stamp out the first stirrings of sympathy, Ināra erupted, 'For heaven's sake, what's it to you?' At which, the woman looked at her sweetly, intensely, and said in her thin voice, 'I am Aina. Jānis Roze's daughter.'

Aina put Ināra in touch with Ainars. Both were there on the front row when a bronze portrait of Jānis Roze was unveiled in the shop's facade on 30 November 1988. There were more than a handful of dissidents in attendance. This was the first open demonstration of independence by the people of Latvia, and Barona iela was teeming. Trams could not get through; traffic came to a standstill. As the covering was carefully pulled away, a tentative applause began. And then, from one second to the next, it burst into an ovation.

Ināra shows me the photographs, points out the people who were there. Standing in the front row, in a long fur coat, is the culture minister, jaws clamped tight, as if swallowing something bitter. Beside her, the people's commissioner for book distribution: another long fur coat, another furrowed brow. Beside him stands a senior party official whose displeasure seems to have turned into a craving for vodka. In the eyes of these apparatchiks, all hell had broken loose, but they remained firm in their conviction that revenge would taste sweet once Gorbachev had been strung up ...

Far more impressive was the gathering inside, in what was still the publisher's office at the time, 'the museum'. Professor Vladislavs Urtāns took the floor. 'I was with Jānis Roze in Siberia, in the forced labour camp at Solikamsk. I am the last person who saw him alive.' Everyone was silent as he recounted Jānis's final moments. 'We hadn't eaten in days. We were exhausted. We did not even have the strength to bury the dead. The frozen ground was too hard, our limbs too weak. The dead were thrown outside. The next day, they were gone, eaten by the wolves. And so it went with Jānis Roze.'

Aina cried, but not because of what had been said. How sad it was, she whispered, that her mother had not lived to see this day. Emma had died three years earlier, aged ninety-seven.

Ainars's father did not live to see it either. He had died just months earlier, after taking one last look at the only painting he had salvaged from his childhood home. A Latvian landscape, a scene he had gazed on half his life.

Nine months after the unveiling, Estonians, Latvians, and Lithuanians formed a human chain that stretched over 650 kilometres from Tallinn to Vilnius. On 23 August 1989, some two million inhabitants of the Baltic states joined hands to mark the fiftieth anniversary of the pact between Stalin and Hitler that had stripped them of their autonomy. Through this vast, non-violent demonstration, they ultimately forced the Kremlin to accept their independence.

It is almost a duty to ask any Estonian, Latvian, or Lithuanian where they were on 23 August 1989.

'In front of the Freedom Monument in Riga,' Ināra replies, 'with all the bookshop staff. After 30 November on Barona iela, we were given a place of honour.'

Latvija, Rīga, foto: H.Burmeistars, skenēja: I.Beišāns.
Latvia, Riga, photo: H.Burmeistars.

23 August 1989. A section of the human chain or Baltic Way, in front
of the Freedom Monument in Riga. Photographs of this scene are still
displayed in Riga's shop windows.

'In front of the university,' Ainars recalls, 'with all the professors
and students. The strange thing was that hardly anyone dared look
straight ahead. Almost all the lecturers and students stood with their
head bowed, so they would be harder to identify in photographs after
the fact. No one was confident things would end well.'

Ainars had been warned repeatedly by his father in the months
before his death. Jānis Jr never recovered from the events of 1941.
Once he had been destined to take over his father's bookshop, alongside his elder brother, Ilmārs, who was to run the publishing house.
But after the war, he had been capable of little more than taking
pictures at parties, weddings, and open days of the Young Communist
League. Not that he was a photographer; these were snapshots at
best. Jānis became a bitter man, with a deep distrust of human nature.
'They're only luring you into the open,' he said of his son's participation in meetings and demonstrations. 'They give you a taste of
freedom, see who takes the bait, then put you on a list and ship you
off to Siberia.'

Ainars is willing to admit that, even on 23 August, he had no conception that two and a half months later the Berlin Wall would come

down. Or that Gorbachev the reformer would be ousted from the Kremlin and communism would be carried off like an autumn leaf on a breath of wind. Let alone that the Latvians would be singing their own national anthem before the year was out. Surely an empire as vast as the Soviet Union could not be brought to its knees so quickly? His boldest prediction had been that, if he took good care of himself and hung on till the ripe old age of ninety, he might just live to see the swan song of Marxism-Leninism.

For Inãra Beļinkaja, it was no different. She still has trouble grasping the chain of events. It all happened so fast, so improbably fast, that a miracle seemed to be unfolding on the streets and on her television screen. A miracle about which, even now — every morning, afternoon, and evening — she still says softly: it can't be true, it can't be true ...

After independence, which was officially ratified on 6 September 1991, Inãra took another dive into the bookshop's archives. She knew nothing about free-market economics, nothing about sales techniques. She found translations of English books from 1933 and 1935, and she lays them out in front of me now. *Practical Hints on Running a Shop. Advertising and Advertisements.* And, not to be forgotten, *Successful Selling.* Hopelessly outdated, but a place to start. 'It was like learning a new language, having to become a different person.'

She subscribed to Western trade magazines, pored over the announcements, attended the Frankfurt Book Fair, the London Book Fair. She registered for conferences and conventions, the first of which was a gathering of young booksellers in Amsterdam. For all her experience, she still *was* a young bookseller, in terms of running an independent bookstore at least. She was starting a new life.

Ainars had the advantage of being an economist, one reason why Inãra was keen to involve him in the firm. The other being that he was a Roze, of course. The family would soon be due state recompense for the nationalisation and confiscation of their home and belongings. And since the fledgling state barely had two cents to rub together, the property on Barona iela was bound to be returned to the family. Inãra could see it was best to forge an alliance from the off.

Ainars may have been an economist, but he had completed his education in Moscow. To obtain a doctorate in Soviet times, you had to study in Leningrad, Moscow, Novgorod, or Kyiv. Ainars had spent the final three years of his studies absorbing the finer points of the planned economy. Any schooling in free-market economics had been geared towards exposing the enemy's wiles and weaknesses. Those lectures were also the best attended. While this meant that Ainars was not exactly a blank slate where capitalism was concerned, one of the first things he did after independence was book a flight to the United States. For seven months, he attended lectures at a business school.

Back in Riga, he and Ināra embarked on a high-stakes game of poker. He was indeed granted ownership of the office and apartments on Barona iela, but not the bookshop. As compensation for the shop, he was given government bonds. He transferred the office, flats, and bonds to the private company Jānis Roze Ltd. Meanwhile, Ināra continued to run Jānis Roze — the bookshop — as a state-owned enterprise. After all, it was anyone's guess whether the Latvian economy would abandon state control altogether as it opened up to capitalism.

For five years, the building on Barona iela was home to two Jānis Rozes. For five years, Ainars and Ināra bet on two horses. The firms were not merged until 1996.

What benefits did this bring?

'Let me show you,' Ainars says.

The following afternoon, we drive out of Riga, past dreary Soviet-era housing estates and nineteenth-century wooden houses, unpainted and dilapidated. We take the road to the airport in the four-wheel drive shared by Ainars and Ināra: he drives it during the week; she takes it at weekends. Twenty kilometres outside the city, we stop at a huge shopping centre surrounded by birch forests.

Since independence, many such places have sprung up, palaces of glass and steel financed by foreign investors, often German or, in this case, Finnish. The New East houses fifty shops spread over three floors. I find myself amid marble and fountains, on boulevard-style walkways lined with snow-white tiles. Tall trees sprout from wooden tubs. A restaurant on every floor, a tearoom on every corner, stores on either side: Prada, Zara, Gucci, Villeroy & Boch, Esprit, Chanel. In this consumer paradise, Jānis Roze has a branch that covers 1,000 square metres: a bookstore, open seven days a week from 10.00 am to 10.00 pm, except on New Year's Day and Latvia's midsummer holiday, the feast of St John, on 24 June.

At the entrance, bestsellers are displayed against the mahogany wall. Topping the charts is *Putina Krievija*, or *Putin's War*, by murdered journalist Anna Politkovskaya. Number two is the latest book by Paulu Koelju, published by Jānis Roze. Latvian publishers adapt the author's name, so I don't immediately recognise it as Paulo Coelho. At number five, a nonfiction book causing a stir: the tale of a Latvian mayor turned multimillionaire after giving the go-ahead for a gas pipeline running north through his municipality. This is a thoroughly modern bookshop, in other words.

Looking around, it strikes me that there are almost as many Russian as Latvian titles on sale. Officially, half of Riga's population is Latvian. The other half consists of — to use the Latvian term — 'Russian-speaking residents'. Many of these residents have to date been denied Latvian citizenship and are not permitted to vote in elections. To be a Latvian citizen, you must have been born in Latvia before 1940 or to parents who meet that requirement.

Ainars reckons the proportion of Russian-speaking residents in Riga is much higher: two out of three. In this light, it was far from inconvenient that, in the years immediately after independence, Jānis Roze remained a state-run bookshop with good contacts in Moscow: after all, a sizeable chunk of the stock still had to come from Russia.

This construction also saved the firm from more sinister repercussions. When the shopping centre had been completed and Jānis Roze moved into its 1,000 square metres of prime retail space, Ainars received a visit from a Russian-speaking resident of Riga. He introduced himself as a businessman. There was nothing out-of-the-ordinary in that; Ainars explains that Latvia owes much of its impressive economic growth to Russian entrepreneurship. Latvians, like Swedes and Finns, tend towards caution in their business dealings. Russians, on the other hand, are more likely to go for broke. Always in for a game of Russian roulette.

The Russian in question complimented Ainars on his new enterprise, a retail outlet that was sure to attract many customers. Of course, this also meant that its owner needed protection. To make sure the windows remained intact, for example. Not to mention the risk of fire. And, of course, Mr Roze wouldn't want to worry about his own safety, to say nothing of the safety of Mrs Roze. And didn't he have a son? You could never be too careful when it came to your sole male heir.

Ainars told the man he was absolutely right. Only, he was talking to the wrong person. 'You see, Jānis Roze is still a state-owned company. I recommend that you contact the Ministry of Culture. They are the ones in charge of the bookshop.'

The twists and turns of their two-company approach enabled them to shrug off extortion. 'But,' he says, pointing to Prada, Gucci, Esprit, and the rest, 'the neighbours were not so lucky.'

We say our farewells over dinner at Sarkans, which is Latvian for 'red'. The restaurant lives up to its name — from its sofas, chairs, and tables to its napkins, glasses, plates, and even the waitresses' skirts. Ināra lets me in on the gallows humour behind the colour scheme. The restaurant rubs shoulders with a sturdy building on the corner, wider than it is tall: the former KGB headquarters. It has been vacant for years; no business has had the heart to move into the colossus on Stabu iela. For decades, there was a saying in Riga: 'Watch out you don't end up on Stabu iela.' A Latvian artist has turned the building's entrance into a monument: a rusty steel wall that bears the inscription: '1940–1990. Anyone brought in through this door never came out again.'

'What you said to us yesterday is true,' Ināra begins, once the wine — red, naturally — has smoothed away the last of her reserve. 'We have lived two lives. The first one was grim.'

And the second?

'Travel! London. New York. Chicago. We were locked up for so long. Travel is freedom, freedom is travel. Next month, we're off to an international booksellers' conference in Cape Town.'

Ainars has brought another photo with him. He places it carefully between the red napkins. An idyllic photo of a pre-war St John's Day: Jānis, Emma, and the children, surrounded by the writers, professors, and musicians they'd befriended. Three of the men are wearing a traditional garland of flowers.

Out of nowhere, Ainars starts talking about his son.

This third-generation Jānis was thirteen when Latvia gained its independence. After high school, he wanted to study abroad and opted for a business school in Sweden. Jānis III saw a bright future for himself in IT. Returning to Latvia, he founded his own company. The bookshop? Too dull for words. But his startup never quite got off the ground, and for the past four years, he has been working at Jānis Roze Ltd.

Ainars and Ināra at Sarkans, the restaurant next door to the former KGB headquarters.

One evening, he asked to speak to his father. He had something important to tell to him.

'I don't want to hurt your feelings,' he said. 'But this is the real thing. Can I ask her over to meet you?'

Of course. Jānis called her on his mobile.

She arrived an hour later. A beautiful young woman. Blonde. Russian.

'She didn't speak a word of Latvian,' Ainars recalls.

That night, Ainars couldn't sleep. He paced from one end of his study to the other. Snippets of conversations he'd had with his grandmother came to mind. Lines from the 'Letter to My Father' his Aunt Aina had written for the collection *We Sang through the Tears: tales of survival in Siberia*. 'Dear Father, in my mind I have written to you every day since we were separated at Torņakalns Station on 14 June 1941, when, amid a crowd of desperate people, we looked on in bewilderment as you were led away to another train.' Ainars saw before him the broken woman that his Aunt Aina had remained all her life. Thirty-five she had been when she graduated from the

Art Academy of Latvia — thirty-five! Siberia had robbed her of her youth, poisoned her entire life.

Russians had killed his grandfather and reduced his father to a bumbling onlooker, a loser who took snapshots of other people's parties. And now his son had come home with a Russian.

Night became day. From his flat in Jūrmala, Ainars watched the sun rise over the still waters of the Gulf of Riga. He went into the kitchen and started making breakfast. The smell of eggs sizzling in the pan brought Jānis III down from his room.

'I know you must be sad,' he said, visibly affected. 'I kept it from you as long as I could.'

And Ainars said, 'There was no need. It's your life, your future. This is your choice, and I have made my peace with it.'

3

The Architect's Shoes

EISENSTEIN VS EISENSTEIN

Latvia, February 2007
Every morning, I walk the streets of Riga — the same streets. And gazing up at the apartment buildings that line Strēlnieku iela, Alberta iela, and Elizabetes iela, I see them with different eyes. They look new to me each morning because I spend my evenings reading about the architect who designed so many of them: Mikhail Eisenstein, the father of legendary filmmaker Sergei Eisenstein.

That history has given us two illustrious Eisensteins is a fact I have only been aware of since my arrival in Riga. Not that this is especially obtuse of me: even Sergei's first biographer, Marie Seton, had no idea what position his father held, referring to him rather vaguely as 'a successful engineer' in her 1952 account of his celebrated son's life story.

Eisenstein Sr was to Riga what Otto Wagner was to Vienna, the architect who gave the city on the Daugava the allure of Austria's capital. He designed nineteen residential complexes, sixteen of them in Jugendstil, the German counterpart to Art Nouveau. Standing in the same district of Riga, some side by side, these are buildings with facades of white, green, sky blue, amber yellow, or garnet red. They feature columns and pilasters, goddesses and mermaids, sphinxes and dragons. Their balconies have wrought-iron railings; there are flower motifs in their stained-glass windows. They are buildings that make an overwhelming first impression due to their abundance of detail.

All of these apartment buildings follow the same pattern. The kitchens and stairs for the domestic staff are located at the back; the reception halls and living rooms, designed to prompt the admiration of visitors, are at the front. This layout alone gave Eisenstein Jr enough reason to despise his father.

A detail from the facade of Strēlnieku iela 4a,
designed by Mikhail Eisenstein and built in 1905.

Mikhail Eisenstein in Riga.

Mikhail Osipovich Eisenstein settled in Riga in 1897. He had been born thirty years earlier and 400 kilometres away, in St Petersburg, to parents of German and Jewish origin. His career got off to a brilliant start. The ink on his diploma from the Institute of Civil Engineers in St Petersburg had barely dried when he won his first commission, and soon after moving to Riga, he landed a senior position at the Ministry of the Interior. Mikhail took up residence in a grand home at Krišjāņa Valdemāra iela 6, a desirable location to this day. Back then, it bore the name of Tsar Nicholas.

Mikhail was able to afford this townhouse thanks to his wife's fortune. Yulia Ivanovna Konyetskaya's fabulously wealthy parents owned Konyetsky, one of Russia's largest inland shipping companies. Based in St Petersburg, it operated a fleet of barges that plied the waterways between the Baltic, the Neva, and the Volga.

Though Yulia could hardly be described as a classic beauty — she had the jawline of a boxer and a disproportionately high forehead — she was far from unattractive, and the low-cut gowns she wore at parties and receptions showed her sculpted shoulders and ample bosom to great effect. She took equal pride in accentuating her wasp waist and flaunting the silver, crystal, Chinese porcelain, and furniture in her home. The entire interior, complete with paintings and piano, had been part of her trousseau.

Mikhail was a product of the lower middle classes. With a bank clerk for a father, he had every patron saint in Russia to thank for the chance to graduate as a civil engineer. He was equally indebted to Tsar Alexander II, who had removed all legal impediments to Jews pursuing university studies or entering public service. Nevertheless, Mikhail Eisenstein left his Jewish background behind him. To curry favour with Yulia's family, he converted to the Russian Orthodox faith. He wasn't out to marry a rich woman so much as a Russian woman, whose family name would command the respect of the bourgeoisie.

Once in Riga, Mikhail became a fervent supporter of Nicholas II. The first major honour to come his way, the Alexander III Medal, had been conferred on the occasion of Nicholas's accession to the throne. From that moment on, he threw in his lot with the tsar.

His wife, who had no noble title, shared her husband's devotion to the Romanovs and anything associated with the 300-year-old Russian

Yulia Konyetskaya in 1905.

royal house. Revelling in distinction was the one thing the couple had in common. It was a marriage of attrition from the start.

Mikhail became a workaholic. Combining his government position with his own architectural firm, he designed the sixteen residential buildings that would change the face of Riga in less than a decade.

'When I think of him,' son Sergei noted, 'it is blueprints, templates, set squares, protractors, and drawing pens that I see.'

It was Riga's 1901 crafts-and-industries exhibition that gave Mikhail Eisenstein wings, a World's Fair in miniature to mark the burgeoning port and commercial city's 700th anniversary. A central theme was the Jugendstil and Art Nouveau movements that had found their way north from Vienna, Paris, and Brussels. For Eisenstein, this new, exuberant approach to architecture came as a revelation. The first building he designed after the exhibition, the residential complex at Elizabetes iela 33, is so pearly white, fresh, and expressive that it could have been plucked from the heart of a Mediterranean city. The six buildings that followed are all located on Alberta iela, each one surpassing its predecessor in eccentricity. This has nothing to do with their proportions: the buildings Eisenstein designed after 1901 are all the same width, height, and depth. The contrast lies in their colour and ornamentation. Eisenstein favoured shades that stood out like theatrical costumes, not so much bright as striking. A blue so blue that it transports you to the islands of Greece. A green that reminds you of olives. Eisenstein's hues are more southern than northern. He gave Riga a warm glow.

He was not alone in taking inspiration from this new style. A third of all houses built in Riga between 1901 and 1911 bear the hall-mark of Jugendstil. It's the abundance of ornamentation that makes Eisenstein's designs leap out at you.

The early twentieth century was a period of dramatic expansion; the population of Riga doubled within fifteen years. After Moscow and St Petersburg, it became the third city of tsarist Russia. Newcomers flocked from the provincial towns of Germany and Russia, and many of them were Jewish. In 1905, Riga was home to 90,000 Jews out of a population of 700,000. The city enjoyed a reputation for tolerance that was comparable to Amsterdam.

Most of the Jugendstil architects were of Jewish origin. They had surnames such as Mandelstam (an uncle of Riga-born poet Osip Mandelstam), Aschenkampff, Scheel, Medlinger, Seiberlich, Friesendorff, Bockslaff, and Lindberg. And Eisenstein, of course, who designed the most outlandish buildings of all.

Riga's development was not an isolated phenomenon. The period 1890–1910 was something of a golden age for Central and Eastern

Europe. This economic and cultural boom changed the face of Riga, Budapest, Oradea, Breslau (now Wrocław in Poland), and Berlin within two decades. Entire districts were built in the flamboyant spirit of Jugendstil: Kaiserwald (now Mežaparks) in Riga, Rosenhügel (now Rózsadomb) and Stadtwäldchen (now Városliget) in Budapest, Grunewald in Berlin. All of these districts later fell into disrepair. Both the communist authorities and the National Socialists loathed Jugendstil: too bourgeois and decadent for communist sensibilities, too effeminate and fussy for the Nazis.

Under Soviet rule, Riga's lavishly decorative architecture went uncared for and was left to rot. Doors and windows were wilfully neglected. The woodwork was denied even a lick of paint; no crack was plastered over. Soviet bureaucrats wantonly allowed past splendour to deteriorate. To hasten their decline, houses in these districts were mainly allocated to poor tenants with large families.

Restoration began shortly after Latvia's independence and, at the time of writing, around half of the buildings have been saved. A recovery operation on this scale calls for craftsmanship and very deep pockets. It will take some time for the atmosphere of the 1910s to return to the entire district, and for Riga to regain its bygone reputation as the second city of Jugendstil after Vienna. For now, at least the blue-and-white facade at Strēlnieku iela 4 has been restored to its former glory. Eisenstein designed the building, with its castle-like contours, in 1905. Commissioned by the Mitusov Private School, it was the only one of his buildings to serve a public function. Since 1995, it has been home to Riga's branch of the Stockholm School of Economics.

Sergei Mikhailovich Eisenstein had no respect whatsoever for his father's work. To his schoolmates, he dismissed his old man as 'a cake maker' and urged them to go and take a gander at 'all that whipped cream' stuck to the facades of the buildings his father had designed.

Born in 1898, Sergei remained an only child. If his memoirs are to be believed, he devoted the first fifteen years of his life almost exclusively to laying bare his father's faults. In Sergei's eyes, the man did not possess a single virtue. But it was his self-importance that rankled most. Mikhail Eisenstein insisted on acting the gentleman, at all times.

To Sergei, it would always remain a mystery why his mother put up with his father for twenty years. In size and stature, to say nothing

Stunning: the blue-and-white building at Strēlnieku iela 4a.

of his facial features, Eisenstein Sr could have stepped straight from the pages of a children's book. He was the bumptious oaf with whom illustrators have a field day: fat, balding, and pompous, with round cheeks, huge whiskers, and dozy, watery eyes. To make matters worse, since being appointed head of the Department of Roads and Railways for the region of Livonia, he paraded around in a uniform with a cap that was far too small, even wearing it on family trips to the forests outside Riga. A kind of brass-band uniform, in which he was all too happy to be photographed.

Yet friends, colleagues, and clients typified him as a bright, jovial, and talkative fellow with an exceptional sense of humour and prone to irrepressible flights of fancy. When he entered a room, people may have sniggered at his appearance, but they were soon laughing at his jokes and usually ended up hanging on his every word. He spun his yarns with the ease of a commercial traveller and succeeded in securing one assignment after another.

Mikhail may have been a snob and a member of the nouveau riche, but he was nobody's fool. In addition to Russian, his mother tongue, he spoke fluent German, French, and English. His bookcase contained the collected works of Gogol, Tolstoy, Zola, Dumas, and Hugo, along with a whole range of historical and cultural-historical

The Eisensteins with little Sergei in 1900.

works. Mikhail was an admirer of Napoleon Bonaparte and read stacks of biographies about his hero.

There was even a cultural component to the jokes that Mikhail made at his own expense. Whenever *Die Fledermaus* by Johann Strauss was performed in Riga, he would invite his friends and colleagues, sit in the front row, and sing along with the chorus at the top of his voice: 'Eisenstein has gone to jail, gone to jail, gone to jail.'

At other times, Mikhail took himself extremely seriously, or so his son maintained. No letters, diaries, or notes written by Mikhail himself have survived. Even his business correspondence was lost. His reputation has been posthumously defined by the ill-tempered viper who observed his every move at close quarters. When it came to his son, Mikhail had it anything but easy.

According to Sergei, Papa devoted much of his energy to keeping up appearances as an upstanding member of the bourgeoisie. Above all, no one in Riga could be permitted to think that money was in short supply. 'Father had forty pairs of patent leather shoes,' his dear son wrote in his memoirs. 'He did not acknowledge any other sort. And he had a huge collection of them "for every occasion". He even listed them in a register, with any distinguishing feature indicated: "new", "old", "a scratch". From time to time, he held an inspection and roll call.' To maintain order, Eisenstein Sr tasked his valet with administering the shoe register and classifying the footwear according to function: ballroom dancing, riding, and numerous other uses. He even designed a special cabinet to house his collection.

Yulia and Mikhail squandered much of their fortune on hosting dinners, balls, and parties, to which they invited Riga's elite: the Baltic German landed gentry, who spent most of the year in the city, Russian aristocrats, the governor-general, and the highest-ranking officials in the tsarist regime. Sergei characterised his father as a 'staunch representative and admirer of the Russian bureaucratic class'. Mikhail collected honours like other people collected paintings: the Imperial Order of Saint Anna, 3rd class; the Imperial Order of Saint Anna, 2nd class; the Imperial Order of Saint Stanislaus, 3rd class; the Imperial Order of Saint Stanislaus, 2nd class.

The tsarist regime kept its public servants in line with such decorations. The Order of Saint Stanislaus, 2nd or 1st class, conferred a noble title on the holder and merited an entry in the *Government Gazette*, a publication pored over by every official as a measure of where they stood on the ladder that eventually gave access to the elevated realms of aristocracy. The system explains why so many Russian novels are teeming with aristocrats: beaver away obediently at your desk and you too could end up a count, provided that you resist even the slightest urge to institute change or renewal. No system of governance was as conservative as the tsar's; it despised innovation in all its guises.

In the summer months, the Eisensteins relocated their dinners, balls, and receptions to their residence on the coast. A railway line ran from Riga to Jūrmala, which literally means 'by the sea'. With Riga a mere thirty minutes away, father could simply carry on working. From June to September, all of Riga's businessmen, judges, lawyers, publishers, and architects became commuters.

Jūrmala is a ribbon of villages and hamlets that winds through the dunes and the pine and spruce forests on the Gulf of Riga. Turn your back on the sea and the elongated form of Lake Babīte stretches out before you. All this water means that the area is bathed in light. To this day, the wooden villas stand dreaming at the side of sandy roads.

The most well-to-do of all the coastal villages was Majori, and of all the houses in Majori, Mikhail and Yulia's was the grandest. Even by the seaside, the couple liked to show off. When they were not playing tennis — the most modern, Anglophile, and upper-class pastime of the day — the Eisensteins could be found riding their horses through the woods. The governess, who travelled with them for the summer, was an Englishwoman. She taught Sergei to write verse in English. His first ever poem contained only a single spelling mistake.

At school and at play, Sergei spoke German; although Riga was a city under Russian rule, its German roots ran deep. Before he went to school, he also spoke fluent French. Classmate Erwin Mednis described him as 'always very sociable and invariably good-natured, and there can be no doubt at all that intellectually he was extremely gifted ... physically he was slightly built and rather frail. There was something rather feminine about his appearance, so that he often looked more like a girl than a boy.'

According to another classmate, Maxim Shtraukh, who went on to become a prominent actor, Eisenstein Sr was too busy working to pay any attention to his only son. Sergei's autobiography tells a different story. Whenever a circus came to Riga, Mikhail would take his son to the big top in the park. Mikhail loved to see the riders performing breakneck tricks on horseback — or 'high-class equestrianship' as he liked to call it — while Sergei was mad about the clowns.

Mikhail also took his son to the theatre; the plays could be German or Russian — both were well-represented in Riga. By the age of

Sergei Eisenstein in Riga.

thirteen, Sergei had seen so many operas — Tchaikovsky, Borodin, Suppé, Bizet, Glinka, and, of course, Strauss — that he wrote his own libretto for a comic opera, drawing cartoons to illustrate the scenes.

In Riga, the Eisensteins did not skip a single opera or theatre production. Yulia and Mikhail sat through the entire cycle of Wagner's *Der Ring des Nibelungen* in 1902 and 1903, and took Sergei along to the final performance.

Music had a calming effect on Mikhail. Coming home after a long day's work, he would sit down at the piano and play Schumann or Brahms. If he was in high spirits, he might bang out a Strauss polka. Much to the disdain of his son, as evidenced by the comic Sergei drew as an adolescent entitled 'A Day in the Life of a Bourgeois Family'. A day that culminates in a marital spat.

For no matter how distinguished, cultural, varied, and extravagant the Eisensteins' life was, Sergei's mother was bored senseless by what felt to her like an interminable winter in a remote, stifling provincial town. Longing for yet more distinction, yet more excitement, Yulia began an affair with General Bartel, the father of Sergei's close friend Alyosha. Fearing the scandal would jeopardise his position as a prominent architect and pillar of society, Mikhail bombarded her with bitter recriminations. Young Sergei spent many a night in bed listening to their blazing rows.

In 1905, Yulia returned to St Petersburg for several months. After the events of 13 January, when the tsarist army opened fire on 15,000 demonstrating workers in Riga, the unrest in the Latvian provinces simmered on. Yulia cited the uncertain political situation in Riga as the reason for returning to the city of her birth, but in all likelihood, she had already made up her mind to divorce Mikhail and regain her independence. In any case, she bought a spacious flat in the heart of the city.

Yulia had taken her son with her, and at the age of seven, Sergei proceeded to fall madly in love with his mother. Her every kiss, her every tender gesture, enchanted him. But this blissful attachment ended abruptly when Yulia sent him back to his father without so much as an explanation. She escorted her young son to the train, reserved a compartment for him, and instructed the conductor to lock the door. For the entire nine-hour journey, Sergei was trapped.

Back in Riga, to use his own words, Sergei became a David Copperfield–like figure. Bitterly, he listed what this entailed:
'Frail,
rather thin,
small,
defenceless
and very shy.'
Mikhail and Yulia separated for good in 1909, though many

more years passed before their divorce was sanctioned by the civic authorities and the church. After a brief spell in Paris, Yulia settled permanently in St Petersburg, and had the tableware and all the furniture shipped from Latvia to her new home. In the house in Riga, only three beds remained (for Mikhail, Sergei, and the housekeeper), along with the piano and the piano stool. For weeks on end, Mikhail took out his anger and misery on the keys — piercing onslaughts that echoed through empty rooms.

The breakdown of his parents' marriage dealt Sergei a blow from which he would never recover. It scarred him for life. 'It poisoned the atmosphere of the family,' he wrote in his memoirs, 'the cult of family principles, the joy of the family hearth, in my ideas and my feelings'.

The look in Sergei's eyes turned spiteful. There was something unsettling about his whole appearance: short arms, stumpy legs, a lean body, and his disproportionately large head with its wide, high forehead. In his younger years, the tangle of blond curls had given his face something intriguing and engaging, but as he grew older, his expression became more intense, some might say demonic.

Sergei was eleven years old when his mother left and he was entrusted to the care of his Latvian nanny Maria Elksne and Russian housekeeper Tyotya (Aunt) Pasha. He witnessed his father's mental decline, yet continued to blame him for the divorce and absolve his mother entirely: Yulia had been worn down by Mikhail's vanity and petty ambitions. She was the victim, he the pompous ass.

Meanwhile, Mikhail was doing what he could to make his son's life a little more bearable. He selected a darling governess for the boy, and even took him to Paris. The trip only compounded Sergei's resentment. He would recall their visit to Napoleon's tomb as a particular low point.

In 1915, shortly after his seventeenth birthday, Sergei said farewell to his native Riga and the home in which he was born. From his perspective, the move made all kinds of sense, but the route he chose was surprising to say the least. He opted for the same institute from which his father had graduated, the Institute of Civil Engineers in St Petersburg (now renamed Petrograd). There he resolved to become a structural engineer, again following in his father's footsteps. He entered the world of set squares, protractors, and drawing pens, the instruments he had so despised as a boy.

He wanted to beat his father at his own game, to surpass him as a master builder. History put an end to his plans — Sergei was caught up in the Revolution of 1917, the subject of his later films. Though he would never design a single building, he sketched his film sets with an architect's precision.

The final building designed by Sergei's father was a plain affair. Constructed in 1911 at Lomonosova iela 3, its facade is bereft of ornaments and sculptures. Only the colour scheme — the sandy yellow of the lower floors, the azure above — betrays something of Mikhail Eisenstein's bygone taste for the exotic. The link between this shift and the architect's personal woes — his wife's departure, the ongoing conflicts with his son — is easily made. But it's worth noting that, within a matter of months, Riga's other Jugendstil architects had also radically toned down their approach, until precious little of their trademark exuberance remained.

The death knell had been sounded in Vienna by Adolf Loos, a leading architect and designer in his own right. In his essay 'Ornament and Crime', published in 1908, he slated the artists of the Vienna Secession so ruthlessly that every architect worth his salt refrained from sticking a nymph on a facade from then on. In one fell swoop, the Vienna Secession, Art Nouveau, and Jugendstil were rendered passé.

Clarity of form, Loos argued, had been buried under an excess of ornamentation. Led astray by patrons who craved extravagance in the homes they commissioned to showcase their spending power, a young, fresh architectural style had degenerated into stale and superficial frippery within a matter of years.

Loos might have written his denunciation with Riga's most eminent architect in mind. Eisenstein had taken his penchant for extravagance to the extreme. He had erected six opulently styled apartment buildings at Alberta iela 2a, 4, 6, 8, 11, and 13, three residential blocks at Elizabetes iela 10a, 10b, and 33, and a housing complex at Brīvības iela 99. He had turned the corner of Alberta and Strēlnieku into a sculptural showroom. On two occasions, he had been invited to dream up the figurative elements for a design by another architect. He

Sergei Eisenstein.

had become the cake decorator among Riga's master builders.

The goal pursued by Eisenstein and the other Jugendstil architects was noble and progressive: to give residential buildings a sense
of the palatial, to apply the exceptional craftsmanship once reserved
for cathedral altars and castle staircases to the windows, doors, balconies, and railings of the home. Jugendstil was both the pinnacle of
bourgeois democracy and its architectural endpoint. From 1910 on,
artisans were no longer in a position to deliver work that was halfway
to being art.

The sphinx in front of the building on Alberta iela.

Yet in addition to Loos's criticisms, the style was far from novel. In Riga, this is evident. In both structure and decoration, Eisenstein consistently appropriated the ideas of others. The designs of Otto Wagner invariably provided the template for the buildings themselves, while the ornaments were plucked from catalogues of the 1898 Vienna Secession exhibition and the 1900 World's Fair in Paris. Unsurprisingly, the accusation that Eisenstein was nothing but a diligent copyist is noted in the memoirs of his ungrateful son.

Mikhail yearned for symbolism, for the goddesses of Greek and Roman mythology, mermaids of the Scandinavian sagas, dragons and *walküre* of Germanic folklore, and shepherdesses of German romanticism. His pilasters recalled eighteenth-century neoclassicism, while the sphinx at the entrance to Alberta iela 2a is a faithful copy of a print by Félicien Rops. The effigies on other facades are infused with the spirit of symbolists Gustave Moreau, Fernand Khnopff, František Kupka, and Franz von Stuck. Together, they form a kind of swatch of European symbolism, as practised in Brussels, Paris, or Vienna.

Mikhail was unable to conceive a building without the image of Medusa, Apollo, Artemis, or Pan, without peacocks, eagles, or lions.

About those plaster lions, his son remarked: 'Father himself was a *lion de plâtre* ... Vainglorious, petty, too stout, industrious, unlucky, broken — but still he wore his white gloves (on weekdays!) and his collars were perfectly starched.'

Jugendstil was the swan song of the bourgeoisie. Walking through Riga, I am haunted by the lament of composer Erik Satie: 'I came into the world very young, in an age that was very old.' In that very old world, the bourgeoisie had revived the symbolism of Western civilisation in an exquisite display of splendour, but without the youthful vigour of innovation.

Nevertheless, for Mikhail, Jugendstil came with eruptive force. His first building in the style was completed in 1901, his last, at Alberta iela 2a, in 1906: an average of three apartment complexes a year. As his building plans show, he drew every detail of the facades himself, applying lines, arches, decorations, and sculptures to every section of wall. The windows and railings of no two buildings were identical; he must have spent entire days and nights at his drawing board.

Then came a five-year hiatus. Perhaps his clients had tired of him. Or — and this strikes me as a more plausible explanation — the 1905 uprising had made the moneyed classes less inclined to indulge in displays of affluence. Jugendstil confections were too conspicuous, too likely to catch the eye and fuel indignation. Throughout 1905, townhouses and country manors had gone up in flames.

In 1910, Eisenstein received two commissions at long last. In the spring of 1911, the residential complex at Strūgu iela 3 was completed, followed in the autumn by the residential complex at Lomonosova iela 3. Both were no-frills affairs: austere buildings, devoid of sculptural elements. Arched windows on the upper floors and a turret on either corner were his only gestures towards frivolity.

Upon their completion, Eisenstein once again channelled his energies into his official position: ordering the construction of road and rail links. After the outbreak of World War I, his duties were restricted to overseeing road maintenance. His role as an architect was played out. Or, as I muse on my daily walk down Alberta iela, Eisenstein's orgy of statuary had come to an end.

In the first week of July 1917, Sergei Eisenstein joined the Bolshevik demonstrations against Alexander Kerensky's provisional government.

The facade of Alberta iela 2a before restoration.

This was not a decision born of political conviction: Sergei had never heard of Marx or Lenin, and spent much of 1917 immersed in the writings of Leonardo da Vinci and Sigmund Freud. As he later confessed, he had taken to the streets so as not to lose face with his fellow students.

When police snipers on the rooftops above Nevsky Prospekt opened fire on the protesters, Sergei found himself in the middle of the crowd. People scattered in all directions. 'I saw people quite unfit, even poorly built for running, in headlong flight. Watches on chains were jolted out of waistcoat pockets, cigarette cases flew out of side pockets. And canes. Canes. Canes. Panama hats.' As Orlando Figes notes in *Natasha's Dance*, it's almost as if Sergei were already writing the film version of events and had started work on the screenplay of *October*, his third major film, completed in 1928.

'The Revolution gave me the most precious thing in life — it made an artist out of me,' Sergei revealed in his autobiography. 'If it had not been for the Revolution, I would have never broken the tradition, handed down from father to son, of becoming an engineer … I had already felt the ability and desire, but only the revolutionary whirlwind gave me the main thing I needed, the freedom of self-determination.'

After the Bolsheviks seized power, he studied for exactly eight more months. The outbreak of civil war in 1918 led him to join the Red Army's northern front as an engineer, where he was deployed to defend buildings of strategic importance. 'The reason why I came to support social protest had little to do with the real miseries of social injustice,' he would go on to say with remarkable honesty, but came 'directly and completely from what is surely the prototype of every social tyranny — the father's despotism in a family'. In other words, it all came down to Mikhail Eisenstein.

All the bourgeois characters he later brought to life on screen, from the corpulent factory manager in his first film, *Strike* (1924), to Prime Minister Kerensky in *October*, would share a trait associated with his father. For no fewer than forty steps, half a ministerial staircase, Sergei trains his camera on Kerensky's perfectly polished shoes. Not his head, shoulders, back, or legs, just his shoes.

For three years, Sergei fought for the Reds against General Yudenich's White Army, which, in the autumn of 1919, stood at the gates of Petrograd. His father fought there too, on the other side, with the Whites.

Mikhail had left Riga a good two months before the October Revolution, on 10 August 1917. Unable to stomach the removal and exile of Nicholas II, he was willing to lay down his life for the restoration of the tsarist regime — a life which had come to mean very little since his wife had so shamelessly abandoned him. In 1918, he joined the White Army, also as an engineer, and spent all of the following year on the battlefield.

The White Army was defeated at Petrograd, and in the chaos that followed, Mikhail managed to escape to Berlin. In his final years, he led an anonymous and poverty-stricken existence among the tens of thousands of Russian migrants who had fled to the German capital. In 1919, he married his landlady, Elizabeth Michelsohn, which was the only way for him to avoid eviction. She was twenty years his junior. In 1920, Mikhail Eisenstein suffered a fatal heart attack and was buried at the Russian Orthodox cemetery in the Tegel district.

Three years passed before Sergei learned that his father had died. At the same time, he found out that he had fought against his father at Petrograd. They had literally faced each other in battle; they could have killed each other. This discovery had little impact on Sergei. To him, his father's decision to side with the counter-revolutionaries was little more than resounding proof that he had grown up in a despicable environment. In his later films and writings, he would settle the score with his father once and for all. From his perspective, Mikhail would always be the prototypical bourgeois.

Sergei lied about his father to biographer Marie Seton. He claimed that Mikhail had died in 1926 or early 1927, after making a new life for himself as an engineer in Berlin. In his version of his father's life, it was unthinkable that someone so dreadfully bourgeois could have died jobless and destitute.

Sergei's inner struggle was that he closely resembled Mikhail. As a film director, he pursued exactly the same ideals as his father, the architect. He embraced aestheticism and symbolism, and went in search of a powerful visual style. He left little to chance, and sketched sets and scenes on large sheets of paper with the precision of a blueprint.

On leaving the battlefield, Sergei had gravitated to Moscow, where he took up with the avant-garde movement Proletkult, a mash-up of 'proletarian' and 'culture'. Leading director Vsevolod Meyerhold brought the spirit of Proletkult to life in his stage productions. An adherent of symbolism, Meyerhold saw theatre as a stylised, almost abstract art form, as opposed to an imitation of reality. He stressed the importance of mime and gesture to convey ideas to the audience, and rejected naturalistic theatre and Stanislavsky's ambition of depicting everyday life on stage. In Meyerhold's view, the actor who made an audience forget they were in the theatre was the worst of all actors. Actors were supposed to avail themselves of a technique he called 'biomechanics' to *show* that they were acting, in much the same way as an acrobat or a clown performs. In a new world symbolised by the machine, he believed stagecraft should involve a continuous emphasis on the mechanical.

As one of the few groundbreaking artists of his time, Meyerhold had the wholehearted support of the Bolsheviks. Having nationalised the theatres, they entrusted him with running the theatre department of the People's Commissariat for Education and the State School for Stage Direction. One of Meyerhold's first students was Sergei Eisenstein.

Meyerhold's influence would remain visible in every film that his pupil went on to make. Right down to the editing, Eisenstein worked hard to achieve a stylised aesthetic driven by visual symbolism. The white horse that plunges from a bridge into the waters of the Neva in *October* is a reference to Napoleon Bonaparte. The Bolsheviks put their own spin on this Napoleonic emblem: in their propaganda, a general on a white horse was a general of the White Army, a leader of the counter-revolution, a reactionary. Lenin had denounced Alexander Kerensky, the prime minister of the Provisional Government, as a Bonapartist counter-revolutionary, a denunciation that resonated with Eisenstein's personal preoccupations. After all, Papa had revered Napoleon and, like Kerensky, had ended up a Bonapartist counter-revolutionary.

Through his films, Eisenstein illustrated historical events such as the October Revolution and the mutiny on the battleship *Potemkin*, but his myth-making cinematic images often ran counter to historical fact. He reinvented history, embellished it, shaped it to his liking, or sought to amplify historical reality. In this too he followed Meyerhold, who, when a play featured soldiers, had actors walk among the audience in military uniform to raise money for aircraft that would bolster the strength of the Red Army.

When filming the storming of the Winter Palace in St Petersburg, one of the most iconic scenes from *October*, Eisenstein moved the action to the central staircase; the left staircase that the Bolsheviks had actually climbed was far too mundane and narrow for the crowd scene he had in mind. In Eisenstein's cinematic version, the assault takes place on the Jordan staircase, which the tsars descended during state processions. For the scene, he drummed up 5,000 Russian Civil War veterans, when in reality no more than a few hundred sailors and Red Guards had stormed the palace. Many of these extras brought their own guns and fired live ammunition during the scene; arguably, more people were injured in the filming than in the events of 1917. An elderly caretaker sweeping up the shards of broken china reportedly commented, 'Your people were far more careful the first time they took the palace.' Incidentally, it was Eisenstein himself who preserved this remark for posterity, by chronicling it in his memoirs. Like his father, he was not averse to having a laugh at his own expense.

In 1925's *Battleship Potemkin*, Eisenstein went even further in distorting reality than he would in *October*. As the uprising that began on the ship spreads through the city, Eisenstein slows down the action by alternating close-ups of faces in the fleeing crowd with recurring images of soldiers marching down the Odessa steps. The sequence culminates in footage of a baby's pram, which, having slipped from the grasp of a young mother who has been shot, bumps down the steps, slowly at first, then steadily gaining speed. There has seldom been a more powerful symbol of slaughtered innocence, and dozens if not hundreds of directors since have sought to create their own variations on this scene.

Masterful though it is, almost everything about the scene is an invention. A massacre did take place in Odessa, but at the foot of the steps and along the docks by the water, not at the top or even halfway up. The mutiny on the *Potemkin* started with a lump of maggot-ridden meat. The sailors complained to the captain, whose response was to have their ringleader Grigory Vakulenchuk executed. In retaliation, the crew killed seven officers, raised the red flag, and sailed the ship to Odessa, where striking workers had already brought public life to a standstill two weeks earlier. Here, the sailors placed Vakulenchuk's body at the foot of the steps, surrounded by a guard of honour. This, of course, was a scene drenched in symbolism, and Eisenstein uses it in its entirety.

The next day, thousands gathered at the port. As the demonstration spiralled out of control, tsarist troops fired into the crowd at random. With nowhere to run, hundreds of panicked protesters jumped into the sea. Very few of the bullets missed their target: 2,000 people were killed, another 3,000 seriously injured.

By reimagining the entire scene on the white steps, Eisenstein ramps up the symbolism and creates a starker contrast for the blood that was spilled: the city's poor senselessly mown down in a monumental setting built to embody civic pride.

Eisenstein defended his approach by insisting that his audiences were already familiar with the key historical facts. In his dramatised documentaries, he was more interested in 'chains of psychological associations' and providing his own 'visual commentaries' on events. But in doing so, he underestimated the impact of his images. Both within the Soviet Union and beyond, the revolutions of 1905 and 1917 would go on to be imagined as Eisenstein had visualised them. In people's minds, the storming of the Winter Palace took place in broad daylight and not in darkness. The director had lacked the technical resources to shoot the scene at night.

Eisenstein was a master at splicing images. It's no exaggeration to call him the inventor of montage. For him, the editing process was so much more than assembling a succession of scenes. By intercutting contrasting images to produce arresting sequences, he created a compelling rhythm to tell the story as it needed to be told. Through montage, he engineered collisions between individual elements rather than a smooth flow of images. The resulting shock effects heightened the symbolism.

For all his brilliance as a filmmaker, Eisenstein lacked subtlety. When tsarist police shoot protesting workers in *Strike*, his cinematic debut, he alternates the brutal crushing of the demonstration with footage of a bull being slaughtered. Rewatching the film a decade later, even he

Sergei Eisenstein
lounging on the throne
of the Winter Palace in
St Petersburg.

The actor who
played the scene
in *October*.

was shocked and dismissed it as an example of 'the infantile malady of leftism'. The only aspect he was still willing to defend was the extreme violence of some scenes, a direct consequence, he said, of witnessing the bloodshed of the 1905 Riga workers' uprising at the age of seven. From his bedroom window, he had seen protesters being shot from the barricades. In another sense too, that event would have a lasting influence on him. While bourgeois cinema centred on individual histories and tragedies, Eisenstein took inspiration from the mass movements that would define the twentieth century. With *Strike* and *October*, he brought collective action to the cinema screen for the first time.

With his potent mix of historical myth and symbolism rich in pathos, Eisenstein won greater adulation outside the Soviet Union than among the communist leadership. The avant-garde filmmakers of Germany, France, Italy, Britain, and Japan admired *Strike* and *Battleship Potemkin* and saw Eisenstein as a director with almost superhuman gifts. Stalin, however, had little regard for a director who neglected to make films for the masses. The dictator harboured a secret preference for westerns and Hollywood blockbusters.

October came in for harsh criticism in the party press for its formalist preoccupations with montage, for its lack of individual heroes, for the wooden actor (a factory worker) who played Lenin, and for including Trotsky, the military leader of the October Revolution. Trotsky had been expelled from the party by Stalin and all but erased from Soviet history; Stalin therefore took the film's heroic depiction of his former rival as a personal slight. Party leaders felt that Eisenstein was not doing enough to promote the lie, and the scene with Trotsky was cut from the film.

In 1947, while filming the third part of his epic *Ivan the Terrible*, Eisenstein had another run-in with Stalin. The director had no choice but to bow to the party leader's wishes, and the second part was banned, unreleased, while the third part was destroyed, unfinished.

The following year, Eisenstein died of heart failure at the age of fifty. Stalin would go on to class him as one of the Jews — along with poet Osip Mandelstam and painter Marc Chagall — responsible for the 'ugly distortions' of the avant-garde.

Eisenstein was Jewish on his father's side. Since his mother was Russian, he was not a Jew by Orthodox Jewish standards. His father had renounced the Jewish faith, and in Riga, young Sergei had never seen the inside of a synagogue or come into contact with the Jewish community. Being Jewish held no meaning for him; he defined himself as Russian, and even more so as a patriot.

A firm believer in communism, it was only in later life that he became a prisoner of the system. He was free to travel and attend conferences, congresses, and festivals in Berlin, Paris, Brussels, London, and New York. There were no security guards in tow when he travelled to Central America to shoot *¡Que Viva México!*, a film he never completed. In Mexico, he rubbed shoulders with other staunch communists, not least the husband-and-wife painters Diego Rivera and Frida Kahlo (if anything, even more devoted to the communist cause) and American writer Upton Sinclair, who financed Eisenstein's Mexican film as an anti-capitalist statement.

Eisenstein spent most of 1930 in Hollywood. Had he been so inclined, he could easily have applied for political asylum in California. Instead, he returned to Moscow to make his contribution to furthering the advancement of the socialist state.

'Biologically, we are all mortal,' he said in a lecture to students at the All-Union State Institute of Cinematography in Moscow. 'But we become immortal through what we achieve for society — in those contributions, we aim for the future by passing on the torch of social progress from one generation to the next.' Words that resound like an article of faith.

His only period of genuine unease with socialism came in the 1920s, an aversion prompted not by party doctrine but by licentiousness and loose morals. The millions of men uprooted by the civil war had little truck with moral fortitude, but when the revolutionaries also began preaching the end of civil marriage and the advent of free love, Sergei found himself a man out of step with the times. Both men and women seemed happy to change partners as often as they changed outfits. Any woman who had not slept with a man by the age of twenty could expect to be openly mocked; for men, the humiliation was even greater. Sergei dared not confess to any of the actors at Proletkult that, at the age of twenty-six, he was still celibate as a monk.

The 1930s were well underway before he finally began to develop feelings for a woman. Pera Atasheva already looked like a

Pera Atasheva.

long-suffering mother when they first met. From the very start, she called him the Old Man, a mark of respect that almost made a caricature of their relationship. Sergei hired her as a secretary but refused to live with her. Before these tentative advances, he had tended to fetishise abstinence, deluding himself that maintaining his celibacy would somehow safeguard his genius. This was the period in which he made *Strike, Battleship Potemkin, October,* and *The General Line.*

Sergei viewed Stalin's ascent to power with a measure of relief: the new ruler put an end to the sexual abandon sparked by revolution. Stalin himself was no advocate of marriage — wed or unwed, it was all the same to him — but his preoccupation with discipline and obedience left no room for the decadent high jinks of the first wave of revolutionaries. The fact that Stalin's definition of decadence came to include progressive or avant-garde concepts of art was something Eisenstein only discovered with the passing of the years. In 1939, two years after Stalin had exiled many hundreds of thousands of Jews to Siberia, the director was awarded the Order of Lenin, the highest civilian decoration in the Soviet Union. His fall from grace was an exceptionally long time coming. It was only from 1947, perhaps even 1948, that he came to be seen as beyond the pale, a bourgeois formalist who played fast and loose with the ideals of Soviet art.

Sergei's time in Hollywood remains the most curious episode of his life. In the US, he embraced the role of snobbish socialite with as much relish as his father had back in Riga. Paramount Pictures paid Sergei and his inseparable sidekicks — cinematographer Eduard Tisse and screenwriter Grigori Aleksandrov — 900 dollars a week. This sum was to be increased to 3,000 a week once shooting started. The three of them explored the possibility of filming Theodore Dreiser's successful novel *An American Tragedy*.

Nine hundred dollars a month — never mind a week — was enough to bankroll a life of luxury in 1930. Sergei, Eduard, and Grigori moved into a Spanish-style residence at 9481 Readcrest Drive in Coldwater Canyon, Beverly Hills. Work on the script progressed at a snail's pace, constantly derailed by fine dining and readily accepted invitations to parties and receptions.

Sergei developed a taste for fame and welcomed every opportunity to hobnob with fellow celebrities. He lunched with Douglas Fairbanks, Ernst Lubitsch, D.W. Griffith, and Josef von Sternberg, and dined with Charlie Chaplin (very earnest and not the least bit funny), Marlene Dietrich (a bore), and Greta Garbo (dismissed as stupid for asking 'Who was this man called Lenin?' as her opening gambit). Sergei began looking the part and even splashed out on a pair of expensive shoes. Perhaps that was when he again found himself face to face with the spectre that had haunted him all his life: he caught himself emulating his father's self-indulgence. From one day to the next, Sergei stopped shaving, dressed sloppily, and let the negotiations on *An American Tragedy* come unstuck. He turned up for his final US press conference drunk as a skunk, though as a rule he barely touched alcohol.

In the end, it was his surname that drove him out of America. More specifically, his shock at the response it triggered. In Riga and during his student years in Petrograd, he had never encountered anything that resembled anti-Semitism. But in Hollywood, a retired major launched a smear campaign against him, claiming to represent a group of film producers. In a series of pamphlets and letters to the press, he referred to Eisenstein as 'the Moscow Jew', 'the Jewish Bolshevik', and 'the international Judas of the cinema'. Sergei could well understand the fear that he might turn *An American Tragedy* into a critical or an outright anti-capitalist film. But to be so blatantly portrayed as an untrustworthy and pernicious Jew offended him to his very core.

Back in Moscow, he could sense a wave of anti-Semitism rising there too. He made a point of engaging with patriotic issues to show that he was more Russian than the Russians. In 1937, he completed *Bezhin Meadow*, and in 1938 the epic feature film *Alexander Nevsky*. He composed Slavic prince Alexander's campaign against the Teutonic Knights as a sweeping drama set to Sergei Prokofiev's incomparable soundtrack, with the Battle on the Ice as its visual and musical climax. Party officials had given the rural drama *Bezhin Meadow* a lukewarm reception, but after the premiere of *Alexander Nevsky*, Stalin reportedly slapped the director on the back and said, 'Sergei Mikhailovich, you are a good Bolshevik after all.'

In November 1940, Sergei was given the dubious honour of directing *Die Walküre*, a cultural seal on the non-aggression pact between Hitler and Stalin. The production of the Wagner opera so adored by Eisenstein Sr premiered at the Bolshoi Theatre. The war gave Sergei a few more years of respite. Between 1941 and 1945, he completed the first part of *Ivan the Terrible*, filming in the Kazakh capital Alma-Ata.

This last film project was commissioned by Stalin, who greatly admired Ivan IV. The Soviet leader was so impressed by the first part that he awarded Eisenstein a Stalin Prize. However, the second part of the film, in depicting a more human and fallible Ivan, incurred the wrath of Stalin. In 1948, he delivered his damning verdict: Eisenstein was a Jew who had betrayed the revolution.

Sergei's father had become the laughing-stock of Riga's Russian bourgeoisie. Abandoned by his wife and hung out to dry, Mikhail was left to rattle around an empty townhouse with little more than a piano for company. Shunned by his son, whom he had visited one more time — in Petrograd in the summer of 1916 — and from whom he had heard nothing since.

Sergei himself became the laughing-stock of the Communist Party leaders. They believed the filmmaker to be far too preoccupied with style and not concerned enough with propaganda, despite his unceasing efforts to prioritise the political message over historical reality in his films.

'He was a great man with a distant vision,' actor Maxim Shtraukh said after the film director's death, 'but his life was tragic from the days I first knew him. He was seeking to find his way to the home he never knew.'

Sergei Eisenstein in 1946: tired, old, and out of favour.

Sergei Eisenstein did not marry and fathered no children. We can be forgiven for assuming that he had never been intimate with a woman. Or with a man.

In the summer of 1929, while attending a congress in Switzerland, he went for a walk in the mountains with a small group of film critics, including Frenchman Jean George Auriol. It was a warm day. On reaching a mountain lake, the men undressed and jumped into the water. Only Sergei was left on the shore.

'Why don't you join us?' Auriol shouted.

'I'm not belonging to myself,' Sergei called back. 'I'm too old.'

'So, you think you are wiser than we are,' Auriol remarked.

With some trepidation, Sergei took a step back. 'You must see me as an older man,' he said. 'I have done so many things that it is too late for me to go by an alternative way. You can't live two lives at the same time. I feel old because it is too late.'

Bizarre language. The others had no idea what he was talking about. Sergei was thirty-one at the time, young and strong with a huge mass of blond curls. It did not occur to them for one moment that the revolutionary filmmaker was too ashamed to undress in front of them.

From Switzerland, he travelled to Berlin. After visiting Eldorado, the most famous and notorious nightclub in 1920s Berlin, featuring the wildest transvestites decked out in flamboyant make-up and rubber breasts, he went to the Magnus Hirschfeld Institute of Sex Research to seek treatment for what he saw as his sexual deviance. What, he wondered, would become of a man who rejects every woman and every form of sex?

Following therapeutic sessions with Dr Hanns Sachs, who had learned the trade from Sigmund Freud himself, he concluded that for him homosexuality was 'a dead end'. 'A lot of people say I'm a homosexual,' he confessed to biographer Marie Seton. 'I never have been, and I'd tell you if it were true. I've never felt any such desire, not even towards Grisha.' Grisha was his close collaborator Grigori Aleksandrov, who openly admitted his love for men. 'I think I must in some way have a bisexual tendency — like Zola and Balzac — in an intellectual way.'

After this 'treatment', he resolved to finally take an open, cordial, joyful interest in women. But when the artist Fernand Léger introduced him to the painter's model Kiki de Montparnasse in Paris, he froze. Kiki, muse and model to Léger, Man Ray, Chaïm Soutine, and Jean Cocteau, among others, was a boyish girl of dazzling beauty. To everyone's surprise, she promptly fell for the Russian filmmaker with the oversized head. She sought him out and turned the tables by sketching his portrait: he became her model. What could be more thrilling? But no ... assailed by memories of his mother fleeing to Paris with her lover in 1909, Sergei removed himself from Kiki's orbit.

In the summer of 1946, he moved into what he described as a 'little dacha' near Moscow for a few weeks. The wooden house, which had two floors and seven rooms, conjured up vivid recollections of childhood summers in Jūrmala.

Sergei did his best to unwind in the woods; by then, he was afflicted with a serious heart condition. A distinguished, elderly lady was in attendance, to look after him and make sure he did not overexert himself. She took the handful of friends and acquaintances who visited Sergei in the countryside on long walks to give the ailing director some peace. 'Who is she?' they asked Sergei on their return. And he replied casually, as if it were a completely self-evident arrangement, 'Oh, that's my mother.'

Left destitute and starving in the aftermath of revolution and civil war, Yulia Eisenstein had turned to her son. Her aim had been to come to Moscow and take up residence in his house. Instead, Sergei arranged a one-bedroom flat for her in Leningrad and asked her to leave him be from then on. In 1924, he had Pasha — the Russian housekeeper who had raised him with his Latvian nanny — come over from Riga. She continued to live at his Moscow home until his death. He had no further need of his mother.

Even so, Yulia found a way to get close to him again, looking after him in the weeks he spent at his dacha recovering from a long period of illness and fatigue. Sergei's mother was seventy-nine when at last she once more took over the care of her only child. She died that same year.

4

The Will of the Father

Latvia, March 2007
My time in Riga brings me closer to another tormented father, another tormented son. Not surprising, perhaps, in a country where every son wonders which side his father was on in 1919, 1934, 1940, 1941, 1945, 1949, 1958, or 1989, to name but a few crucial turning points in Latvia's turbulent history. For almost a century, Latvians were condemned to pick a side: the Germans or the Russians, the Reds or the Whites, Stalinists or fascists, democrats or authoritarian nationalists. At the same time, they faced the precarious task of finding the spiritual resolve to withstand the suffering inflicted on every family, every adult, and every child.

One Wednesday evening, I attend a concert by the Latvian National Symphony Orchestra, the Latvijas Nacionālais simfoniskais orķestris. It is being held at the Great Guild Hall, a nineteenth-century neo-gothic building in the heart of the old town, with foundations that date back to the fourteenth century. At the time, it is a dingy building undergoing phase after phase of restoration. I enter through an emergency exit.

The concert starts early — seven o'clock — and in my eagerness to arrive on time I landed a taxi driver in a whole lot of trouble. By day, Riga feels like a tranquil, provincial city, until about six in the evening, when the cars have to squeeze their way across two bridges to the suburbs and traffic chokes the avenues. Arriving in the old town with no time to spare, I asked the driver to drop me off in front of the Freedom Monument. He pointed out that this meant stopping in a no-stop zone. 'Don't worry,' I said, rounding up my fare, 'keep the change … I'll only be a second.' He stopped, I hopped out, but as he was about to drive away, a siren began to wail.

'This is all my fault,' I said in English to the policemen who had pulled the taxi driver over and were demanding to see his driving licence and permit. *'Weg, weg,'* they growled at me in the kind of German you only hear in war films. The driver too gestured that it would be better if I made myself scarce, but the fault was entirely mine, and turning to the officers again, I offered to pay the fine. 'You keep out of this!' the older of the two barked at me, and his colleague repeated, *'Mensch, geh doch weg!'* I crossed the wide road and watched the scene unfold from the far side of Freedom Boulevard: in the end, the driver had to surrender his licence. The same offence in Amsterdam wouldn't have earned him so much as a reprimand. It was quarter to seven. I was outside the concert hall, bang on time, but it had hardly been worth all that. Feeling wretched, I stepped inside.

Riga has a long musical tradition. Before making a name for himself as a composer, Richard Wagner had been musical and artistic director of the city's opera house, giving him a wealth of ideas that he would later bring to fruition at his own theatre in Bayreuth. When he arrived in Riga at the tender age of twenty-four, Wagner was already living beyond his means, and three years later, he had to flee the city to escape his creditors. With his wife, the actress Minna Planer, and a giant Newfoundland dog by the name of Robber, he raced through Courland in a small horse-drawn carriage. By this time, the Wagners' passports had been confiscated and the three of them had to sneak across the Russian border on foot, under cover of darkness. This humiliation would haunt Wagner for the rest of his life, spurring him to seek out powerful, wealthy, and above all, generous patrons. Richard, Minna, and Robber were able to continue their journey by coach to the German port of Pillau, near the city then known as Königsberg, where they boarded a ship called the *Thetis*, bound for London. The ship sailed into a fierce storm, and, so the story goes, it was on this hellish voyage that Wagner hit upon the majestic opening bars of *The Flying Dutchman*. The opera premiered in January 1843, and made his name as a composer.

Clara and Robert Schumann visited Riga and toured Latvia, as did many of Germany's performing artists. Nineteenth-century Riga was a German city with a German-speaking aristocracy, German tastes, and a German lifestyle. Robert expressed irritation at the noisy and inattentive audience, but then he complained of a similar reception in Düsseldorf.

As the most northerly of the German-speaking cities, Riga held a certain fascination for musicians from Vienna and Germany's southernmost cities. They joined the orchestra of the city's German Theatre, as the opera house was then called. In their eyes, there was a purity about the north, something pristine and elusively romantic. In the twentieth century, Riga produced musical luminaries such as pianists Eduard Erdmann and Naum Grubert, cellist Mischa Maisky, and violinists Gidon Kremer and Philippe Hirschhorn. They went on to study in Moscow or Leningrad. The same was true of Mariss Jansons, who went from Riga to Leningrad and back to Riga, making his debut as a conductor with the Latvian National Symphony Orchestra.

This long and illustrious past is not exactly evident as I take my seat and look around the concert hall. Both the interior and the audience appear to have seen better days. Pricking up my ears, I hear more Russian than Latvian spoken. Two out of three residents of Riga are Russian-speaking, and in newly independent Latvia, they play second fiddle and often have inferior jobs, if they are employed at all. I am surrounded by stooped ladies in faded velvet and men in well-worn suits, grizzled before their time. I can't help thinking they wore the same outfits to the First of May celebrations back in 1986 or 1987.

The front rows are packed with denim-clad youngsters, most with a score on their lap: conservatory students, cherishing the hope that music will be their ticket to success. I soon understand that they are under the tutelage of members of the orchestra. The string, woodwind, and brass sections take their places to rapturous applause.

The atmosphere takes me back to concerts I attended in Leningrad and Moscow in 1975, when music was the only escape from the dreariness of everyday life under communism. If you had talent, music could be a lifeline. Few twenty-year-olds aspired to a glittering career in the party or the unions; instead, they saw themselves on stage as a soloist or in an orchestra. In Leningrad and Moscow, up to twenty young men would be standing at the back of the hall, conducting along.

Nothing before the interval gives me the least inkling that I'm in for a musical revelation. The orchestra, led by young Estonian conductor Olari Elts, performs Rachmaninoff's Second Piano Concerto.

Germany's Bernd Glemser is the soloist, forty-something with a look of Liszt about him. A true virtuoso, he doesn't miss a note, which in a piece by Rachmaninoff is saying something. Even so, I can't help feeling slightly short-changed, and search in vain for the Slavic pathos I had hoped for.

Cantus by Estonian composer Arvo Pärt comes after the interval. Within seconds, I am bolt upright in my seat. This is Baltic music, rooted in this region and written by Pärt — a completely isolated figure at the time — in memory of English composer Benjamin Britten. The piece begins with the ringing of bells, then the strings come in, the first and second violins, violas, cellos, and basses, sixty stringed instruments in all. Brass and woodwind are silent. With the exception of the first violinist, the second cellist, and the six bassists, the entire string section is female. Women expressing centuries of suffering in the Baltic countries through slow waves of sound, as if lamenting every man, woman, and child deported to Siberia's penal colonies, sent to World War II battlefields or Nazi concentration camps. The piece lasts exactly five minutes. As I concentrate on each extended note, it stretches to five times that length. *Cantus* begins thin and high, then sinks deeper and deeper through a constantly repeated motif that resounds with the sense of life slipping away. For the final notes, the deepest, the very deepest, the cellists hunch over their instruments, as if stooping to drop a flower or a handful of earth into an open grave. The dark tones vibrate in my stomach and give me chills. Rarely have I been so transfixed. And in that moment I recall the book that violinist Gidon Kremer wrote about his child-hood in Riga.

I shook hands with Gidon Kremer once, and spoke to him twice on the phone. The first call was to tell him of the death of pianist Youri Egorov. Though Kremer was seven years older than Egorov, they knew each other from the conservatory in Moscow. Youri went there to study at the age of seventeen, while Gidon was completing his training, having started out in Riga and Leningrad. After their flight from the Soviet Union — Youri emigrated to Amsterdam in 1976, Gidon to Munich in 1980 — they had kept in touch.

I always heard Youri speak of Gidon with respect and sympathy. In Youri's eyes, Gidon was a discerning and ultra-sensitive human being and a passionate, sincere musician. Friends had wanted to spare him the ordeal of learning about Youri's death from the press, and so I agreed to call him. He was stricken. As if stunned, he kept repeating 'Thirty-three, thirty-three, so young …'

A year later, I picked up the phone again, to ask Gidon if he was willing to participate in a benefit concert in Brussels to be held in Youri's memory. The proceeds were in aid of young musicians who had fled the Eastern Bloc countries. He agreed immediately and dismissed any notion of a fee or reimbursement of his travel and hotel expenses, despite having to make the trip from Munich. That night, he played as if it were his last concert. His interplay with Argentinian pianist Martha Argerich was phenomenal. After the performance, he was distraught, intensely sad.

From that moment on, I bought all of Gidon Kremer's recordings, regardless of the repertoire. There were plenty of surprises in store. Through his performances, I got to know the work of Arvo Pärt — religious music, ahead of its time considering the ten thousand churches that have been built in Russia in the last decade. But he also introduced me to the violin concertos of John Adams and Philip Glass, to Alfred Schnittke, to Olivier Messiaen's *Thème et variations* for violin and piano, Pēteris Vasks's *Distant Light*, and Astor Piazzolla's tangos. On the violin, Kremer's tone is austere, even a little constricted at times, as if determined to keep frivolity at bay, but that same tone enriches the pieces he plays. In his choice of repertoire, he is often a pioneer.

In 1993, he published his childhood memoirs in Germany, under the title *Kindheitssplitter* (Fragments of a Childhood). A French edition was published six years later, under the more inviting title *Une Enfance balte* (A Baltic Childhood). I bought it, read it, and forgot about it. Until that night in Riga's concert hall, when the last note of *Cantus* died away and I had to swallow hard.

Marianne Brückner, Gidon Kremer's mother, was a violinist with the Latvian National Symphony Orchestra. Her father, Karl Brückner, was a well-known violinist who had grown up in Sweden. After his marriage to a German violinist, he moved to Karlsruhe in central Germany, and from there this musical family relocated to Latvia. Daughter Marianne married Markus Kremer, a Latvian Jew who had spent his youth in Riga and become a young widower at the beginning of World War II. Like Marianne, he played violin in the Latvian National Symphony Orchestra.

It was a miracle that Markus Kremer had escaped the concentration camps. Thirty-five members of his family were killed in the Holocaust, including his first wife and their fifteen-month-old daughter. In 1941, he had been able to escape when Jews in Riga were being rounded up on a large scale. At random, he rang the doorbell of an apartment building and a young woman answered. She agreed to take him in. One day, then two. Two days in hiding became two weeks, two months, and eventually two full years. She was in a position to offer him safety because, as the mistress of an SS officer, she was above the suspicion of the Nazis. In 1943, when the officer began to sleep at her apartment more often and it became too dangerous for Markus to stay there, the Nazi's Latvian mistress rented an old workshop. There, Markus dug a hole under the floor where he spent the last two years of the war, along with another Jew in hiding. The woman made sure she was paid for her help and paid handsomely, Gidon suspected. Not that this makes her any less courageous: had the men she was hiding been discovered, her fate would have been summary execution. Long after the war, Markus continued to visit her once a year, on 13 October, the day of Latvia's liberation from the Nazis.

Gidon, born in 1947 and raised in the long shadow cast by the war, grew to dislike his father. It was not an intense hatred, nothing terrible; more like a nagging pain that never goes away. His father was a reader. Every spare hour, every moment when he was not rehearsing, performing with the orchestra, or teaching violin, he read books about the war, about the Holocaust. Nothing but the war, nothing but the Holocaust. He found something of himself in the horrors that were chronicled, and no description was too exhaustive or detailed for him.

An unresolvable conflict was tearing him apart from within. Why had fate spared him but not his wife, his child, and the thirty-three other members of his family? Guilt tainted every minute of the day. He did not say so, not in so many words, at least not to his second wife and his son. Instead, he pushed his personal suffering aside; compared to that greater suffering, what did it amount to? Markus talked about the terror of the Nazis, as detailed in the books he read. No atrocity was left unspoken.

Listening to his father was a torment for Gidon, not least because he saw how much pain these accounts of the war and the Holocaust inflicted on him. Kremer Sr seemed compelled to seek out facts even more terrible than those he already knew, to dwell on the family suffering that he alone had escaped. Poring over the most harrowing details was a form of self-castigation. Markus Kremer described the gas chambers with such precision that a child could have drawn them.

His father's unending tales of war stirred up anxieties in young Gidon. The Daugava river sweeps past Riga in a wide bend; when it froze and the ice cracked, the sound shook Gidon to the core. In it, he heard the cracking, the breaking of war. The sound haunted his nightmares, an echo of events he had not experienced himself.

Listening to Markus's litany of wartime atrocities also weighed heavily on Gidon's grandmother. She reproached her son-in-law for wallowing in his suffering and asked him to his face what he thought he was doing. Was it the pity of his wife, of his son, that he was looking for? If so, why not tell them what had happened to *him*? Why take this endless, roundabout route? She could no longer listen to his stories about the death camps. But when she cried 'enough', Markus made her out to be a fascist, and that hurt. Or he called her 'a typical German', which in her eyes was even worse.

It was up to the son to restore his father's lost pride and self-respect. Gidon, named after the Old Testament warlord Gideon, was to become an authentic Jew. In the fourth week after his birth, he was circumcised without anaesthesia, a practice prohibited under Latvian law. His father ordered him to give 'Jew' as his nationality on all official Soviet papers. Gidon had to learn Hebrew, Gidon had to become a violinist. A famous, a world-famous violinist. 'I had to crown my life with success,' Gidon wrote. 'In the depths of my father's soul, I was his heir. Or more to the point, I was the justification of the fact that he had survived the war. Gidon, the second life of the man who had been spared.'

Gidon never stopped practising the violin. When he wasn't practising, he felt as guilty towards his father as his father felt towards his murdered

Gidon Kremer in 1960.

family. He rehearsed for hours and hours, not because he particularly wanted to become a violinist or enjoyed music, but because it was what his father wanted. Gidon understood from an early age that his father would suffer a mental collapse if his son abandoned the violin. He did his best, his utmost. In his memoirs, Gidon includes a note he wrote at the age of ten, a promise to his father to practise a thousand times. He had already done his homework ahead of time so that he could work on improving his technique all the next day. It was the Christmas holidays, and he asked his father to wake him at 8.30 am or at 7.15 if need be. The letter ends, 'Forgive me, forgive me again. Your Gidon.'

Gidon grew into a pale, nervous youth, whose cheeks flushed bright red whenever a waitress in a cafeteria spoke to him. A bumbler, who wondered furiously why he was so shy. Furtive too, watching the girls from behind his glasses and out of the corner of his eye. A spotty teenager who, whenever he performed, would sweat profusely. A teenager who knew that he possessed no charm. Most painful of all is that this is how he describes himself thirty years later, with a precision bordering on self-castigation, quite possibly inherited from his father. He too wallowed in past horrors: the horrors of his youth.

For Gidon, music was a matter of diligence rather than abandon. It gave him little genuine pleasure. The only exception was when he paced the floors of the dance studios of the building shared by Riga's conservatory and ballet school with his violin tucked under his chin, keeping time for the young ballet dancers, male and female, exercising at the barre. These sessions gave Kremer his idiosyncratic on-stage movements; when giving concerts, he bends deep at the knees and sweeps past the accompanying piano or orchestra. Seeing this for the first time, Russian violinist David Oistrakh branded Kremer a poseur and refused to teach this upstart from Riga. But for Kremer, music and movement were inseparable: little wonder that he went on to record three tango albums. Eventually, Oistrakh relented and took him on as a pupil. A strong bond formed between master and apprentice. Oistrakh too was Jewish, and although he did not speak to Gidon at length about his background, he understood where his pupil was coming from.

One of the young dancers Gidon played for at the ballet school was a stocky country boy with meaty thighs and stiff hair the colour of straw. There was nothing to suggest that he would become the greatest dancer of all time, except perhaps the look in his expressive ice-blue eyes. Unbeknownst to each other, Gidon Kremer and Mikhail Baryshnikov had something in common: a troubled relationship with their father and a tense, traumatic childhood.

Baryshnikov's father was a Soviet soldier stationed in Riga. Even after Stalin's death in 1953, he continued to hold Stalinist views, which made him doubly hated. Even back in the 1950s, Russians were considered outsiders in Latvia, though they still ruled the roost. At home, Baryshnikov Sr was every bit as authoritarian as he was in the barracks. Mikhail's mother committed suicide when he was twelve years old. His father was quick to remarry and no longer wanted his son around. A friend of his mother's took him under her wing and encouraged him to pursue the path his mother had set out for him. She had wanted him to become a ballet dancer.

As a boy, Mikhail Baryshnikov was every bit as nervous as the young Gidon Kremer, a boy who could never keep his legs still under the table. The stage, he says, was where he found peace, self-assurance, inner purity, and exaltation. It was where he discovered his true nature. He slept on a wooden board because he was told it would make him grow faster. He trained so fanatically that the fat disappeared from his thighs. He worked to sculpt his own body, the position of his shoulders, the angle of his elbows.

He completed his training at a renowned drill school: the Vaganova Ballet Academy in Leningrad. At the Kirov Ballet, he became a star, in New York a megastar. I saw him dance there in 1981 and could only agree with every superlative that had been lavished on him in the West. He was beautiful, strong, masculine, mysterious, and melancholy. On tour in Canada in 1974, Baryshnikov had escaped his handlers and sought political asylum in the US.

It was only in 1998 — at the age of fifty — that he dared to return to Riga. He laid flowers on his mother's grave and accepted a lofty Latvian honour. In an interview that featured in Dutch daily *de Volkskrant*, he said, 'I didn't actually have a childhood. I found a home in dance that I did not find with my family. It is a fact of life. Not belonging to anything gives me the freedom I have always sought. I have no roots, and every step I take is a shock. For me, living is about change. I can do anything, be anything.'

Substitute 'music' for 'dance' and Gidon Kremer might have said those very words.

From a very young age, Gidon had taken part in competitions, without ever winning. The feeling that he alone had the needle and thread to stitch up the deep wound in his father's soul put unbearable pressure on him. On occasions when he had to dig deep and give his all, his arms and fingers stiffened. He lost his touch.

Gidon would never have become a renowned violinist had he not encountered another, very different violin student at the Riga music school: Philippe Hirschhorn. In Kremer's eyes, Hirschhorn was a go-getter; he was quick, sharp, direct, proud. 'You might call him an anarchist.' That was putting it kindly. I met Hirschhorn several times in Amsterdam in the early 1990s: he was nervous, moody, unpredictable, and sometimes incredibly difficult. He was also exactly the kind of friend that Gidon needed.

Philippe Hirschhorn, son of a German Jewish father and a Latvian mother, was a brilliant violinist who did not care what anyone thought of him. During one competition in Moscow, as Gidon looked on, he simply left the stage because he was not in the right mood. Felik, as his friends from Riga called him, had been playing superbly, but to his ears it lacked a certain warmth. Unmoved by the music he was making, he broke off the performance and walked away, leaving both judges and audience stunned. Felik himself was impassive. Back in the dressing room, he said coolly, 'It was the right decision.'

On another occasion, after Gidon had given a concert in Leningrad, Felik went back to the soloist's dressing room, embraced his friend, and said, 'Congratulations, that was really very bad.' This was not him poking fun; he meant it. It was this unremitting force of nature with whom Gidon had to compete, in Riga and at the Leningrad Conservatory, where they were live-in students and roommates.

Of the two, everyone expected Philippe Hirschhorn to take on the mantle of world-renowned violinist, not Gidon Kremer. In 1967, it was Felik who won the prestigious Queen Elisabeth Competition in Brussels, while Gidon took third prize. Both were congratulated by Belgium's King Baudouin and Queen Fabiola after the event; in the photograph, you can see Felik thinking, 'Of course I won,' while Gidon hides his shame behind a smile as forced as the king's. But Gidon fought back, year upon year, and ultimately won the International Tchaikovsky Competition in Moscow.

After their first major successes, both Felik and Gidon defected to the West. There, Gidon began his steady rise, while Felik slowly sank into ever-increasing cynicism. Felik ended his career as a violinist with the Utrecht Symphony Orchestra and a teacher at Utrecht Conservatory. Accomplished as he was in both these roles (his pupils include the world-famous violinist Janine Jansen), this was no life for an astounding virtuoso, praised by cellist Mischa Maisky as possessing 'mystical, hypnotic gifts'.

In 1996, aged fifty, Hirschhorn died of a brain tumour.

In their documentary *De winnaars* (The Winners), Paul Cohen and

King Baudouin and Queen Fabiola congratulate Philippe Hirschhorn
(m) and Gidon Kremer (r) on winning first and third prize at the
Queen Elisabeth Competition in Brussels, 1967.

David van Tijn explore the fortunes of former winners of the Queen
Elisabeth Competition. Hirschhorn emerges as the most brilliant of
the great musicians who won the competition in Brussels and yet
failed to fulfil their vast potential. The reason? One contributor to the
film posits that, at a young age, Hirschhorn briefly inhabited a realm

where mere mortals never dwell — the realm of absolute perfection — a shock to the system from which he never fully recovered. For a fleeting moment, he had been untouchable, a god; he had transcended his peers and every earthly criterion, an unbearable state that casts a young man into profound loneliness. He was like Icarus flying too close to the sun, or Bobby Fischer taking the 1972 world chess title in unparalleled fashion. Hirschhorn didn't just win in Brussels, he left the audience and the jury breathless. Thereafter, motivation had been hard to come by. He had reached the pinnacle; there was nothing higher. Above God there is nothing, bar madness.

In Moscow, where he completed his studies at the conservatory, Gidon Kremer kept a diary. For the first time, he dared to rebel against his father.

> My father's criticism irritates me (although I know my weaknesses).
> It irritates me just as much when he compliments me (which is
> rare). Every time, I hear the same contradictions in his remarks, and
> these have become far too familiar to me.

In ugly, biting sentences, he wrestles free of his father. Even then, he remembers the good times: the games of chess they played, or the occasions when his father took him fishing at the lake near the coast by Jūrmala. Gidon was happy as a sandboy when his father sent him a book, a brilliant book, despite the bitterness of the title: *All People Are Each Other's Enemies*.

Encouraged by the cynicism and perhaps the unattainable brilliance of his friend Felik, Gidon was finally able to banish his father from his mind. When he walked onto the stage in Moscow to play in the final of the International Tchaikovsky Competition, it was not to rescue his father from the suffering of war. If it had been, he would have lost. Instead, he said to himself, 'I have to prove that this profession, which I did not choose myself, has become my own.'

Latvian composer Pēteris Vasks read *Kindheitssplitter*, and closing the book on Gidon Kremer's memoirs, he heard a high, thin E on the violin. This note, sustained and tremulous, became the opening of his violin concerto, a single thirty-minute movement entitled *Distant Light*.

Gidon Kremer, dancing his way through the recording
of *Fratres* by Arvo Pärt, October 1983.

Born in Aizpute in 1946, Vasks could look back on a childhood
less traumatic than Kremer's, which is not to say he'd had it easy. His
father was a pastor by profession, and this excluded Vasks Jr from
admission to the conservatory in Riga. In 1968, the Soviets were still
combating religion as fiercely as they had in the immediate aftermath
of the October Revolution. To make matters worse, Vasks Sr belonged

to a small, intensely devout denomination, the Baptists. His son had to escape to Vilnius, where for years he played in an orchestra because no music publisher would touch his work. Only after the collapse of the Soviet Union was he able to establish himself as a composer.

He described his violin concerto as 'a song, coming from silence and floating away into silence, full of idealism and love, at times melancholy and dramatic'. The light in the title was a reference to the reflection of distant memories.

Distant Light — *Tālā gaisma* — in Latvian, premiered at the Salzburg Festival on 10 August 1997. The soloist was Gidon Kremer. It must have been a strange experience for him to play such a haunting piece, music that sprang from the fragments of memory he himself had committed to paper.

Vasks creates distance between the violin and the orchestra, between — we may assume, given the inspiration for the piece — son and father. A silence lies between them. Towards the end of the middle section, violin and orchestra come closer in a crazed waltz and finally unite in dark, sustained tones. The concerto ends as it begins, with a high, thin E played by the violinist, lonely and alone.

Fathers and sons … I walk out of Riga's Great Guild Hall and feel the cold nipping at my cheeks. Fourteen, fifteen, sixteen below zero. At the same time, I remember the only words Gidon Kremer spoke to me, in Brussels.

'I want to leave again.'

He wanted to travel to the far north. Not to Latvia, Estonia, or Finland, but further still, to the North Pole. For a period of loneliness, of hardship.

'That's something I need from time to time.'

At that time, I knew nothing of his book. There was nothing to know. It had yet to be published and may not even have been written. But his words spoke of a pain that never passes.

The snow creaks under my shoes. The war weighed just as heavily on my own father's shoulders, cast just as much gloom over my childhood. It's tough to grow up with a war you did not live through.

I cross a deserted square and walk through a city haunted by the ghosts of Kremer, father and son. A city where even three metres of snow cannot blanket history.

5

What Made the Chameleon Burst

ROMAN KACEW FROM VILNÉ

Lithuania, March 2009
One bleak winter's afternoon in Vilnius, I attend a class on Yiddish, taught by Professor Dovid Katz. Every Wednesday, he welcomes his students in the Jewish community centre at Pylimo gatvė 4. Once met, never forgotten: few live up to that billing better than Dovid Katz. Larger than life, you might say, but I've encountered many a larger-than-life character who pales by comparison.

A slice of poetry in a pizzeria brought us together. Dining alone, I heard a man a few tables away recite a verse of forty lines or more in resounding and melodic English. It was his voice that caught my attention, followed soon after by his stature. He was a broad, bulky man in his fifties, his black trousers held up by crimson braces. Jet-black hair down to his shoulders, matching beard down to his breastbone. He pushed his square-rimmed glasses higher on his nose and there was something gentle, almost defenceless in his expression. Across from him sat a woman with ash-blonde hair, a timeless beauty whose youth was unmistakably behind her. Visibly moved by the declamation, she smiled throughout. I got up, went over to their table, and asked the man what he had recited with such passion.

'An American folk song.'

He shook my hand and introduced himself.

'Dovid Katz.'

'*The* Dovid Katz?'

'That depends what you mean by *the*!'

'The man who wrote the preface to *Sounds of Silence: traces of Jewish life in Lithuania*.'

'Sit yourself down, sir. With that opener, you've made a friend for life.'

He ordered a bottle of San Pellegrino.

Professor Dovid Katz in Vilnius.

'About the book,' I said. 'I bought it yesterday afternoon and read your preface last night.'

'It wasn't well received in these parts. Here, they prefer to forget.'

Sounds of Silence is a book of photographs that seeks to capture what remains of Jewish life in Lithuania.

'Remembering can't hurt, can it?'

'Forgetting is easier. Isn't that right, Maria? Let me introduce you to my friend: Maria Krupoves-Berg, Lithuania's most celebrated singer.'

'Hence the folk song.'

'Yes. Maria always wants to hear what's being sung elsewhere.'

Maria shook my hand and asked me where I was from.

My answer induced a mild state of euphoria.

'I just did a show in the Netherlands,' said Maria. 'In Friesland, Leeuwarden ... The sweetest audience I've encountered anywhere.'

'Audiences are like that wherever you go,' Dovid said decisively. 'You bring out the sweetness.'

'Do you specialise in folk music?' I asked.

'No, I'm a professor of Yiddish. With a fondness for American folk songs.'

'The title of the book, *Sounds of Silence* ...'

'Yes, it's a nod to Simon and Garfunkel. Their Jewish forebears hail from Vilnius. Same goes for the grandparents of Bob Dylan, Bob Zimmerman if you will. It's an aspect of the American folk song that often gets overlooked: the Yiddish influence from Central Europe. What brings you to Vilnius?'

'The childhood of Romain Gary, the writer.'

'Well, what do you know!' Maria exclaimed. 'My grandmother's sister was Romain Gary's nanny.'

'And? Was he a difficult child?'

'Incredibly sensitive.'

'I can well believe it. Even as a grown man, he could burst into tears and sit sobbing in public for a full fifteen minutes.'

'What do you expect?' Dovid burst out. 'He was from Vilnius!'

His laughter echoed through the pizzeria, where we were the only guests.

'Do you live here?' I asked.

'Two months a year in Ireland, four months in New York, and six months in Vilnius. Not a day more! I couldn't take it.'

'Why not?'

'The suffocating, right-wing nationalism. Nothing to do with the man in the street, mind. I've never encountered anti-Semitism in a bar or restaurant here. No, the xenophobia comes from the politicians, the civil servants, the journalists, and often from the cultural elite ...'

We talked for hours that night. Maria was sharper and more combative in her views. She could clearly afford to be more outspoken than Dovid, who occasionally made a guarded remark. Maria had a deep animosity towards nationalism.

When we said goodbye, Dovid invited me to attend his weekly

class. 'It will give you an idea what's left of Jewish Vilnius.'

'Not to be missed,' Maria urged.

Two days later, I am sitting at an oval table in a late-nineteenth-century building that once housed the Jewish Lyceum. The class is attended by three students — a red-haired boy, a red-haired girl, and a woman in her early forties — and an audience of eleven, all aged between seventy and ninety. The last survivors of the Vilnius ghetto. They are not here to learn; they were raised speaking Yiddish. In 1940, it was the most widely spoken language in the city. After 1945, they no longer heard it anywhere, and slowly but surely, they also lost the ability to read the Hebrew scriptures.

Professor Katz covers a short story by Isaac Bashevis Singer. The elderly Jewish men and women take it in turns to read a passage. One man still has two teeth, the second none at all. The third man, well into his eighties, is wearing glasses that are held together by tape. The eight women look even shabbier, except for one old lady whose thin hair is dyed a coquettish shade of purple. They bow over the text, perfecting their pronunciation. Every now and then, I pick out a word that echoes German or catch a phrase I know from the shops in Amsterdam's Jordaan district.

Halfway through the proceedings, Professor Katz introduces me.

'We have a Schriftsteller from Mokum as our guest today. Mokum being the Yiddish name for …?'

The old folk nod. 'Amsterdam.'

'Our guest has come to Vilnius to visit the places where the Jewish writer Romain Gary spent his childhood. Romain Gary moved to Poland when he was twelve and France when he was fourteen. He became a war hero and a famous French writer, in that order. Do any of you know Gary?'

They all shake their heads.

'Romain Gary was born Roman Kacew. Which may explain why he decided to change his name!'

Laughter erupts, and I learn that Kacew means 'butcher'.

'Did anyone know the Kacew family?'

No, no one.

'Do you have any questions for our guest?'

Seconds tick by.

Then the old lady with the purple hairdo gets to her feet and addresses me in Yiddish. She speaks slowly, and when I cannot follow her, Dovid Katz translates.

'There were many of us in Vilnius,' she says. 'Now, hardly any of our people are left. There was a synagogue on every street. Only one still stands. We had our own culture, our own language. We also had our own name for our city: Vilné. These days, everyone talks about Vilnius. Vilné no longer exists. I would like to ask you to call your story "Roman Kacew from Vilné". So that the name Vilné will live on a little longer.'

She makes a slight bow and sits down.

The student sitting next to me, the woman in her forties, puts a palm to her jaw to calm a twitch.

I nod slowly. The realisation of sharing a room with these trampled souls dawns, and I cry without making a sound.

Romain Gary, Roman Kacew.

His father abandoned him. Not his mother, no; *him*. At least, that is how he took it: as a rejection, a denial of his existence. Going by his own version of events, he was a toddler at the time; in reality, he was about ten years old. He continued to see his father until the age of twelve, a stranger who visited from time to time. Later in life, he had no desire to remember anything about those rare encounters.

As an adult, he took his revenge. In interviews and private conversations, Roman not only changed his father's nationality — sometimes Polish, sometimes Russian or Tatar — but also his identity, claiming that the man whose name he bore was not his father. He had been sired by none other than Ivan Mosjoukine, a famous Russian actor. The fact that his mother had never met Mosjoukine and that his only connection with the film actor was a signed photograph bought at a flea market was neither here nor there. A fabrication was better than an accurate family tree.

Roman was determined to be free of his actual father. Never again was he to be associated with Arieh-Leib Kacew, a Jewish furrier and trader from Vilnius. To be on the safe side, he adopted a pseudonym. First name Romain, surname Gary. In time, it would become the name of a literary phenomenon. Looking back on his vagabond existence, he wrote, 'Everybody knows the story of the willing

Roman Kacew, aged twelve, in Vilné.

chameleon. He was put upon a green cloth and obligingly turned green; he was put upon a red cloth and obligingly turned red. Upon a white cloth he turned white, and on a yellow one, yellow. But when they put him upon a Scottish plaid, the little fellow burst.'

In the year that he committed these lines to paper, he had already taken another alias: Émile Ajar.

His mother's name held no such shame: Mina Owczyńska. To him, she would always be Mina. He did gloss over the fact that she was registered as Mina Bregsztein, the surname of her first husband, a Polish Jew. Roman said nothing about that first failed marriage in any language. He also drew a veil over where Mina had given birth to him: in Moscow, in Kyiv, or in Kursk. Or at a station on the Russian–Polish border, where the train from Crimea stopped. Or in the palace of a khan, a Tartar ruler, in Samarkand. Or an unspecified location somewhere on a steppe … Often in Russia (St Petersburg also got a mention), sometimes in Poland, but rarely in Lithuania, let alone a Jewish ghetto. Without a father, he must have thought, what's the point in having a fatherland?

His mother insisted that one day he would become a French ambassador: a curious dream for a penniless Jewish woman more than 2,000 kilometres from Paris, swept along in a maelstrom of mass migration and struggling to see a way out for herself and her son. But in the mud, the mire, and the cold of Lithuania, it was a dream that kept Mina alive.

We can picture Mina as a full-figured woman with short, dyed-blonde hair, large, worried eyes, broad cheekbones, and a wide mouth. A faded beauty and, according to her son, an actress who, in her heyday, had charmed theatres packed with Russian soldiers. Pearl earrings, still something of a flirt, a hint of the common in the ever-present cigarette at the corner of her mouth: brown tobacco, no filter. Something akin to Simone Signoret in her final film, as impressive as she was short of breath.

Ambassador. This was the prospect she held out to her young son through every stage of her diaspora: in Vilné, in Święciany, in freight wagons, in Warsaw. Even when she finally moved into a two-room flat in Nice and, insisting she was vegetarian, fed her boy steak for dinner only to wipe the gravy off his plate with a chunk of bread in the far corner of the kitchen to give herself a little taste of meat. All the while she clung to the wish that her Roman would one day be France's diplomatic representative to a large and powerful country.

A good thirty years later, her dream would come true. Her son,

Mina Owczyńska in her twenties.

her only child, became the French consul-general in Los Angeles, having held lower-ranking diplomatic posts in Bulgaria, Switzerland, New York, Peru, and Bolivia. By then, Mina was long dead.

For young Roman Kacew, there were other dreams. He saw himself high in a blue sky, in a cockpit, as an aviator. In 1938, he began his training at an air-force base in the south-east of France, but was the only officer trainee not to be promoted to lieutenant. He may have obtained French citizenship and changed his name to Romain Gary (derived from the Russian 'to burn'), but in their eyes he remained someone with a murky past. Russian or Pole, Jew or half-Jew, military intelligence never quite knew what to make of him.

Lieutenant Gary on board a French bomber, just before take-off in
England.

With the outbreak of World War II, he took to the air at last,
first in Central Africa and Sudan, then Egypt and Damascus, and
ultimately in Western Europe. In the desperate year of 1942, a low
point for the Allies in the conflict, he was recruited by Lorraine, a free
French squadron stationed in England as part of the Royal Air Force.

Up in the clouds, Roman dared to indulge a far bolder dream,
that of becoming a celebrated writer. He flew one bombing raid
after another over Germany at a time when two out of every three
aircraft failed to make it back to base in England. As the navigator, in
a small glass dome in the nose of the aircraft, he was a sitting duck for
German fighter pilots, and his most likely prospect was an early grave.
In January 1944, it looked like his final hour had come: his bomber
was strafed by German machine-gun fire and he sustained serious
injuries. His survival was nothing short of miraculous. The pilot in
the cockpit, separate from the navigator, had also come under fire in
the attack and was blinded by a hail of glass splinters. He had to be
talked back to England over the radio and execute the landing purely
on Gary's instructions, a feat that earned both pilot and navigator the
highest military honour.

Recovering from the injuries to his abdomen in an army hospital,

Gary wrote a novel. Set in Poland, the book was first published in Britain. Publication in France followed in 1945, under the cynical title *Éducation européenne* (A European Education). It was the beginning of a literary career; eleven years later, he would be awarded the Prix Goncourt.

For a Jewish boy from Vilnius who had grown up fatherless, he had reached the pinnacle. But no, not quite. To become a fixture in the society pages and the glossies of the early 1960s, there was one more step: to marry the most beautiful woman in the Western hemisphere, a film star adored by millions. An American with big, dreamy eyes, short light-blonde hair, a not-quite-turned-up nose, full lips, and a delightful accent. From the moment he married Jean Seberg, he was pursued by an army of photographers. Romain Gary became famous the world over. The relationship would last for the decade, and produced a son.

The film star took her own life in 1979. Fifteen months later, in December 1980, Gary did the same. He had failed to give Seberg the fatherly protection she had sought from him. Like his own father, he had fallen short as a carer and protector. He had abandoned the girl with the boy's name and boyish haircut to her fate.

In a district of south-east Vilnius, I go in search of the house where Roman Kacew came into the world on 21 May 1914. According to my information, it should be on Subotnikų gatvė, number 6a, at the corner of an alley, on the edge of the old Jewish quarter. But the street names have since been changed to Lithuanian and the houses renumbered, as if to make life impossible for anyone trying to trace past inhabitants. On Subotnikų gatvė, things could be worse: the street now goes by the name of Subačiaus gatvė, and the house on the corner is number 8.

I have only known for a year or two that Romain Gary was born in Lithuania. Throughout his life, he maintained that he was Russian, half-Jewish, a quarter Jewish, a little Jewish, according to his mood. Once, at a press conference in Israel, he was put on the spot when an elderly journalist who bore a striking resemblance to Ben-Gurion asked him if he was circumcised. He took a deep breath, wiped the sweat from his brow, and answered in all honesty, 'Yes.' Afterwards, he dismissed the incident with a quip; for the first time in his life, he had been asked to publicly divulge the state of his member, something he had always assumed would only be of interest to his lovers.

Following his dramatic death, journalists were keen to delve into the final mysterious years of Gary's life, but no one was overly concerned with his origins or his birthplace. Twenty-six years would pass before I read in a four-line report in French regional daily *Sud Ouest* that a memorial stone had been placed on the facade of the building where he was born, in Vilnius, the capital of Lithuania.

It turns out that the stone is affixed to another building, where Gary spent most of his childhood, and not to the building where he was born, still remarkably intact after the ravages of two world wars. A middle-class residential block of reddish-brown stone from the late nineteenth century, with Art Nouveau influences in its tapering windows and its wrought-iron railings and gate. From the first floor, Gary's parents could see the dome of the Orthodox Church of the Holy Spirit, as well as the towers of the Church of St Theresa and the Carmelite monastery.

Vilnius was, and still is, a beautiful city. It has the unmistakable air of what was once the capital of a great empire, a grand duchy that stretched from the Baltic to the Black Sea in the fourteenth and fifteenth centuries. A river city, on the banks of the Neris, into which the much narrower Vilija flows. A city of hills, studded with churches. From each hill, other spires and towers catch the eye. On my fourth day in Vilnius, mist rolled into the city's low-lying districts and along the river valley. From the highest hilltop, all I could see were the towers rising above the mist. It was a breathtaking sight.

Historian Karl Schlögel describes the towers of the various churches and monasteries as engaged in a mutual rivalry, seeking to outdo one another. There was a time when they vied for prominence with the city's synagogues and Jewish places of worship. The main synagogue in Vilnius was the largest in the world and could hold 3,000 worshippers. Ninety-nine of the city's one hundred shuls were burned to the ground, bombed, smashed to rubble, or in the most favourable circumstances, simply demolished.

What we are left with is the round tower in front of the gleaming white cathedral, the tower of what used to be St John's monastery, the twin towers of St Catherine's, the tower of the Bernardine monastery, the three spires of St Anne's (a church so magnificent in Napoleon's

The apartment building on Subačiaus gatvė where Roman Kacew was born.

eyes that he wanted it dismantled stone by stone and rebuilt in France), the tower of St Theresa's, the Church of the Assumption of the Blessed Virgin Mary, St Michael's, the dome of the Church of the Holy Spirit, and the tower of the Sacred Heart church. Another baroque tower still standing belongs to the Chapel of St Casimir, built by the Jesuits in the early seventeenth century. Under the tsars it became a Russian Orthodox church; under the Soviets it housed the Museum of Atheism. A few hundred metres away, the elegant yellow-and-red tower of the Church of St Nicholas overlooks the buildings of the main shopping street.

'Where so many towers rise,' Schlögel continues in his book on the cities of central Europe, 'it cannot be purely in honour of God. Such a thing comes about only where people are crowded together in a very small area, where the great variety and jumble of houses and buildings grow together into a single house, in a growth process that has taken centuries, stone by stone, staircase by staircase, arch by arch … Generations have built on the work of their predecessors. Vilnius is not a city set down somewhere in the country, with no conditions and ending just anywhere. Every plot of land has been covered and viewed multiple times from all sides.'

Lithuanian-born Polish writer Czesław Miłosz writes of 'narrow cobblestone streets and an orgy of baroque; almost like a Jesuit city, somewhere in the middle of Latin America'. Yet while the monumental cities of Peru and Bolivia teem with life, Vilnius feels empty somehow. If we want to know why, Schlögel writes, we should read the indictments of the war criminals who faced prosecution at the Nuremberg trials. The vibrant heart of Vilnius, the Jewish ghetto, was cut out of the city. What remained was an artfully restored corpse.

Vilnius bears as many names as it has had masters in the course of its chilling history. In Polish, the city is called Wilno, in German Wilna, in Russian Vilna, in Yiddish Vilné or Wilne, and in Lithuanian Vilnius. Present-day Vilnius, Lithuanian through and through, is a shining example of how to rebuild a city. It is a neat city, a clean, tidy city, and this alone jars with the Vilnius of old, where visitors were always complaining about the dirt. It is a city that looks to the future after a turbulent past. But with every step, you notice the absence of something essential. Along with the Jewish population, an entire culture, a language, a way of life disappeared from Vilnius. In this respect, the city bears a strong resemblance to the collected works of Romain Gary, in which Vilnius is no more than a phantom, a city he and his family only ever visited in passing. Or so Gary made it appear.

In 1914, the year in which Roman Kacew was born, an estimated 350,000 Jews lived in Lithuania. Most Jewish families had come to

Lithuania from Russia in the late eighteenth century, a time when the
tsarist regime permitted only wealthy Jews to remain. A decree issued
by Catherine the Great expelled the poor to the Pale of Settlement
(or Chertá), the area in the west of the empire that included present-
day Latvia, Lithuania, Belarus, and Ukraine. In many Lithuanian
towns and villages, 50, 60, or even 70 per cent of the population was
Jewish. And as Czesław Miłosz wrote, 'it would ... be hard to count
any group whose numbers in the cities varied from 30 to 70 per cent
a minority'. In Lithuania, many Jews took charge of undeveloped
areas and set up farms. This stirred ill feeling among the locals.

Things had begun to improve for Russian Jews under the rule of
Alexander II, but following his assassination, these improvements were
swiftly reversed. The May Laws of 1882 left Jews even worse off than
they had been under Catherine the Great, so that they were only permitted to settle in the urban areas of the Chertá. These new measures
were accompanied by pogroms in Latvia, Lithuania, Poland, Ukraine,
and Belarus. Anti-Semitism coloured the already grey history of those
countries pitch-black. The people of Riga, Vilnius, Warsaw, Vitebsk,
and Minsk actively resisted the arrival of tens of thousands of Jews.

In Vilnius, the number of Jews came to exceed 100,000. In 1914,
this was half the population and earned the city the nickname 'the
Jerusalem of Lithuania' or 'the Jerusalem of the North'. Jewish culture flourished there, both in Yiddish, the language of the common
people, and Hebrew, the language of the literate.

Vilnius published two daily newspapers in Hebrew and countless
books by Jewish writers, poets, philosophers, and scholars. Romm,
a publishing house founded in 1795 by Baruch Joseph Romm, went
on to become one of the world's largest Jewish publishing houses in
the nineteenth century. To this day in Israel, the Talmud is printed
in a typeset developed by Romm. Remarkably for the time, it was a
woman who brought this local printer to international renown. In the
second half of the nineteenth century, Deborah Romm headed the
company. She published the Babylonian Talmud and numerous other
standard religious works.

In his cradle, Romain Gary must have heard the rattle of the type-
setting machines. Romm's printing house was just around the corner
from Subačiaus gatvė, on A. Strazdelio gatvė. Though the walls are
still standing, the buildings are in a desperate state. If they are ever

restored, the result will be an architectural monument to rival the Hospices de Beaune. After the Germans invaded in 1941, Romm was dismantled and the buildings succumbed to neglect. Gales, snow, sleet, and rain did their work; no wrecking ball was required. Moss grew over the brickwork, roofs started leaking, windows were broken. It seems that since 1945 not a living soul has set foot inside. My only company is a single stray dog, slinking along behind me with its tail between its legs, whining softly.

Once this place offered employment to hundreds of typesetters and printers. In the narrow streets and alleys, you could hardly move for people. For Alfred Döblin, author of the classic German novel *Berlin Alexanderplatz*, Vilnius was the beating heart of Jewish culture in Europe. He visited the city in 1924, and the descriptions in his resulting memoir are so lyrical, it's hard to imagine that a man so enchanted by Vilnius could have given life to a character as caustic as Franz Biberkopf.

I find German Avenue, the Jewish street. Here, I understand the language. Store by store, countless people, Jews, hauling, lugging, standing in groups. A rare caftan, usually European provincial garb. Very narrow side lanes, street peddlers all the way into courtyards. The shops are open, often windowless, rows of meat and poultry stores cheek by jowl. Arches span a few streets. They mark the boundaries of the old ghetto. There is an energetic life, here and at the castle hill, on the water, where the soldiers exercise.

I enter the 'Jewish Courtyard'. Under the arch, boys distribute Yiddish leaflets, publicity and an invitation to a meeting. A medium-size courtyard with small plain houses. Steps lead up to some of them. Prayer room next to prayer room. At one point, steps lead down; to my amazement, I find myself in a huge, very dilapidated temple …

I can't help thinking as I go out: What an impressive nation the Jews are. I didn't know this nation; I believed what I saw in Germany, I believed that the Jews are the industrious people, the shopkeepers, who stew in their sense of family and slowly go to fat, the agile intellectuals, the countless insecure unhappy refined people. Now I see that those are isolated examples, degenerating, remote from the core of the nation that lives here and maintains itself. And

what an extraordinary core is this ... What events occurred in these
seemingly uncultured Eastern areas. How everything flows around
the spiritual. What tremendous importance is placed on spirituality,
on religion! Not a minor stratum, an entire mass of people —
spiritually united. Few other nations are centred in religion and
spirituality as this one.

Döblin not only portrays Vilnius as a new Jerusalem, he declares
it to be a metropolis of civilisation. His observations were primarily
intended for his home market, of course: Germany 1924, where
anti-Semitism was spreading like an epidemic. A doctor in the slums
of Berlin during the 1920s, Döblin wanted to impress upon his fellow
Germans what they would be missing if they banished Jewish culture
from their midst. But however noble his intentions, in the heat of his
argument, he bypassed reality.

Most of the Jews of Vilnius lived in miserable conditions. Visitors
to the Jewish quarter recoiled at the filth and the stench. The district
was not connected to the sewage system and the houses, the hovels,
had no plumbing. Wastewater ran over the pavements and through
the alleys to the river valley, and most of the children went barefoot.
The poorest families lived in cellars and rarely saw daylight. In winter,
the cold claimed the lives of infants and old people by the dozen,
and in summer, they succumbed to the humid, oppressive heat. One
eyewitness, the historian Simon Dubnow, wrote, 'The poverty seeped
from the walls.' The ghetto was a sinister place; to escape it, you had
to be a prodigy such as Jascha Heifetz, who conquered the world with
the violin under his chin.

This level of poverty did not really impinge on the world of Roman
Kacew. We know this since the publication of Myriam Anissimov's
biography, *Romain Gary, le caméléon*, in 2004, and the revised edition
in 2006. In over 1,000 pages, Anissimov was the first person to fill in
the details of Gary's childhood, a Herculean task. The writer himself
did a thorough job of concealing three-quarters of his past, and then
set about distorting or wilfully mutilating the remaining quarter.
Only a handful of the details he revealed about his life in books and
interviews have turned out to be true.

His parents lived with his paternal grandparents, as was common among Jewish families at the time. At home, the Kacews had a telephone, a rare luxury in 1914. The shop run by grandfather and father Kacew was located at number 31 Niemiecka gatvė, later Daytshe Gas or Deutschegasse (German Street), the Jewish street described by Alfred Döblin in his travelogue. One of the few childhood memories Roman kept intact concerned walking around barelegged in a short fur coat, and seeing pieces of fur scattered around the house. That said, most of the fur was probably confined to the shop and sewing workshop.

Daytshe Gas was broad, full of shops, and took its name from the Lutheran church at the top of the street. Many of its buildings were destroyed during World War II, but its wholesale destruction took place during the Soviet era. In the late 1940s, all of the buildings on the east side were demolished to widen the street. The Kacews' shop was one of the properties razed to the ground. When Lithuania gained its independence, the street was renamed Vokiečių gatvė.

Roman spent the first year of his life in Vilnius and was raised there between the ages of six and twelve. World War I was responsible for this interruption, a time of chaos that ended with Poland's annexation of Lithuania. Between 1914 and 1921, Vilnius passed from one sphere of influence to another, changing sovereignty a total of eight times. Roman's father was mobilised as a reservist, and Roman and his mother began a nomadic existence. First, they found a safe haven in Święciany, eighty-four kilometres north-east of Vilnius, the town where Mina had been born and raised and where her parents still lived. Born? No, even this fact stated by the biographer has had to be revised. More recent research reveals that Mina was born in Kursk, 500 kilometres south of Moscow. Which means that Romain Gary's claim that his mother was 'the daughter of a watchmaker from Kursk' was not simply plucked from thin air. She must have moved to Święciany with her parents in the late nineteenth century.

These days, Święciany is called Švenčionys. I travel there, first by taking the train to Švenčionėliai, a ninety-minute journey. We pull out of the capital and are soon enveloped by forests that extend all the way to Lithuania's northern border. Snow is falling steadily. The train stops in every village, most of which appear to consist of three or four wooden houses — shack-like structures with small windows and

roofs of corrugated iron. Švenčionėliai's station is a red-brick building
that dates from 1862. Ever since, an inscription on the wall proclaims,
Švenčionėliai has been linked to Warsaw and St Petersburg.

I pass through the station building and find myself on a flat patch
of wasteland. The wind is whipping up a storm, throwing snow in
my face; I begin to worry that Švenčionys might be a bridge too far.
Half an hour later, a rickety bus arrives. The driver gets out and goes
for a smoke in the bus shelter. Meanwhile, a private taxi van rolls up,
and the passengers pile on. The taxi driver — twenties, leather jacket,
shaved head — charges four litai per person. For less than one euro
fifty, I am whisked off to my destination. A soundtrack of blaring
electro dance renders any attempt to talk to my five fellow passengers
superfluous. Up hill and down dale we go. Snow-covered fields fly
past, interspersed with stretches of forest. The landscape reminds me
not of Gary's books — for him, Lithuania was a country without a
face — but of Czesław Miłosz's *Native Realm*:

> Contrary to what inhabitants of warmer countries might imagine,
> the countryside is neither sad nor monotonous. There are no
> mountains, but it is hilly. And probably it was these first visual
> impressions that taught me my abhorrence for completely flat
> terrain. The land is fertile and, in spite of the severe climate, it is
> possible to grow sugar beets and wheat. There is an abundance of
> lakes and forests, both coniferous and mixed. The latter contain a
> number of oak trees, whose role in pagan mythology was, and in my
> own personal mythology continues to be, so important. Because of
> such childhood memories, I tend to classify the places I have lived
> as 'better' or 'worse': 'better' means that there are lots of birds. The
> beauty of spring and summer in my region makes up for the long
> winters. Snow falls in November or December and melts in April.

A green, friendly landscape, alive with birds. And although this
is not spring or summer, but March, the coldest month of the year,
and the only birds are black flocks of crows in the snow, it is not hard
for me to imagine how wonderful this place must seem to a child. I
know, appearances can be deceiving. Ecologically, everything appears
fine here: no industry, no intensive agriculture, no factory pig farms,
but it's only a short drive to the Ignalina nuclear power plant, a carbon

copy of Chernobyl that has been shut down by order of the European Union. Until it is finally decommissioned, the Russian-built plant remains a time bomb.

This pleasant region was also home to another time bomb, one that did explode: anti-Semitism. At the end of the nineteenth century, Švenčionys had a population of 6,790, including 4,850 Jews. Fifty years on, the number of Jews had been reduced to fourteen. According to Professor Dovid Katz, two remain. 'I know them both. One was born in Švenčionys, the other is from out of town. No, the only trace of Jewishness you'll find in Švenčionys is the cemetery.'

The snow continues, as if nature is intent on erasing every trace of the past. Thick flakes fall steadily on the forests. Švenčionys's one edifice of note is the Russian Orthodox church, a basilica of white and lilac-blue stone that emerges from the snow with fairytale beauty. The charm of the wooden houses is overshadowed by the five-storey Soviet flats plonked down among the original buildings. No one knows where I can find the Jewish cemetery. Nor is there a cafe. For a toilet, I am directed to Maxima, the local supermarket.

The most striking thing about the town is its location: as you leave the flats and wooden houses behind, next stop is the border with Belarus. This place really is in the shadow of Russia. And in the shadow of communism: Belarus is Eastern Europe's last Stalinist dictatorship.

'Picture yourself walking on,' Dovid Katz told me in Vilnius. 'That will take you to the town of Lyntupy, or, time-wise, back to 1928. In Lyntupy, there's a giant vodka factory with a seven-metre statue of Lenin in the central hall, gazing down on the shop floor from on high.'

The snow creaks beneath my shoes. Trudging towards the border, I am reminded of one of the vivid anecdotes from historian Geert Mak's travelogue *In Europe*. When a fresh-faced British diplomat spoke up for Estonia and Latvia at the 1919 Paris Peace Conference, the British chief of staff, Sir Henry Wilson, led him to an enormous map of the Russian Empire. 'Now, my boy,' he said. 'Look at those two little plots on the map and look at that enormous country beside them. How can they hope to avoid being gobbled up?'

Roman Kacew experienced the gobbling of the Baltic countries firsthand. At the start of World War I, Mina and little Roman found

In 1900, Švenčionys had a population of 6,790, 4,850 of whom were
Jews. In 2009, the Jewish population was two.

shelter in rural Švenčionys for a few months at most. Then all hell
broke loose. In spring 1915, a German offensive ousted Russian
forces. This led the region's Russian citizens to accuse the Jews of
aiding and spying for the Germans. Amid brutal acts of violence, the
Jews were driven east, deep into Russia. Every Jew in Lithuania and
Courland was carted off by cattle wagon, 600,000 people in total.
These deportations were accompanied by arson, theft, and looting.
Everything the Jews possessed was ripe for the taking.

The mass deportation to the east was chaotic. Trains were shunted
onto sidings, and sometimes stood there for days. Deportees died of
hunger, thirst, or disease; they suffocated or succumbed to the cold
or the heat. Tsarist Russia became Bolshevik, but for most Jews, this
made little difference. Two thousand pogroms took place on Russian
soil between 1917 and 1921.

In Švenčionėliai, Mina and Roman were put on a transport to
Belarus. It is possible that they managed to make their way eastwards
from there. They may have headed for Kursk, the city Romain Gary
often referred to subsequently as his place of birth. Or perhaps to
Moscow, which he also claimed as his hometown on more than one
occasion.

The Russian Orthodox church in Švenčionys.

The Germans occupied Vilnius until late 1918. Jews were not allowed to return until January 1919, by which time the city had become Polish. We do not know what Mina endured in the course of those five years: it was something she never spoke of to Roman. Across the 2,000 kilometres she travelled with her child during the deportations, she must have seen unimaginable misery. And as a single woman caught up in the retreat of an utterly demoralised army, she must have been easy prey.

Roman's first impressions were chaotic. Where exactly was he? Where was he going, where did he come from? The first words he remembered were Russian. Little wonder, then, that he was later unable to bring any kind of order or chronology to his memories. In his mind, the macabre scenes he witnessed must have bled into each other, a grim turmoil played out in a bleak no man's land. It was with good reason that he called one of his last novels *Pseudo* (translated into English as *Hocus Bogus*). It is the book of a damaged mind. Seething with self-hatred, it teeters on the brink of anti-Semitism.

For him, peace did not come until 20 September 1921, the date on which the reunited Kacew family settled into a spacious apartment behind the soft yellow facade of Wielka Pohulanka 16. The building was on the fringes of the more affluent section of Vilnius's Jewish quarter, close to the wide central thoroughfares of Zavalnaya and Trokskaya. Their balcony overlooked the lower part of the city.

The Kacew family were among the fortunate ones. Of Vilnius's original Jewish population, only 3,000 men, women, and children returned. The others did not survive deportation or remained stranded in Russia, too poor to return to their former homes. Jews from Vilnius who had sought refuge in Warsaw also did not return. The lucky ones made it to Hamburg, Rotterdam, or Antwerp and set sail for America as third-class passengers; those less fortunate were robbed, raped, or lost their lives along the way. At the age of seven, Roman could already call himself a survivor.

The Poles went to war against the Ukrainians, against Bolsheviks holed up not far from Vilnius, and against the Soviet Union, with the aim of annexing parts of Lithuania, Belarus, and Ukraine: a bloody and bewildering game of musical chairs. The Treaty of Riga, signed in March 1921, put a provisional end to these hostilities and established a set of borders. Estonia and Latvia gained their independence; so too did Lithuania, but with Kaunas as its capital. The Poles refused to cede Vilnius to the young republic and retained control of the city.

This meant that Roman Kacew grew up in a Jewish Russian city governed by Poland, where Polish was the official language. Caught between the Poles and the Russians, the residents of Vilnius once again faced a choice between the devil and the deep. The streets were given Polish names, and the schools and the university became Polish, though the Poles only outnumbered the city's other ethnic groups by the slimmest of margins: close to 38 per cent of the population of Vilnius was Polish.

Roman was finally able to go to school. We do not know what kind: Polish non-denominational, Polish Catholic, Jewish, or Hebrew. We do know that he at least learned to speak Polish, in an accent denoting that he lived a long way from Warsaw. At first, his mother wanted him to become a violinist like Jascha Heifetz, who was a shining example for all Jewish parents in Vilnius. When Roman turned out to have no musical talent whatsoever, her next thought was to mould him into a ballet dancer, the next Nijinsky, and when that too failed, an Olympic fencing champion. French ambassador was Mina's last resort: if nothing else, it was a profession that did not require a particular talent from a tender age.

Gary would later write an affectionate send-up of his mother's aspirations in *La promesse de l'aube* (Promise at Dawn). In the novel, he portrays Mina as an indefatigable and infinitely adaptable optimist kept afloat by her outlandish fantasies. In Vilnius, she poses as the representative of a distinguished Paris fashion house and dresses the city's well-to-do ladies. But this too could be another of her son's fictions. Biographer Myriam Anissimov was only able to confirm that Mina occasionally made hats to earn some extra cash, which relegates Gary's descriptions of ladies in various stages of undress to the realm of fantasy. In his own account, as a ten-year-old, he often witnessed bourgeois ladies disrobing in order to try on the gowns sewn by Mina — a delightful episode that conjures up a palpable sense of his budding sexuality.

Walking along Wielka Pohulanka, still a broad and distinguished street, another scene from the book comes to mind. Number 16 was home to a certain Mr Piekielny, which means 'hellish' or 'diabolical' in Polish. This gent, a mouse of a man, developed a soft spot for the kid who lived two floors below. He gave Roman tin soldiers as gifts, invited him in, and fed him chocolates and Turkish delight. One day, he asked the boy, 'So what do you want to be when you grow up?' Roman gave the answer his mother had instilled in him: 'A French ambassador.' Not the least surprised, Mr Piekielny said, 'Perhaps you will meet the famous and the great of this world. And when you meet them, promise me one thing. Promise me to tell them there was once a Mr Piekielny who lived at number 16 Grand Pohulanka in Vilna …'

Twenty years later in England, towards the end of World War II, the Queen paid a visit to Lorraine squadron headquarters at RAF Hartford Bridge. Lieutenant Gary stood to attention in front of his fighter plane. The Queen, the mother of Queen Elizabeth II, nodded kindly and asked him which part of France he was from. 'From Nice,' he said, cutting it short. The Queen nodded again, and before Gary knew what had got into him, he said, 'At number 16 Grand Pohulanka in the town of Vilna, there lived a certain Mr Piekielny …'

He would go on saying it, to General de Gaulle, to high-ranking dignitaries at the United Nations, and to tens of millions of American television viewers. He did so, he wrote, in memory of 'the friendly mouse of Vilna [who] long ago terminated his tiny existence in a

Nazi crematorium, along with several million other European Jews'.

With Gary, an anecdote is never innocent. Never, not for a moment, did he lose sight of his own narrow escape. If, in 1925, his father had not moved in with his mistress Frida Bojarski, seventeen years younger than his wife Mina, and if Mina had not left the house on Wielka Pohulanka one year later because Frida had given birth to a son, Roman would have followed the path of his father Arieh-Leib Kacew. 'To the gas chambers,' as he wrote. Another detail that turned out not to be true.

Wielka Pohulanka has since been renamed, twice in fact: the Polish Wielka Pohulanka became the Russian Bolshaya Pogulanka, and in 1990, the avenue was named after Lithuanian nationalist Jonas Basanavičius, founder of the first Lithuanian monthly newspaper in 1883, the first Lithuanian daily paper in 1905, and the Lithuanian National Democratic Party in 1907.

Despite the changes, the building where Roman grew up is easy enough to find: a statue has been erected on the street corner. After that first memorial stone, the Lithuanians caught on quickly, and Gary's recognition went from strength to strength: a plaque, a statue, and a cafe with walls covered in pictures of the aviator, diplomat, society figure, and author. Vilnius has embraced Roman Kacew and counts this prodigal son among its greatest writers, an honour he is destined to share with Czesław Miłosz, who was awarded the Nobel Prize in Literature in 1980.

I wonder what Gary would have thought of this posthumous recognition. For all he cared, Vilnius — that murderous city — could sink into a swamp never to be seen again. Yet the interest in his person helps ensure that the shameful stain that clings to the city will never fade. The bronze statue, a work by Lithuanian sculptor Romas Kvintas, shows a little boy looking skywards and pressing a broken shoe to his heart. The look recalls the dreamer, the broken shoe his five years as a deportee during World War I. For all its simplicity, it is a striking image, and if he'd had the chance to see it, I think Gary could well have shed a tear or two.

Cafe Mano Guru — a meeting place for the latest generation of writers and poets — is 300 metres away. As I walk, it occurs to me that Gary only ever described the interiors of Vilnius, never the outdoors,

Lithuanian sculptor Romas Kvintas's statue of Gary as a boy. It stands on
the avenue in Vilnius where Roman Kacew lived until he was twelve.

its streets and its squares. It's as if he had spent all of his seven years
there cooped up indoors. To sample the atmosphere of Vilnius as it
once was, it's not Gary but Miłosz you need to read:

> In winter, the town acquired a polar look. Small sleighs, presided
> over by drivers in fur caps, who resembled centaurs, served as

a means of transportation. City buses also ploughed their way assiduously through the snowdrifts. Children used the middle of the sloping streets for sledding — they usually lay on their stomachs and steered with their feet — or for skiing.

A delightful city for children — at least if they were Catholic, like Czesław Miłosz. Jewish children were better off staying in the Jewish quarter. As Miłosz acknowledged:

> There was no bridge between these two groups in our city. The Catholic and Jewish communities (some districts were almost entirely Jewish) lived within the same walls, yet as if on separate planets. Contact was limited to everyday business matters; at home, different customs were observed, different newspapers were read, different words were used to communicate — the vast majority of Jews spoke Yiddish, an emancipated minority spoke Russian, and a very small percentage used Polish.

Among that small minority was Roman Kacew.

I meet Dovid Katz again that evening. 'Did you see Gary's house?' he asks.

I nod.

'Which number?'

'Sixteen.'

'Ha, then you've seen the wrong house. Those dimwits put up a plaque at number 16. But the houses were renumbered. Gary lived one building along, at number 18. I'll wangle you an invite.'

The present occupant of the Kacew family home is Professor Irena Veisaitė, a sociologist in her early sixties. She is knowledgeable about Gary's work.

'He has written next to nothing about this building, other than a mention of looking out at the tree in the courtyard. There's also that beautiful scene in *Promise at Dawn*, where his mother asks him to stand by the window because, from a distance, in the soft afternoon light, he looks so much like his father ... Strange, but he doesn't say a word about the significance of this place in Jewish history. Two floors above the Kacews' flat, Max Weinreich founded YIVO, the Institute for Jewish Research, in 1925. Albert Einstein and Sigmund Freud were among the honorary members of the presidium. YIVO played a pioneering role in the emancipation of the Jews. It did so much to preserve the Yiddish language and Jewish cultural heritage of Central Europe. In 1935, YIVO invited Marc Chagall to Vilnius and honoured him with an exhibition of his graphic work. The mood was already grim: Jewish students were made to sit at the back of the lecture hall, on "ghetto benches" that were painted yellow. Max Weinreich was beaten up during a pogrom and lost the sight of one eye. The institute continued to be based here until war broke out. After the war, New York became its headquarters. I can't understand why Gary doesn't say a word about this in his books. Any Jew would be proud to have been Max Weinreich's neighbour as a boy, don't you think?'

'I don't think he knew,' I reply. 'Or if he did, then he had forgotten. He had nothing against YIVO; all the information about Yiddish words and expressions he used in his books was mined from YIVO publications. But little about Vilnius appears to have stuck in his memory. He always told French journalists he was Russian or from Russia.'

Gary's insistence on his Russian roots starts to make more sense to me during my time in Lithuania. Looking left as he stepped out of his home on Wielka Pohulanka, Roman would have seen — high on the hill at the end of the avenue — the bright-green domes of the Russian Orthodox Church of St Constantine and St Michael, popularly known as the Romanov Church because it was built to add lustre to the Romanov dynasty's 300th anniversary in 1913. Every morning, he clapped eyes on the onion-shaped domes of the recently completed Romanov Church, and coming home from school every afternoon, he would hear its bell ring out.

Recent guidebooks describe Vilnius as a Catholic city (80 per cent of the current population is Catholic), but that was not always the case; throughout Roman's childhood it was Jewish and Russian. From the end of Subotnikų gatvė, the street on which he was born and where many of his father's relatives still lived, Roman could walk a few hundred metres and leave the city behind him. Among the hills of the surrounding countryside, the setting was distinctly Russian, with wooden houses on either side.

After exactly a kilometre, the road began to rise, arriving at a dacha where Alexander Pushkin's daughter-in-law lived. The poet's youngest son, Grigory, had married Varvara Melnikova in 1884; from an earlier marriage, she had come into possession of a manor house and the surrounding parkland on the outskirts of Vilnius. Grigory died in 1905 and Varvara in 1935, leaving the house and the eighteen-hectare park to the state in her will. It was turned into a museum: the Alexander Pushkin Literary Museum.

Nothing about the place seems to have changed since Grigory Pushkin's death. I spend the best part of a morning treading its creaky floorboards, and imagine myself deep in Russia. Grigory, the curator tells me, was a tireless defender of his father's work, even though he had hardly known him: Pushkin lost his life in a duel when his youngest son was just four years old. In later life, Grigory gave weekly lectures at schools in Vilnius and invariably broke the ice by asking the pupils to name the poet's worst work. After waiting patiently for them to mention a few poems they didn't think were up to much, he would point to himself.

In 1914, the year Roman Kacew was born, poet Anna Akhmatova stayed at a hotel on the corner of Subotnikų gatvė (now Subačiaus gatvė) and Aušros Vartų gatvė. Her husband, the poet Nikolai Gumilev, had been given a few days' respite and was permitted to leave the front not far from Vilnius. 'In the morning,' Akhmatova wrote in her diary, 'I saw through the window of the hotel room pilgrims making their way on their knees to the chapel where an icon of the Black Madonna hung above the Gate of Dawn.' The next day, Akhmatova herself knelt before the icon to pray for her husband's soul. The icon of Mary, Mother of Mercy, still hangs above the Gate of Dawn, a place where almost every passer-by, old or young, male or female, genuflects or makes a sign of the cross.

The poet Osip Mandelstam spent a few weeks in Vilnius, the poet Joseph Brodsky a few months. For two centuries, Vilnius was not only the most Jewish but certainly also the most Russian city in the western reaches of the Russian Empire.

For Jewish boy Roman, another exodus began in 1926. With Mina, he moved from Vilnius to his grandparents' house in Švenčionys. A few months later, mother and son left for Warsaw, where they would spend two years in circumstances Gary would later describe as dire. To begin with, they stayed with a brother of Mina's, a lawyer, and later with a sister of Mina's, who was a dentist. There, they slept in the waiting room and had to clear away their bedding first thing every morning.

Half a million Jews lived in Warsaw in the late 1920s. The city's grammar schools only accepted Jewish students whose parents were willing to make a hefty donation. Roman received private tuition in French to prepare him for his new homeland. Mina's only reason for staying in Poland was that it was relatively easy to obtain a French visa; this called for a tidy but not excessive sum in cash and a spurious doctor's certificate prescribing medical treatment in the temperate climes of the Côte d'Azur. Applicants were numerous, however, so plentiful supplies of time and patience were also required.

In the course of their two years in Warsaw, young Roman saw anti-Semitism gaining ground all around him. Trade unions called for a boycott of Jewish-owned shops, and the clergy encouraged campaigns against Jews in their parish newsletters.

Mina saw a greater danger looming for her son. Already on the brink of adolescence, it was only a matter of time before he acted on his sexual urges. She took him to a photographic exhibition that showed the effects of syphilis: the sores on the skin, the toothless mouths …

With that life lesson firmly embedded, Mina and her son bade farewell to what would become the dark heart of Europe to settle in a two-bedroom flat on Avenue Shakespeare in Nice.

The divorce between Arieh-Leib and Mina was pronounced in Vilnius on 17 October 1929, one year to the day after Mina and Roman arrived in Nice. Before the month was out, Arieh-Leib had married Frida Bojarski. After their son, a daughter was born, but it is unclear whether Roman ever knew he had a half-sister. None of the family survived the war.

By his own account, as penned in *Promise at Dawn*, Romain Gary learned the truth about his father's death days after receiving the Prix Goncourt. By 1956, the literary award had already become a media event: it was the top story on French radio and television news bulletins, and the winning writer became a nationwide celebrity overnight. In the wake of Gary's win, an unsigned letter arrived at his publishers, Gallimard, supposedly written by an eyewitness to Arieh-Leib Kacew's final moments. Just before entering the gas chamber, knowing what fate awaited him, Roman's father had dropped dead of fright. Gary read the letter and was close to passing out when Albert Camus, who as editor of the literary magazine *La Nouvelle Revue française* had his own room at the publishing house, ushered him in and tried to calm him.

It is painful to read in Myriam Anissimov's biography that this scene is another of Gary's fabrications. The supposed witness, Albert Camus, did not live to tell the tale: he died in a car crash in 1961. The letter in question was never recovered. And, most importantly, the facts contradict Gary's version of events: only a few hundred Jews from Vilnius were transported to the gas chambers; the others, including Roman's father, were killed at a site near the city, usually in their thousands.

The war came late for the Jews of Vilnius, but the horror was immediate. The Hitler-Stalin pact had given the Jewish population some respite until mid-1941, when Hitler unilaterally abandoned the agreement and Eastern Europe was transformed into a battlefield within days. The Soviets withdrew from Vilnius on 22 June 1941, and the Germans rolled in on the 25th. In anticipation of the arrival of the Nazis, Lithuanian nationalists killed more than 15,000 Jews in three days. The Nazis took over the executioners' work, assisted in many cases by Lithuanians. Gas was not involved: the Jews were shot dead.

Initially, the Kacews managed to escape this fate, thanks to a clever deception by Arieh-Leib. In 1942, the Nazis transferred them to ghetto number 2 on Šiaulių gatvė. In the initial selection, Arieh-Leib would have been classified as elderly and, serving no useful purpose in the eyes of the Nazis, would have been killed without delay. But Arieh-Leib took ten years off his age and, by passing himself off as forty-nine, was given a job as a chimney sweep. Concerned about the fire risk within the fortified walls of Vilnius, the Germans had the ghetto chimneys swept. The chimney sweeps, Verena Dohrn reveals in her book on Jewish Vilnius, smuggled weapons into the ghetto in their double-bottomed toolboxes, to arm Jewish resistance groups. Some of the resistance wanted to fight to the bitter end from within the ghettos; others wanted to get as many young people as possible out to join the partisans in the forests. Arms smuggling was punishable by death, yet almost all of the chimney sweeps did their bit.

Meanwhile, the liquidation of the ghettos continued. Between July 1941 and September 1943, group after group of ghetto residents were selected to walk two by two to the Paneriai extermination camp. After they were killed, their bodies were thrown into pits they had dug themselves, or which had been dug by previous victims. The SS and their Lithuanian accomplices shot the men first, in groups of ten, followed by the women and children.

When every chimney had been swept, Arieh-Leib was able to return to his former profession for a time. At the former electrical-appliances factory Electrit, furriers were put to work in two buildings, making fur coats and fur-lined boots and gloves for the German army. Leaving the ghetto for the factory early in the morning and returning early in the evening, they were the only Jews permitted to cross the city. They carried identity cards that guaranteed the safety of the bearer and three members of his family: his wife and two of his children under the age of sixteen. This was documented down to the last detail by the Germans in extensive written regulations. It makes you wonder what for, when the ultimate goal remained the total extermination of the Jewish population. The exemptions that applied to the furriers meant that the Kacews were spared until September 1943. Then the SS informed the Jewish Council that the 3,000 workers at the factory would be liquidated and the 2,000 Jews still living in the ghetto would be deported to labour camps in Estonia and Latvia. For most of the women, this meant Kaiserwald concentration camp near Riga. The men, along with some women and children, were killed far closer to home, in Paneriai. The massacre that took place there stained the grass red, and the skin and limbs of the children shot to pieces hung from the trees.

The last of the ghetto's survivors were deported to Klooga concentration camp in Estonia. As the Red Army approached and the dull salvos of the Russian artillery could be heard, the remaining prisoners were hastily shot or burned alive on pyres doused in petrol. The SS resorted to this medieval method in the hope of wiping out the traces of mass extermination. The barracks also went up in flames. The lives of 2,500 deportees were lost in the fires, including those of Frida Kacew and her children, Pavel and Valentina, Roman's half-brother and half-sister. Their father, Arieh-Leib, was probably among the victims of the mass killings on 24 September 1943, in the oak forests of Paneriai less than seven kilometres south-west of Vilné.

Romain Gary cannot be blamed for failing, in the aftermath of the war, to do what his biographer Myriam Anissimov would do half a century later: conduct a painstaking investigation of the true circumstances of his father's death. The events were too horrific, especially for a son who despised his father. It is also possible to understand why Gary took refuge in less brutal fabrications about his childhood, versions that were, at best, bittersweet. He rejected the role of victim to the point where he did not even care to be associated with the Jews of Vilnius. Like his mother, he had become a combative survivor. In the 1930s, anti-Semitism also took hold in France; once in Nice, Roman soon recognised the expediency of covering up his background and his ancestry. But after the war, it would have been better for him not to devote a single word or letter to his father's death. In Gary's version of events, his father even lacked the backbone to enter the gas chamber. An accusation so crude, you are left to infer that young Roman left Lithuania as a deeply disturbed child.

Mina saved her son's life during World War I. During their deportation to Russia, she kept him from hunger and thirst in conditions that left many young children dead of dehydration. Roman remembered nothing of that time, though it did leave him with a deep distaste for drunks, a reaction, perhaps, to the alcohol-fuelled, demoralised Russian soldiers they had encountered in those chaotic years. As an adult, he did not drink a drop of alcohol, not even the smallest glass of wine with dinner.

In the 1920s, Mina saved his life a second time: she took Roman to Italy, where he overcame a mysterious kidney ailment.

But her most miraculous intervention came at the beginning of World War II, when, from a distance of 800 kilometres, she saved her son from certain death. In June 1940, Mina was living in Nice, where she ran a simple family guesthouse. On 16 June 1940, her son was leaving for England with three friends to join the forces of General de Gaulle. He had already boarded the small plane when a man came cycling towards them over the runway at Bordeaux-Mérignac airfield. Urgent call for Gary! He knew right away it was his mother, ringing with some last-minute encouragement. As he stood at the phone, chatting to Mina, the plane — an experimental Den-55 — took off for a test run. Suddenly it seemed to stall in midair. It lurched to the left and plummeted to earth, exploding on impact. Gary's friends were killed instantly. Yet again, Mina had been her son's guardian angel.

Gary also maintained that she saved his life a fourth time: throughout the war, he continued to receive letters from her, in Africa, the Middle East, England. They never failed to lift his spirits. Only after the war did he discover that Mina had died in 1941. On her deathbed, she had written 250 letters in a matter of weeks and instructed an acquaintance to send them to her son one by one, at weekly intervals.

At any rate, that's how Gary tells it in *Promise at Dawn*. None of these letters have survived, and it is almost inconceivable that Gary would have destroyed such tangible evidence of his mother's love. He treasured even the smallest, fuzziest picture of Mina as if it were a lock of her hair.

Romain Gary became a war hero. In 1943, Lee Miller photographed him in the uniform of Les Forces aériennes françaises libres. It is an image that radiates self-confidence, though by then he was one of only a handful of survivors. Of the fifty airmen who joined the Lorraine squadron, only three lived to see liberation.

After the near-fatal sortie of 25 January 1944, Gary spent a month in hospital. He had barely recovered when he boarded a bomber again on 25 February. Until 10 April, he flew mission after mission. Not that he was a warrior addicted to battle: Gary abhorred violence and wholesale destruction, but part of him could never forget that he had come from the ghetto of Vilnius. From the first day of the war, he was prepared to give his life for a democratic Europe free from racial hatred, to give his life for freedom. He became one of the French nationals of foreign origin serving under de Gaulle during the earliest, most difficult phase of the conflict, when the general spoke with barely concealed contempt of being surrounded by 'nothing but dirty immigrants'.

Gary married English journalist and writer Lesley Blanch, who was ten years his senior and by no means a beauty. More than his lover, she became his confidante. They slept in separate beds. Blanch

Mina, who saved her son's life at least three times.

was far too independent to fulfil a maternal role. She loved Gary's
Slavic side; her role model was Russian adventurer Isabelle Eberhardt,
about whom she wrote extensively in *The Wilder Shores of Love*,
a book that made her a bestselling author in the UK and the US.

During the war, she had earned herself a reputation as one of Britain's outstanding reporters, and several leading publishers had been keen to woo her. With Blanch at his side, Gary was practically guaranteed a UK publisher for his debut novel.

A European Education, the French edition of which was published in 1945, is set in Poland and Lithuania and recounts the fortunes of a Polish-Jewish resistance group during World War II. Gary's biographer Myriam Anissimov notes that such groups did not in fact exist. The small numbers of Poles and Jews who took up arms against the Germans did so separately: the Poles' aversion towards Jews precluded cooperation, and for their part, the Jews distrusted the Poles.

In Lithuania, I am given a different take on this situation. To join the resistance, Jews first had to escape the Vilnius ghetto, a feat which was nigh on impossible. Seen in this light, the number of Jewish partisans was considerable: about 1,650. In the forests, they banded together in small, tight-knit, autonomous groups, or threw in their lot with Belarussian resistance fighters — Soviets from the east, that is, rather than Polish partisans.

Even so, it was Gary's version of events, a tale in which Polish and Jewish resistance fighters worked together heroically, that made the book a success, first in Britain, then in France, and ultimately in Poland. Though its tone is sober, it is a paean to the partisan mentality, and it earned Gary a diplomatic post courtesy of a panel of war veterans, French novelist André Malraux among them.

A photograph taken in 1949 shows Gary and Blanch in the unheated service quarters of the French legation in the Bulgarian capital, Sofia. Her hat is fur, his is astrakhan. Gary's next posting was New York, where he became part of the French delegation to the United Nations. After this, he and Blanch moved to Los Angeles. It was there that he met Jean Seberg and began a legal battle with Blanch that lasted years, after she refused to give him a divorce.

He wrote seven, eight, nine novels in powerful, punchy, high-flown French. Rich in colloquialisms, it was a style that played fast and loose with grammar and syntax, more reminiscent of American writers than the likes of André Malraux or François Mauriac. Interestingly, he wrote four of his novels in English, before translating them into French. For him, translation almost always became rewriting. Even the books he had written directly in French were subject to tinkering with each new edition, ten or fifteen years later.

Like Joseph Conrad and Vladimir Nabokov, Gary was one of those miraculous writers with an astounding command of a language other than his mother tongue. In Gary's case, this was all the more remarkable given that he did not have a true mother tongue. In his dreams, he sometimes spoke Russian, sometimes Polish, usually laced with Yiddish words and expressions. His pride in his French rivalled that of Guillaume Apollinaire — real name Guillaume Apollinaire de Kostrowitzky — whose mother was Polish and who had mastered French at the same lycée in Nice where Gary would one day astound his fellow pupils with his exceptionally rich vocabulary.

Gary would never be a poet, but he was an outstanding storyteller with an exceptional talent for humour and irony, both mild and acerbic. His fluid narrative style won him hordes of readers. Here was a writer who drew you in, who could make you laugh, squirm, shudder, and cry. Qualities that were frowned upon by the French literati. His admiration for Charles de Gaulle meant that he was shunned by the likes of Jean-Paul Sartre, Albert Camus, Simone de Beauvoir, Boris Vian, and Raymond Queneau. In the 1960s, Gary became a completely isolated figure on the French literary scene.

This did not lead Gary to temper his esteem for de Gaulle, in whom he had found a father figure: a courageous man, as steadfast as he was intractable, an erudite and incorruptible soldier, and above all, a virtuous husband who would remain eternally faithful to his devoted Yvonne. In the fidelity department, Gary was de Gaulle's absolute opposite: during his marriage to Lesley Blanch and later, when he was married to Jean Seberg, he had a series of lovers, some famous (actress Romy Schneider), some young (writer Katherine Pancol, forty years his junior). In the meantime, Gary became a father himself: Jean bore him a son. He made sure little Diego was well cared for, but without toning down his lifestyle. Though he despised himself for it, Gary had become addicted to fast sex and fleeting encounters. At the same time, knowing full well it was a sham, he clung to the image of the ideal father: the man presiding at the family dinner table every evening. A man you can depend on, who will look you straight in the eye. A man like Charles de Gaulle.

Gary's loyalty to the general never faded. He seemed to have an unshakeable bond with war veterans, and with the mouthpieces of Gaullism: *Le Figaro* and *Paris Match*. As a diplomat, he reaped the benefits; as a writer, he bet on the wrong horse. In the eyes of the Parisian literary set, he had become a reactionary veteran who lived more in the past than in the present.

His marriage to Jean Seberg did little to change things. Seberg had become the face of the nouvelle vague thanks to her leading role in Jean-Luc Godard's *Breathless*, the explosive film in which she played the lover of gangster Jean-Paul Belmondo. As the cream of the French cultural world saw it, she then ripped up her cutting-edge credentials by falling for a much older man who turned up in uniform every year at the national Remembrance Day ceremony and continued to back de Gaulle even amid the upheaval of May 1968.

Proving her detractors wrong, Seberg became an active supporter of the Black Panther Party in the US. Though from a diffident middle-class background, she gravitated towards radical politics and came under the influence of Hakim Abdullah Jamal, a former associate of Malcolm X. She gave thousands of dollars to Jamal and the Black-rights movement, enough to prompt the FBI to keep close tabs on her, even to the point of having her shadowed and listening in on her phone calls day and night. Time and again, the trail led to Jamal, with whom she fell passionately in love.

Gary watched all this unfold from a distance. He wanted nothing to do with the radical Black leaders ('all anti-Semites'), and even less to do with any person or movement he judged as willing to exploit an impressionable actress for their own ends. Yet at the same time, he was outraged that the FBI seemed bent on making Seberg's life a misery in every possible way. It drove her to the brink of paranoia, alienated her from those around her, from the film world and, ultimately, from her husband. Gary had since left the diplomatic service, but when he and Jean returned to Paris, it was to live at different addresses.

As a writer, Gary had reached a dead end. Nothing he produced had any merit in the eyes of the leading literary critics of the day. He saw only one way out of this impasse: to adopt a pseudonym. Under the name Shatan Bogat, he published *Les têtes de Stéphanie*, a novel he had initially written in English under the title *A Direct Flight to Allah*. The ploy failed: Gary was soon exposed as the author, and the subsequent reprint of the novel was issued under his own name. To pull off his escape into anonymity, a change of publisher was required. Instead of submitting the manuscript of *Gros-Câlin* to Gallimard, he sent it to Mercure de France. This debut novel by the unknown Émile Ajar received scant attention, but Gary held firm and published a second title under the same pseudonym. *La vie devant soi* (The Life Before Us) became a bestseller and was awarded the Prix Goncourt in 1975. As the Prix Goncourt's statutes prohibit a writer from winning twice, Gary had no option but to maintain the facade of his assumed identity. He nudged a maternal cousin, Paul Pavlowitch, into the spotlight to claim the nom de plume of Ajar and looked on in silence as *La vie devant soi* garnered ever more success, thanks in part to the film adaptation, featuring a tour de force by Simone Signoret.

Purely by dint of his writing, Gary had taken his revenge in style. But living with a fame you cannot celebrate is far from easy. The young philosopher Bernard–Henri Lévy, who lived round the corner from Gary and had coffee with him every morning, became fascinated by the writer, in whom he saw an older version of himself. Gary was every bit as cosmopolitan, as heroic, and as Jewish as Lévy wanted to be. He contacted the chief arts editor of the weekly *Le Nouvel Observateur* about interviewing him and was told, 'Oh man, Gary is out, completely out. Interview his cousin! Interview Ajar! He's the real writer, the real wordsmith. He is the true genius.'

I first read *La vie devant soi* when only three people knew Émile Ajar's true identity: Gary, his cousin, and his publisher. It has a purity of tone that I have seldom encountered. I reread it during my time in Vilnius, and its gentle irony moves me once again. The first time, I warmed to the deep humanity in the story of a jaded madam receiving help from Momo, the young boy who lugs the wheezing old woman's shopping bag up the stairs and dispels her dark thoughts with his amusing stories. When I realise now that Madame Rosa is none other than Mina, when she was running her Nice guesthouse, the book becomes even more poignant for me.

Gary had previously portrayed Mina in *Promise at Dawn*, filmed in 1969 with Melina Mercouri in the role of the mother. Halfway through the premiere, Gary fled the auditorium in tears, weeping with rage. In one scene, the young boy in the film — Gary himself, in other words — says to his mother, 'Mama, I don't want to be

Jewish.' That was when Gary ran out of the cinema, suddenly realising how far he had gone in his self-loathing. Hours later, he had still not recovered from the shock; sobbing, he walked the boulevards of Paris for an entire afternoon.

Mina came to life on the silver screen a second time, as Madame Rosa in *La vie devant soi*. Initially, Simone Signoret had turned down the part, considering herself too much of a beauty to play a decrepit madam. After reading the book, she changed her mind, and turned Madame Rosa into the most moving creation of her career — her face puffy, wrinkled, and stripped of make-up. Gary did not attend the premiere, but watched the film at a Paris cinema one week later. This time, he stayed until the end.

It was only after his death that Gary was revealed as the writer behind the pseudonym Ajar. Revisiting the novel in that knowledge, it strikes me as an even greater accomplishment. As well as his mother, Gary also transformed himself — little Roman, living in a one-bedroom flat — into the Arab kid, Momo. As if to say: Jewish, Muslim, it doesn't matter. What Jewish boys were to Vilnius, Muslim boys are to Marseilles or Nice or the banlieues of Paris. They belong to a large, widely disparaged minority. They are every bit as caring as German, Polish, Russian, or French boys, but can only show that side of themselves to a figure like Madame Rosa, someone who is treated with the same contempt.

Gary needed his imagination to escape the horrors of his childhood. He did this with unerring skill at first, a lightness of touch that grew steadily more warped. The low point came with the lies he told about his father in 1956. He made a glorious recovery with *La vie devant soi*, but one year later he was back plumbing the depths. As Émile Ajar, he published *Pseudo*, followed a few years later by *L'angoisse du roi Salomon*. In particular, *La danse de Gengis Cohn*, written under his own name in 1968, is torture to read. Describing a scene in which mothers with children are waiting to be shot by the Nazis, he writes, 'I don't want to sound anti-Semitic, but nothing screams like a Jewish mother when her kids are being murdered.'

However hard he tried, Gary was unable to overcome his self-loathing. Fearing old age and deterioration, he took his own life at the age of sixty-six. On 2 December 1980, at his home on Rue du

Bac in Paris's seventh arrondissement, he placed a towel on the pillow, lay down on the bed, put the muzzle of a revolver in his mouth, and pulled the trigger.

Fifteen months earlier, on a Paris street, the body of Jean Seberg had been found on the back seat of her Renault. After seven suicide attempts, the eighth had proved fatal. Jean died of an overdose of barbiturates and alcohol, parked a few hundred metres from Rue du Bac.

A note was found on the bed where Gary had pulled the trigger.

> D-day.
> No connection with Jean Seberg. Lovers of broken hearts are kindly asked to search elsewhere.
> Obviously one could blame this on nervous depression. But then, one would have to admit that it had lasted since I reached manhood and had permitted me to carry on my literary work.
> Why then? Perhaps one should seek the answer in the title of my autobiography *La nuit sera calme* (The Night Will Be Peaceful). And in the last words of my last novel: 'Because it could not be said better.' I have explained myself fully.
> Romain Gary

Thus ended the life of a man who had escaped the hell of Vilnius and survived two world wars, the first in the east, the second in the west ... A few hastily worded sentences, ugly sentences that scream loneliness.

Walking through Vilnius, I am constantly reminded of another passage from *La danse de Gengis Cohn*, which Gary wrote shortly after visiting Warsaw in 1966. He had been invited to give a lecture at the university. Jean Seberg travelled with him. This reunion with Poland was a shock to his system, one that is still palpable in his novel, published two years later.

> There are some dead who never die. I would even say that the more often they are killed, the more they are there. Take Germany. Today it's a country entirely inhabited by Jews. Of course, you can't see them, they don't have any physical presence, but ... how shall I put it? They make themselves *felt*. Walk around in German cities, as well

as in Warsaw and other places rich in German history, and you feel a strange, heavy, Jewish presence in the air. Yes, the streets are full of Jews who are not there. It makes a poignant impression. By the way, there is an expression in Yiddish that comes from Roman law: the dead take the place of the living. That's exactly it. I don't want to hurt an entire people, but Germany is a country that has become completely Jewish.

Five thousand Jews still live in Vilnius, most of whom were born in Russia, Belarus, or Ukraine. One synagogue still stands, the Choral Synagogue at Pylimo gatvė 39.

At the only museum that tells the city's Jewish history, I have to come back twice before someone answers the doorbell. The place consists of four rooms of photographs: pictures of the ghetto symphony orchestra, the ghetto choir, the ghetto dramatic society (which gave 120 performances), the school where the children were taught until their deportation. At the Holocaust Museum, a green, single-storey wooden house, I am the first visitor in five days. The images of women's bodies lying pale and naked in ditches turn my stomach.

The former ghetto has been absorbed into the old city. And yet, on every street corner, in every square, down every alley, it feels as if something is missing. As if the city cannot quite come to life without its Jews. It is only when you imagine them, in their thousands, in their tens of thousands, that you find yourself walking through a city you can love.

Gary wanted nothing more to do with Vilné. On my last day in the city, I begin to understand why. In *The Baltic Times*, I read a report that the Lithuanian government has finally agreed to pay compensation for the buildings lost to the Jewish community during World War II. The payment of 376 million litai is due to begin in January 2011 and end in March 2021.

In 2021? Seventy-eight years after the last Jews from the Vilnius ghetto were killed?

I call Simonas Gurevičius, the head of the Jewish community in Lithuania. That same afternoon, I sit opposite him in his study. Aged 81, Gurevičius is eating Turkish delight and trying to appear as calm as possible.

'But surely this is a disgrace?' I say, again and again. 'Three-quarters of a century after the war, and finally they start paying ...'

Previous efforts to pay compensation led to so much tension in Lithuania that the government reneged on its promises. 'We are satisfied that the present government is serious about compensation,' Gurevičius tells me. 'Note that this is compensation for the loss of community buildings — synagogues, places of worship, schools, and buildings used by associations — not houses or other private property. We will spend the money on public facilities that will be open to all Lithuanians. On libraries, for example. We want to keep everything as transparent as possible and avoid creating any further tensions in society.'

Libraries, public facilities for all Lithuanians; these are the words of a wary man. Simonas Gurevičius speaks softly, in a voice that is wavering, almost apologetic. He is keenly aware that one word out of place is all it will take for the hatred to flare up again.

On leaving his office, I bump into Dovid Katz. I give him a brief account of my conversation, and he nods. 'A few years ago, there was a big demonstration by right-wing extremists here in Vilnius. They railed against everything and everyone. Against Jews, Russians, Belarussians, foreigners, communists, socialists, homosexuals ... The next day, the Polish embassy issued a press release. "We are deeply disturbed that the protesters did not mention Poles in their slogans. Since when have we not been counted among Lithuania's enemies?"' Katz wipes away tears of laughter. 'That's Polish humour for you. The Poles got it: the one response that shows up hardline nationalists for what they are is hilarity. And that was exactly the attitude Romain Gary took. He could have written deeply tragic books about the fate of Lithuania's Jews, but he embraced sardonic derision and laughed away his anger.'

'Yes,' I say quietly, 'until he couldn't laugh anymore. And then he picked up his gun.'

6

The Child Who Paid the Price

LORETA ASANAVIČIŪTĖ FROM VILNIUS

Lithuania, April 2009
Every ethnic group in the Baltic countries has its own heroes, its own saints, its own martyrs, and its own villains. Good and evil intersect at every turn. One person's righteous crusade is another's rage, despair, or sorrow. Lithuania's nationalists are often characterised as rightwing, chauvinist, and Catholic, but they were on the front line in the fight against the communist oppressor. Without their commitment and courage, Lithuania would not be the free European nation it is today.

Loreta Asanavičiūtė was a girl you could easily fall in love with — wavy, shoulder-length black hair, parted to the left; dark eyes, straight eyebrows, and full lips. She was slender, with a long, graceful neck. Perhaps the most touching thing about her was her earnest expression. In the last surviving photo of her, she is gazing sternly into the distance, as if watching a calamity unfold.

By all accounts, she was a quiet girl, shy, and prone to reflection. Loreta was not fond of loud music and had no time for rock. She sang in a choir, where she wore a long, burgundy dress with a lace collar. A good girl, you might think, if you hail from Amsterdam. As decent and well-behaved as her sister Renata, who was also a choirgirl. Loreta sang in the union choir, her sister in a folk choir. Not that there is anything exceptional about this in Lithuania, or Latvia, or Estonia for that matter. If one fanatical pastime unites these neighbours, it is singing. The Baltic countries are home to hundreds, if not thousands of choirs.

A song festival is held in Riga every five years, a tradition that dates back to 1873. One thousand singers took part in the original festival, 10,000 in 1988. Towards the end of the Soviet regime, singing

Loreta Asanavičiūtė in 1988.

became an even bigger craze in Riga, Vilnius, Tallinn, and the provincial towns. The pent-up rage of the Baltic people had to be vented somehow, and it found expression in song. The Gaudeamus song festival in Vilnius went from being a convivial celebration of national

Loreta (right) in Lithuanian costume and her sister Renata (playing accordion), with members of a Lithuanian musical ensemble.

folklore to an annual protest gathering. Vingio Park, where the choirs came to perform their dainas, would be teeming with people.

The daina stands at the centre of a strong cultural tradition, a four-line poem performed as a folk song and expressing all aspects of life and nature. Their use of internal rhyme and alliteration is reminiscent of haiku. New anthologies are published every few years, but the standard work remains Krišjānis Barons's six-volume edition from 1915. Travelling through Latvia and northern Lithuania, he collected 35,000 dainas with more than 200,000 variations over the course of eleven years. These two, three, and four-part songs deal with love and death, lakes and forests, summer and winter, reaping and sowing, pain and pleasure. They describe the rituals of the feast of St John, when men, women, and children are crowned with floral garlands. The daina is the most profoundly characteristic aspect of Baltic cultural life, a singing tradition they have nurtured and kept alive through wave upon wave of conflict and foreign occupation. When it comes to part-song in particular, the Baltic countries are unrivalled. There is no better place for choirs than Estonia, Latvia, and Lithuania.

In light of all this, there was nothing especially straitlaced about Loreta's singing or about song being a primary outlet for her Lithuanian identity. That said, she was cautious by nature. Perhaps this had something to do with her father's absence. He had left by the time she was born. Her mother, a bookkeeper, had to work hard to raise her two daughters and her son. Loreta studied at the School of Finance and Credit and earned herself some extra money at the Dovana garment factory. At home, she made music with Renata; one would play the piano, the other the accordion, and of course they sang together. Sweet daughters who gave their mother no cause for concern. Who could have thought that Loreta would go down in history as a rebel?

I walk the length of Gedimino prospektas, a distance of two kilometres. In the 1950s, the avenue bore Stalin's name, followed by Lenin's from the 1960s to the late 1980s. Its department stores spent years behind scaffolding, until the communist drabness had been chipped away; today, the grandeur of the early-twentieth-century plaster shopfronts has been restored, in pastel shades that give them a fresh, modern feel. Here, contemporary Vilnius finds expression in an appealing mix of old and new. Gedimino prospektas has become a pretty-in-pink shopping street, a place for a pleasant stroll: the road is only open to public transport.

Reaching the end, I take the bridge across the river and board a bus heading west to the modern district of Karoliniškės. Before long, I find the block of flats where Loreta grew up. A 1950s building, blackened by the exhaust fumes of the traffic that races past. On every balcony, laundry has been hung out to dry in the feeble spring sunshine. Crates of beer are stacked beneath the trousers, shirts, and towels. Lopsided satellite dishes cling to the railings to catch foreign TV channels. Children wail; radios blare.

This was the environment Loreta hoped to escape when, in 1990, she got engaged to an older man. A balding chap with a good job. With him, she hoped to start a better life in a pleasant neighbourhood across the river.

The *televizijos bokštas* is hard to miss, a television tower rising 326 metres above the city. I consider taking the lift to the revolving restaurant halfway up (360 degrees in sixty minutes) to admire the magnificent views. Instead, I enter an exhibition space on the ground floor, a tribute to the country's Defenders of Freedom.

The first thing to catch my eye is the floor with its wooden crosses.

Lithuanians have a thing for crosses. Near Šiauliai, 180 kilometres from the capital, an entire hill is covered with tens of thousands, perhaps even hundreds of thousands of crosses. On three separate occasions, Soviet bulldozers rumbled up to the site to clear it of religious symbolism, but every year, on the third Sunday in July, pilgrims would arrive and plant more, a staggering number. The cross became the symbol of Lithuania's national consciousness.

I take a closer look at the photos and recognise Loreta Asanavičiūtė. The words of Dutch songsmith Boudewijn de Groot pop into my head: 'Poor child / sixteen springs old / how still you lie / by the side of the road.' Sixteen is poetic licence. Loreta was older, twenty-three, almost twenty-four. But in the pictures, she looks much younger. She really is still a girl. A girl who wrote poetry, who dreamed of love and woodland holidays.

In the first week of January 1991, Loreta woke up screaming. A nightmare, she told her mother. She had screamed when, in her dream, a metal object had struck her head. Her mother edged onto the bed beside her and told her she should be dreaming about her hope chest instead.

Loreta may have shared the ideas being expressed by Lithuania's dissidents, but she lacked their courage. Like many others of her generation, she steered clear of anything that smacked of politics. Until 1988.

At Dovana, she was one of forty women working in the same factory workshop, stitching pictures and decorations onto sweaters. It was mind-numbing work, and to stop themselves being driven mad by the rattling of the sewing machines, the women listened to the radio. One hour they tuned into a popular Russian music station, the next a Lithuanian station — a compromise given that half of them were Russian and the other half Lithuanian. One day, one of the Russian women stood up and exclaimed that she could not listen to 'that godawful language' a minute longer. To Loreta, this felt like a slap in the face. On 23 August 1989, she joined the two million Estonians, Latvians, and Lithuanians who formed a human chain, a Baltic Way that stretched over 650 kilometres from Tallinn to Vilnius. She took part in every demonstration from that day on.

When the Soviets decided to halt the steady grind towards

The Hill of Crosses near Šiauliai.

independence by seizing control of the television station, Loreta was among the protesters again. Her sister was there too; so was her mother. On 12 and 13 January 1991, she sang as one with the determined crowd. After standing firm for hours, she returned home with her mother, but the dull boom of distant artillery fire drew her back to the tower. Her mother planned to join her later and bring an umbrella. By the time she arrived, it was snowing heavily, and she was unable to find her daughter among the crowd.

Close to two in the morning, Loreta found herself on the front lines, where the protesters stood shoulder to shoulder, arms linked. Her main motive for standing there, for facing the Russian tanks, was that she was sick to death of singing in Russian. What she was feeling could only be expressed in her own language, in Lithuanian. And perhaps there was a personal barb in her protest too: her absent father was of Russian descent.

During those January days, the situation was chaotic. Eighteen months of protests seemed to be coming to a grim end.

The uprising had begun with the Baltic Way on 23 August 1989. That mass demonstration, exactly fifty years after the signing of the Molotov-Ribbentrop Pact, would go down in history as the Singing Revolution. A cappella, two million protesters signalled the start of what would turn out to be a monumental change. The Singing Revolution had the strength and spontaneity of the Prague Spring, the May 68 protests in Paris, and Portugal's Carnation Revolution. Loreta was one of those singing revolutionaries.

On 20 December 1989, the Communist Party of Lithuania split from the Communist Party of the Soviet Union. On 11 January 1990, protesters disrupted a visit to Vilnius by Mikhail Gorbachev. Cameras zoomed in on the unsuspecting Soviet leader's face as he strolled down Aušros Vartų gatvė to acknowledge the cheers from the crowd. Suddenly, a man stepped forward. A figure in workman's clothes, with broad shoulders and short grey hair. Security guards tried to shove him aside, but he held firm and stood directly in front of Gorbachev. 'You have exploited us for fifty years,' he said. The Russian party leader was visibly shocked and asked the man what he meant. 'You have humiliated us for fifty years.' Gorbachev's expression was a mixture of anger and bewilderment. Such sentiments were never voiced within the walls of the Kremlin, views that local and regional party leaders had never dared relay to him. The footage was broadcast live on Lithuanian television. Gorbachev barely knew what to do with himself as the man confronted him fearlessly and told him in five sentences what was wrong with the Lithuanian Soviet Socialist Republic. Gorbachev took this as a personal affront. He turned and strode away. Onlookers booed. The Black Madonna surveyed the scene from above the city gate. The camera caught her halo and her smile.

The next day, Gorbachev addressed around 1,000 union and party executives. Assured of a warm response, he delivered his speech as planned, but it was met with a meagre applause that stopped before it had properly begun. Again, there was surprise on Gorbachev's face. Before leaving the lectern, he asked an off-the-cuff question: 'Do you really want independence?' A thousand voices answered: 'Yes.' He asked again, unable to believe their resolve. 'Do you really want independence?' Their answer came as a roar: 'Yes.' That same afternoon, Gorbachev broke off his visit to Vilnius and flew back to Moscow.

On 24 February, the independence movement Sąjūdis won a parliamentary majority in the country's first free elections. On 11 March, Vytautas Landsbergis — the newly elected speaker of Lithuania's parliament, and its de facto head of state — proclaimed independence and demanded the withdrawal of Soviet troops. On 17 April, the

Soviets responded by imposing an economic blockade on Lithuania. This stalemate held for eight months, then nine: the calm before the storm. On 1 January 1991, food prices shot up, and even the most basic foodstuffs had to be rationed. This was the last straw, even for Russians living in Lithuania.

On 8 and 9 January, the Soviet Union dispatched a number of army units to Lithuania. They came under the command of General Vladislav Achalov, the Soviet Union's deputy defence minister, who was hastily flown into Vilnius. On 10 January, Mikhail Gorbachev demanded that the constitution adopted by the Lithuanian parliament be repealed and the Soviet constitution reinstated. On 11 and 12 January, Russian troops tried to enter parliament, an action prevented by the foresight and leadership of Landsbergis.

Up to this point, there had been nothing to suggest that Vytautas Landsbergis would be the man to save his country. He had received many an ovation in his time, but only as a pianist. He had addressed many a packed hall, but only at the conservatory and the university, where he lectured in musicology. Landsbergis, the great connoisseur of painter-poet-composer Mikalojus Konstantinas Čiurlionis (1875–1911), had more than fifteen publications to his name when he entered the political arena in 1988 and founded independence movement Sąjūdis with a small group of like-minded individuals. Two years later, he declared independence, and Lithuania became the first Soviet republic to take its fate into its own hands.

Landsbergis never became what you might call a dyed-in-the-wool politician. With a voice as soft and mournful as the opening bars of the *Moonlight Sonata*, he was ill-equipped to stir the hearts of the nation's voters. At the lectern, his head was bowed and his shoulders rounded, as if his hands were unconsciously searching for the keys of a piano. For Lithuanians, he was and would remain the man who brought about the country's independence. But once that milestone had been achieved, he gradually lost his grip on the country, and his electoral support shrank to a mere 15 per cent.

In 1991, however, he played a crucial role. He kept a watchful eye on the process as it unfolded, a skill that comes in extremely handy in a crisis. Nothing escaped his attention; he listened intently, gathering as much information as possible, appraising the situation from hour to hour, and turning events in his favour.

He trusted Gorbachev no more than a slave trusts his master, and refused to be taken in by the man's air of good-natured lenience. Gorbachev's smile may have worked well on Western television, but behind that affable demeanour, Landsbergis could see a spooked and manipulative leader determined to prop up the Soviet empire to the bitter end. He was not mistaken. During those turbulent January days, he called Gorbachev three times in an effort to reason with him and calm the situation. The Russian party leader would not come to the phone.

Gorbachev saw Lithuania's declaration of independence as a provocation and decided to intervene. The first blood flowed in Vilnius on 7 January at the Press Building in Karoliniškės. The Soviets wanted to seize control of the building but about a hundred Lithuanians were on hand to stop them. Their approach was unconventional to say the least: a young man by the name of Vitas Lukšys wielded a pipe and blew water in the direction of the Russian soldiers. A Soviet colonel reached for his gun and shot him. The bullet grazed Lukšys's head, causing a gaping wound. A Norwegian cameraman captured the shooting on film, and it made news around the world.

This gave Landsbergis the idea of making active use of television. Until that time, Lithuanian broadcasting had been a sedate affair, with programming from seven to nine in the morning and from six in the evening until midnight. Landsbergis ordered wall-to-wall coverage, turning Lithuanian television into a kind of low-budget CNN, delivering nonstop news round the clock. He dispatched camera crews to parliament, where up to 60,000 people had gathered. The demonstration was broadcast without a break, and viewing figures hit 90 per cent. Anyone who wasn't out demonstrating in the bitter cold — the temperature had dropped to minus fifteen — was glued to the television screen. The broadcast continued throughout the night. Landsbergis was interviewed repeatedly, calling on his fellow Lithuanians to defend parliament, the television studios, the television tower, the telephone exchange, and other key government buildings. Cameras followed the crowds, and with the eyes of the world upon them, the Soviets were reluctant to intervene.

Most of the television crews were concentrated at the parliament. In the dead of night, around 2.00 am on 13 January, Russian soldiers cut the cables relaying footage to the studio in Vilnius. The

technicians got to work and succeeded in rerouting the signal through
the television studio in Kaunas. All night long, TV Kaunas took over
the Vilnius broadcasts.

At the television studios in Vilnius, Soviet soldiers became increasingly worried that they would be filmed from inside the building.
By this time, the crowd was delirious and began chanting, '*Fashisty,
fashisty, ubiytsy.*' 'Fascists, fascists, murderers.' For the Soviets, 'fascist'
was the worst of all insults. In fury, they reached for their guns and
began shooting over the heads of the protesters. Meanwhile, their
T-72 tanks and BTR-60 and BRDM armoured vehicles began firing
salvo after salvo.

When the Soviet army did launch a full-blown assault, it was
three kilometres away, at the television tower, where only one camera
crew was on hand to record the events. First, the military tried to
sow confusion among the protesters. Through the loudspeaker of an
armoured vehicle, one of the last of the Moscow faithful, Communist
Party ideologue Juozas Jermalavičius, called on the protesters to give
up the fight. 'Brothers, Lithuanians! The nationalist and separatist
government has fallen! Return to your parents and your children, all
of you!' His appeal was met with a chorus of whistling, followed by a
chant of 'Freedom now! Freedom now!' At that moment, a command
sounded from another loudspeaker, and the tanks advanced.

One of the protesters, Algirdas Šukys, gave a detailed account the
next morning.

> I barely had time to pull my foot back ahead of the tank tracks. To
> my left, I heard a scream. I turned and saw a woman, a girl, lying
> on her back. It was hard to see her face in the shadow of the tank,
> but I could tell she was wearing a light-coloured scarf or hat, and a
> dark or grey coat. Her legs were trapped under the tracks. Men were
> trying to push the tank away so that they could pull the casualty out
> from under, but it was no use. That thing was far too heavy, colossal.
> I started banging on the top of the tank, shouting in Russian that
> there was a woman underneath. A soldier lunged at me, swore
> loudly, thumped me on my back, in my stomach, and shoved me
> off the tank. The tank began to move, but before it shot forward,
> it rolled back a little and crushed her even more. Then several men
> lifted the young woman and carried her away.

A cameraman registered the protesters' attempts to push the tank away and filmed the tank rolling back, over Loreta, at close range. Her lower left leg was severed by the tracks. These images, which can still be found on Lithuanian websites, are horrific.

A total of fifteen people were killed at the television tower that night: thirteen protesters, including eight students (the youngest had yet to turn eighteen) and five workers (the oldest was sixty), an onlooker who died of heart failure, and a Soviet soldier hit in the chest by a ricocheting bullet at the entrance to the tower. Between 600 and 700 people were injured.

Loreta Asanavičiūtė was transferred to the Red Cross Hospital. As she was being admitted, she asked the doctor, 'Will I survive?'

A television journalist held out a microphone to her. Loreta was so numb from the cold that she could barely move her lips, never mind speak. She turned her head and looked straight at the lens. Ask any Lithuanian: no one who saw it has forgotten that look, the suffering on her face.

A team of doctors and nurses worked for hours to save her. It was then that she asked one last question, later read out on Lithuanian television; a question that brought an entire nation to tears and left it incandescent with rage. A question that turned Gorbachev's affable expression into something far more sinister and ultimately led to the withdrawal of all Soviet troops from Lithuania.

'Can I still get married?' she asked. 'Will I be able to dance at my wedding?'

The Russian tanks attacking the protesters at the Vilnius television tower escaped the gaze of the rest of the world. Soviet television reported that several people had died in 'road accidents' near the Lithuanian television station and that an onlooker had died of heart failure. Only that last detail was true.

The images of Loreta Asanavičiūtė lying fatally injured on the ground did not make headline news in the West. Another conflict had entered the spotlight: the outbreak of the Gulf War. The only tanks shown to television viewers across Western Europe and the US were those advancing through the deserts of Kuwait and Iraq.

The only protest to the UN Security Council came from the

Loreta crushed by the Russian tank, as protesters try to push it away.

Norwegian government, which called for an investigation of the events in Lithuania. The government of Poland declared its solidarity with the Lithuanian people and condemned the actions of the Soviet army. The government of Iceland considered recognising the new republic of Lithuania six days after the massacre and eventually did so two weeks later, on 11 February. The government of Sweden decided to open an embassy in the Republic of Lithuania. The United

States and the United Kingdom kept quiet for months, as did the governments of most of the European Union's member states, the Netherlands included.

This lukewarm response left a bitter taste in the mouth of Vytautas Landsbergis. When he was later elected to the European Parliament, he proposed a ban on all Soviet communist emblems, such as the hammer and sickle, along the lines of an earlier law that banned Nazi emblems such as the swastika. It earned him a furious reaction from the Italian Communist Party and the backing of Alessandra Mussolini and her neo-fascist Alternativa Sociale.

Loreta Asanavičiūtė was buried in the Pantheon of Antakalnis Cemetery in Vilnius, alongside the thirteen other Lithuanians who lost their lives on 13 January 1991. Fresh flowers are laid on her grave each day. Lithuanians say her voice can always be heard whenever they sing the national anthem.

Young, well-educated women like Loreta were among the greatest beneficiaries of the change that came to Lithuania. More than their male counterparts, they took advantage of the opportunity to travel and complete their studies in Berlin, Stockholm, or Oslo. They went on to fill many of the plum positions in the new Western companies that sprang up around Vilnius and Kaunas. They moved into apartments in the renovated properties of the old city centres, purchased a VW Golf or an Audi, dined out in trendy restaurants, dressed up for an evening at the Philharmonic, and shopped at Giorgio Armani, Hugo Boss, Pierre Cardin, Max Mara, and Prada, the stores that give the square in front of Vilnius City Hall its Western allure. The trappings of a bright future in a free country, a future denied to Loreta Asanavičiūtė.

7

A Neighbourhood of Composers

SAULĖ GAIŽAUSKAÍTĖ'S YOUNGER YEARS

Lithuania, April 2010
Nostalgia is not the right word, she says. Nor does she look back with regret. It was *her* youth, that's all, and it unfolded like a spring sonata.

Saulė Gaižauskaítė was born in the last month of 1963, the tenth child of composer Jurgis Gaižauskas and his wife, Zofija Meyer. Vilnius is her home town and she grew up in a neighbourhood of composers, on a street where sixteen musical families lived side by side, in a stretch of woodland behind the headquarters of the Composers' Union.

Music, or the beginnings of music, could be heard coming from every home. When Saulė thinks back to her childhood, she hears notes in search of a melody, sudden bursts of inspiration punctuated by long silences. A note or two, then nothing for a time. And all the while, the children played, chalking pictures on the paving stones.

The composers' neighbourhood is set on a hill that rises from the right bank of the Neris, on a street named after Polish poet Adam Mickiewicz, who was born on a country estate east of Vilnius. It winds through the trees, more path than road, cobbles that only gave way to asphalt in the 1980s. Saulė tells me all this as we walk there one bright spring morning.

Two houses under one roof, designed in the late 1950s by an architect whose watchwords were 'clean lines' and 'clarity'. If a Lithuanian filmmaker in the 1960s or 1970s was in search of a modern Western backdrop, the composers' neighbourhood was their first stop. Inside, the walls were the most distinctive feature, one of smooth, yellowish wood, the other built of glass bricks that let in the light. Outside, the flat roofs and wide windows caught the eye, an open invitation to the spirit of the surroundings.

Even today, it makes an exceptional setting: an urban oasis, green and tranquil, where pines tower high above the houses. Saulė tells me her father named a tree after each of his ten children. Returning from an early-morning forest walk at the start of a day's composing, he would tell his daughters and sons, 'I thought of you all, tree by tree, and didn't skip a single one.'

Saulė immediately notices a change compared to the old days: hedges planted behind the houses to demarcate the gardens — shoulder-high bushes, barbed with thorns. A sign of the times, she muses: nowadays life is about what you own.

'In communist times ...' I begin, intending to ask: was it different, was it ... ?

'Stop right there,' she bursts out. 'Those are the words of an outsider.'

'I didn't mean anything by them.'

'You said communist.'

'That's what it was called, right?'

'Yes. No! You don't get it!'

In the Soviet Socialist Republic of Lithuania, the word 'communism' encompassed so much that it could only be uttered with due reverence and the utmost awe. As a child, Saulė only used it five times, six at most, and on at least half of those occasions she used it incorrectly.

Saulė imitates the voice of her primary-school teacher explaining this to the children. 'We are living in an advanced stage of socialism. We will not reach communism for another fifty or even 100 years. You may not live to see the day. Communism, for example, means that you can take anything you need from a shop. You will no longer have to buy it, everything will be free. This demands complete honesty and great self-control, things that we have yet to achieve. We have to shed our selfishness to practise socialism in our daily lives. But ... it is something we will attain, step by step.'

Walking home from school, Saulė was inclined to believe her teacher. At the bottom of the street, there was a vending machine. A glass of mineral water cost one kopeck, lemonade cost three. The machine contained a glass that you had to rinse with cold water after use. Nobody ever took the glass, and it always looked clean.

'In our high-school history classes,' Saulė recalls, 'we spent a lot of time studying China. The Chinese had no qualms about calling

Saulė Gaižauskaitė, aged four, in front of Lenin's statue in Vilnius.

themselves communist. We thought that was presumptuous of them: they were nowhere near that far along the road of socialism! China had no right to call itself communist; that was an ideological aberration of the highest order! Here in Lithuania, we had a much purer take on the doctrine. We knew we still had to try terribly hard to achieve a state of communism.'

In one of her earliest photos, four-year-old Saulė is pictured standing in front of Lenin's statue. Like all the other children from the nursery, she is clutching a bunch of flowers wrapped in cellophane. It must have been the birthday of the Father of the Revolution (22 April) or the anniversary of his death (21 January). The children look frozen but cheerful. This was an outing; there was no need for them to grasp its purpose.

At primary school, whenever major sporting events were held at the stadium, the children had to march past a podium where the party leaders stood before the sports began. They were expected to smile and sing about how wonderful it was to be living in their socialist homeland. Again, they did this without registering the cold or what they were singing about — it was simply a welcome change from the classroom routine.

Saulė and her five sisters slept in the large room that was intended as the composer's study, big enough to accommodate a grand piano. The four boys slept in the other two rooms, and an additional small room that had been made in the basement. In summer, one of the boys slept out on the balcony. They lived in comparative comfort: few families in Vilnius had a whole house at their disposal.

Each of the children played an instrument. After school, they attended music school from four to six. These days, music lessons for a family of ten would be unaffordable; then, it cost next to nothing.

With their parents, the Gaižauskas children formed an ensemble that performed all over Lithuania. Father played the violin, mother tambourine, the eldest son piano, the eldest daughter cello, the second son double bass, and the third played the flute; the younger children sang and danced. The twelve of them performed works by their father, the odd folk song, and a few classical pieces, anything from Mozart to Shostakovich. The show was compered by an actor, who also performed two comic intermezzos. Sometimes they wore

Saulė (left) with her classmates, off to commemorate Lenin again.

traditional Lithuanian costume on stage, with the exception of the eldest son, who had been called to arms and performed in uniform. When the occasion demanded it, they dressed all in black, with fetching white collars for the girls.

The family ensemble travelled from kolkhoz to kolkhoz in a Latvija minibus that belonged to the Composers' Union. Each performance was followed by a long and hearty meal, interrupted only occasionally when Gaižauskas Sr reached for his violin. He could make the strings sing and weep. For the men and women who worked all day in the fields, on the thousands of hectares of these collective farms, this was entertainment of the highest order.

In the villages and provincial towns, the Gaižauskas Twelve performed in the Houses of Culture. They could be on the road for days at a time, which meant spending the night in hotels. The children noticed that their mother and father always slept in the same bed, even in a twin room. However small the bed, they always shared it.

Their mother also used to accompany their father to the Composers' Union conference, which was held in a different Soviet

Nine-year-old Saulė, singing in the music ensemble that consisted of
her parents and siblings.

city each year. Most of the composers left their wives at home. The
Gaižauskases were a devoted couple, and this instilled a natural calm
in their children. Even the youngest were strangers to stage fright.
'We enjoyed the attention and applause.'

They performed in a hospital, in a prison, and at an institute for
the visually and hearing impaired. 'We wondered why deaf people
would want to listen to music, but they gave us a rousing reception.'
Their show took them to schools, universities, and the film festivals in
Vilnius and Klaipėda.

The Gaižauskas family became the subject of a documentary in the
best Soviet tradition: a paean to the exemplary socialist family who
put their artistic gifts at the service of the working class. For months
on end, the film was screened in cinemas across the country ahead
of the main feature, alternating with a documentary about a labourer
who was a piano virtuoso in his spare time.

The Gaižauskases were well paid for their family concerts. Jurgis
was the kind of father who liked to reward his children for their
achievements: a school report card with straight A's earned its recipient a bicycle. An impossible challenge — nobody ever got that many

A's — but one of Saulė's brothers managed it. The sum of 5,000 roubles was on offer for the son or daughter who gave Jurgis five grandchildren. One of Saulė's sisters got him to pay up. A family trip to Japan was another promise, at a time when no Eastern European made it further than Prague or East Berlin. For the Gaižauskases, Japan would remain a distant dream.

Saulė describes her father as a cheerful man whose optimism was infectious. The torment of the creative artist was certainly in evidence among the composers in the neighbourhood, but not at number 32-2. Jurgis Gaižauskas was not an exceptional violinist, but his passion made up for his lack of brilliance. As soon as he clamped the violin between his chin and shoulder, a smile appeared on his face. He always cast a tender glance at the strings.

He composed 500 instrumental and 600 vocal works. His short pieces for violin deliver fireworks. When he performed them himself, the response from the audience was ecstatic. Yet it rankled with him that he was not a true virtuoso, neither on the violin nor the piano. Like many a composer, he had to acknowledge that others performed his works better than he ever could himself. The thought that Ravel had been a mediocre pianist and Prokofiev a lousy conductor offered some consolation at least.

As a composer, his greatest success came with his children's opera *Buratinas*, the Lithuanian version of the Pinocchio story. It became an annual event at the Vilnius opera house, an experience shared by thousands of children. As the composer of *Buratinas*, he was known to almost everyone in Lithuania.

With a dozen mouths to feed, Gaižauskas took on commissions and wrote a great many short pieces to order. Aged seventy, he sighed in a newspaper interview that if he'd had fewer children, he would have composed more symphonies and string quartets. It was one of the few occasions when Saulė was taken aback by her father. Her siblings were equally surprised: they had never heard him complain about the burden of a large family. When they were young, he used to tell them he was trying to father his own basketball team. So what was all this about fewer children?

In his serious works, Gaižauskas had little need to make concessions. He had a gift for combining the modern and the traditional. Listen to his symphonies, string quartets, and sonatas and you can hear that they come from a place between Shostakovich's Russia and Penderecki's Poland. In the slow movements, he sought to connect with Čiurlionis, the greatest of Lithuania's composers, but what he missed in Čiurlionis was fire. The spark of nature meant everything to him. His love of music that made you forget it had been written saved him from reckless experimentation; he was not one to shock.

'Life has changed,' he wrote in one gloomy diary entry. 'There is more and more noise. Must we make our music noisier too?'

He rarely lacked inspiration. Saulė recalls how the children of neighbouring families would have to tiptoe through the house when father was composing; at her house, that was never an issue. Father sometimes shut himself away in his study, but he could just as often be found scribbling notes on a scrap of paper at the kitchen table. He heard the music in his head, with a level of concentration that no child's voice could break.

Jurgis Gaižauskas was born in 1922, in Karužalaukis, eastern Lithuania. When he was three, his family moved to the small town of Telšiai in the north-west. His father was a local doctor who, in World War I, had spent the best part of three years sawing off arms and legs on the Russian front. In Ukraine, he was assisted by a nurse with eyes so beautiful that some of the wounded forgot that the amputation would be performed without anaesthesia. Before the war had ended, they were married. Of all their granddaughters, Saulė most resembles her Ukrainian grandmother: hair as black as the soil of Crimea, eyes a translucent shade of brown. 'Only I'm shorter than my grandmother,' Saulė says as I study the yellowed photographs she shows me.

In the 1920s and 1930s, Telšiai was a prosperous town. Outside the family circle, Saulė's father said very little about the good times he remembered. In his eyes, that was asking for trouble. The good times began with socialism, after all, an official premise that was not to be undermined. Saulė's father was a member of the Communist Party and understood the art of keeping his head down when needed. 'Every adult was a member of the Communist Party,' Saulė says. 'Without a party card, you were sidelined and could forget about a career.'

Her mother, who also came from Telšiai, was equally circumspect. Due to her heritage — her father came from a German family — she kept things vague whenever her childhood came up in conversation. Only after Lithuania gained its independence did her children learn that she had grown up in a wealthy household, with live-in staff that included a seamstress. As a girl, Zofija Meyer had looked around and asked, 'Mummy, how far do our lands`reach?' To which her mother replied, 'As far as your eye can see, child.' Saulė's father, intent on keeping Zofija's feet on the ground would often interrupt her reminiscences with a 'Come now, my dear ...'

Jurgis took to the violin at an early age and never considered being anything but a musician. In 1940, at the age of eighteen, he was admitted to the conservatory in Kaunas, Lithuania's capital at the time. As the war raged, he studied violin, piano, and music theory. In 1942, the conservatory was closed by order of the German occupying forces, and Jurgis played in an operetta orchestra for a few months before continuing his studies in Vienna.

Zofija Meyer went to Germany to complete her training as a teacher. She had a crush on Jurgis Gaižauskas's brother and sent him a postcard that went unanswered. Jurgis felt sorry for her and wrote her a note. A few weeks later, Zofija was in Vienna, where Jurgis was both student and a jobbing viola player with the Vienna Radio Symphony Orchestra. Boy and girl were both devout enough Catholics to sleep in separate rooms at the boarding house. In mid-spring 1945, they eloped to Germany and were married in the small town of Barth.

After Germany's capitulation, they returned to Vilnius. In the Soviet Socialist Republic of Lithuania, Jurgis continued his studies, first with a Lithuanian teacher, then with a Russian. In 1958, he joined the Composers' Union, and in 1966, he and his family moved into the first house in the composers' neighbourhood.

As soon as the door swung open, they could tell this was a house designed for musicians. The staircase was so far back that a grand piano could be rolled in with ease, and the staircase itself was wide enough for instruments to be carried up and down. The insulation was far from ideal: outside you could hear note for note what was being played within. Any composer dawdling down the street risked whispered accusations that he was fishing for some neighbourly inspiration.

Any pilfering of ideas never went beyond a single line of melody.

The residents of the composers' neighbourhood formed a good-natured clan with a lifestyle that bordered on bohemian. On special birthdays, they were known to serenade each other, gathering at seven in the morning beneath the window of the person turning forty or fifty to parp a merry tune on tuba, trombone, trumpet, and clarinet. Later in the day, this would be followed by a festive concert given by fellow musicians at the Composers' Union Hall. This inevitably culminated in a song that extolled the virtues and vices of the birthday boy. The lyrics came courtesy of librettists from the opera or operetta, whose services the composers enlisted.

At Saulė's house, cooking was an activity that took up the entire afternoon and half the evening. The windows of number 32-2 were constantly fogged up. Neighbours often pulled up a chair at mealtimes, knowing that Mrs Gaižauskaítė always cooked to feed an orphanage. Her signature dish was the napoléon, a cake that went down a treat for dessert; so good, the composers maintained, that it could soften the blow of any bad review or lost commission. Zofija even made her own puff pastry from scratch.

There were neighbours who found it hard to compose without a generous swig of vodka. If there was a furtive knock on the kitchen door late in the evening, Saulė's mother would pour the caller a glass without a second thought. The excuses given were as transparent as a child's: they had forgotten to buy some, or the lady of the house had hidden the bottle again. The glass was downed hurriedly in the kitchen, so Jurgis would be none the wiser. He liked a drink himself, but the sight of a fellow musician begging for booze filled him with vicarious shame. He particularly disapproved of smoking and card games, and even set fire to a pack of cards one of Saulė's elder sisters had drawn on pieces of cardboard.

A bit of a puritan, I conclude, but Saulė begs to differ. At a foreign festival, her father met a Japanese dancer, with whom he struck up a correspondence that lasted years. She sent him pictures of her future husband, her wedding day, her children, as well as a calendar of scantily clad Japanese women. It was no secret among the children that their father had stuck one of the pictures on the inside of a wardrobe door.

The real surprise was that the bare Japanese breasts had escaped the notice of the censors. No letter or parcel arrived from abroad without

undergoing a thorough inspection. A book about the American astro-
nauts who had walked on the moon, sent by a former classmate who
had emigrated to the US, never reached the Gaižauskas household.

Soviet censorship provided the composers' children with a weekly
outing. Secretly, they were able to attend private screenings of foreign
films in the main hall of the Composers' Union. These were films
that had already been approved in Moscow, but a separate panel was
drafted in to assess whether they were equally suitable for Lithuanian
cinema and television audiences. The films had yet to be subtitled,
so an interpreter was on hand to provide simultaneous translation.
Officially, only adults were allowed to attend the screenings — more
specifically, members of the Composers' Union and employees of the
nearby film studios — but as soon as the lights went out, the children
sneaked in too. Saulė saw French comedies, the *Fantômas* trilogy
starring Louis de Funès, the Ingmar Bergman classics *Wild Strawberries*
and *Autumn Sonata*, the latter piquing the interest of the composers
because of its musical form. She must have been about seventeen
when she saw Martin Scorsese's *Taxi Driver*, approved by the censors
because it painted such a harsh picture of the free-market economy.
To Saulė, it was propaganda in reverse: '*Taxi Driver* was supposed to
scare us silly about capitalism.'

When summer came, Jurgis would take his children on an eight-day
trip, camping in the wild and canoeing on Lithuania's lakes and rivers.
Nowadays, that would be impossible: pitch your tent anywhere and
a landowner will soon show up demanding payment. But then they
had their pick of fields and riverbanks, stoking a fire to dry their wet
clothes and roast the fish they had caught. Every year, Jurgis chose a
different region to navigate; Zofija stayed at home to recover from a
year's worth of cooking, washing, and ironing.

These annual canoeing trips reinforced Saulė's idea that Lithuania
was the most beautiful country in the world. It was an idea that would
never leave her, even when, as an adult, she travelled to the West, got
to know Germany and France, and enjoyed an extended stay in the
Netherlands. Albums full of idyllic photos prove her point: there is
something almost pristine about 1970s Lithuania.

In August, the family would spend two weeks by the sea. Always
in the same region: Neringa, on the long narrow peninsula of the

Curonian Spit. Saulė recalls one summer at an artists' colony in
Nida, the village where, before the war, Thomas Mann had a house
among the dunes. The atmosphere was mad and merry, and for the
children, it was one big party. Out of nowhere, musicians formed a
jazz orchestra; actors imitated well-known Lithuanians at dinner; a
painter made portraits of the artists and members of the Gaižauskas
family and pegged them to a clothes line strung between the trees, an
impromptu exhibition entitled *The Ineradicable People*.

Around this time, more and more Russian was being spoken in the
schools, and less and less Lithuanian. People were being issued with
Soviet passports, and Russian took precedence over Lithuanian on
birth certificates. Public life was growing more Russian by the day,
and it began to feel as if the Lithuanian people were being absorbed
into Mother Russia. But as the Lithuanians liked to say, 'We are
ineradicable.'

That was the extent of the protests at the artists' colony, where
sculptors made carvings for the Hill of Witches in the neighbouring
village of Juodkrantė and nature lovers admired the colonies of cor-
morants and grey herons. The teenagers sneaked off into the dunes,
knowing every kiss would be observed by the border guards. The
Curonian Spit was an outpost of the Soviet empire, and the watch-
towers were manned day and night.

In the Gaižauskas household, early autumn was dominated by the
humble mushroom. The family spent hours tramping through the
yellow-brown forests in search of fungi. Distinguishing between
poisonous and non-poisonous specimens was never an issue; it was
something the children learned at primary school. For Lithuanians,
foraging for mushrooms provides a tasty treat, an outing, and an
intense encounter with nature all in one; as they hunt, they become
one with the forest. Saulė's father was a fervent practitioner. The hunt
was followed by the domestic rituals of cleaning and pickling. All
winter, they ate mushrooms on Sundays and holidays — an absolute
delicacy for Lithuanians, who liken the taste of chanterelles to a tender
cut of meat. The family could spend anything up to eight weekends
a year roaming the forests in search of enough supplies. Boletes were
the real prize: you could wander for hours without coming across a
single one.

Jurgis Gaižauskas with five of his ten children on their annual canoeing
trip in the Lithuanian countryside.

The rewards of berry picking were more immediate. The children
were dispatched with a small bucket each, to be emptied into father's
big bucket; all except Saulė. As the youngest, she only had a cup
to fill, though she rarely succeeded, unable to resist the temptation
of eating every blueberry she found. Her father came to her rescue,
slipping a handful of berries into her cup when the others weren't
looking. Nothing made more of an impression on Saulė than that
simple handful of blueberries. Her father was her hero.

The winters seemed endless, though Saulė's parents were allowed
to travel to other Soviet republics as part of the Friendship of Nations
exchange program, or further afield, to Czechoslovakia, Romania,
and even Greece, Spain, and the Netherlands. In 1981, they spent
three months in the United States.

The Soviet authorities had no concerns about the Gaižauskases:
with ten children back home, they were sure to return to Lithuania.
Besides, nothing about Jurgis Gaižauskas suggested he was a rebel or
a dissident; in the words of his youngest daughter, he was 'a survivor'.
If he was told to write a song about Lenin, that's exactly what he did.
And, Saulė recalls, it ended up being such a moving song that she loved
singing it with her sisters as part of the family ensemble's repertoire.

Saulė saw her father as a dreamer. He dreamed his music and he dreamed his way through life. Putting more faith in dreams than reality meant that he could live within any political system. He sidestepped confrontation with a smile. Saulė never saw him argue with anyone. Her father taught harmony at the music academy, and harmony suffused his entire way of thinking.

Not all the composers were this compliant. Up the road lived Benjaminas Gorbulskis, a writer of pop songs and something of an eccentric. If you rang his bell during the day, there was every chance he would open the door in silk pyjamas. Gorbulskis was Jewish. He travelled extensively, made friends with foreigners, and corresponded with Lithuanians in Israel, Germany, Australia, and the United States. Well aware that his correspondence was scrutinised by the Soviet censors, he took to adding a pleasantry in Russian before starting his letter proper. 'Hello, fellow reader.' Or finishing with 'All the very best, bye now.' When Saulė began writing to a pen pal in the Netherlands, she imitated Gorbulskis's joke, much to her father's alarm. If you wanted to avoid trouble, it was important not to poke the bear.

Saulė skipped down the same path as millions of children in the Soviet republics. From the age of seven, she was an *oktyabryonok*, from the age of ten a *pionerka*, and from the age of fourteen a *komsomolka* — a member of Komsomol, the young communist league. She did not see this as coercion. The communist youth movement enabled her to travel cheaply to East Germany and Kyiv. Photos from that time show a teenager with a thick black ponytail draped fetchingly over her right shoulder and breast. For Saulė, her Komsomol years were less about the membership pin with its image of Lenin and more about puppy love and flirting.

The contrast with the West was mainly a gulf between lifestyles. Westerners were guests at Saulė's parental home in the mid-1970s. It was clear that they pitied the composer and his family, an attitude that extended to all Lithuanians: not poor perhaps, but shabby and lacking the most basic of home comforts. Oppressed. Saulė was indignant: they weren't to be pitied! They lived in a wonderful house, they had it good. What a cheek! Yet the ban on speaking openly about the time when Lithuania was free and honouring Lithuanian heroes revealed a nasty side to the Soviets. During a summer holiday by the sea, she

Zofija, Saulė, and Jurgis Gaižauskas in the Lithuanian countryside.

and a couple of friends had tried to get as close to Brezhnev's villa as they could. A villa for the party leader ... what was that all about? She began to ask questions, though more about how the system operated than the system itself.

'We knew we were being indoctrinated, at school, through radio and television. Teachers didn't tell us what they thought but what they were supposed to think — we could hear it in their voices. We knew that we were constantly being exposed to propaganda. The difference with you in the West was that you *didn't* know. You still don't. We had to undergo it, but we knew what was happening. We weren't stupid or crazy.'

The first dark cloud in Saulė's young life appeared when she was interrogated by one of her high-school teachers. Not just any old teacher, but the deputy head, a known KGB informant. The questions were short and precise. Who was she in regular contact with? Who did she correspond with abroad? Who were her friends?

There she stood, just shy of her sixteenth birthday, in her school uniform: pleated brown woollen dress, black tunic, white collar, white cuffs, ribbons woven into the neckline. She was presented with a statement that she had shouted a Russian swear word. Nothing to write home about, a Russian equivalent of 'fuck'. That word had indeed been shouted in the changing room after gym class, but not by Saulė. She knew who was responsible, a tough girl who was always mouthing off. Even so, Saulė signed the statement. Otherwise, she thought, her father might suffer the consequences.

The reason behind the interrogation was anyone's guess. It may have had something to do with an initiative she had taken not long before: organising a folk-music festival at the school. The response from the teachers had been lukewarm at best, but she had persevered. In response to their main objection ('we have no instruments at school'), she had asked her father for a violin and with great difficulty had managed to borrow her sister's cello. From home, she had also brought the kanklės, a traditional Lithuanian instrument that resembled a zither. The performance had been a great success. Only — and Saulė can back this up with photographs — there had been three strangers in the front row, members of the KGB no doubt. Folklore had never been contrary to socialist principles, until Lithuanians had started promoting their culture with verve to bolster their desire for independence. It was 1979, and the tide was beginning to turn.

A few months later, Saulė was listening to the Lithuanian broadcast of Radio Free Europe. Her parents were in America at the time. The news bulletin reported that six girls had been arrested at a religious festival in Telšiai. It went on to say that three more girls were suspected of illegal activities, including Saulė Gaižauskaítė.

She practically fell off her chair.

Her surname was far from common in Lithuania, and as far as she knew, her father had coined her first name. In all of Vilnius, she did not know a single Saulė. Her sister who was ten years older and had just obtained a position as cellist in the Lithuanian State Symphony Orchestra called in a panic. Someone from the orchestra had heard the broadcast and asked, 'What the hell has your sister been up to?' Saulė only found out later that she did have a namesake in Telšiai, the town where her father grew up. For a while, she was convinced that she had been blacklisted and was wanted by the authorities.

Saulė wanted to train as a singer and had to audition for one of only eight places available at the music academy. Her voice was too light for opera, the listening panel concluded, but excellent for popular song. Even so, a place was denied her: two of the eight who had made the grade were composers' daughters, and the panel thought this was one too many. Saulė could understand the panel wanting to avoid the impression of favouritism, but why was she rejected and not the other girl? Her disappointment was such that for ten years, she could not bring herself to listen to songs or opera.

After sitting her final exams, the head of the school said to her, 'Well, Saulė, the doors of the university will always be closed to you.' Why? Because of the statement she had signed? Because of a swear word she had never uttered? Her father had always been an exemplary party member. Her brothers had steered clear of politics: one had become an organist, another an actor. And two of her sisters had gone into music. She herself had always believed in the ideals of socialism. So what was the problem?

With the benefit of hindsight, she thinks that, on one occasion, she may unsuspectingly have been in the wrong place in the wrong company: a boy who had contacts in the dissident movement. Could that have been the cause? That one evening, by a pile of withered leaves, when someone had whispered, 'This is where he is buried.' Nothing more, just that simple phrase: 'This is where he is buried.'

Had 'he' been Romas Kalanta, the nineteen-year-old student who, on 14 May 1972, had doused himself in three litres of petrol and set fire to himself in the public square in front of the Kaunas State Music Theatre? The place was symbolic: the theatre's steps were where the Lithuanian Soviet Socialist Republic had been proclaimed in 1940. Kalanta had been hastily buried in an unknown location: in the Romainių cemetery it later transpired, in a hole three metres deep and covered by a layer of concrete. At the time, nobody knew the details. The authorities had been afraid Kalanta's grave would become a place of pilgrimage for dissidents and disaffected youth. They were equally concerned about a chain reaction: in 1972 alone, twelve students had followed Kalanta's example and publicly killed themselves, in most cases by self-immolation.

It might have been him, Romas, who lay buried there. Or one of the other twelve martyrs. After hearing that ominous message, Saulė had not immediately backed off. It had given her a thrill. Perhaps, behind a nearby tree, a camera had clicked. She remembers one of the boys joking about it. 'I bet we'll be photographed.' No, hang on, he said, 'I hope they get our good side.'

If Gorbachev had not come to power, Saulė would never have seen the inside of a university. After sitting her final school exams, she had to wait two years before starting her studies. She took English and teaching, but would not complete either course.

The struggle for independence took two full years. Her mother attended the demonstrations, bringing soup for the protesters who had formed a cordon around the parliament building. Those people had to eat after all! Her mother was a kind woman, Saulė says. Lending a helping hand was second nature to her. Later, she helped clean the church buildings that had been used as warehouses during the Soviet era.

In the composers' neighbourhood, independence created a curious paradox. Every morning and every evening, the presidential limousine could be seen crawling along the asphalt path between the composers' houses, so narrow that one car had to pull over before another could pass. The black limousine would always stop for a moment outside the Gaižauskas family's kitchen window so that the chairman of the Supreme Council of Lithuania could give Zofija a wave. Vytautas Landsbergis had always been a fan of her home-baked napoléon.

As previously noted in the chapter on Loreta, there had been nothing to suggest that Vytautas Landsbergis would be the man to save the country. He was the son of a prominent architect and a renowned eye specialist. Having graduated from the Lithuanian Conservatory of Music in 1955, he was awarded a doctorate from Vilnius University in 1969 for his research on Čiurlionis. Some ten years later, he moved into a house in the composers' neighbourhood.

Landsbergis became the leading expert on Mikalojus Čiurlionis, often dubbed the devil's artist. A musician, composer, poet, and painter, he died in a Warsaw asylum in 1911 at the age of thirty-five, exhausted, desperately ill, and all but insane. Čiurlionis was among Eastern Europe's first abstract painters, a kindred spirit of Wassily Kandinsky and Kazimir Malevich. His output was prolific: 300 of his paintings have survived. He wrote poetry, swapped Polish for Lithuanian, and astonished his contemporaries with poems that foreshadowed surrealism. To perfect his Lithuanian, he took lessons from

Zofija Kymantaitė, whom he married in 1909. Kymantaitė would go on to become one of Lithuania's best-known writers.

Čiurlionis began his artistic career as a musician. He received his first music lessons from his father, an organist in Varėna, Lithuania's second-southernmost town, and then in Druskininkai, the very southernmost town, on the border with Belarus. There, his father was dismissed by the Polish priest for speaking Lithuanian in public. Mikalojus continued his music studies on the other side of Lithuania, in Plungė, close to the Baltic Sea, at Prince Ogiński's Orchestra School, located in the castle of the noble Ogiński family. He completed his studies at the Warsaw Music Institute and the conservatory in Leipzig.

From Leipzig, he returned to Warsaw, where he enrolled at the School of Drawing and two years later at the Academy of Fine Arts. He alternated between painting and composing symphonic poems, piano works, string quartets, and choral works. In his 356 compositions, he sought an impressionistic way to turn images into sound. In his paintings, he did the opposite: his Sonata of Spring, Sonata of Summer, and Sonata of the Sun each consist of four paintings, which he titled *Allegro*, *Andante*, *Scherzo*, and *Finale*.

His compositions sparked the interest of the young Stravinsky, but around 1900 the international set still regarded Lithuania as a rural backwater, incapable of producing anything modern. Čiurlionis remained a figure on the European margins, though he himself knew exactly what place he would one day occupy in Lithuania's national consciousness. 'My works,' he wrote, 'will be the link between folk music and the music of the future.'

The spirit of Čiurlionis unmistakably haunts the early string quartets, symphonies, and symphonic poems composed by Jurgis Gaižauskas. No Lithuanian composer could escape the great man's influence. That said, the slow, introverted, and melancholic mood of Čiurlionis was not in keeping with Gaižauskas's character. The young Vytautas Landsbergis took a different view, relishing the ways in which Čiurlionis broke new ground.

As a pianist, Landsbergis was a regular participant in events organised by Fluxus. From 1962, this international arts movement embraced the same goals that Čiurlionis had pursued half a century earlier: making interconnections between music, the visual arts, architecture, design, and dance. In Germany, Poland, and the United States, Fluxus attracted artists such as Joseph Beuys, John Cage, Krzysztof Penderecki, Merce Cunningham, and Yoko Ono. They organised happenings in New York, Wiesbaden, Paris, and Nice, and even underground events in Vilnius. Alive with the spirit of the old Dada manifestations, these were a determined attempt to keep the avant-garde torch burning. Landsbergis was often in the thick of things, spurred on by the aim that music should carry an idea far beyond the concert hall. Fluxus stood for strong political engagement.

Vytautas Landsbergis was married to Gražina Ručytė, a fellow pianist and an exceptionally gifted one. Their two daughters chose the same musical path and studied at the conservatory, while their son became a writer and documentary filmmaker — an artistic family with a deep distaste for the Russians. Vytautas's grandfather had been one of the first dramatists to write in Lithuanian. Gabrielius Landsbergis-Žemkalnis founded a daily newspaper, wrote fiercely critical editorials, and was exiled to Smolensk by the tsarist police. Vytautas's father, the architect, had to flee the Soviet authorities in 1944 and was only able to return to Lithuania fifteen years later.

In the composers' neighbourhood, Landsbergis was known to all as the musicologist, the thoughtful professor. But also as an ardent patriot. The one side of him seemed at odds with the other. In appearance too, Landsbergis was far more the retiring scholar than the dissident activist, yet whenever the subject of Lithuania arose in conversation, he was implacable: the country deserved to be free and independent.

For Saulė, Landsbergis was just one of the neighbours. A nice man, even if he did maintain a certain distance. He was not the type to give you a hearty slap on the shoulder. A man of integrity: a promise was a promise. He kept his word, even in his later life as a politician. And beyond that? A stout, bespectacled fellow who came by to congratulate her father on turning seventy, seventy-five, eighty; who attended his birthday concerts in the hall of the Composers' Union; and who took part in the neighbourly morning serenades with the rest of the musicians.

When he was elected speaker of the Lithuanian parliament and de facto president of the country, Landsbergis kept life simple and continued to live in the composers' neighbourhood. He was proud that he had led Lithuania to independence, but would always prefer the title of 'professor' to 'president'.

Jurgis Gaižauskas had known Vytautas Landsbergis since his student days at the music academy in Vilnius. Jurgis, who was ten years older, taught there. From the moment Vytautas moved into the composers' neighbourhood with his wife and children, a bond was forged that went far beyond a dutiful association between fellow musicians.

The most moving photo of the two friends was taken shortly before Zofija's funeral, in 2007. Vytautas came up to offer Jurgis his condolences. In Lithuania, this is done before the funeral, rather than after. The family were sitting in a circle around the open coffin. Zofija was laid out in traditional Lithuanian dress in the hall of the Composers' Union, Jurgis sitting so close that he could touch her feet. Landsbergis took a seat next to the widower, put a hand on his arm, and inclined his head towards him. Jurgis was incapable of speech, Vytautas spoke words of comfort. He shared his memories of Zofija Meyer, who had made life so much more bearable amid the hardships of the Soviet era, for her husband, her family, and all the residents of the composer's neighbourhood. 'Ah, Zosele,' he murmured, using the pet name the neighbours had for her.

The years between 1989 and 1992 had been memorable; wonderful years in which Lithuania took shape as an independent nation once again. Then came the years of organised crime, which would last until 2003, years marred by extortion, by the threat of violence. Anyone starting their own business had to budget for large sums in bribes.

Saulė spent most of the 1990s abroad, but her siblings kept her informed. When she came back to visit her family, it was to a Vilnius where only the foolhardy ventured out after dark. Robbery was so rife, it was dangerous to walk the streets. 'In the old KGB days,' Saulė scoffed at her sisters, 'at least you knew someone was keeping an eye on you.'

In the winter of 1993, she found her father in a freezing house wearing three jumpers and a body warmer. The Russians had cut off gas supplies to Lithuania. In 1994, she returned bearing gifts, among them a pair of ski pants; he kept them on all winter.

Her father had a decent pension; he had no reason to complain. However, he found living in a country where suddenly money was

Vytautas Landsbergis (right) comforts Jurgis Gaižauskas at his wife
Zofija's funeral.

doing all the talking hard to bear. Prices shot up, including tickets for
the opera, concert hall, and theatre. Music and drama became the
prerogative of the new elite. In the old days, packed buses from the
kolkhozes used to pull up outside the opera house; culture had been
for everyone.

Sometimes Saulė would say to her sisters, 'Life was better back
then.' And they would reply, 'You're forgetting the empty shops, the
lack of meat, fish, clothes. You're forgetting that we weren't free to
travel abroad and that all the news on TV was censored.' And she
would concede that her sisters were right.

I cannot tempt Saulė to further statements about the current state
of Lithuania. She immediately downplays every assertion, swallows
every criticism. 'Don't quote me on that,' she says, 'it will only get me
into trouble.' Fear, I realise, is quick to take hold and hard to unlearn.
Readiness to express an opinion is a luxury that has to be cultivated
from early age, a luxury Saulė was denied throughout the Soviet era.
Today she has the freedom to speak her mind and voice criticism, but
she is not quite bold enough to take it. She has come to resemble her
father: cautious, always searching for harmony.

On 25 May 2009, the evening news in Lithuania opened with the death of Jurgis Gaižauskas, at the age of eighty-six. After the newsreader had delivered the sad tidings with an earnest expression, a compilation of scenes was shown, a look back at his life. More than a tribute to a beloved composer, it was a farewell to an era.

The news item has been preserved on YouTube. The first images show an upbeat Jurgis, conducting a troupe of folk musicians, violin in hand. He is dressed in a white shirt with puff sleeves, a dark red waist-coat, and a red sash. From colour, the images fade to black and white. A much younger Gaižauskas fronts the Lithuanian State Symphony Orchestra in a performance of one of his symphonies. There follows a few stills of the composer, poring over a score, pen in hand. Colour returns, and we see Jurgis at home, in his later years; he is at the piano, playing some kind of polka with his stubby fingers. Zofija accompanies him on the tambourine. The final images show the Gaižauskas family, parents and all ten children, dressed in Lithuanian costumes and performing a stirring piece at a provincial music festival in the late 1960s. The audience — farmers and workers from the nearby kolkhoz — jump up from their seats and start dancing around the musicians. The girl on the right, so small that she barely peeps out above her sister's cello, is Saulė. A girl with jet-black hair and wide eyes that shine with happiness.

Saulė in Vilnius, spring 2010.

8

Copulation in Bronze

LIPCHITZ'S SCREAM

Lithuania, August 2009

Forest, endless forest. The road dips and rises through what feels like one endless park. The trees stand so close together that their branches interweave, leaves washed by dew. The nights are already turning chilly, though today's weather forecast has promised the warmest day of summer. Ash, alder, and aspen flash by. A huddle of lime trees. Or are they elms?

I am travelling in a minibus packed with tourists, travelling from Druskininkai to Varėna along a road named after Čiurlionis. Beside me sits a Polish priest. Lithuania is home to a quarter of a million Poles. Most of the tourists who visit the south of the country are Polish too, lured to Druskininkai by the prospect of spa treatments and warm mud baths. The priest knows the town and the region like his own parish. 'You should see this place in a month's time,' he tells me in German. 'Stalls lining the road. Forty varieties of mushroom to choose from.'

How old would he be? Thirty, forty, fifty? It's hard to tell. Age means more here than it does back home. Age tells you the regime someone grew up in. He has hitched up his cassock a little, like an actress anxious not to tread on the hem of her evening dress. His shoes haven't been polished in a while. His stiff white collar appears to divide one man from another. The comical, slightly cheeky face above is the spitting image of Roman Polanski.

Every two kilometres, the minibus stops at a sculpture. Mikalojus Konstantinas Čiurlionis moved from Varėna to Druskininkai at the age of three. To mark the centenary of his birth, a permanent exhibition was installed along the road that links the two towns. That was in 1975. Twenty artists working in wood contributed sculptures, which were given pride of place along the forty-kilometre route. Each refers in one way or another to Čiurlionis's work: to his paintings, of course, not least the strangely muted colours he liked to use, but also to his poems and musical compositions.

The Soviet authorities were none too pleased with this initiative. Čiurlionis had been a driving force behind a national cultural reawakening in Lithuania. He had started writing in Lithuanian, sought out Lithuanian motifs in woodcarving and Lithuanian rhythms and melodies in folk music. From the centralist Soviet perspective, he was a divisive figure in the region. Yet in his letters and writings, he had shown himself to be a fierce opponent of the tsarist regime and an advocate of the just aims of socialism. What self-respecting communist could argue with that?

'What brings you to these parts?' the Polish priest asks.

'I want to write about Lipchitz.'

'Lipchitz? The sculptor? I once visited his birthplace in Druskininkai.'

The home where Chaim Jacob Lipchitz was born on 22 August 1891 now houses the Jacques Lipchitz Memorial Museum, part of the Vilna Gaon Museum of Jewish History. It is located one street behind the wooden house where the Čiurlionis family lived.

For a period of six years, up-and-coming artist Lipchitz and established painter-composer Čiurlionis lived sixteen metres apart. In Amsterdam, Antwerp, or Paris, that would have been nothing special. 'But here,' says the priest, 'in the winter of 1900, just a few kilometres from Belarus, surrounded by forests where you still had to watch out for wolves and lynxes, you would never expect such a concentration of creative talent.'

The previous evening, I had attended a concert in the garden behind the Čiurlionis family home. A young Lithuanian pianist performed preludes and nocturnes composed by the former resident. She sat in the parlour of the wooden house, while the audience were seated outside. The atmosphere was extraordinary; the music and the setting were a perfect match. This was visual music, forest music. It reminded me of Scriabin's preludes, the piano music of Janáček, the early piano works of Szymanowski (Čiurlionis and Szymanowski had been contemporaries at the Warsaw Conservatory). At times, I picked up traces of the chamber music of Sibelius and Wagner's long melodic lines. But I was most struck by a choral quality in the music. It was

Four-year-old Chaim Jacob Lipchitz in Druskininkai, Lithuania.

almost like listening to a lone piano in the foreground, backed by a whole choir.

Folk songs were a profound influence on Čiurlionis. Southern Lithuania has produced the country's purest voices and its most musically interesting songs. Time and again, they drew him back to the small town of his youth; between 1896 and 1910, he frequently spent months at a time in Druskininkai, painting and composing.

'Čiurlionis is completely unknown in Western Europe,' I tell the priest.

'Here he is everywhere — it's enough to drive you mad, like Chopin in Poland. I don't know quite what to make of him anymore. He must have been remarkably modern in his time.'

'Last night, I heard *Lakštingala*.'

'The Nightingale ...'

'One minute and four seconds.'

'And?'

'Anyone who can create such breathtaking music with so few notes can count themselves among the greats.'

'Yet in my opinion, the real genius was Lipchitz. Have you seen much of his work?'

'After my time in Africa, yes ...'

'Africa?'

'For a while, I was obsessed with Africa. I travelled through Burkina Faso, Mali, Côte d'Ivoire, Gabon, collected books on masks, totems, sculptures, and amassed a modest collection of Senufo sculptures, Baoulé rice spoons, Bobo and Fang masks. Lipchitz was a very early collector of African art: long before Giacometti, long before Picasso and Max Ernst. Back in 1916, he bought a wooden bowl from Dahomey, a perfectly shaped piece. Not a single artist was interested in those days, only the occasional anthropologist. Twenty years on, Lipchitz owned more than sixty African masks and sculptures. I always thought West African woodcarving had been his main inspiration, but now I'm starting to wonder.' I point at one of the wooden sculptures at the side of the road. 'Those elongated faces: a few years ago, I would have sworn they were influenced by Fang or Senufo. But now I think this might be where it all began ...'

'I'm afraid can't be much help,' the priest replies. 'I know too little about art, especially modern art. It's something we were hardly ever exposed to. There's not one Lipchitz sculpture in all of Lithuania. I had never even heard of him until they opened that little museum in Druskininkai. All I know for certain is that it's our childhood impressions that leave the deepest mark.'

The minibus pulls over, and we get out to see another sixty or so sculptures in Grūtas Park. The collection belongs to Viliumas Malinauskas, a businessman who made millions in the mushroom trade. When independence came, he bought up statues that had been removed from public spaces all over Lithuania and put them on display in a plot of woodland he had acquired in his native region. Heads of Stalin that dwarf a grown man, busts of Marx and Engels, statues of Lenin up to ten metres tall, always in mid-speech with the outstretched arm of a visionary showing the ignorant proletariat the way. There are statues of Lithuanian socialist intellectuals lost in thought, and local heroes with clenched fists. The showpiece of the collection is a monument dedicated to the Soviet partisans, which lined the steps of Pylimo gatvė in Vilnius until 1992.

At the entrance to the park, visitors are required to knock back a glass of vodka and down a bowl of borscht. This is supposed to put them in just the right mood for a tour of Soviet-era heroes, to say nothing of the marching bands and First of May speeches blaring nonstop from the speakers. They have a gift for absurdist humour in these parts. The Polish priest laughs until he cries.

For Lipchitz, sculpture stemmed first and foremost from experience. He began work on *The Scream* a few months after losing his father and his sister, who died in quick succession in a single spring.

Since 1909, Lipchitz had made his home in Paris. In the spring of 1928, both his father, Abraham, and his sister Eugenia passed away. Telegrams were delayed, and the news of their deaths took a long time to reach him. In 1928, the journey from Paris to Druskininkai took at least three days. Both his father's and Eugenia's funeral took place in his absence. 'I would rather have set out on foot,' he later said. At least then, he would have felt that he had done something.

Lipchitz was seized by inner turmoil. Memories surfaced with such force that he could not work. For weeks, he walked around with a cheerless expression. As soon as night came, he resorted to drink. He grew afraid of the dark. When he closed his eyes, memories rushed in, unfocused images that left him frightened as a child in a strange bedroom. He was a man who needed to see hands, ears, and eyes, the curve of a cheek or the line of a neck, clearly in his mind's eye.

But the image of his father's eyes and his sister's lips eluded him. He heard voices. Noises. Terrifying noises. It took him a long time to link them to those June days in 1906.

As long as it was light, he pottered about his studio. He had always been a hard worker, up at quarter to six, even in winter. He was astounded to find himself rising well after eight only to spend the rest of the day brooding. Brooding was too kind a word; it was like staring into a black hole. If he picked up an implement, it would fall from his hand. At first, he thought his joints were playing up again, as they had five years earlier, when he'd been forced to give up stone and chisel once and for all. In a strange coincidence, that had been shortly after his last visit to Druskininkai, his final days with his father, mother, second sister, and younger brother.

The advice to give up working in stone had come much earlier. At the age of twenty, he had been admitted to a sanatorium with tuberculosis, escaping death by the skin of his teeth and undergoing week after week of treatment in Belgium before his lungs were clean again. Dust and grit had become as harmful to him as to an old miner. Since then, he had only indulged his passion for stone two or three times. He had made the transition to bronze, which only required the moulding of a plaster model before the final form was cast.

During those aimless days in 1928, his studio came to feel like a vast, bleak space. It had been specially designed for him by his friend Le Corbusier, who would rather have become a sculptor than an architect. On reflection, Lipchitz would have been quite happy to swap places. It would certainly have impressed his father. 'Allow me to introduce my eldest son, the architect!' His cheeks would have glowed like copper, like burnished gold. Nor would he have lacked for orders: his father ran the largest contracting firm in Druskininkai, employing an army of carpenters, masons, and plasterers. If you wanted a villa or a hotel built in Druskininkai, Abraham Lipchitz was your man.

The demand for villas and country houses in and around the town was hard to keep up with. As for hotels, new ones were springing up every year; it sometimes seemed as if every aristocrat in the tsarist empire simply had to take the waters in the place they knew as

Druskieniki. In those days, the more lilting 'Drus-ki-nin-kai' could only be heard on the tongues of their Lithuanian servants. It gave them a chuckle too, *druska* being Lithuanian for 'salt' and *druskininkai* meaning 'salt panner'.

The town takes its name from the lukewarm, salty water that bubbles from the ground. The first health resort was built there in the mid-nineteenth century, fitted out with fourteen baths. Within two years, fifty baths had been installed. The construction work went on and on: hotels, guesthouses, and later sanatoriums. The year Chaim Jacob Lipchitz left town to attend the drawing academy in Vilnius, 100,000 patients flocked to Druskieniki.

All summer long, the town was inhabited by men in pyjamas, bath-robes, and slippers, always with a tin cup in their hand. At the same time, dozens of men in overalls scaled the scaffolding every morning. The more ailing patients there were, the better it was for business; the town's economy thrived on the upset digestion and failing livers of the Russian nobility.

Until Chaim Jacob's eleventh birthday, his father had been a virtual absentee. Abraham Lipchitz was always working. The boy was raised by his mother, and when she didn't have time for him, she would park him at his grandmother's house. His birth had been followed by five more; his mother was always either pregnant or breastfeeding the latest arrival. Yet she always gave her firstborn son the impression that she lived for him alone. It was also his mother Chaim Jacob turned to for guidance on God, the prophets, and the Torah. In most Jewish families, religious upbringing was the father's department, but his father barely had time for a cigar, never mind the Almighty. He was a believer, but seldom put his beliefs into practice.

Chaim Jacob's mother, Rachael Leah Krinsky, was of Jewish Polish Lithuanian descent, his father's line was Jewish Lithuanian Russian. It was later claimed that he came from a wealthy banking family, but back then all Jews were said to be descended from Rothschild. His father had founded his business with a single cement mixer, and one carpenter and one bricklayer on the books. It was thanks to his consistently astute choice of materials and architects that the firm flourished.

'Chaimke, why are you always messing about with modelling clay?' His father's voice. 'As a grown man, you'll need to use your head, not your hands …' Chaimke, the firstborn son, was destined to study engineering and take over his father's business — this was written in stone, like the laws of Moses. But Chaimke refused, and high-tailed it to Paris.

In August 1909, he turned eighteen; by September, he had flown the coop. Without valid papers. Not that the Russian authorities would have issued them to a young man who had yet to do his military service. Besides, he would have needed an exit visa: no Jew was simply permitted to leave the Chertá.

Chaim Jacob had at least been open with his mother. A few days before his departure, he had told her he wanted to become a skilled artist and continue his education in Paris. He had also been honest about his fears of a repeat of June 1906. The same frenzied violence could erupt again at any moment, in Druskieniki, Vilnius, or any town in the Chertá.

There was one other person he talked to at length before leaving. Artist Chaïm Soutin — he later Gallicised his name to Soutine — came from a village near Minsk. He and Lipchitz (who at the time was still using the Polish spelling of his name: Lipczyc) had met at Ivan Trutnev's school of drawing in Vilnius. In Soutin, the fear ran even deeper than it did in Lipchitz.

Chaïm Soutin, the tenth child of a tailor who mended old clothes, had a beating to thank for the chance to study art. When he tried to sketch the rabbi in his home village, he was attacked by the rabbi's son, a violent reminder that Jews are not permitted to depict the human form. Young Chaïm was hurt so badly that he had to be hospitalised. The affair was settled with the sum of twenty-five roubles, exactly the amount he needed to enrol at the academy in Vilnius.

Chaïm Soutin saw no future for himself in Eastern Europe. Nor for any other Jew. 'Paris, you fool,' he told Lipchitz in his rasping voice. 'As soon as you can. I may even get there before you. Things are bound to explode here. It will be a bloodbath.' In later years, Lipchitz often had cause to reflect on that advice, by which time Soutin had become Soutine and achieved fame with his paintings of slaughtered oxen and hunks of meat hanging from butchers' hooks.

Lipchitz's mother had understood his need to go to Paris. His father was a different story. He had even objected to his son's lessons with Trutnev in Vilnius. 'An artist?' he had shouted. 'And end up like

Čiurlionis? Destitute, diseased, insane … is that what you want? And our Mikalojus Konstantinas is brilliant! Something you have yet to prove.'

Everyone in Druskieniki knew about the fortunes of the Čiurlionis family. The father, an organist, had been fired for speaking Lithuanian in public. The mother, Adela Radman, of German descent, changed her name to Radmanaitė after her husband's dismissal: an outright provocation. Their daughter, Jadvyga Čiurlionytė, a late addition to the family, went on to study music history in Moscow, then studied at the conservatories of Leipzig and Berlin, and became Lithuania's first ethnomusicologist. Their son was a composer who wanted to paint, and a painter who wanted to visualise music. All this in a sleepy town on the upper reaches of the River Memel (Nemunas in Lithuanian), the last place anyone would expect to find an outpouring of unprecedented artistry.

Influenced by Čiurlionis, Lipchitz sought out the avant-garde in Paris, following developments in music as much as in the visual arts. He was present when a Parisian audience booed Stravinsky at the premiere of *Le Sacre du printemps*. Stravinsky's music moved him more deeply than cubism, which he encountered during the same period. Such power! Such menace! And, as with Čiurlionis, such a riot of tone and colour!

Čiurlionis may have been the embodiment of the starving artist, but this had not scared Lipchitz off. If anything, Čiurlionis's willingness to suffer for his art made him a role model. Admittedly, it was best not to look into his troubled eyes for too long, or you might become a little unhinged yourself. But his was an insanity driven by curiosity. Lipchitz's father had issued a warning: go to Paris and you will not receive another penny from home. It had not stopped him.

On his mother's advice, the wayward son wrote a long letter from Paris, not so much to ask his father's forgiveness as to explain again at length why he had enrolled at the École des Beaux-Arts and the Académie Julian, the sculpture academy in Paris. In November, an unexpected answer arrived: yes, my son, I can see that you have thought all this through. You can count on your father's support, both moral and financial.

How to honour the memory of such a man?

Young Lipchitz had received his first allowance by Christmas. The second followed in spring 1910, the third in the autumn, and the fourth in early 1911. Then came a letter from his mother, with devastating news: your father is virtually bankrupt, and the whole family is in dire financial straits.

The crisis of 1911, the hatred of Jews. Lipchitz didn't even have to sleep on it; he took the train from Gare de l'Est early the next morning and returned to Druskieniki. Though he was unable to be of much help, his return meant the world to his father.

When he departed in 1909, Lipchitz had left behind a father who was hale and hearty. He returned in 1911, to find him drawn and angular. He assured his father that he would support himself from then on, and told him what little money was left should be spent on educating his brothers and his youngest sister. He returned to Paris, where he sometimes went hungry for days on end. Yet strangely enough, he continued to look strong: whether he was suffering from tuberculosis or had barely eaten a scrap in days, his shoulders and his face were broad, his cheeks were never sunken.

In 1912, Lipchitz saw his father again, this time on his way to St Petersburg. Still a Russian citizen, Lipchitz had no desire to go through life as a deserter. In St Petersburg, he planned to report for military service. Another decision that his father greatly appreciated.

Lipchitz got lucky. He failed the medical. His lungs were still too weak, and he was granted an exemption. This not only spared him two years of military service but saved him from full-blown combat: in 1914, he would have been sent to the front at a moment's notice.

Instead, when World War I broke out, he was in Spain in the company of Mexican artist Diego Rivera. In Madrid, he made sketches of the bullfighter Joselito for a sculpture eighty centimetres tall. Paradise compared to the mud and the trenches.

Until 1920, there was next to no correspondence from Druskieniki. No one was able to tell him whether the small town on the River Memel belonged to Poland, the Soviet Union, or a newly independent Lithuania. It had in fact become Lithuanian.

In 1923, he returned, not to Druskieniki but to Druskininkai. The town had immediately adopted its Lithuanian name. The Memel had been rechristened the Nemunas. On his arrival, he laid eyes on his mother and father for the first time in eleven years.

Chaim Jacob Lipchitz had hesitated for a long time about whether to take Bertha Kitrosser back home with him to meet his parents. By this time, they had been living together for about eight years. Had Lipchitz been able to obtain French citizenship, he would have married her long before.

Because the paperwork was taking so terribly long, his friend Modigliani had already painted their wedding portrait in 1916. It turned out to be one of his finest paintings. Chaim Jacob in his beret, Bertha with her jet-black hair; he in his turtleneck, she with a collar of white lace. She is seated, he is standing, his hand resting lovingly on her shoulder. It was Modigliani's vision of Eastern European Jews: simple, sincere, devoted, driven.

Modigliani, Soutine, and Lipchitz had become friends in Paris, though Lipchitz found it hard to imagine two people as ill-matched as Soutine and Modigliani. Soutine was moody, unruly, and boorish, his manners sloppy, his clothes filthy. Amedeo Modigliani was a refined Sephardic Jew from Livorno, 'a prince' in the eyes of Marc Chagall — albeit a prince who was stoned every other day, who couldn't work without hashish, and who came to blows with anti-Semites on the streets of Paris. Yet he was every inch the aristocrat, an Italian with impeccable manners. In company, he was infinitely more amiable than Soutine, who had grown up in abject poverty at the mercy of a father who beat him and locked him in the cellar for days at a time. Lipchitz was more taken with Modigliani but at the same time felt a brotherly need to defend Soutine. Modigliani must have felt something similar, judging by the portrait he painted of Soutine, which peels away his gruff exterior to capture his sensitive, contemplative side. Created not long after the wedding portrait of Lipchitz and Bertha, it is a true Modigliani: little more than a line drawing, but every line conveys respect.

Lipchitz and Bertha Kitrosser met in Paris in 1915. By that time, she was already mother to a two-year-old son. Kitrosser was a Russian poet with anarchist ideas. An unmarried mother and an anarchist … not a choice his father would have understood. In the end, Lipchitz decided not to confront Kitrosser with his father's wrath. It turned out to be the right decision. He returned to Druskininkai alone to find a father he barely recognised, an embittered old man at death's

Amedeo Modigliani: Jacques and Berthe Lipchitz, 1916.

door. A man whose feelings he wanted to spare as much as possible so as not to cause him further suffering.

A year after his visit to Druskininkai, Lipchitz finally obtained French citizenship. That same day, he and Kitrosser went to the town hall to get married. He left home that morning as Chaim Jacob and returned as Jacques; without so much as a word, the immigration officer rechristened him. Bertha emerged from the town hall as Berthe. When it came to naturalisation, the French did nothing by halves.

One spring morning in 1928, Lipchitz went to the synagogue in Boulogne-Billancourt to say Kaddish, the prayer a son is supposed to say in memory of his deceased father. That same day, he went into his studio, mixed lime and water, and began to knead it into plaster. All he had in mind was the vaguest of shapes, but he knew what his sculpture would be called. *The Scream.*

In 1902, his father had sent him to the commercial college in Białystok, north-east Poland. The journey from Druskininkai was about three hours by train. There was no border to cross; at that time, the whole region was part of a seemingly endless Russia. All told, it was close enough: a brisk walk to the station followed by three hours gazing out of a train window. A wonderful experience for a boy of ten or eleven. But even on that first trip, it was fear he had felt.

After every school holiday, he found it harder to return to Białystok. By that time, he knew what to expect: another three to four months of confinement in classroom, dining hall, study hall, dormitory. As the day of departure came closer, he could feel the tension rise.

In 1902, 52,000 Jews lived in Białystok, accounting for 76 per cent of the population. Most of them worked in the textile industry. Białystok was a rapidly growing industrial city which, in a strange contradiction, bordered one of the last expanses of primeval forest in Europe. It was also a college town, teeming with Jewish students and schoolkids.

Almost without exception, Jewish textile workers were members of the socialist Bund. During the 1905 uprising, they took to the streets en masse. An anarchist shot and killed the tsarist police chief. He couldn't have picked a worse target: the police chief was a reformist who had never missed a meeting of the Constitutional Democratic

Chaïm Soutine in 1917, painted by Amedeo Modigliani.

Party. In every New Year's speech, he had proclaimed, 'As long as
I live, there will be no pogrom in Białystok.' After the killing, only
one question preoccupied the policemen and soldiers of the garrison
stationed in the city: when could the bloodbath begin?

Seven, eight, nine months passed. The spring of 1906 arrived, then
June. The feast of Corpus Christi was a Christian holiday, celebrated
by both the Roman Catholic and the Russian Orthodox churches
of Białystok with a religious service and a procession. The Catholics
walked to the old city centre, the Russian Orthodox to the city's new
quarter. When the Orthodox procession reached the halfway mark,
a shot rang out. For both denominations, it was the starting gun for
retribution.

Hundreds of vandals and rioters descended on the city's Jewish
quarters, accompanied and spurred on by soldiers and police. They
looted shops, set fire to entire streets, crowbarred their way into
houses and, armed with daggers and axes, chased down the fleeing
residents. Women were raped, eyes gouged, fingernails pulled out.
Fathers who reached for a knife to defend their children were gunned
down by police officers.

The pogrom lasted two days and nights. Tens of thousands of Jews
took refuge in cellars and sewers. Several hundred managed to reach
the station and secure a seat on one of the trains that were ready for
departure. The Polish railway workers set all signals to red to stop
them leaving. With the help of conductors and station guards, the
Polish butchers forced the Jewish passengers off the trains and slit their
throats on the square in front of the station.

At dawn on Saturday, one of the Jewish leaders found a way to
escape from Białystok. At the post office in a neighbouring town, he
was able to send a telegram to St Petersburg, informing the Russian
parliament of the massacre. The Duma, which was almost permanently in session during the chaotic months of 1905–1906, immediately dispatched a delegation to the city.

Three delegates arrived in Białystok at half past four on Saturday
afternoon. To reach the town hall, they had to step over the bodies
outside the station. The violence ended abruptly, even before the delegates had a chance to speak to the mayor. Seventy corpses lay in front
of the hospital; inside, 200 people were awaiting treatment for serious
injuries. Given the extent and duration of the pogrom, the delegates

reckoned things could have been worse. When they inquired why the death toll wasn't higher, they learned that, in some neighbourhoods, sharpshooters from the Jewish Self-Defence League had been able to keep the mob at bay, and that hand grenades had been thrown at the mounted police. This had kept a number of the Jewish colleges and boarding schools safe.

Young Chaim Jacob Lipchitz spent two days and two nights in the cellar of one of those schools. He had run for cover on hearing the approaching screams of a frenzied mob. For years, he had succeeded in banishing the bloodthirsty screams of June 1906 from his memory. Until the spring of 1928 when his father died, followed soon after by his sister.

The Scream. That was to be the title of the sculpture.

The wide-open mouth took shape quickly, upper and lower jaw moulded in plaster. Then something strange began to happen. The upper jaw began to take the shape of a head, and so did the lower. From the heads followed shoulders, one then the other. The process gathered speed. Shoulders, then arms. A back for the upper figure, a belly for the lower. Graceful curves for the legs, pressed together in the upper figure, spread wide in the lower.

He stepped back, viewed it from a distance. It made him smile. In memory of his father and his sister, and perhaps all the Jews of Lithuania and Poland, he could not sculpt an image that was terrifying, macabre. From his hands, an act of love had emerged. The screams of the many had become the cries of a couple. And so the work became *Le cri (le couple)*. A tremendous relief washed over him. From horror, he had created something pure. From death, he had raised the living; despair had given way to hope. No sculpture had given him more satisfaction. Out of darkness, he had conjured light.

In 1929, the work went on show for the first time, but to Lipchitz's dismay, it was hastily removed from the public eye. Amsterdam slapped a ban on *Le cri (le couple)*, or 'the copulation in bronze' as it had been dubbed in the Dutch press. By order of the mayor, this violation of public decency was expunged from the exhibition at Arti et Amicitiae. Paris too was scandalised: 'obscene' and 'vulgar' were among the reactions. Even so, it remained on view at the Bernheim-Jeune gallery.

Lipchitz's *The Scream* (1928–1929).

These scandals inflamed Lipchitz's rebellious side. His early works had been small enough to grace the hall, living room, or garden of a private home. The events of 1929 fired him up to create monumental works made to stand on tall plinths, colossal statues that would command attention in public spaces, upstaging ministries and other government buildings. He began work on *David and Goliath* and *Prometheus Strangling the Vulture*.

But there was something about Amsterdam. Not unlike Białystok, the city had a way of stirring fear in him. In 1936, he was one of 150 artists to take part in a major international exhibition against National Socialism organised in Amsterdam in protest at the Olympic Games being held in Berlin, the capital of Nazi Germany. Artists from the Netherlands, Belgium, France, Denmark, Sweden, the UK, the US, Czechoslovakia, and Germany submitted work for the exhibition, De Olympiade Onder Dictatuur. Both the full title (Dutch for 'The Olympiad Under Dictatorship') and its acronym, D.O.O.D. (Dutch for 'death'), pulled no punches. Max Ernst, Frans Masereel, Ossip Zadkine, André Lhote, and Robert Capa all took part. As did Jacques Lipchitz, who, with his first New York solo exhibition under his belt, was at least as well known as Zadkine.

The German ambassador in The Hague and the German consul in Amsterdam railed against the exhibition as 'an almighty provocation' that was 'highly insulting to the head of the German state' (i.e. Hitler) and 'a clear example of a Marxist and Jewish smear campaign'. They exerted all kinds of pressure on the Dutch government, the attorney-general, the mayor of Amsterdam, and the chief of police to ban the show, a campaign that nearly succeeded: the Netherlands was still pursuing a policy of strict neutrality at the time. By order of Amsterdam's mayor, Willem de Vlugt, 'only' nineteen works were ultimately excluded, including several drawings by German artist Karl Schwesig, inspired by his experiences in the Brownshirts' torture chambers in Düsseldorf.

Although Lipchitz's drawings were not censored, the controversy in Amsterdam came as a warning. Fascism was unmistakably on the rise, and anyone who did not see it, did not *want* to see it. The following year, 1937, Lipchitz's highly symbolic sculpture *Prometheus Strangling the Vulture* was given pride of place in front of the Palais de la découverte in Paris on the occasion of the Exposition Internationale. In 1938, it was destroyed by right-wing extremists.

A 1935 trip to Soviet Russia had already taught Lipchitz that life under Stalin was not much better. He had gone there to track down Berthe's son, André, who seemed to have disappeared. Lipchitz's brother Paul was under constant surveillance and would perish in a Stalinist purge not long after. After a difficult search, he finally found André, who had gone into hiding from the state security service. A few months after their reunion, André was deported to Siberia.

Experiences like these led Lipchitz to conclude that there was only one place in the world where an artist could still work in freedom. On the day that Germany declared war on France, Jacques and Berthe Lipchitz left Paris for Toulouse. In 1941, they set sail for the United States — New York, to be precise.

In New York, MoMA offered him a workspace. Ukrainian sculptor Chaim Gross lent him chisels and other tools. Lipchitz immediately began work on a sculpture that expressed his despair about the war: *Mother and Child*.

The works that followed saw him return to biblical themes. He grew more religious by the month. In 1944, he met sculptor Yulla Halberstadt, who had fled Berlin with her two sons the day after the Kristallnacht. In the United States, she had converted to Orthodox Judaism. Under Yulla's influence, Lipchitz too became Orthodox.

In 1946, Jacques and Berthe Lipchitz returned to Paris. For Jacques, the trip had a single purpose: to collect what was left of his belongings from his studio. For Berthe, it was a homecoming. She decided to stay on in Paris. To her, America had never been home, and she had continued to feel a strong physical connection to Europe. This did not stop Jacques from taking the next boat to New York. He continued to correspond with Berthe until the end, but he could no longer live in Europe.

Lipchitz settled in Hastings-on-Hudson, a village in New York state. In 1948, he married Yulla, and he became an American citizen in 1958. He travelled frequently, to Israel and to Italy. Lipchitz died on Capri in 1973, aged eighty-one. His body was interred at Har HaMenuchot cemetery in Jerusalem.

His work *Le cri (le couple)* ultimately found a home in the Netherlands, the country where it had once been banned. In the 1950s, it was acquired by Abraham Hammacher, director of the Kröller-Müller Museum. A leading expert on sculpture, he wrote an outstanding book on Lipchitz, in which he praised the Jewish Lithuanian's 'immense sculptural power'.

It was Hammacher who took the initiative to create an extensive sculpture garden on the museum grounds in the De Hoge Veluwe National Park, with a central place for *Le cri (le couple)*. The sculpture suits its surroundings. Or, perhaps more accurately, the surroundings are a good match for the sculpture. *Le cri (le couple)* was made in Paris, but its origins lie in Białystok and Druskininkai. It belongs to the forests. Forests where, if you listen closely, you can still catch chilling echoes of the past.

Lipchitz never spoke about what he experienced in Białystok in 1906. I discovered the true course of events through David Sohn's 1982 publication *The Białystoker Memorial Book*, for which he collected as many eyewitness accounts as he could. They make it clear that young Chaim Jacob, hiding in the cellar of his school, must have heard screams that pierced the thickest stone.

Lipchitz at his studio in Hastings-on-Hudson.

9

Hannah Arendt's City

KÖNIGSBERG

Kaliningrad, May 2009
Hannah Arendt's city has vanished. Nothing remains of its monumental buildings, its university, its castle, its theatres and concert halls. Nor is there any trace of the narrow streets, the shops, the tea-scented warehouses and patrician residences from the era of the Hanseatic League, which dominated northern European trade from the thirteenth to the fifteenth century. Time has marched on. Prussian turned to Russian; Königsberg became Kaliningrad. In the mid-twentieth century, the merchant city was transformed into a hermetically sealed Soviet navy garrison town, and by the century's end it had become a mob town, as lawless as Al Capone's Chicago. The stock exchange, an imposing Italian Renaissance-style building and one of the few restored to its original grandeur, served as a Cultural House for Sailors during the Soviet era and a casino cum nightclub during the Yeltsin era, when 'Monetny Dvor' appeared in neon on its facade. It was a place to avoid unless you wanted to witness firsthand how Russian Mafiosi settle their scores. From Prussian order and discipline to blackjack and shootouts: Königsberg's metamorphosis could not have been more radical.

The city was destroyed in three stages. Firstly, by the Nazis, who created a colossal bunker for themselves inside the castle walls and turned the city into a fortress. Then came the Allied bombers. The Soviets saw to the rest.

With the bombing of Königsberg in August 1944, the Allies ushered in the final phase of World War II. It became a dress rehearsal for the destruction that would engulf the city of Dresden six months later. RAF squadrons dropped tons of high explosives and incendiaries, unleashing a raging firestorm in the heart of the city.

Königsberg on a postcard from 1905.

Trees and bushes sprang up among the ruins. The past disappeared under parkland. Kaliningrad became a sprawling, green city, its centre bisected by wide thoroughfares. The House of the Soviets was its most eye-catching building, a gargantuan structure that largely stood vacant and showed such signs of neglect that it was nicknamed The Monster. Nothing recalled the bustle of densely populated Königsberg with its warren of streets, the German empire's easternmost port, where there was barely space to walk along the crammed quays, and where you could inhale innovative ideas like the scents emanating from the hold of a ship. There were few cities where the flame of Enlightenment burned brighter, and few cities where it was extinguished so abruptly.

Unless, of course, you take a different view. The view that Hannah Arendt's city lives on in her thinking. That the spirit of Königsberg is preserved in the free and frank tone of her writing.

Königsberg — or Kenigsberg as the nasal twang of its Prussian citizens would have it — was also the city of Immanuel Kant. He taught there at the Albertina, the university named after Duke Albrecht of Brandenburg-Ansbach, founded in 1544 and brought to prominence by Prussian Protestant thinkers in the seventeenth and eighteenth centuries. Kant rarely left the city. Königsberg was a cosmopolitan port, and the philosopher could state without exaggeration:

German soldiers flee the centre of Königsberg during
the Allied bombing in August 1944.

A city such as Königsberg on the River Pregel — a large city, the
centre of a state, the seat of a government's provincial councils,
the site of a university (for cultivation of the sciences), a seaport
connected by rivers with the interior of the country, so that its
location favours traffic with the rest of the country as well as with
neighbouring or remote countries having different languages and
customs — is a suitable place for broadening one's knowledge of
man and of the world. In such a city, this knowledge can be acquired
even without travelling.
(*Anthropology from a Pragmatic Point of View*)

After World War II, Königsberg's cathedral remained roofless for
years, its windows reduced to dark hollows. It was 1995 before restoration was completed and its four bells rang out again as they had in
Prussian times. During that half-century, Kant's lonely tomb leaned
against the ruins. It had been robbed in April 1945, when Russian
tanks advanced, German troops withdrew, and the civilian population
fled on foot or by horse and cart in a chaotic exodus, through the

The former House of the Soviets in Kaliningrad,
nicknamed The Monster.

snow and biting cold, to the fishing villages on the coast. The tomb
had long been left in its sullied state, with a bullet hole below the
sarcophagus. But it was not demolished. Even now, it is brightened up
daily by a red rose or two, laid no doubt by those grizzled souls who
still keep the communist faith. Kant was a philosopher the Soviets
could live with.

Through his doctrine — always behave in such a way that your
actions may serve as a law for all humanity — he exerted a considerable influence on Marx and Engels. And on Hannah Arendt, who, at

the age of fourteen, took Kant's collected works from the bookcase at home in Königsberg and began to read them intently, an act that would shape her thinking and the course of her life.

In the end, she broke with Kant. His categorical imperative did not go far enough for her; his moral philosophy no longer held up after the Holocaust. 'We — at least the older ones among us — have witnessed the total collapse of all established moral standards in public and private life during the 1930s and 40s, not only ... in Hitler's Germany but also in Stalin's Russia.' In times of crisis — and the entire twentieth century was characterised by devastation, as her Königsberg proved — human beings could not rely on regulations and the rule of law. The key for each individual, as Arendt saw it, was to say: 'I must be true to myself. I must not do anything that I cannot live with, that I cannot bear to remember.'

Arendt was late to lose her respect for Marx; it was a gradual process. In *The Origins of Totalitarianism* (1951), she was still making a clear distinction between Lenin, who had tried to put Marxist doctrine into practice, and Stalin, who had squandered Marx's legacy. It was a position that sparked a spirited correspondence with her friend and philosophical mentor Karl Jaspers.

'You speak favourably of Marx's passion for justice, which links him to Kant,' he wrote. 'Marx's passion seems to me impure at its root, itself unjust from the outset, drawing its life from the negative, without an image of man, the hate incarnate of a pseudo-prophet in the style of Ezekiel.'

In her response, Arendt defended Marx as a rebel and a revolutionary who had truly understood the 'de-naturing' of man and nature by the economy of commodities.

Jaspers was having none of it and hammered on about Marx's intolerance, yes, and even the alarming obsessiveness revealed in his character. 'There is an unbroken continuity from him to Lenin ... He was probably a figure of destiny, like Luther, not as important for his ideas as for the character that carried those ideas.'

Arendt did not answer him for a while, reread Marx, and wrote, 'The more I read Marx, the more I see that you were right. He's not interested in either freedom or justice.' Obsessed with social issues, Marx refused to engage seriously in anything relating to state and government. This would become the central theme of her subsequent fundamental studies, *The Human Condition* (1958) and *On Revolution* (1963).

Hannah Arendt fled Germany in 1933, without valid papers, escaping through a house which had its front door in Germany and its back door in Czechoslovakia. She lived in Paris for seven years, was imprisoned in an internment camp at Gurs in the south of France at the beginning of the war, only to be released after a few weeks. From there, she swiftly fled to Lisbon, and in 1941 emigrated to the United States with her mother and her husband. New York became her new home, but her language, her dearest friends, and the thinkers who inspired her remained German. Deep down, she never left her homeland.

Sixteen of the twenty-seven years she actually lived in Germany were spent in Königsberg. Even as a student in Marburg, Freiburg, and Heidelberg, she would return to East Prussia at Christmas and during the summer months. When she wrote about being at home, she meant Ke-nigs-berg. The only book from her father's library that travelled with her to New York was the 1795 first edition of Kant's *Zum ewigen Frieden* (Perpetual Peace). In her mind, Kant and Königsberg were one. In the troubled final months of her life, she read 'good old Kant' and did not bother much with anyone else. That was what made her happiest.

Kant lent Königsberg a magnetic appeal. He was born in 1724 and died in 1804, just shy of his eightieth birthday. This long life, exceptional for the eighteenth century, meant that he had a profound influence on the spirit of the city. Freedom was central to his doctrine: freedom of action and freedom of thought. He broke with both divine destiny and the laws of nature. Each human being had their own responsibility and a duty to take it.

Students from Lübeck, Gdańsk, Memelland, Latvia, and Estonia flocked to Königsberg to hear Kant lecture. Johann Gottfried Herder was one of them. So too was Jakob Michael Reinhold Lenz, son of a clergyman from Livonia (then part of Russia). After studying in Königsberg, Herder became the founder of Romanticism, and Lenz a leading dramatist of the Sturm und Drang movement. If, as Lenz had learned from Kant, each individual was in a position to take their own responsibility, they were also allowed to rebel. In his eyes, the next step was socialism and everyone's right to demand human dignity.

Hannah Arendt always considered it a stroke of luck that she had been given the chance to grow up in Königsberg, a city that was both part of Germany and on Germany's border, both Prussian and Baltic. Old Prussian, which died out in the eighteenth century, was a Baltic language, related to Livonian and Latvian. Königsberg drew on centuries of Prussian tradition for its rigour and industriousness; it left the militarism to Berlin.

Königsberg avoided power struggles and traded with the northern German cities, Denmark, and Sweden on one side, and with Russia on the other. Königsberg passed on Western products and Western ideas to the East. It became a transit hub and a centre of knowledge.

If we see the Baltic countries as a piece of amber, Königsberg and Riga formed the western, German facet; Tallinn and Tartu the northern, Scandinavian facet; and Daugavpils and Vilnius the eastern, Russian facet. The forces of history would pulverise that gem and redistribute the dust, leaving Königsberg a Russian city. But the Königsberg Hannah Arendt knew was still very much Prussian, with strong Baltic and Russian influences.

Hannah's mother was a Cohn. Her grandfather Jacob Cohn came from Lithuania, which had been under tsarist rule throughout the nineteenth century. In 1851, Nicholas I issued a decree that declared prosperous or skilled Jews to be 'useful' and the rest to be 'non-useful'. As well as being a crude expression of anti-Semitism, this was also a way to round up as many recruits as possible to fight in the Crimean War: the 'non-useful' were called up for military service. Jacob Cohn's father emigrated to Königsberg, where he set up a business importing Russian tea. J.N. Cohn & Co. became the city's largest tea merchant.

One of Hannah's fondest and most abiding childhood memories was the smell of black tea that hung in her grandfather's warehouses. The Cohn children and grandchildren lived a pleasant, comfortable life, with trips to Memelland in spring (an area north of the River Memel, then part of East Prussia, now a region of Lithuania) and long holidays at a summer house on the Baltic coast. But rampant inflation during the final months of World War I caused the family's wealth to shrivel.

Generations of Arendts had lived in Königsberg. Max Arendt,

Hannah's paternal grandfather, was the embodiment of an assimilated Jew. To Zionists, he responded with a nationalist motto. 'When my Germanness is attacked, I prepare for murder.' His German credentials were questionable to say the least: his mother came from Russia. Even so, the Arendts were more Prussian and straitlaced than the generous, warm-hearted Cohns, whose family included many *Ostjuden*, Eastern European Jews. Hannah's grandmother, Fanny Spiero Cohn, spoke German with a heavy Russian accent and had a penchant for dressing in Russian peasant clothes. Even in her own home, Hannah was keenly aware that she was living in a border region.

Paul Arendt, Hannah's father, led a tragic life. As a young man, he contracted syphilis. He was treated and given a clean bill of health, but in 1902 the disease was effectively incurable. When he met Martha Cohn, he informed her about his infection, yet it did not discourage her from marrying him. Paul took a job at an electrical engineering firm in Hanover. Since he had suffered no further symptoms, Paul and Martha decided to ignore the risks and try for a baby. Hannah was born in 1906 in the village of Linden near Hanover. Two and a half years later, her father had to seek treatment again at Königsberg university clinic. Not only did his condition steadily worsen, but his daughter also suffered the consequences, undergoing medical examinations for hereditary syphilis every six months.

The family returned to Königsberg, and Paul's condition deteriorated. To begin with, he kept falling over, episodes that came as a great shock to his daughter; later, spastic paraplegia affected his movement. In the end, he went mad. During the summer of 1911, Paul Arendt had to be admitted to a psychiatric institution, where he died two years later.

Martha observed that her seven-year-old daughter did not shed a tear at her father's death. At his funeral, it was only the beautiful singing that moved her. With a wisdom and sense of perspective beyond her years, she told her mother, 'Remember, Mama, that it happens to a lot of women.'

More than anything, Hannah experienced her father's death as a liberation from the oppressive atmosphere at home. Until he was admitted to the institution, she had not been allowed to invite friends over to play. During their walks in the zoo, she was always worried that he would collapse without warning. As an adult, Hannah would

Eight-year-old Hannah Arendt with her mother, Martha, in Königsberg.

Paul Arendt.

portray her father as a kind, gentle, and learned man, but by the age of five, she could barely talk to him and tried to amuse him with card games to distract him from the dreadful pain he suffered. His mental decline reached a point where he no longer recognised his daughter.

Martha Arendt raised Hannah alone, in a grand house on a tree-lined avenue that led to the zoo, one of the most impressive in all of Europe. Today, there is no trace of their house on Tiergartenstraße, or the entire district of Hufen for that matter, but the zoo came through the war unscathed. Children still walk there with their fathers, though nowadays they call out to the monkeys in Russian.

Darja Sviridova was born in Kaliningrad in 1974, the year before Hannah Arendt died in New York, aged sixty-nine. Darja spent her entire childhood in Kaliningrad, without hearing a single word about her famous compatriot. At school and at home, the city's German past was hushed up. The fact that Reichsstraße 1 ran all the way from Berlin's Brandenburg Gate to Königsberg was something she learned from history books, but no one ever mentioned that this trunk road had once been the Kaiserliche Allee. When a German businessman asked her about Memelland, she had no idea he was talking about the expanse of land by the river, nor that the river had once been called the Pregel. She knew, of course, that Kaliningrad was named after Mikhail Kalinin, the long-serving chairman of the Central Executive Committee of the Supreme Soviet and as such the formal head of state of the Soviet Union, and that until 1945 her city had been called Königsberg. But what did a king — *könig* — have to do with anything? It astounded her to read that the castle on the hill — the *berg* of the city's old name — was the site where every king of Prussia had been crowned.

The history Darja was taught began with Hitler's order to defend the city to the last man. 'Total victory or total defeat': the phrase was drilled into her by her teachers, safe in the knowledge that Hitler's fate had been the latter. On 6 April 1945, the Red Army launched its offensive and 250,000 Russian soldiers went into battle against 30,000 German troops. Russian tanks outnumbered German tanks by a hundred to one — she knew these figures as if she had counted the tanks herself. Two-thirds of the population had already fled the city; in the three-day battle that followed, most of the 100,000 Königsbergers who remained would perish, and practically every survivor would go on to die in the epidemics that broke out between April and June. Several thousand Königsbergers had managed to flee aboard German ships, many of which were torpedoed by Russian submarines in the Baltic.

Darja knew nothing of Stalin's 1947 order to deport the 20,000 Königsbergers who had survived the war to Siberia. History as she had learned it consisted of the righteous battles and noble deeds of the Great Patriotic War — the name given to World War II by Russian history books.

It was the soldiers of the 43rd Army who captured Königsberg from the Germans, and 80 per cent of them continued to live in the city, which was quickly renamed Kaliningrad. Later, workers from all parts of Russia were given a financial incentive to settle in Kaliningrad and its suburbs in the wider province, Kaliningrad Oblast.

The Baltic climate was more forgiving than that of Russia's heartlands, and from the 1950s, once the rubble had been cleared and the first housing blocks sprung up, you could obtain a brand-new home there up to twice the size of a newly built flat in Moscow, Kyiv, Minsk, or Leningrad. It was just such a home — a two-bedroom flat of seventy square metres, practically a palace — that brought Darja's parents to Kaliningrad. Of course, it helped that her father had a desk job with the navy.

Growing up, Darja could still see traces of the city's distant past — statues of Kant and Friedrich Schiller continued to stand tall — and yet that past was subject to a kind of a ban. History was concentrated in the bunker, in Fort No. 5, wrested from the grip of the Nazi's by the Red Army. It did not extend to the Altstädtische Kirche, which was razed to the ground.

In 1996, Darja Sviridova travelled abroad for the first time, a trip that would become a defining event in her life. In London, she decided to abandon Russian and study English instead. Someone asked her where she was from. 'Kaliningrad,' she replied. There was a pause before the person said, 'Ah yes, Königsberg, the city of Immanuel Kant and Hannah Arendt.' She asked who Hannah Arendt was. 'A philosopher. A Jewish philosopher.' She nodded and said nothing more. Back in Kaliningrad, she typed 'Hannah Arendt' into a search engine and found some information. Years later, this episode came back to Darja when her dying mother said she had something to tell her. 'Your grandmother was Jewish,' she said, hours before her passing, immediately followed by the advice: 'Do what I did and never tell a soul.'

Only 200 kilometres separated Königsberg and Riga. Three hundred kilometres lay between Königsberg and Vilnius. Yet the contrast with both cities could hardly have been greater. At the beginning of the twentieth century, Jews accounted for half the population of Riga and Vilnius; in Königsberg they numbered less than 5,000. By the end of the eighteenth century, Jews were already being admitted to the high schools and Albertina University — the young men, that is; women were not permitted to study at the Albertina until after World War I, but that ban applied to all women, regardless of their background. Affluence was the other prerequisite. The poor Eastern European Jews lived in the slums in the south of the city and rarely crossed the River Pregel to attend school. They learned to read and write from the rabbi. The other difference with Prussian Jews was that they were strictly Orthodox.

Hannah Arendt's father obtained his engineering degree at the Albertina. Her mother had to make do with home schooling, but also had the opportunity to go to Paris, where she spent three years studying music and French language and literature.

In her youth, Hannah was not especially aware of anti-Semitism. Königsberg offered a safe and sheltered haven, and the fact that she had learned to defend herself from an early age may also have been a factor. In an interview with Günter Gaus in 1964, she said:

> I came from an old Königsberg family. But the word 'Jew' was never mentioned at home. I first encountered it — though really it is hardly worth recounting it — in the anti-Semitic remarks of children as we played in the streets — then I became, so to speak, enlightened ... As a child — now a somewhat older child — I knew, for example, that I looked Jewish ... That is, that I looked a bit different from the rest. But not in a way that made me feel inferior — I was simply aware of it, that is all ... My mother was not very theoretical ... the 'Jewish Question' had no relevance for her. Of course she was a Jewess! She would never have had me christened, baptised. And she would have given me a real spanking if she had ever had reason to believe that I had denied being Jewish. The matter was never a topic of discussion. It was out of the question that it be.

Hannah went on to recount her schooling in self-defence, a description that offers a telling portrait of her mother, Martha Arendt:

You see, all Jewish children encountered anti-Semitism. And the
souls of many children were poisoned by it. The difference with
me lay in the fact that my mother always insisted that I not humble
myself. One must defend oneself! When my teachers made anti-
Semitic remarks — usually they were not directed at me but at
my other classmates, particularly at the Eastern Jewesses — I was
instructed to stand up immediately, leave the class, go home, and
leave the rest to school protocol. My mother would write one of
her many letters, and with that, my involvement in the matter ended
completely. I had a day off from school, and that was, of course,
very nice. But if remarks came at me from other children, I was
not allowed to go home and tell. That did not count. One had to
defend *oneself* against remarks from other children. And, so, these
things did not become really problematic for me. There existed
rules of conduct, house rules, so to speak, by which my dignity was
protected, absolutely protected.

Defending yourself, standing up for yourself, being politically
aware, and not denying your own identity: these are the constants in
Hannah Arendt's work. In one of her most uncompromising essays,
she aims her criticism at Stefan Zweig. She did so at a delicate time,
in 1943, shortly after the publication of the English translation of
Zweig's memoirs, *The World of Yesterday*, and a year after Zweig and
his wife, Friderike, had taken their own lives. This tragedy did not
make Arendt go any easier on them. Zweig was both the type of
writer and the type of Jew she despised.

But deeply as the events of 1933 had changed his personal existence,
they could not touch his standards or his attitudes to the world and
to life. He continued to boast of his unpolitical point of view; it
never occurred to him that, politically, it might be an honour to
stand outside the law when all men were no longer equal before it.

In Arendt's eyes, none of Zweig's responses from that time show
any political conviction.

Instead of hating the Nazis, he just wanted to annoy them. Instead
of despising those of his coterie who had been *gleichgeschaltet*, he

thanked Richard Strauss for continuing to accept his libretti. Instead
of fighting, he kept silent, happy that his books had not been
immediately banned.

Then again, Zweig came from conservative, bourgeois, convivial
Vienna, not free-thinking, progressive Königsberg, where intellectuals
had been politically aware from the mid-eighteenth century onwards.
Arendt writes:

> Naturally, the world which Zweig depicts was anything but the
> world of yesterday; the author of this book lived only on its rim.
> The gilded trellises of this reservation were very thick, depriving the
> inmates of every view and every insight that could mar their bliss.
> Not once does Zweig mention the most ominous manifestation of
> the postwar period, which struck his native Austria more violently
> than any other European country — unemployment ... It is
> astounding that there were still men among us whose ignorance
> was so profound, and whose conscience was so clear, that they
> could continue to look on the prewar period with the eyes of the
> nineteenth century. They could regard the impotent pacifism of
> Geneva and the treacherous lull before the storm between 1924 and
> 1933 as a return to normalcy!
> (Hannah Arendt from 'A Review of *The World of Yesterday: an
> autobiography*')

Even as a girl, Hannah had known better. In the aftermath of World
War I, inflation had decimated the Cohn family's capital. Her grandfather's firm went bankrupt. Her mother had to take in a female boarder
to keep her household running. In 1920, Martha Arendt remarried.
Martin Beerwald was a widower with two daughters, aged twenty and
nineteen. With fourteen-year-old Hannah in tow, Martha moved into
Martin's home on Busoltstraße, just two blocks from Tiergartenstraße.
While Martha never referred to it purely as a marriage of convenience,
presumably it helped that Beerwald was a partner in a flourishing hard-
ware firm and did not lack for income. That is until surging inflation
in the late 1920s put paid to his business too.

Hannah acquired her political awareness at home. Before they had
turned twenty, both Paul and Martha Arendt had joined the Socialist

Party, still banned in Germany at the time. They did not miss a single clandestine meeting. For them, politics was about obtaining freedom, equality, and prosperity for all citizens, including Jews. Neither of them could be described as religious. Occasionally, they would allow their daughter to accompany her paternal grandparents to the synagogue, so that she would not be a complete stranger to the Jewish faith and traditions. They were on friendly terms with the liberal rabbi of Königsberg, Hermann Vogelstein, but primarily because he was as ardent a social democrat as they were.

When the world tilted on its axis, Martha and Hannah were at the Cohns' summer house in the fishing village of Neukuhren on the Baltic coast. As soon as World War I broke out, they returned to Königsberg to find the city in panic and disarray: the Russians were advancing. On 23 August 1914, Martha and Hannah headed for Berlin on a train packed with farmers and landed gentry from Livonia and Courland, whose houses had been looted or torched by Russian soldiers. The aisles were crammed with the bags and suitcases that held what was left of their possessions. '*Die Kosakken kommen!*' was the warning that Martha and Hannah heard from countless mouths. But the Cossacks did not come, at least not in 1914. Their offensive was halted in its tracks by the German army at the savage Battle of Tannenberg. Ten weeks later, Martha and Hannah were able to return to Königsberg. But when eventually the Cossacks did come, in 1945, they came to stay. The friendly fishing village of Neukuhren, where Hannah had spent all her summers until 1920, became Pionersky, Town of the Pioneers, a name it bears to this day.

Hannah became ill, frequently ill. That is to say, she became ill every time a trip was scheduled and she had to leave her home and her hometown for a few days or weeks. Shortly before another journey to Berlin, her temperature soared and she developed a nasty cough. Ahead of a departure for the Bavarian Alps, she was diagnosed with diphtheria; the trip was cancelled and a serum injection appeared to quell the disease with remarkable speed, leaving the doctor to wonder if it had been diphtheria at all. This was followed, in her mother's words, by 'a happy and successful return to school'. Hannah was afraid to leave Königsberg. Each time, she feared her departure would be final and she would never see her city again.

A few weeks after Russia's October Revolution, thousands of

workers in Königsberg demonstrated against the war and the resulting high cost of living. The German army intervened and opened fire on the protesters. Immediately after World War I, East Prussia was cut off from West Prussian Pomerania by the Polish Corridor, and Königsberg became an exclave. Hannah's fearful premonitions were beginning to come true.

During the first days of 1919, there were echoes of revolution in Berlin. Martha Arendt, a reformist social democrat, had little time for the communist-revolutionary Spartacus League, though she did have a genuine admiration for Rosa Luxemburg's commitment and passion. In the first week of January 1919, she took her daughter to a meeting in Königsberg where news of the uprising in Berlin was discussed. Running through the streets, Martha shouted to her daughter, 'You must pay attention, this is a historical moment.' She was proved right: days later, on 15 January, Rosa Luxemburg and Karl Liebknecht were captured and killed by members of the Freikorps in Berlin.

From a young age, Hannah Arendt lived in the constant realisation that the world could change overnight, whether through personal suffering — the death of her father — or the grinding wheels of history.

The realisation that events can take a strange turn in your city, your country, and your life also dawned on Darja Sviridova. At the age of seventeen, she took her final exams. The text she had to comment on was obviously one by Lenin. But four years later, the statues of Father Lenin disappeared from the streets of Kaliningrad, and anyone who quoted him invited the suspicion of hankering back to a time when party officials called the shots. Newborn boys were given every name imaginable but not Lenin's first name, though Vladimir had once been as popular in the Soviet Union as Jesús in the heartlands of Catholicism.

Free trade had always meant the black market, but suddenly the city was teeming with market stalls. From one day to the next, you could buy anything on the streets. People on television began to speak a different language, everyday language with everyday words, a far cry from the usual propaganda clogged with Marxist-Leninist jargon. The hardest part was changing the way you thought. From a staunchly collective mindset, you suddenly had to start from an individual perspective, from yourself and your own self-interest. Gaining your independence was difficult and demanding. Comrade Sviridova became Darja Sviridova. 'Comrade' meant: shut up and do what's expected of you. Being Darja required her to form her own views. She barely had a view of herself, beyond the obvious: blue-grey eyes, blonde hair that needed bleaching more often (but she had to do it herself, and it was such a hassle), five feet ten inches tall, legs too sturdy for gymnastics or ballet (which was fine, as she didn't like either), seventeen, eighteen, nineteen years old and still no boyfriend. Her own views had always been secondary. You didn't have a view, unless you wanted to get into trouble; you said what everyone else said and kept your head down. You barely even wondered whether what you were told actually made any sense. You deactivated your own opinion. An opinion was asking for trouble. Did the Soviet Union have to go back to being Russia? Yes, but how? The answers used to descend from on high; these were not the kinds of questions you went around asking yourself.

For Darja, there was another issue to consider. For some time now, she had known she was Jewish, or at least had Jewish roots. She had no idea what this entailed or even if it held any meaning for her personally. It made her curious; it frightened her. This was 1996: did it really matter whether your forebears were Jewish, Armenian, or Georgian? Did her mother's deathbed confession hold any significance at all? She had always thought of herself as a Russian, as living on the very edge of Russia. Is that how things would stay? Or should she count herself among the Russian Jews, about whom she knew next to nothing?

Darja started to read Hannah Arendt.

As an adolescent, Hannah was trouble. Her fierce intelligence and the speed at which she drew conclusions meant her teachers were often glad to see the back of her. The situation at home forced her to stand her ground. She developed a strong sense of self, hiding her shyness behind outspoken opinions and overconfident actions. Since they had moved in with the Beerwalds, she'd had to share her mother's attention with two stepsisters. The eldest, Clara, was startlingly intelligent and also went on to become a brilliant pianist. She studied mathematics, chemistry, and several languages before turning to the study of pharmacy, which, according to the wisdom of the age, was a profession better suited to a woman. Martha Arendt had her hands full just trying to keep her stepdaughter on track. With her pinched face and panicked gaze, Clara scared men off. Following a string of broken love affairs, she became suicidal. Psychiatry could not help her, and at the age of thirty, she ingested a lethal amount of poison. Her sister, Eva, was less gifted and more accommodating by nature. That said, she saw no reason to play second fiddle to Clara and demanded equal attention from her stepmother. Hannah suddenly found herself with formidable rivals. She and her stepfather did not get along. With his patriarchal Bismarck moustache and a tail coat as his daily attire, Beerwald was every inch the conservative. Intellectually, he was no match for Martha or her daughter.

By the age of sixteen, Hannah had mastered Greek and Latin so thoroughly that she formed a club dedicated to the reading and study of classical literature. Yet she refused to attend Greek classes, because they started early. A notorious late-sleeper, Hannah insisted that no one had the right to inflict Homer on students at eight in the morning. Following negotiations with her mother and the school board, she was permitted to study Greek and Latin on her own time and take an end-of-year exam that was specially drawn up for her. These remarkable concessions — this was East Prussia in 1919, remember, when teenagers were expected to keep quiet and toe the line — did not make her more amenable. She refused to learn English, because she disapproved of the teacher. Following a conflict with another teacher, in which her mother sided with Hannah, she was expelled. In Berlin, she attended lectures by the philosopher Romano Guardini, began reading Kierkegaard, and prepared for her final school exams, which she eventually took as an external student in Königsberg.

In Berlin, she had already heard about Heidegger. 'The rumour about Heidegger put it quite simply: thinking has come to life again; the cultural treasures of the past, believed to be dead, are being made to speak, in the course of which it turns out that they propose things altogether different from the familiar, worn-out trivialities that they had been presumed to say. There exists a teacher; one can perhaps learn to think.' Heidegger taught in Marburg. To enter the orbit of that teacher, Hannah left her beloved Königsberg for Marburg and moved into an attic room close to the university. Her short hair and striking clothes ensured that all eyes were on her.

'The most striking thing about her was the suggestive force that emanated from her eyes,' wrote her one-time boyfriend Benno von Wiese in his memoirs. 'One virtually drowned in them and feared never to come up again.' Another fellow student, Hermann Mörchen, recalled how in the dining hall, conversations sometimes dropped away when Arendt spoke. One simply had to listen to her. Her probing intensity, her unceasing search for essence and depth, cast a kind of spell. She also developed a great talent for friendship. For her, a friend always remained a friend. In a letter, she wrote, 'I cannot say no to someone once I have said yes to them.' It is hard to find a better definition of loyalty.

Her relationship with Martin Heidegger began five months after her arrival in Marburg, as the very height of romance. From her seat in the lecture theatre, she saw herself reflected in his eyes, not narcissistically as the object of his desire, but as the woman he brought to life in her, a being she had not encountered before. According to Elżbieta Ettinger, who reconstructed the affair by piecing together excerpts from their letters to create a breathtaking love story, Heidegger had already spent two months observing her when he invited her to his office in early February. The impression she made on him at that meeting reads like a scene from a film: 'She came in wearing a raincoat, a hat pulled low over her face, now and then uttering a barely audible "yes" or "no".'

In deepest secrecy, she received Heidegger in her attic room over the course of two semesters. She was eighteen; he was thirty-five. She had had two boyfriends; he was a married man and the father of two sons. She dived headlong into student life; he was a brilliant scholar who maintained a safe distance from his colleagues and from the other students who idolised him. She wore elegant green dresses; he preferred simple peasant clothes. She chain-smoked or lit a slender pipe with a metal mouthpiece; he believed that a healthy mind resided in a healthy body and was an avid skier who enjoyed giving ski lessons. She had a toughness born of timidity; he had a stiffness born of awkwardness. She wrote poems with lines such as 'I no longer know how love feels / I no longer know the fields aglow'; he formulated poetic phrases as intense as they were pompous.

Arendt during her final year in Königsberg.

Despite his poetic zeal, he was petrified of his ambitious wife, Elfride, who kept a close watch on her family's reputation. He sent Arendt cryptic notes telling her to the exact minute when he expected her to turn up for their next assignation at his country cabin, and came up with a boy-scout system of lights switched on or off to indicate that the coast was clear. Their relationship could not last: she knew that from the start.

In an intimate, confessional piece of writing called *The Shadows*, which she sent to Heidegger, Arendt is tormented by the feeling of not really being present in their relationship. Nevertheless, she clung to it, describing her love as an 'unbending devotion to a single one' and hoping that Heidegger would put an end to her confused disposition, which perhaps only stemmed from her 'helpless, betrayed childhood'.

She never wanted to make the direct connection to her father's early death, or to her lack of a father in general. She scorned psychoanalysis. Painful experiences, she felt, should be allowed to slip to the bottom of the soul, where they could no longer cause harm. Or as she said to her mother, aged seven, not long after her father's death: 'We must not think too much about sad things.'

In 1927, Hannah returned to Königsberg for several weeks, at her mother's invitation. On what would have been her parents' twenty-fifth wedding anniversary, she and her mother treated themselves to a lavish lunch — three courses, with wine — at a restaurant right next to the civic court where Martha and Paul Arendt had been married all those years ago. In Martha's eyes, Hannah had taken her late husband's place, something that did not trouble Hannah in the slightest.

After her time at Marburg, Hannah studied theology in Freiburg with Edmund Husserl, and philosophy in Heidelberg with Karl Jaspers. A world of difference. Martin Heidegger was to philosophy what Nikolaus Harnoncourt was to music: he wanted to return to the sources of thinking just as Harnoncourt, half a century later, wanted to rediscover the original intentions of Bach and Mozart. The Viennese conductor sought out original instruments from the eighteenth century to get as close as possible to the composers' world, while the sage of Marburg developed a method of thinking that enabled him to explore the thinking of the past and unearth all the stages that had remained 'unthought'.

Karl Jaspers was a less abstract, less fundamental, and less rigid thinker than Heidegger; his profound engagement with the world also made him more playful and humane. He was, as he wrote of himself, 'more conjectural than knowing, groping, not sure of anything'. He too became enamoured of Hannah — her intelligence, humour, ferocity, and even her impetuousness — but he was happily married to Gertrud Mayer and belonged to the rare group of men who were, in Arendt's words, 'inviolable, untemptable, and unswayable'. In him,

Arendt in her student days, with ever-present cigarette.

she found the true substitute for Paul Arendt. 'I naturally count myself especially lucky,' she wrote in a letter in 1952, 'that he is in such great measure pleased with me; because it is like a childhood dream come true.' Above all, Jaspers was open-minded and understanding. When, after the war, Hannah told him about her affair with Heidegger, his reply was, 'Ach, but that is very exciting.'

The affair was certainly exciting for Martin, who got a kick out of furtive sex in a twilit country cabin. He had a perverse side, although for one so inclined to use the word 'pure', sex of any kind qualified as depraved and sinful, a consequence of his strict Catholic upbringing. It was also a thrill for Hannah, who wanted to lose her innocence, but not in the arms of a boyfriend. The budding romance of girlhood was a stage she was intent on skipping, though friends from that time describe her as very shy and withdrawn, and at least as romantic as the older man she loved.

Until 1929, the year in which Hannah wrote her dissertation, Martin only had to send her a note telling her to come and she would drop whatever she was doing and jump on a train. 'Come' was not the word he used; he 'called for her', as a general might call for his aide. He became a tyrant, a petty dictator in love. And she, the provincial lass from Königsberg, became dazzled by the role she was allowed to play. She became his passion and his muse — it was at this time that he wrote his magnum opus, *Sein und Zeit* (Being and Time). Although he did not discuss its content with her in any great depth, it is clear that he felt encouraged and admired by her.

In the postwar period, on discovering that she understood his ideas much better than he did, or could at least express them more clearly and precisely, he grew jealous. His response to the German translation of Arendt's *The Human Condition* was an outburst of hostility. He was done with her. She wrote to Jaspers:

> I know that he finds it intolerable that my name appears in public, that I write books, etc. All my life, I've pulled the wool over his eyes, so to speak, acted as if none of that existed and as if I couldn't count to three, unless it was in the interpretation of his own works. Then he was always very pleased when it turned out I could count to three and sometimes even to four.

The idea that his sympathy for the National Socialists implied a deep contempt for her and who she really was, was something he failed to grasp. Heidegger saw the Nazis as gatekeepers of German culture. With his fondness for mountains, forests, farmers, and shepherds, he believed the Brownshirts would restore the pastoral values of the pre-industrial age. He was an inveterate romantic for whom nothing ranked higher than the German language, German poetry, and German thinking. The great thinker proved to be staggeringly unworldly — to hear Goethe in Hitler's speeches, you had to be dreaming rather than listening.

When he actually lent his support to the Nazis and joined the party, Arendt ended their relationship. But on meeting him after the war, she once again fell for his poetic language and went a long way towards forgiving him, a bitter illustration, perhaps, of the incomprehensible traces left by love. She quoted Jaspers: 'Loyalty is the sign of truth.' But Heidegger was undeserving of her loyalty. Even after the war, he did not recant his earlier views and hauled Jaspers, who had resumed tentative contact with him, over the coals for marrying Gertrud Mayer, who was Jewish. The essence and the enormity of the Holocaust never seemed to get through to him.

Heidegger would outlive Arendt. Until the very end of her life, she continued to correspond with him and see him occasionally. A framed picture of Heidegger hung above the door of her New York study, which overlooked the Hudson. 'At bottom, I was happy,' she wrote to Jaspers, 'at the confirmation — that I was right never to have forgotten.' It was her relationship with Heidegger she was talking about. Yet while her tumultuous relationship with Heidegger would always stay with her, it was her husband Heinrich Blücher who gave her the fulfilment she sought: 'It still seems to me unbelievable, that I could achieve both a great love, and a sense of identity with my own person.'

Darja Sviridova noted, 'There's a certain appeal in making the wrong choice against your better judgement. Plenty of women fall for the wrong man.'

Aged twenty, she herself had an affair with a soft-spoken man who commemorated the anniversary of Stalin's death every year, a man who dismissed the gulag as Western propaganda. Her next flame was out to get rich, at any cost. 'I honestly believe he would have killed to get what he wanted.' She had less trouble forgetting him: he was an indifferent lover.

'Did Arendt marry?' Darja asked me.

Having read Elisabeth Young-Bruehl's biography, I knew the answer: twice. Hannah's first husband was a fellow philosophy student who, like her, came from a well-to-do Jewish family. Günther Stern was his name, and he went on to become a well-known writer under the pseudonym Günther Anders. Martha Arendt adored her son-in-law, but it wasn't long before the marriage foundered. Martha was less enthusiastic about Hannah's second husband, a German émigré she met in Paris. He was neither Jewish, middle-class, nor well-to-do; he had little education, no title, and no profession, let alone a career of note. As the son of a Berlin washerwoman and an unknown, nameless father, Heinrich Blücher could lay claim to no status of any kind. He was a revolutionary proletarian who had spent years working as a junior clerk and was among the founders of the German Communist Party. Above all, he was a brilliant talker who could think aloud for hours on end, pipe in hand. For Hannah, he became more friend than husband, the finest and most committed of friends, and would remain so all his life. What she loved most about him was his 'real understanding of people'.

Darja immersed herself in Arendt. First came the essays on Jewishness: 'The Jew as Pariah' and 'Antisemitism'. Then her journalistic work *Eichmann in Jerusalem: a report on the banality of evil*. And finally, a much harder slog with the dictionary at hand, she tackled Arendt's major political analyses *On Revolution*, *The Human Condition*, and *The Origins of Totalitarianism*. Much of the writing was hard to follow. Reading Arendt made your head spin; it required a depth of knowledge and culture that few people in the late twentieth century possessed, that few people have ever possessed. Darja knew firsthand what it was to live through dictatorship and revolution, but on turning every page she thought, 'What do I really know about these things?'

On finishing *The Origins of Totalitarianism*, Darja couldn't help thinking that Arendt had drawn a faulty conclusion. As Arendt saw it, the crushing power of a totalitarian regime could only be stopped by external resistance from non-totalitarian countries. By the armies of Britain and the United States, for example, which had brought the Nazis to their knees. But had Arendt forgotten that the tipping point of the war had begun at Stalingrad? That it was Stalin's Red Army advancing towards Berlin that had dealt the decisive blow? Arendt's whole conclusion was wide of the mark. Nor had external resistance from the free world brought about the fall of communism. In Poland, trade-union leaders had taken matters into their own hands; in Berlin, young East Germans had begun hacking at the Wall with pickaxes. The people of Estonia, Latvia, and Lithuania had joined hands and sung their way to independence. And Kaliningrad, her own Kaliningrad, became a free city because the communist system had corroded down to the last screw, not as a result of outside intervention.

These doubts aside, Darja was keenly aware that Arendt forced you to think and judge for yourself and, most importantly, to take responsibility. If, like Eichmann, you simply said who am I to judge or have my own thoughts, then you were already ruined. Yes, that summed it up exactly. Like the phrase 'the banality of evil'; Eichmann did what his country demanded of him, without stopping to think that its laws were wrong. He had carried out 'administrative massacres'. The same could be said of many Soviet officials. Kant had argued that human beings cannot be devils. Arendt claimed more or less the same thing: human beings are ordinary by nature. But in their blind zeal, a human being can act like a devil, with horrific consequences: 'the fearsome word-and-thought defying banality of evil', to quote the final sentence of *Eichmann in Jerusalem*. For Darja, the book was as much about faceless Soviet officials as it was about Eichmann. 'About people who are not even bad or stupid, but who do not want to think and simply do what is asked of them.'

Her own father could have become an Eichmann, she realised with a shock as she read Arendt's book. Fortunately, the Kremlin did not direct the Soviet fleet to Gdańsk in 1980 when the shipyard workers rebelled. Fortunately, the submarines and missile-armed frigates did not sail from the port of Kaliningrad in 1989 when Estonians, Latvians, and Lithuanians formed a human chain from Tallinn to Vilnius. Had Darja's father been ordered to press the yellow button, the signal to launch missiles with nuclear warheads, it would not have occurred to him to ignore the command. That was just his way; not an evil man, but an ordinary apparatchik. She was also pretty sure that he had made her mother promise never to speak a word about her Jewish origins. In his mind, it paid to be as vague as possible. In all things.

I met Darja Sviridova on the train from Kaunas to Kaliningrad. She sat down opposite me, without so much as a glance. Another Lithuanian for whom I don't exist, I sighed. The Baltic had made me homesick for the Dutch for the first time in my life, for their frank and friendly curiosity. Without question, it's their history that leads the people of the Baltic countries to keep a safe distance from foreigners, but after a while the effort of breaking through yet another wall of suspicion becomes wearing.

For the first few hours of the journey, she looked at her nails or her mobile phone. Then, for some unknown reason, the train ground to a halt. We were not far from Kaliningrad. In recent years, the Lithuanian government had made every effort to ensure that rail and road traffic to and from the Russian exclave ran as smoothly as possible. Day-long delays and impromptu border blockades had become a thing of the past. Self-interest ensured that the Russians cooperated: all land transport has to pass through Poland or Lithuania. Since the former Warsaw Pact countries gained their independence, the Russians of Kaliningrad have been living like rats in a trap.

The train showed no sign of moving. A technical defect, a signal malfunction, a go-slow by customs or border police — it was anyone's guess. The residue of communism that lingers in the Baltic countries means that official explanations are seldom forthcoming: as an ordinary citizen or passenger, these things are none of your business.

There wasn't much to see. A few houses in the distance, storks' nests perched above their roofs, so characteristic of East Prussian villages. The early spring sun, still low in the sky, was shining straight in. Behind the double glazing designed for bitterly cold winters, the temperature began to rise, and the windows could not be opened. Having learned from previous train journeys in Lithuania, I had packed a few cans of mineral water. I offered her one. Almost instantly, her face softened, and she began to talk. Another lesson learned: once an inhabitant of north-eastern Europe starts talking, there's often no stopping them.

It was a full five hours before the train began to move again. Was I the first to mention Hannah Arendt? Probably. By then, having read much of what had been written by and about her, I had grown to love the woman. 'One sensed an absolute determination to be herself,' her old college friend Hans Jonas said at her funeral. Isn't that what we all long for: to be ourselves? Could I claim to be myself? These are the questions Arendt teaches you to ask. 'I somehow enjoy the handling of facts and concrete things,' she wrote to writer Mary McCarthy.

That too is something I recognise. The same goes for her cult of friendship, the veneration of loyalty that she shared with Jaspers. I also loved her persistence in provoking debate and her unashamed displays of knowledge, which led German writer Hermann Broch to exclaim, 'No one should be allowed to know so much!' Most of all, I loved how she had lived: the smart Jewish girl who threw herself at life with Russian passion and Königsberg boldness.

I may well have said those very words to Darja: Russian passion, Königsberg boldness. I think that was when she first smiled at me, when a measure of understanding first began to develop between us.

It was dark when the train pulled into Kaliningrad station. The five hours had passed in a steady stream of words. I still had so much to ask Darja, about her city and the life she now led there as a teacher of English and history, the subjects in which she had finally chosen to graduate. We parted company but agreed to meet the next day at Med, a restaurant in the city centre where they served fifteen kinds of blini.

I ate blinis with salmon, with melted cheese, with halibut, with caviar. Darja did not appear.

I explored Kaliningrad alone and was pleasantly surprised. The mood was far less tense than I had been led to believe, the undercurrent of crime less evident. Everywhere, in the streets and parks, boys and men sat at tables playing chess, draughts, or cards. Young women and girls with spring on their minds sought out patches of grass where they could hitch up their skirts and tan their legs. There was a sense of expectation in the air.

Most of the Soviet Navy had been reduced to scrap metal. Since 2003, a colossal statue of Elizabeth of Russia has stood on the pier of the Baltiysk naval base, her searching gaze turned westward. At a kiosk behind the cathedral, I was able to buy the German-language *Königsberger Express* as easily as I could pick up a copy of *The Baltic Times* in Riga, Tallinn, or Vilnius.

The small island in the Pregel on which the cathedral stands was called Kneiphof in Prussian times. Thereafter it took a Russian name, and recently it was renamed once again: after Kant, appropriately enough. I was impressed by the scholar's mausoleum, the simplicity of its plain, rectangular pillars. Eschewing all manner of pomp, it did

Königsberg cathedral, restored with German money.

justice to Kant's clarity and consistency.

The cathedral was restored with German money. The Russians preferred to invest in the construction of the octagonal Cathedral of Christ the Saviour, completed in 2006 with space to accommodate 3,000 worshippers at its dedication. At seventy-three metres, the tallest of its four spherical towers reduces the old cathedral to the dimensions of a friendly village church. It's as if the Russians were keen to get one up on the Germans, a rivalry that looks set to define the future.

Some of the young people I chatted to over a beer said they hoped Kaliningrad would become the Hong Kong of the north, a city whose links to Russia are as self-evident as those of early-2000s Hong Kong and China, but with greater scope for independence. Others went further and saw a Singaporean haven for free trade emerging in a matter of years, a place where Germans could compete with Russians and Lithuanians, Latvians with Swedes and Finns.

I left with the impression that this was a city in waiting, impatient for a new purpose, a new future, and a new name. For there was one thing everyone I spoke to in Kaliningrad agreed on: the city should no longer bear the name of a schemer, a cunning backer of Stalin's rise to power. The name Kaliningrad had the ring of dictatorship, the clunk of a cell door locking. In those conversations, the door appeared to be opening, if only a chink.

10

The Baltic Baroness

ON OLD FAMILIES AND STUBBORN PREJUDICES

Lithuania, March 2009; Courland, February 2007
'She's sitting right there … go and talk to her!'

Is it the bronchitis that's holding me back? Five hours on an unheated train have reduced me to a spluttering, shivering wreck. I am no longer myself, and my main concern has become working out how much paracetamol I need to stay on my feet.

'Go over there. Introduce yourself. Strike up a conversation.'

Could it be her noble title that's getting to me? Am I afraid of being put in my place? Or worse, of being on the receiving end of a reactionary tirade laced with anti-Semitism?

I am staying at the Grotthuss Hotel, on a narrow street in the southern section of downtown Vilnius that, before the war, marked the boundary of the Jewish quarter. The hotel has twenty rooms and occupies a building that once housed Jewish orphans; it has since been restored from the ground up. The reason for my choice is purely economic: a 50 per cent discount in February and March for a stay of five nights or more.

The rooms are furnished with antiques. I write at a desk that may well have been around when the people of Vilnius took to the streets cheering and waving flowers to greet 200,000 Napoleonic soldiers as they descended from the hills. Napoleon, they hoped, would put an end to feudalism. I read in one of two armchairs in which an exhausted general might have slumped. Only 30,000 of Napoleon's vast army returned from Russia, the majority felled not far from Vilnius by starvation and the fierce winter cold — a mass grave containing the bodies of 20,000 Frenchmen was discovered only recently. Musing on their cruel fate, I can bite into a piece of fresh fruit — the bowl on the coffee table is replenished daily. Or I can sit out on the balcony in the steadily falling snow, gazing at the church tower built in the early fifteenth century under the watchful eye of the knights of the Teutonic Order. Mine is the only room with a balcony. But as fever takes hold, I resist the temptation.

Apart from the occasional vehicle racing through the narrow, cobbled street below, or a car alarm blaring in the dead of night, there are no sounds from outside. Inside, the quiet is almost unsettling. I am the only guest. The world is in the throes of a financial crisis, and Lithuania and Latvia have been hardest hit of all. In the first quarter of 2009, turnover and production shrank like wool in a hot wash. Shops, restaurants, and hotels stand empty. Western business travellers are nowhere to be seen.

After six days of solitude, two delegations descend on the hotel: one Russian, one German. The Russians are eager to take a stake in companies run by the cash-strapped Germans. Listening in on their negotiations, I am treated to a mismatch between Russian bluntness and German prevarication.

Until that seventh morning, I sip coffee in an empty breakfast room and gaze alone upon a buffet table brimming with eleven kinds of sausage, smoked mackerel, carp and herring in yoghurt sauce, salmon, and halibut. A breakfast fit for a king, with sour cream and blueberries for dessert.

Not quite alone, however: on Saturday and Sunday morning, the hotel owner takes a seat ten paces away, at the round table by the entrance. Across from her is an empty chair.

'Go on!' I urge myself. 'It's flu you're suffering from, not chronic shyness. Get over there and start talking.'

Baroness Edith von Grotthuss is dressed in black. A woman of around fifty — my best guess — in a black sweater buttoned to the neck, a black skirt, and black slippers topped with black pompoms. No jewellery: true nobility needs no adornment. I may be getting her name wrong. Shouldn't it be Edith Baroness von Grotthuss? I could go over and ask her. She sits distinguished and aloof, an impregnable fortress above marshy lowlands. Her back is straight, her hair is dark. Her dark eyes settle on nothing and no one in particular. Her curt nods to the blonde Lithuanian waitress are commands in themselves.

I know from the receptionist that the baroness has done a remarkable job. Edith von Grotthuss comes from a German family who traded Münster for Lithuania in the thirteenth century. Seven centuries later, the family was sent packing back to Germany, a fate that befell all Baltic Germans in 1939. In 1992, she decided to move to Lithuania herself. After years spent consulting contractors and pleading for a building permit, in 1999 she was able to embark on the restoration of the dilapidated property on Ligoninės gatvė. Judging by the photos in the foyer, it was a Herculean task.

The hotel is a success. Her guests, the majority of them German, appreciate being spoken to in their own language. Those Germans come to tour the Baltic countries in search of the houses and villages in which their ancestors lived like princes. In Edith von Grotthuss's hotel, they have come to the right address. A member of the Baltic nobility, the baroness speaks their language in more ways than one.

The *Baltenritter*, Germany's Baltic Knights, are hated to this day across the region. Until the abolition of serfdom, they maintained a glorified form of slavery, and until 1920, they owned 90 per cent of the land. Their mindset ranged from conservative to outright reactionary, more German than their compatriots who lived in Germany. This made them more courteous but also considerably more austere, class-conscious, and high-handed. Caught up in centuries-old conventions and as stingy as they were wealthy, they treated their horses with more kindness than they did the local population. Not infrequently, they were anti-Semitic. Or is this too much of a caricature?

Their history has its romantic side. They were directly descended from the Crusaders. In the thirteenth century, the Livonian Brothers of the Sword began their *Drang nach Osten*, or push eastwards. As if embarking on a new crusade, they threw themselves with indomitable fighting spirit into the conversion of the pagan Estonians, Livonians, Latvians, and Lithuanians. In full regalia, they charged on horseback across the eastern plains. It must have been quite something: the knights in their white cloaks and white tunics bearing the red sword-and-cross insignia, followed by the clergy in their white robes and blood-red sword and cross. Their servants formed the rearguard, clad in black or brown habits. The knights took Dorpat (present-day Tartu) in 1215 and Tallinn in 1227, renaming it Reval. They built fortresses and six fortified monasteries, including Riga. Initially they had the support of the Danish king, but after the capture of Tallinn (literally *Taani Linn*, Danish city), they came into conflict with Valdemar II, and the Pope sided with the Danes.

In 1236, the Brothers of the Sword suffered a heavy defeat at the Battle of Saule (Šiauliai in Lithuania) and in 1237 their order was subsumed into the Teutonic Order. The branch that was active in the territories on the Baltic coast became known as the Livonian Order. These Teutonic Knights took possession of the entire region.

Forward, ever forward, was their motto. In a race with the Swedes, who were advancing from the north, they pushed on into Russia. Alexander Nevsky, Prince of Novgorod and Kyiv, halted their advance during the famous Battle on the Ice in 1242. As described earlier in this book, this clash was famously filmed by Eisenstein, with music by Prokofiev. To this day, Alexander Nevsky's victory is considered the first heroic milestone in Russian history.

The Teutonic Knights retreated to the Baltic. There, they ruled for two more centuries, until their defeat at the Battle of Tannenberg (*Žalgiris* in Lithuanian) in 1410 — a traumatic blow to German pride that resonated through time. In 1914, when General Ludendorff halted the advancing Russian troops near the lakes of Masuria, south of Königsberg, he urged Kaiser Wilhelm to give the victory the name Tannenberg. After five centuries, the defeat of the Teutonic Knights had finally been avenged.

In the first (and only genuine) Battle of Tannenberg, half the Teutonic Knights lost their lives. The other half laid down their armour and settled in Livonia and Courland. A direct line runs from those knights to the German counts and barons who later lorded it over the Baltic region. From the fifteenth century, these nobles built castles, mansions, and manor houses at the edge of lakes, meadows, hills, and forests in the vast lands by the Baltic Sea. The von Grotthuss family acquired an estate in Gedučiai on the border between Lithuania and Courland, not far from Bauska.

In the seventeenth century, the history of Courland fell out of step with that of Livonia, which roughly comprised present-day Estonia and northern Latvia. The Duchy of Courland became a fief of the Polish monarch, while the northern territories came under Swedish rule. Courland enjoyed a high degree of autonomy. As long as the duke paid his fees to the Polish king on time, he was free to go about his business.

Under the leadership of Jacob Kettler (1610–1682), the region experienced its own golden age. As Duke of Courland, he oversaw significant advances in agriculture, industry, trade, and shipbuilding. Windau (Ventspils) and Libau (Liepāja) became the home ports of a fleet that sailed the world's oceans. Tiny Courland even acquired two colonies: the Caribbean island of Tobago and Fort Jacob in the Gambia.

Jacob Kettler — Jēkabs Ketlers in Latvian — led his country like an entrepreneur. From the age of two, he was raised in Königsberg. At thirteen, he was sent to Leipzig University, and between the ages of twenty-four and twenty-seven, he travelled Europe, spending extended periods in Amsterdam, Paris, Warsaw, and probably England. One country in particular inspired him: Holland. Returning to govern his duchy in 1642, he resolved to transform Courland into the Holland of the North and Windau into Amsterdam on the Baltic. He went on to achieve this at a miraculous pace.

One lesson Jacob had learned in Amsterdam was that a country with trading ambitions needs its own means of production. Following the Dutch example, he modernised agriculture by pumping dry the marshy fields: the yields doubled. He established forges, glassworks, production facilities for saltpetre and soap, paper mills, and textile mills. He shook up the landed gentry and encouraged them to process flax in mills, hops in breweries, and barley in distilleries, in addition to running their country estates.

Trade also requires a fleet. On a sandbank off Windau, Jacob had a shipyard built. To draw on the necessary experience, he brought Dutch maritime carpenters, rope makers, and sailmakers to Courland. He set up workshops in which cannon were cast and nails, chains, anchors, and ammunition were manufactured. To obtain the necessary iron, he purchased a mine in Norway.

Once again following Amsterdam's example, he had a hospital and an orphanage built. By paying good wages, he kept productivity among his craftsmen high. One hundred and fifty ships were launched from the yard, including sixty-one warships. England boasted three times as many, but for a country the size of Wales, this was a respectable number. Occasionally, Jacob Kettler would lend a few warships to a major power, for a fee of course.

In 1654, *Das Wappen der Herzogin von Kurland* set sail from the port of Windau, a two-decker with forty-five guns. On board were twenty-four officers, 124 soldiers, and eighty Courland settler families. On

the bridge stood Willem Mollens, a Dutch captain with experience
of Antillean waters. Mollens sailed the Duchess of Courland straight
to Tobago, took possession of the island, and christened it New
Courland. For twenty years it remained an important trading post,
until little Courland was intimidated into selling its colonies to the
English.

Jacob Kettler was not solely fixated on expanding his power and
his territories. Another lesson he had learned in Holland was that a
country could only earn from trade if it imported spices, the petro-
leum and natural gas of the seventeenth century. Kettler deliberately
selected small colonies, conveniently located trading posts that could
be controlled without a full-blown occupation force. In this too he
took his lead from the Dutch, whose primary source of spices was the
Moluccas.

With a population of one and a half million souls, Holland was
a Lilliputian among the world powers of the day. As such, it was a
country that Courland, with its population of 200,000, might emulate, a more realistic model than England or France. Kettler was in
many ways the equal of Dutch stadtholder Willem III and would go
on to inspire another smart and ambitious monarch: Peter the Great
of Russia. He too headed for Holland and established a fleet with the
help of Dutch shipbuilders.

Thanks to Kettler, Courland had prospered and soon found itself
under threat from every side. The Swedes, the Russians, and the Poles
all wanted in on the action. After countless conflicts, Courland was
absorbed into Russia in 1795. The Baltic barons barely missed a beat:
they were just as happy to strike a deal with the Russians as they
would have been to do business with the Poles or the Swedes.

The possessions of these fabulously wealthy noble families were
beyond imagination. The von Medems owned ten manors and 55,000
hectares of land, the von Wolff-Stomersees thirty manors and estates
totalling 290,000 hectares. In 1910, the estates of the Manteuffel
family were tended to by 4,000 farmers and at least three times as
many farm labourers.

The Baltic barons spoke the language of the ruler; at first this was
Polish, and later Russian. They seldom spoke the languages of those
who worked their land. For the vast majority of barons, Latvian,
Estonian, Lithuanian, and Livonian (a language spoken in northern

Courland) were as foreign as Chinese. In their own circles, they continued to speak German. They transacted their business with German
lawyers and notaries, were treated by German doctors, purchased
their medicine from German or at least German-speaking pharmacists, and ordered their carts, ploughs, and carriages from German
suppliers. They surrounded themselves with manservants called Klaus
or Lukas, with nurses and governesses who — bet your eyeteeth —
were named Christa. Their nannies, on the other hand, tended to
be French — a mischievous indulgence. They sent their children
to German primary and secondary schools, followed by a German
university in Königsberg, Riga, or Dorpat.

The barons' concerns were considerable and revolved around three
main issues: training their horses, profiting from their estates, and
marrying off their children. They married among themselves. Anyone
visiting the stately homes of Courland will come across the same
names again and again: von Schlippenbach, von Fircks-Okten, von
Lieven, von Grotthuss, von Pahlen, von Manteuffel, von Behr, von
Medem, von Simolin, von Hahn, von Fölkersahm. Just seventy-one
families bore the title of baron. The Baltic nobility was a closed shop,
and a German one at that.

The hegemony of the Baltic German barons lasted until 1905.
That was the year of Bloody Sunday, an uprising in St Petersburg
that spread like wildfire across Estonia and Latvia. Incensed peasants
stormed the homes of the nobility, strung up the occupants, and
smashed the furniture or set the place on fire. The revolt raged all
year, but it was the end of World War I before the barons' power collapsed completely. The finale was chaotic: throughout 1919, Latvian
nationalists battled Bolsheviks in the forests of Courland, aided by
members of the Freikorps. The latter were demobilised, ultra-reac-
tionary soldiers who dressed in long black cloaks and committed one
desperate act after another. The nationalists came out on top.

In 1918, Estonia, Latvia, and Lithuania all declared their independence. International recognition followed: for Estonia in 1920,
Latvia in 1921, and Lithuania in 1922. The first measure taken by
the newly formed national governments dealt a crushing blow to the
Baltic German landed gentry. The maximum landholding per person
was set at 110 hectares, with the vacated land to be nationalised and
distributed among local farmers. Some barons returned to Germany,

devastated to be leaving behind a Baltic family history that in some cases stretched back eighteen generations. In 1939, Hitler did the rest, ordering the remaining Baltic Germans to return to the fatherland: a move as painful as it was unexpected.

In February 2007, I took a short trip through Courland. It would have been longer, but a sudden thaw left many a road impassable. Latvia's roads are generally in a bad way. In Courland, they are missing a good fifty years of maintenance.

In other respects too it was like stepping back in time. Nothing had changed in Courland for half a century. I set out from Riga and, within a hundred kilometres, found myself in the years immediately after World War II. Let's say 1949, the year I was born. I saw country life not at all dissimilar to my early childhood impressions of the village in which I grew up. There were blacksmiths shoeing horses. Dank, low-ceilinged shops with wood crackling in a pot-bellied stove took me back to Groenenboom's sweet shop on the old dyke. The castles were as sprawling and neglected as Rhoon Castle in the 1950s.

The only asphalt was to be found on the trunk roads and access roads to the towns. To negotiate the rest — little more than dirt roads turned to mud by the thaw — you needed caterpillar tracks.

When Latvia became part of the Soviet Union, the Russians cut off strategically located Courland from the rest of the world. To the west, it borders the Baltic Sea, to the east the Gulf of Riga. In the event of an attack, Courland's flat terrain would have made an ideal launch pad for invasion. Stalin was paranoid enough to fear exactly that, a fear amplified by Cold War deadlock. Courland was turned into a military zone, shielded by naval bases at Ventspils, Liepāja, and Kaliningrad further south. Latvian farmers and fishermen could continue to live on the land, but no newcomers were allowed to settle. For half a century, a permit was required to even set foot there. Visitors were discouraged. Courland's forests went untouched, its lakes the domain of ducks and migrating birds, its beaches left to the gulls. Along its 250-kilometre stretch of coastline, there was not a shack or a cabin to be found; the sands of Courland remained primordially white.

Rather than demolish the region's castles and mansions, the Soviets gave them a public purpose. The largest became sanatoria, the rest were given over to schools, libraries, and village or town halls. As the years passed, they fell into disrepair, though their civic functions saved them from complete ruin. Leaking roofs were plugged, broken windows replaced. The stoves burned through the winter and kept the damp at bay.

After the Soviets left, the buildings of greatest architectural value could be restored to their former state relatively quickly, the only trouble being that there were an awful lot of them. Dozens of castles and manors still await restoration and continue to operate as schools or libraries.

My curiosity about Courland was sparked by a film. Back when I knew nothing of the Baltic countries and had only the vaguest of notions about this corner of northern Europe, I saw Volker Schlöndorff's film *Coup de Grâce (Der Fangschuß)*. Its ghostly atmosphere stayed with me, like mist descending on forests and snow-covered fields and, finally, on the face of the lead actress, Margarethe von Trotta.

In the 1970s, Schlöndorff and von Trotta — a married couple — filmed one literary masterpiece after another. Made on a shoestring budget, these black-and-white gems derived their power from mood and compelling storylines. Von Trotta's talent was evident both on screen and off; in addition to acting, she co-wrote the screenplays with their strong echoes of Ingmar Bergman. Her reverence for the Swedish writer/director was palpable in almost every scene.

For four films, the magic remained intact. *Young Törless* was based on Robert Musil's short novel, *Man on Horseback* on a novel by Heinrich von Kleist. *Coup de Grâce* was adapted from Marguerite Yourcenar's novella, and *The Lost Honour of Katharina Blum* from the novel by Heinrich Böll. After *Katharina Blum*, Schlöndorff and von Trotta went their separate ways. Schlöndorff went on to direct *The Tin Drum* and von Trotta made *Rosa Luxemburg*. Both achieved commercial success, but the films lacked the oblique intensity of their earlier work.

It was *Coup de Grâce* that made the deepest impression on me. Schlöndorff dedicated it to Jean-Pierre Melville, the French master of film noir, and it is every bit as dark as *L'Armée des ombres* (Army of Shadows), Melville's masterpiece about the Resistance. Schlöndorff and von Trotta had little choice but to keep their audiences in the dark. The novella by Brussels-born Marguerite Yourcenar gave the screenwriters only the sketchiest of frameworks. Yourcenar had never experienced the sights and smells of Courland; her story and its trio of protagonists were based on a description given to her by 'one of the best friends of the principal person concerned', as she wrote in the preface to the 1971 edition. She kept the plot and the setting deliberately vague. 'It was not my intention,' she wrote, 'to recreate a particular social group or period.' Proudly, she adds that, in the interest of plausibility, she studied ordnance maps and old illustrated magazines, and that men who had fought in the Baltic during the war made a point of letting her know that *Coup de Grâce* corresponded to their own memories of that time and place. In her memoir *Quoi? L'Éternité*, published seventeen years later, she gave a different version of events, insisting that a friend of her mother's by the name of Egon de Reval had been her inspiration for Erich von Lhomond, one of three protagonists. A fairly obvious attempt at mystification, Reval being the German name for Tallinn.

Yourcenar could have saved herself the trouble. A literary work, she herself once wrote, always has 'a long, partly underground, pre-history', and the facts were bound to surface when her biography was written. Since 1990 and the publication of Josyane Savigneau's *Marguerite Yourcenar: l'invention d'une vie* (Marguerite Yourcenar: inventing a life), we know that Yourcenar worshipped the man who inspired the character Erich von Lhomond as if he were her father.

First, the story: the year is 1919 and in the forests of Courland, troops of the defeated Imperial German Army are engaged in a desperate battle with the Bolsheviks. The Prussian soldiers neither want to surrender, nor to return to their homeland. Baltic countess Sophie falls in love with Prussian soldier Erich von Lhomond (Eric in Yourcenar's book), who secretly lusts after Sophie's brother Conrad. When Sophie fails to seduce Erich, she gives herself to any man who will have her and finally takes revenge by siding with the Bolsheviks. Sophie is taken prisoner and asks Erich to put her out of her misery, the coup de grâce of the title. She does this wordlessly, with nothing but a look. On a railway platform, Erich shoots her dead and then retreats with his fellow soldiers by train.

The man on whom Erich is based was Conrad von Vietinghoff, a Baltic baron. The real-life tale begins with two best friends in

Brussels, Fernande and Jeanne, on the cusp of worldliness. Both are exceptionally beautiful and exceptionally intelligent, and both have a noble pedigree: Fernande comes from the Walloon family Cartier de Marchienne and Jeanne from the Dutch family Storm de Grave. They are out to bag themselves a husband with a title, and before long, it's mission accomplished: Fernande weds Michel Cleenewerck de Crayencour, a nobleman from the Flemish north of France, and Jeanne marries Conrad von Vietinghoff, a direct descendant of the Teutonic Knights. Fernande and Jeanne fall pregnant at almost the same time, and they vow to take care of each other's children if one of them should not survive the birth. Fernande gives birth to Marguerite, Jeanne to Egon. But fate takes a cruel turn: Fernande dies. Jeanne keeps her word and looks after Marguerite until the day she dies. Marguerite de Crayencour grows up to write as Marguerite Yourcenar.

Conrad von Vietinghoff had spent his early childhood in Courland and his youth in Tallinn. Tomes on Baltic nobility reveal that the Vietinghoffs owned country houses all over Estonia, some for longer than others: in Audla, Kaali, and Sandla on the island of Saaremaa; in Sänna and Viitina (named after Vietinghoff); in Kehtna, Kabala, and Adavere. Conrad was ill-suited to life under the tsarist regime and moved to Dresden, where he studied at the conservatory. It was in Dresden that he met Jeanne. They married in The Hague and settled in the Vietinghoffs' family home in Courland, where they lived for two years. For Conrad, it was the prelude to a career as a concert pianist. The couple moved to St Petersburg and then to Germany, followed by Brussels and Lausanne. Vietinghoff performed throughout Europe, and Jeanne began writing: novels and psychological treatises. The five books she published would not only impress Marguerite but also influence her decision to become a writer.

Jeanne and Conrad had two sons, Egon and Alexis. Even so, their love was more platonic than erotic. Conrad had little desire to mix with counts and barons, and just as little time for the Romanovs and the aristocratic clique at the tsarist court. Nor was he enamoured of the Estonian and Latvian nationalists, and yes, when he laid eyes on a young, impeccably well-mannered Prussian officer with a proud bearing, blue eyes, dark-blond hair, and a shy blush on his cheeks, he realised that even his marriage was a painful mistake. He had a

The final scene of *Coup de Grâce*: Sophie (played by
Margarethe von Trotta) at the station.

fondness for men who feigned a strength they did not possess and
who carried their family's tragic decline with them like an invisible
but crushing burden.

Yourcenar first portrayed Conrad in *Alexis ou le traité du vain combat*
(Alexis or The Treatise of Vain Struggle). In this novella in the form
of a letter, a renowned musician confesses his homosexuality to his
wife. Conrad then reappears in the figure of Erich von Lhomond in
Coup de Grâce. Sophie is given the looks of Jeanne von Vietinghoff:
tall, lean, distinguished, once stunningly beautiful, yet from one year
to the next tired, downcast, and sickly, a body that seemed to express
the spirit of the age. Jeanne died young.

Growing up with the Vietinghoffs, Yourcenar must have heard
all about the noble families of Courland and Livonia. Not that
she was in a position to probe the family's secrets. Jeanne did look
after Marguerite, but from a distance. She saw her during holidays,
then disappeared for months on end. During World War I, she
lived in Lausanne, remote and unreachable, and died shortly before
Marguerite's nineteenth birthday.

More than anything, Conrad and Jeanne came to occupy an

important place in Marguerite's imagination. She dreamed their lives and brought those dreams to life in *Coup de Grâce*. Twenty-five years after the book was published, she wrote to a young student that the novella was much more about loneliness than frustrated sexual desires:

> one can surely speak of solitude, but of a very particular type of solitude, due in large part to the vagaries of history, by which I mean the collapse of a caste and a world. Erich remains almost belligerently faithful to codes of discipline rendered useless by a transformed human milieu, and this is his tragedy ... What is hard about him, and almost irremediable, is a function of his desperate qualities.

This sets the tone for the book. The atmosphere of a manor half-destroyed by war, of broken windows, doors that no longer close and which clatter when the wind picks up; the atmosphere of a park grown wild, of fog and drifting snow, of decay and decadence, blood-lust, eroticism, and half-concealed homosexuality. Resignation to the downfall of the aristocracy can be read on the younger brother's face, making him as defenceless as he is attractive. A crazed old aunt walks the floors, babbling in French. The end of an era is fast approaching, but even as she plays at being a woman of easy virtue, Sophie's every gesture marks her out as the descendant of an ancient, noble family.

Margarethe von Trotta's identification with the character of Sophie is total. Like Yourcenar, she had a deeper connection to the story: her own mother came from a Russian aristocratic family. On the railway platform, Sophie is a spent woman, stripped of all her illusions. The final scene encapsulates her downfall: a small, deserted station in a lost country. Travelling through Estonia, Latvia, and Lithuania, I would come across many such stations — and every time, I saw Margarethe von Trotta as Sophie.

The castles and manors of Courland breathe the same atmosphere of rise and fall, grandeur and decay, ingenuity and insanity. In Jelgava, Alsunga, and Nogale, I half-expected an elderly aunt to appear and start berating me in French. Instead, I stumbled upon another lost soul.

A little church brought me to a standstill in the small town of

Schloss Tels-Paddern near Aizpute, the birthplace of Count Eduard von Keyserling.

Aizpute. Suddenly there it was, right in front of me, lonely on a hill, its walls turned white by the salt air of the Baltic. A modest tower rose above the tapering facade. Simple, clear, beautiful.

A young man came and stood next to me. He wanted something — a lift, it turned out later — but couldn't bring himself to ask straightaway. There's a shyness to the people in these parts. To soften me up, he advised me to visit Schloss Tels-Paddern, a manor just south of the town. I might not notice it immediately, he said. These days it was a school, the Kalvene school. Assuming I was German, he said I was sure to know the man who had been born there.

'A German. A writer. Von Keyserling.'

My guidebook made no mention of him. The section on famous writers only listed authors who wrote in Latvian. Such is the Latvians' hatred of the Baltic German nobility that even their notable descendants have been erased from the country's history.

Keyserling. His name rang the vaguest of bells. Back in the Netherlands, I would end up reading every novel of his that I could lay my hands on. Only then did it dawn on me that on impulse I had once bought a slim volume published by Actes Sud, intrigued by the dreamlike cover. It turned out to be the French translation of a Keyserling novella.

Count Eduard von Keyserling was born in 1855 at Schloss Tels-Paddern, near Hasenpoth, present-day Aizpute. Ravaged by a long illness and having lost his sight completely, he died in Munich in 1918.

Having spent his early childhood at the palatial family seat, he attended the German high school in Goldingen, present-day Kuldīga. To continue his education, he moved hundreds of kilometres north to the University of Dorpat, now Tartu, in Estonia, where he studied law from 1875 to 1877. This was a family tradition. 'A calm, sensible starting point that opens the paths both to other areas of study and the practical side of life,' he wrote in one of his novels. But for Eduard, it didn't work out that way. A scandal forced him to pack his bags and avoid disgrace by heading thousands of kilometres south, to Vienna.

The nature of Eduard's offence remained unknown. According to his cousin Baron Otto von Taube, it was no more than a trifle, an indiscretion out of keeping with his background and his noble title. Did Count von Keyserling fail to greet a professor? Default on a gambling debt? Make a rash declaration of love to a peasant girl, maid, or married baroness?

In the autumn of 2009, I made enquiries, but the University of Tartu was unable to enlighten me. No record was kept of the incident, for the simple reason that Eduard von Keyserling had not been formally expelled. He may have left under a cloud, but he abandoned his studies of his own free will. We will never know why.

What we do know is that, in the glory days of the Baltic aristocracy, the slightest misstep could cost a count or baron his reputation, not for a month or a year, but for the rest of his life. Count von Keyserling's membership of the Curonia student fraternity was revoked, he was shunned by aunts, uncles, most of his cousins, and almost everyone who was anyone in Courland high society. His marriage prospects had been reduced to zero. At the age of twenty-two, he was persona non grata in Baltic noble circles.

For Keyserling, a young man already racked by insecurity, being the subject of gossip was unbearable. He withdrew from public life, resolved never to fall in love and never to marry. His desire for women and sex increased in inverse proportion, and he began to frequent brothels. There was the occasional affair with a prostitute that lasted longer than a week or a month, but if his letters are to be believed, he never had sex beyond the confines of a brothel or a hotel room. He steered clear of balls, salons, and the company of noble ladies, and not just because of the university scandal: Keyserling saw himself as hideously ugly and was convinced that no self-respecting woman would ever want to be seen with him.

The portrait that artist Lovis Corinth painted of him in Munich shows a scarecrow's face and a distinct lack of physical charm. Yet, according to contemporaries, he judged himself far too harshly. He was an intensely kind, exceptionally intelligent, and often gregarious man whose affability and impeccable manners made him every inch the aristocrat. In *The World of Yesterday*, Stefan Zweig praises him as a conversationalist to rival Paul Valéry and Hugo von Hofmannsthal. It was a pleasure to engage him in discussion.

Beauty became an obsession for Keyserling. In his novel *Bunte Herzen* (Gay Hearts), he has old Count Hamilkar von Wandl-Dux say to his friend Professor von Pinitz:

> But poor youth. Do you think 'being beautiful' is easy? Beauty complicates destiny, imposes responsibilities, and above all it disturbs our seclusion. Imagine, Professor, that you were very beautiful. With every human being you encounter, your face establishes some relation, affects him, forces itself upon him, speaks to him, whether you will or no. Beauty is a constant indiscretion. Would that be agreeable?

Keyserling had gone to study law primarily to appease his father, and the news of the old man's death came as something of a relief: it gave the young count the freedom to take his life in a whole new direction. In Vienna and Graz, he studied philosophy and art history. Vienna granted him his long-desired freedom. Almost every evening was spent at the theatre, almost every night at a brothel. On completing his studies, he returned to Courland to manage his mother's estates, taking on the role of executor following her death in 1894. In early 1895, he settled in Munich with three of his sisters. Having personally inherited most of the family's lands, it never occurred to him

The portrait of Count Eduard von Keyserling, painted by Lovis Corinth
in 1900.

to worry about his finances. Yet he would die practically destitute.
Like all Courlanders, he held Russian citizenship, and the outbreak of
World War I deprived him of the revenues from his Baltic property:
Germany and Russia were at war, and the transfer of funds between
the two countries was halted. And after the October Revolution of

1917, the count's chances of ever seeing another penny were gone for good.

By the time Keyserling moved to Munich, his first novels had already been published. With *Fräulein Rosa Herz: Eine Kleinstadtliebe* (literally *Miss Rosa Herz: a small-town love*, 1887) and *Die dritte Stiege* (1892, translated as *Number 2, Margaretenstrasse*), he had stolen the hearts of thousands of readers. Keyserling was a subtle, elegant stylist, whose keen sense of mood and emotional undercurrents had a formative influence on the nineteenth-century German *Schloßroman*, novels characterised by their aristocratic setting and romantic intrigue. Initially, he had hoped to make a name for himself as a dramatist, but his breakthrough came as a novelist with *Beate und Mareile*, published in 1903 and later translated as *The Curse of the Tarniffs*. From then on, he turned to writing prose, doubtless spurred on by the fact that literary success had more or less restored his reputation with his family in Courland. Nothing heals old wounds faster than fame, however brief Keyserling's brush with it would end up being.

The titles of his novels instantly evoke a particular mood: *Sultry Days, Experiences of Love, Waves, Houses at Evening, On Southern Slopes, In a Quiet Corner, Princesses* (his best-known), and the posthumously published *Holiday Children*. But Keyserling had a knack for narrative twists that lent his titles a certain ambiguity.

In *Sultry Days* (German: *Schwüle Tage*), eighteen-year-old baron Bill has been sent to a remote country house by his father as a punishment. He has failed his final exams, and his father wants to make sure he devotes the summer months to his studies. The eager boy shares this familial outpost with his two female cousins and a peasant girl who calls him 'our young master' and indulges his every desire. He cannot choose between them. The sultriness of the title is found in the maid's heavy breasts, in his younger cousin's Lolita braids, and the skin-tight riding breaches of her elder sister. Then Bill discovers that for years his father has been having an affair with the elder cousin. That summer, his father dies of a morphine overdose, but not before he has forced his young lover to marry a wealthy cousin. In the space of a single summer, the young baron is introduced to the passions and the poison of his class. Bill's cousin Ellita may be an irresistible horsewoman, but she must have been fourteen at most, perhaps not even thirteen, when his father seduced her.

In terms of style, Keyserling can be compared to Turgenev, in psychology to Chekhov, in irony and atmosphere to Theodor Fontane. What he shares with all three is a willingness to describe rather than judge. Yet he has always remained in the shadow of the literary greats. Despite these qualities, his work has been forgotten, rediscovered, and forgotten again. Most of the interest arose in France and in East Germany, after the fall of the Wall, when younger generations wanted a taste of the decadence so despised by the communists.

Keyserling's novels bear more than a passing resemblance to one another. Life proceeds at a sedate pace within the walls of a Courland castle, a whitewashed Courland manor, or a seaside retreat. A chasm gapes between the interior and the outside world. 'You are the Baroness von Buttlär, are you not,' says one of the protagonists in *Waves*, 'and I am the widow of General Palikov, and that means we are both fortresses, admitting no one who is not of our rank.' But inevitably there will be an intruder: an artist, a countess living in sin, or an unannounced guest who falls in love with one of the daughters of the house. A cat among the pigeons. The big bad world will not be shut out, or as one of Keyserling's intruders puts it: 'You were talking dismissively before about potato soup. I have to say that no life, even the most perfect, is possible in which, for a few hours a day, it doesn't smell of potato soup.'

Love breaches conventions. Love creeps like a flame into the thick velour curtains that shield the nobility from prying eyes. It exposes the narrow-minded constraints of the aristocratic world. To use Keyserling's words: *eine kleine Spielzeugwelt*, a little toy world. Ever since the scandal at Dorpat, the count detested the circles in which he had been raised.

He was a true Baltic soul: an outcast in his own world; an uprooted figure who longed to be anything but; a mild, mocking observer desperate to disguise how rejected he felt; and at the same time someone who harboured an insane love for the setting in which he had been raised. German literary scholars like to call Keyserling 'the Baltic Fontane' or 'Fontane in minor', but in fact — the slimness of his novels notwithstanding — he is the Baltic Proust. He describes fir trees, snow-white beaches, and lakes aglow in the evening sun as if they were cherished first loves, and country estates as if they were a model for his mother.

Keyserling's novels end in drama, usually a suicide. After the 1905 uprising and the outbreak of world war in 1914, the count knew his world was lost for ever. He had no pity for the aristocracy, but nor could he gloat over the harm that befell them. In his final novels, he constantly appears to be holding back. No, he does not want to grieve, but in his youth, aristocracy stood for good taste, social graces, civilised expression, sophisticated sarcasm, and erudite discussions on art, philosophy, and politics. No evening was complete without music, and though he never names a composer, you know that the young baritone sang Schubert and the eldest daughter conjured all of nature from the piano with Tchaikovsky's *Song of the Lark*. The girls were so pretty in their white gowns with a red rose at the waist, the young men were so distinguished. Unobtrusively, perhaps even unconsciously, Count von Keyserling asks for a measure of understanding, like a pro bono lawyer aware that later generations will look harshly on these centuries of rule by the landed gentry and wishing to present a few mitigating circumstances. They were so elegant, he seems to want to say. So improbably beautiful. So thoroughly sensual. But blinkered by their upbringing, they did not know what they were doing.

In *On Southern Slopes* (German: *Am Südhang*), he draws a comparison between the Baltic barons and baronesses and an old Russian aristocrat:

> I once knew an old duke in Petersburg. He possessed an estate in
> the south of Russia and spent several weeks there each summer. A
> story says that one day he goes for a walk and sees a windmill that's
> not moving. He calls a farmer over and asks: 'Why isn't the windmill
> turning?' 'Because there's no wind, your Excellency,' says the farmer.
> At that, the duke booms: 'Tell the estate manager that where I have
> windmills I expect them to be turning!' 'Very good,' says the farmer …

They saw no need to busy themselves with the farming life on their estates. The pastimes of the barons and baronesses were primarily amorous.

It should come as no surprise that this introverted bachelor possessed an unerring ability to describe love with great precision from a female perspective. Eduard von Keyserling was the tenth child in a family of twelve; he had eleven sisters. With three of them, Henriette, Elise, and Hedwig, he moved to Munich. In 1899 and 1900, he took an extended trip through Italy with Henriette and Elise. During the final years of his life, he was bedridden and had to dictate his novels to his sisters. Following the deaths of Henriette in 1908 and Elise in 1915, the third sister, Hedwig, took over the role of stenographer and nurse. Keyserling discussed the inner lives of his characters with all three.

In 1897, on one of his many visits to a brothel, Keyserling had contracted syphilis. One symptom of the disease was a steady decline in his eyesight, and by 1908, he could see next to nothing. In his blindness, he dictated ever more elaborate descriptions of the shade, the light, and the colours of Courland's landscapes. Eleven of Keyserling's thirteen novels are set on summer evenings, when Courland's skies never turn dark and daylight is spun endlessly into a warm, soft glow. 'To this unending light,' Keyserling wrote, 'you would like to say "leave me in peace".' But it forces itself upon you, intensely, improbably red.

If you have a fondness for this kind of atmosphere, Keyserling is your man. Reading his work allowed me to effortlessly extend my travels through the Baltic countries. All I had to do was flip open *Schwüle Tage* to revisit that northern light and the emotions it kindles.

Not much remains of Schloss Tels-Paddern manor these days; it is home to an agricultural school. As for the young man who drew my attention to Keyserling, I gave him a lift to the port of Liepāja. The weather was too bad to drive back to Riga, so I stayed that night there.

The next morning, I drove east. In Aizpute, the architecture alternated between wood and brick. The wooden houses were lopsided and unpainted, meltwater dripping from their sheet-iron roofs. The telephone poles brought back memories of a sound. As boys, we used to throw stones at the porcelain insulators. When we hit one full square — quite an achievement — we were rewarded with a dry bang.

Eight kilometres down the road, I hit the brakes. Kazdanga Manor was too beautiful a sight to pass up. Even under grey skies, the roof seemed to give off a bluish light. I parked the car and, slipping and sliding, made my way up to the building. Slowly, the facade of

Kazdanga Manor, once home to the von Manteuffel family. Destroyed
during the 1905 peasant uprising, it was rebuilt between 1928 and 1932.

the robust three-storey building emerged in all its glory. I counted
fifty-five windows. The six Ionic columns bearing the portico could
have signified the entrance to a temple.

Kazdanga Manor too had been repurposed as a technical-agrarian
college, was in much better condition than the von Keyserling
family seat. Until 1919, it had borne the name Schloss Katzdangen,
and it was owned by the von Manteuffel family until 1939. For fourteen generations, they lived on this land. Construction of the manor
began in 1800 and was completed in 1804. I took a look at the hall,
the staircase. Then Ilmārs Berg took me for a walk.

Ilmārs was well on his way to graduating as a landscape architect.
His ambition was to go to North America, Canada to be precise,
where many Latvians have made a new life for themselves. Among
them was a cousin of Ilmārs's, who had agreed to put him up for the
first few months. He hoped to find a job with a landscaping firm
there, but before emigrating, he wanted to make a study of every
park in Courland, to unpack the wealth of hydrological and botanical
knowledge they represent.

Kazdanga Manor, he explained, was the largest park estate in Latvia, and with 113 non-native species of plants and trees growing in its 173 hectares, it was also the most interesting. The park had existed long before the manor and had its beginnings in the early eighteenth century. Turning up in the dead of winter, I was hardly seeing the place at its best, but for Ilmārs it was a much more instructive season than summer. The lack of foliage and flowers meant he was better able to focus on planting patterns and the structure of the earthworks and waterworks. A park's success, he informed me, hinged on the effective drainage of groundwater.

Ambling along the muddy lanes, he filled me in on the von Manteuffel family, 'the mad barons of Katzdangen' as they were known locally. Whether they were actually bonkers, Ilmārs could not say. 'No doubt they behaved decadently at times. These were circles where a brother could easily fall for his sister-in-law, and a lady of standing lust after her sister's husband. That said, the last baron to live here, Karl Gustav von Manteuffel, looked more like a Lutheran preacher, albeit one with dodgy ideas. He spouted Nazi racial theories and dismissed Latvians as *deutsches Mischblut*. You can read all about it in his memoirs, published in Leipzig in 1942, which tells you all you need to know! But mad? You hear all kinds of nonsense about the von Manteuffels. Some say they're not a noble family at all but descend from a servant who used to walk the dog of the German bishop in Riga.'

Ilmārs laughed long and loud. He clearly appreciated the Baltic nobility for their entertainment value. He himself was 'descended from just about every nationality that ever settled in these parts'. On his father's side, his ancestors were German, Latvian, and Polish, on his mother's side Latvian, Swedish, Belarussian, and Ukrainian Russian. His German ancestors could well have included both Prussians and Jews. 'That's an avenue I've yet to explore. To be honest, this stuff gets me down. What does it matter? All these Latvians making such a big deal of being Latvian nowadays — how Latvian are they when it comes right down to it?'

The Baltic counts and barons exercised the same rights as the Russian ruling classes. 'Until the abolition of serfdom, anyone working on their estates was fair game. If they spotted a comely farm girl, they could take her for a roll in the hay no questions asked, a mindset that continued until the 1905 peasant uprising. The barons came to their country houses in summer, with their sons, daughters, cousins, aunts, and uncles in tow. By the time harvesting began, in the third or fourth week of August, the noble ladies and gents had returned to the city. They spent the endless summer evenings here, when no one could sleep and everyone got a little horny. There's a saying that all Courland Latvians are bastards of the Baltic nobility. Another exaggeration, but the hatred shown to the Baltic Germans was partly the hatred of bastards towards the lords who sired them.'

Listening to Ilmārs, I get a sense of the region's complexities. 'If a Latvian farmer had a problem with a neighbour or the Russian authorities, he turned to his landowner. The baron, in other words. On Karl von Manteuffel's land, there was a long queue in the yard every morning. After breakfast, he would go outside and hear the complaints one by one. More often than not, he promised to address the problem. And he usually kept his promise.'

The Latvians also owed a lot to the German speakers in another respect. 'In the first half of the nineteenth century, the Russians paid scant attention to their Baltic territories. From 1860, things changed, and the Russification of Estonia and Latvia began. This provoked a backlash. The intellectuals — professors, teachers, educators, lawyers, journalists, writers, and, not to forget, the clergy — were exponents of the German language and German culture. In the spirit of German Romanticism and poet and philosopher Johann Gottfried Herder, they also became increasingly interested in the traditions of the region, in folk stories and folk songs, the dainas handed down through generations of Latvian oral tradition. In an effort to capture the language, German pastors began translating the Bible into Latvian and compiling German–Latvian dictionaries. Without their efforts, Latvian as a language would have died out, and precious little Latvian culture would have survived. German-speaking clergymen, teachers, educators, and journalists played a significant part in preserving Latvia's cultural identity.'

And the von Manteuffels? 'As far back as the early nineteenth century, they set up schools for Courland peasant children, to the indignation of most other barons, who preferred to keep the riffraff down. That's why, when all hell broke loose, the von Manteuffels were astounded that the Latvian peasants and servants made no distinction between them and the other barons. During the great uprising of

1905, Katzdangen Manor was looted and torched like most of the other grand country houses. But — and this was typical of the von Manteuffels — rather than resign themselves, they engaged the services of a prominent architect, a connoisseur of Palladian classicism, and got him to rebuild the place in the original style. Much of that work took place in the late 1920s and early 1930s, when newly independent Latvia had long since nationalised the von Manteuffel estates and carved them up among local farmers. Yet despite having had lost their land and most of their income, the family restored their seat to its former glory.'

Ilmārs looked me deep in the eye and smiled emphatically as he continued, 'In other ways too, they refused to resign themselves to the end of their rule. Between 1906 and 1910, they brought German farmers to Katzdangen from Russia. These were Germans who had been lured to Russia in the nineteenth century as part of a campaign to scale up and modernise Russian agriculture and who were then driven out by the 1905 revolt. Karl Gustav von Manteuffel offered 4,000 German farmers work at Katzdangen, which of course made him doubly hated by Latvian farmers and labourers. And the German settlers weren't exactly brimming with gratitude either. On arrival, they refused to work in the rain, a bit of an issue considering it rains here all autumn and two out of every three days in spring and summer. No wonder von Manteuffel began to lose faith in humanity.'

Walking as we talked, we had come to the low-lying section of the park, on the banks of a small river. I was shivering like a lapdog, but Ilmārs, a giant of two metres ten, seemed oblivious to the cold. With expansive gestures, he pointed out the different types of pine trees and the magnificent sweep as they increased in height the further they got from the river. 'I have no time for those barons,' he bellowed at me in English. 'I compare them to the white tobacco planters in Virginia: the Latvians were their slaves. And yet ... Karl von Manteuffel's memoirs include a description of Countess von Medem, a widow approaching the end of her life. After World War I and the Latvian government's nationalisation drive, Karl gave the destitute baroness a roof over her head at Katzdangen Manor. Day after day, in her widow's weeds, she sat at a table in the library poring over botanical works and descriptions of early nineteenth-century herbariums. She wanted to preserve Katzdangen Park, to save it from destruction. And to do that, she needed to know everything about trees and plants. A woman well into her eighties. There's something moving about that, don't you agree?'

The Baltic barons certainly spoke to the imagination. Tall men who dwelled in desolate places, striding through the snow in riding boots, hat, and long black coat with fur-trimmed collar. In summer, they mounted their horses and cantered for hours through the forests or along the Baltic shoreline. Every account of Courland describes it as a remote outpost, a forgotten area. The nearest city was Riga, where the barons invested in a townhouse so as not to miss a play or an opera at the German Theatre. But to truly escape their isolation, they had to travel to St Petersburg, Warsaw, Leipzig, or Berlin. They were welcome guests at court. 'Loved by the nobles, hated by the peasants,' as they still say in Latvia.

Because the Baltic nobles had no claim to a throne but possessed vast estates and handsome fortunes, they made bankable spouses for members of Russian and European royal houses, principalities, and grand duchies. When the von Grotthuss family allied itself to the von Rosen family, it gained in influence. Firstborn sons succeeded their fathers as trustees of the family properties. In Eduard von Keyserling's novels, these are almost always men who are financially exploited by every other family member and abandoned by their baroness wives for being so unspeakably dull. The younger sons ended up as loafers, addicted to card games, or as diplomats in the service of the tsar or the German emperor — in the latter case, they had to be naturalised. The more serious-minded among them threw themselves into scholarly pursuits.

One of Keyserling's cousins, whose father owned vast tracts of land east of Pärnu in Estonia, distinguished himself as a philosopher and sought to provide an academic foundation for pacifism. Hermann von Keyserling studied at the University of Dorpat. He travelled the world and corresponded with his writerly cousin on philosophical issues and the politics of peace. German militarism, he insisted, was finished; the torch of the Teutonic Knights had been extinguished once and for all by the shameful defeat of 1918. He died in 1946, living just long enough to see how misguided his assessment had been.

The royal houses of Europe would never forget that the Baltic nobles had taken care of Louis XVIII. The von Königsfeld family offered the last of the Bourbons a home at Blankenfelde Manor, right below Jelgava, on the border with Lithuania. It was there that Louis, brother to the beheaded Louis XVI, endured the most miserable months of his existence.

I pay Blankenfelde a visit. Nothing but the occasional crow for miles around. For a prince born in Versailles, who had spent his childhood in mirrored halls, the desolate chill of this stately pile must have been almost as crushing as the impotence from which he suffered. After fleeing France in 1791, he had been expelled from one country after another. Fearing French reprisals, no king or prince dared offer him protection. Even in far-off Blankenfelde, he was not safe; the King of Prussia demanded his departure. A vagabond existence in Poland and Sweden followed, before finally he was able to take up residence in Mitau Palace: back to Courland, back to the cold. He stayed there until 1807.

Mitau, now called Jelgava Palace, and nearby Rundāle were both designed by prominent Italian architect Bartolomeo Rastrelli. At first glance, Rundāle appears to be a hallucination: in a small village, you suddenly find yourself face to face with a copy of the Winter Palace in St Petersburg. This echo of the Hermitage is by no means accidental: both are the work of Rastrelli, who later became court architect to Elizabeth of Russia. Rundāle was his practice run for the tsar's winter residence in St Petersburg. He designed the 138-room palace in 1736 for Ernst Johann von Biron, a confidant of Anna of Russia.

The Russians viewed the German Baltic nobles as incorrigible schemers, a reputation that stuck thanks to Biron. With the assistance of two Baltic sidekicks, he held the entire tsarist administration in an iron grip. Biron presented himself as a Baltic baron, but his family probably came from Westphalia. He initially called himself von Bühren, then von Biren, before finally adopting the name and coat of arms of the French earldom Biron. He was a rank opportunist who believed honesty was for the feeble-minded.

After studying in Königsberg, Biron became secretary and chamberlain to a niece of Peter the Great, the widow of the Duke of Courland, Anna Ivanovna. He wound her around his little finger, and became her lover too. All this would have remained a minor, Courland scandal had Anna not been crowned Empress of Russia in 1730. Biron, now married for the sake of appearances to one Fräulein

Rundāle, with its striking resemblance to the Winter Palace in St Petersburg.

von Treiden, was appointed grand chamberlain and count of the tsarist empire. He followed Anna to Moscow. His new position earned him an estate, an annual allowance of 50,000 roubles, and the undying hatred of his new countrymen.

Biron wheedled himself into the good graces of Anna's inner circle, but in the wider world he was a monster with giant tentacles, who has gone down in Russian history as an exceptionally nasty piece of work: treacherous, rapacious, untrustworthy, and endlessly vindictive. It was a reputation that would taint the Baltic barons in general, thanks in no small part to the Russian writers of the nineteenth century, who bestowed these traits on every Baltic pedant who appeared in their pages. Both Gogol and Tolstoy displayed a distinct dislike of their ilk.

Of the bribes intended for the Russian court, Biron pocketed half. Along with money, power, and prestige, he acquired vast swathes of land. His lifestyle became steadily more decadent, to the point of establishing a department of state for the upkeep of his mares and stallions. He cemented his place in Anna's good books by showering her with gifts — outsized diamonds went down particularly well.

In her twilight years, Anna appointed him Duke of Courland and, on her deathbed, made him regent to her infant successor, Ivan VI.

This proved to be a step too far: Ivan's mother allied herself with Biron's opponents, and his regency ended in imprisonment. At a show trial, Biron was accused of attempting to usurp the Russian throne. This was potentially a capital offence, but the sentence imposed was lifelong exile in Siberia and the stripping of all offices, titles, and property. He served twenty years.

But the master schemer still had friends in high places. Elizabeth of Russia allowed him to settle in Yaroslavl; Catherine the Great restored his dukedom. At last, he was able to return to Courland, where he enjoyed life at Rundāle for all of five years, until his death in 1772, aged eighty-two.

Rundāle, set in French gardens and surrounded by a seventy-three-hectare park, had been Biron's summer residence. Construction came to a standstill when he was exiled to Siberia, but architect Rastrelli did not despair. Instead, he directed his 1,500 masons, plasterers, and carpenters to nearby Jelgava, where he built another palace for the newly appointed Duke of Courland. After Biron's return, work on Rundāle resumed. All told, the construction and interior design took thirty-two years to complete. Apart from anything else, the palace is a testament to Rastrelli's perseverance. The first stone and the last were laid under his leadership.

Catherine the Great gifted Rundāle to one of her lovers — she had more than you could count on the fingers of both hands. It remained under Russian ownership until 1917. At the end of World War I, the palace was ransacked, and in 1920, the newly independent Latvian state announced that it was to become a museum, without doing anything much about it. Rundāle survived World War II, but successive tenancies by Nazi military personnel and Red Army soldiers left it in bad shape. A stint as a grain warehouse shortly after the war did not help matters. Later, the Soviet authorities shut down all the wings and converted the main building into an agricultural college. It took them until 1972 to begin restoring the building to something like its former glory.

On the outside, it is now once again one of the most delightful palaces in Europe, its soft-yellow walls and pale-blue roofs contrasting with the blood-red of the gatehouse buildings — a bright idea of Rastrelli's. Inside, it is empty, except for a modest museum and a restaurant that occupies the former canteen of the agricultural college. Ninety rooms await restoration. Since Latvia's independence, it has hosted the occasional historical exhibition, with titles such as *The Time of Misery*, the misery in question being the fate of Lutheran churches during the Soviet regime.

For Latvians, Rundāle Palace is a perplexing edifice. 'Italian on the outside, pure rococo,' said the elderly lady who showed me around, 'but the floor plan is French, with vast dining halls and ballrooms intended to evoke the grandeur of Versailles. That said, every step you take brings Russia to mind. Eisenstein could easily have filmed the storming of the Winter Palace here. Look at those stairs — identical! It's a building that stands for the history of Latvia in its disregard for all things Latvian.'

Leaving Rundāle, I turned around for one last look and had to agree with my Latvian guide: it was like saying goodbye to the Hermitage.

The real Courland lay further west. An exclamation mark glowing red on the dashboard of my rental car was a constant warning of the treacherous conditions. The temperature hovered between zero and minus one, snow sticking to the side windows like wet newspaper. Over deserted roads, I made my way to Stāmeriena, formerly Stomersee, in search of a palace that according to my guidebook was set between two lakes. The landscape lay hidden in the fog, out there beyond the creak of my windscreen wipers. 'Poor Tomasi,' I muttered. After spending a single winter here, he begged his wife to let them have Christmas in Rome from then on. She agreed, albeit reluctantly. What was Christmas without snow?

Courland not only fuelled Keyserling's imagination; it also spawned the early drafts of one of the greatest novels in Italian literature. North shaped south, Courland reflected Sicily. It was on the Baltic estate of Stomersee that the seed for *Il Gattopardo* (The Leopard) germinated in the mind of Giuseppe Tomasi, Prince of Lampedusa and Duke of Palma di Montechiaro. The story he wanted to tell was the story of his own family, his own forebears. But where should he start and with whom? With the arrival of an intruder! The idea came to him in Courland.

In 1925, the Sicilian prince met Baltic baroness Alexandra von

Baroness Alexandra von Wolff-Stomersee, who married Giuseppe
Tomasi di Lampedusa.

Wolff-Stomersee at the home of an uncle who was not only Italy's
ambassador to London but also Alexandra's stepfather. On seeing her
jet-black hair, broad black eyebrows, and dark eyes, Tomasi took her
for an Italian. He was only half mistaken. Alexandra was the daughter
of Modena-born mezzo-soprano Alice Barbi, who found success in
Germany, became a close friend of Clara Schumann and Johannes
Brahms, and married Baltic baron Boris von Wolff-Stomersee.

Alexandra helped Giuseppe Tomasi de Lampedusa overcome his
pathological shyness. She was a psychology graduate and had spent
the first twenty years of her life in St Petersburg, where her father was
a high dignitary at the court of Nicholas II. When the Revolution
broke out, the baron returned to Courland and Riga, where he died
not long afterwards. Alexandra continued her studies in Berlin. In
1927, she met Freud in Vienna.

Giuseppe had lived a life of reading, travel, and leisure. True, he
had taken up arms against Austro-Hungarian forces at the Battle of
Caporetto in 1917, but within days he had been taken prisoner. In
captivity, Austrian officers accorded him the respect due to a prince,
complete with occasional nights out at the Vienna opera. After a
year, he managed to escape and return home on foot, a journey that
took months. In the 1920s, he travelled around Italy and Europe,
always in the company of his mother. Against her wishes, he married
Alexandra in Riga in 1932. The young couple moved to Palermo,
where Alexandra went by the name Alessandra and immediately
locked horns with her mother-in-law. Before long, she retreated to

the Wolff family home in Stomersee.

Giuseppe found it hard to choose between mother and wife. Following the death of his father in 1935, it fell to him to manage the family's affairs. He spent most of the year at Palazzo Lampedusa in Palermo or Santa Margherita di Belice, the family's country residence. His summers were spent at Stomersee. Except for that one winter, which left him with a vicious cough.

Courland was where he penned the first drafts of *The Leopard*. Back in Sicily, he wrote letters to Alessandra, or Licy as he called her. Discreet letters in which he tiptoed around his feelings and avoided putting his love into words. However, he was overjoyed when Licy answered him, 'I love you as much as I love Stomersee.'

I arrived at Stāmeriena Palace — formerly Stomersee — to find it closed to the public. From the outside, crumbling plaster and other signs of neglect were clearly visible, yet its imposing square tower and smaller, round tower still gave the place an air of bygone grandeur. In the surrounding park, meltwater dripped from the branches. This was no place for a Sicilian prince. And yet ... perhaps you have to distance yourself from everything you know to gain a clearer view of your old, familiar surroundings.

The Wolff family were permitted to retain possession of Stomersee from 1920 to 1939, a remarkable exception. However, the 290,000 hectares of land that went with it did have to be transferred to state ownership, save for a single meadow and the park immediately surrounding the palace. When Tomasi di Lampedusa settled in Courland, he found a world peopled by penniless barons and counts, and disillusioned baronesses and countesses. Their decline brought his view of Sicily's nobility into sharp focus. Musing on the undeniable end of an era, the character of Don Fabrizio slowly but surely took shape in his mind.

Tomasi was an avid reader with a comprehensive command of German, and I feel sure that he must have read Eduard von Keyserling's novels at Stomersee. At times, *The Leopard* reads like a pastiche of a Keyserling novel. The world inhabited by Don Fabrizio is one of safety; the prince is reading to his daughters from an edifying novel; outside, the wind is howling and the rain is lashing down. Then an unexpected visitor is announced and 'on the top step appeared a

Schloss Stomersee, once home to the von Wolff-Stomersee family.

heavy, shapeless mass' — it is Tancredi, the intruder. Tancredi's arrival ushers in the family's downfall, the same dramatic premise around which Keyserling structures his own narratives. Stylistically too, there is an affinity between the two writers. Tomasi's style is more elegant, but they share an inclination towards precision, nuance, and multiformity. Above all, both men felt a deep need to mourn the loss of their earthly paradise.

> Tancredi wanted Angelica to know the whole palace with its inextricable complex of guest rooms, state rooms, kitchens, chapels, theatres, picture galleries, odorous tack rooms, stables, stuffy conservatories, passages, stairs, terraces, and porticoes, and particularly a series of abandoned and uninhabited apartments which had not been used for many years and formed a mysterious and intricate labyrinth of their own.

For Tomasi di Lampedusa, the world collapsed forever when Allied bombers destroyed the Palazzo Lampedusa in April 1943. Before the attack came, he had already moved in with relatives elsewhere in Sicily.

When he went to Palermo to see the damage for himself, he was so distraught that for three whole days he could not utter a word. It took him ten years to pick up a pen and start writing regularly again. During the last thirty months of his life, he completed *The Leopard*.

Tomasi died in July 1957. His magnificent book went on to spawn a magnificent film. Luchino Visconti perfectly captured the light and atmosphere that suffuse the novel.

For Alexandra von Wolff-Stomersee, centuries of family pride and family history had come to an end before the war began. In 1939, she was forced to leave Stomersee, never to see Courland, Latvia, or her beloved home again. Alexandra became Italy's first psychoanalyst. She died in Rome in 1982.

During the final days of my stay in Vilnius, Baroness Edith von Grotthuss makes no further appearances in the hotel dining room. Not that this bothers me. In the meantime, I have made the acquaintance of Dovid Katz, the professor of Yiddish, who dismisses the Baltic nobles of yesteryear as 'vile, self-important, gutless'. And I have since read novels very different to Keyserling's, not least the work of A.H. Tammsaare, Estonia's answer to Zola, who describes the fate of the country's poor farmers in a five-part saga that begins with an instalment called *Vargamäe* or *Thief's Hill*. I leave Hotel Grotthuss without feeling that I have missed an opportunity.

It is only later that I kick myself. In Hannah Arendt's essay 'Original Assimilation', from *The Jewish Writings*, I read an account of a Jewish woman by the name of Sarah Meyer. She came from a wealthy family and enjoyed the benefits of 'an aristocratic education and cultural instruction'. She was nobody's fool, as Goethe would discover over the course of a long-running correspondence with her. But her Jewishness rendered her persona non grata in society's upper echelons. Then she took a giant leap up the social ladder: she married the Livonian-born Baron von Grotthuss. For her, the marriage could bring only benefits. Her husband, on the other hand, braved the worst that could overcome a member of the nobility in 1799: to be shunned by one's peers, the fate that would later befall Eduard von Keyserling. But Ferdinand Dietrich Baron von Grotthuss was a headstrong man who despised narrow-mindedness and intolerance. It was a risk he was willing to take.

Sarah adopted the name Sophie von Grotthuss after her marriage. Ushered into high society, she found herself absorbed into a milieu of status and flattery. She renounced her Jewish faith, though not at the baron's insistence; her mother had already cultivated a fierce hatred of religion in her. She was barred from some homes, which, Hannah Arendt writes, 'provoked immeasurable vanity in Frau von Grotthuss'. She started a salon in Berlin and cultivated the art of — in her own words — making 'even boredom entertaining'. As a result of the Napoleonic Wars, the baron lost his fortune in 1805. He took a job as postmaster in Oranienburg and bore his fate resignedly. Sophie followed him without complaint. She loved the baron and, until his death, declared herself to be the happiest woman in the world. In the final phase of her life, she set about writing a long story, an essay, a play, and hundreds of letters. She corresponded with Goethe until 1824.

I read all this with growing amazement and go in search of more information about Ferdinand Dietrich von Grotthuss online. I learn that his cousin Theodor von Grotthuss (1785–1822) was a renowned physicist who developed the theory of electrolysis and in 1818 discovered the chemical processes that gave rise to photography. I come across his portrait in an encyclopaedia and the image leaps out at me: the very same portrait hung behind the reception desk at Hotel Grotthuss in Vilnius. Edith von Grotthuss is from the same branch of the family tree as both Ferdinand Dietrich and Theodor von Grotthuss, two men who were well ahead of their time, open to new ideas, and alive to new perspectives on the world.

When you travel, it's best to leave your prejudices at home.

11

The Start of an Unknown Adventure

IN THE LIGHT OF MARK ROTHKO

Latvia, April 2009

At daybreak, I take the train to Daugavpils. Stiff-backed seats, plastic upholstery, sticky floors. Bins overflowing with brown-black banana peels, with newspapers from yesterday and the day before. There's a whiff of shit and urine in the air. Stopping at every station, the Soviet-era train bumps, swings, slows, then gives a sudden, deafening rattle as it struggles to exceed sixty kilometres an hour. Eight of my ten fellow passengers are elderly women. Raised under communism, they avoid the company of strangers and sit as far away from me as possible. I stretch my legs in silence for the entire journey.

Two colours dominate as I gaze out of the window: the red of the sky and the green of the forest. The red sky is aglow and infused with shadowy halftones, the green shot through with the black and brown of branches. They form two planes, one above the other, interdependent opposites. The dark lower plane intensifies the red above; the sky is only sky in relation to the earth.

It's a painting that glides by, a never-ending painting, powerful and disturbing, hushed and profound. A Rothko painting. An artist shows you what has always been there, hovering just beyond habitual perception. Their vision influences your own. And inevitably leads you to ask what shaped or honed the artist's gaze in the first place. 'I live on Sixth Avenue, paint on 53rd Street, am affected by television, etc.,' Mark Rothko told William Seitz in 1953. 'My paintings are part of that life.' True. Or half-true? Are those paintings also part of another life?

Two hours and twenty minutes later, I reach Daugavpils, drab as any North of England factory town. The factories were built by the Russians, the first of them in tsarist times, to capitalise on Daugavpils's convenient location on the Daugava, a river that flows into the Gulf of Riga 200 kilometres away and links the industrial belt with the Latvian capital. It is also where the railway between Riga and Moscow intersects with the line that runs from Warsaw to St Petersburg.

Three stations tell the story of the city's railway past: Riga (where I get off), Libau (where Mark Rothko began his long journey to the west coast of the United States), and St Petersburg. In this last station, a suite of seven rooms was set aside for Nicholas II, who occasionally spent the night in Daugavpils on his way from St Petersburg to Warsaw. Back then, the city was called Dvinsk.

The city's factories, around 100 in all, supplied the entire tsarist empire, and later the entire Soviet Union. They provided jobs for 6,000 workers. Textiles, stone, leather goods, and matches — products with one thing in common: the inhumane conditions in which they were produced. The largest of the match factories employed 200 men, 400 women, and 200 children, some as young as ten. Many lost a hand or a finger in the woodcutting machines; many more died of phosphorus poisoning.

The first major strike broke out in 1901 and lasted six months. The unrest among the workers spread from the match factory to other workplaces, culminating in the 1905 uprising, crushed brutally by the tsar's troops. Twenty-five thousand Russian soldiers were stationed at the Dvinsk fortress, in the heart of the city. As Mark Rothko's brother Moise recalled, 'they were the elite of the city and we were the other half.'

Supporters of the socialist revolutionary cause gathered to listen to their leaders in Dvinsk's Old Park, the only place where the authorities permitted political rallies and demonstrations. The park was a long walk from the centre, which gave the Cossacks time to intervene if a riotous mob decided to march on the government buildings to vent their frustrations. In addition to the revolutionaries, the Jewish Socialist Bund and Zionist groups also had hundreds of members in Dvinsk. More than half the city's 75,000 inhabitants were Jewish.

Daugavpils stands where Latvia ends: a short distance from Lithuania to the south (under Polish rule in the nineteenth century) and Belarus to the east. These borders defined the city: Daugavpils was Latvia's Lutheran stronghold in the face of Catholic Lithuania and Poland. In the end, both faiths had to give way to Russian Orthodoxy. The city was originally German and called Dünaburg, then became Russian and was named Borisoglebsk, then became Polish and reverted to Dünaburg, returned to Russian rule under the name Dvinsk, and finally adopted the Latvian name Daugavpils — 'Castle on the Daugava' — when Latvia gained its independence.

The city's churches jostle for position on a hillside: the Martin Luther Church, the Catholic Church of the Immaculate Conception, the Russian Orthodox Boris and Gleb Cathedral, the Alexander Nevsky Cathedral, and the Old Believers Church. The Russians win by three churches, an accurate reflection of the city's present-day demographics: 85 per cent of its inhabitants have Russian roots, a mere 15 per cent are Latvian. First the Germans were driven out, then the Jews, then the Poles and Lithuanians, and finally the Latvians. The Soviet authorities recruited new residents from Belarus, Ukraine, and the Leningrad area.

At the beginning of the twentieth century, most of the residents were Jewish. Shoemakers, tailors, confectioners, barbers, jewellers, and pharmacists closed their businesses on a Saturday and made their way to the synagogue. Most of the restaurants and all the print shops in the city were owned by Jewish entrepreneurs. The first strikes in the factories were organised by Jewish workers. Jewish activists structured social protest by setting up trade unions and political groups. The seeds of the 1905 uprising and the 1917 revolution were sown in this western corner of the tsarist empire.

It was Czesław Miłosz who brought this distinct mindset into the sharpest focus:

> Jewish boys and girls were possessed very early by the spirit of progress, and their protest against the mentality of their fathers and religion was incomparably stronger than that of the Christians. They ridiculed superstitions, read Lenin, and usually proclaimed themselves Marxists. They took a rather dim view of the country whose citizens they were, and rightly so, since they saw little opportunity in it for themselves … The Communist movement, which was weak and combatted by the police, recruited its militants and sympathisers mainly from among young Jewish people.

In the Lithuanian city where Miłosz grew up, the residents called the First of May 'the Jewish holiday … Then there was a big parade

Jacob Rothkowitz, Mark Rothko's father.

with banners and flags. And indeed in the crowd, which represented
various species of the Left, young Jewish people were predominant.'

The Baltic nationalists lurched to the right. As Czesław Miłosz
observes:

> they were usually fanatical patriots, conservatives and fond
> of ceremonies copied from German universities in the Baltic
> countries ... Their organisations catered to social snobbery or to
> Rightist politics, and their style was a combination of cocky pride

and military honour. In all this they resembled the officer caste. Intellectually, they developed more slowly. Their emancipation and progress to radical positions were accompanied by great suffering and inner turmoil.

Mark Rothko would remain a revolutionary all his life. When, in 1958, the exclusive Four Seasons restaurant in New York invited him to create a number of murals for the space, he accepted the commission with malicious intent. 'I hope to paint something that will ruin the appetite of every son of a bitch who ever eats in that room.'

The factory workers of Dvinsk subsisted on a daily ration of water and dry bread. Rothko could never forget the fate of the Jews in his hometown, nor the repression they suffered: he liked to point out a scar on his nose, left by the whip of a Cossack when, as a child in his mother's arms, he had been caught up in a demonstration that was dispersed by tsarist police. Though barely visible, it was a mark he bore with pride.

Mark Rothko began life as Marcus Rothkowitz, and lived in Dvinsk until the age of ten. He was not raised in poverty; his father, Jacob, was a pharmacist, and his parental home stood on tree-lined Shosseynaya, the city's widest avenue. In 1945, it was named after Lenin, and in 1992, it became Rīgas iela. Number 17, a residential block not far from the river, is still standing: a distinguished three-storey building, painted white. It is still home to a number of the city's dignitaries.

Jacob Rothkowitz had no desire to cosy up to those in power, preferring to side with small tradesmen and factory workers. He provided free medicine to the poor and spent the little free time he had volunteering at the hospital, writing letters for the illiterate, and organising political meetings in his own home.

'My father,' Mark would recall, 'was a militant social democrat of the Jewish party, the Bund … He was profoundly Marxist and violently anti-religious, partly because in Dvinsk … the orthodox Jews were a repressive majority.'

Marcus's father later became a Zionist. This was a dramatic turnaround for an active member of the Bund: the two factions were bitterly opposed. The brutal suppression of the 1905 uprising had everything to do with his radical change of outlook.

Jacob Rothkowitz came from a Lithuanian shtetl about 100 kilometres south-west of Dvinsk. He grew up under the liberal rule of Tsar Alexander II (1855–1881), who improved the lot of Russia's five million Jews and permitted them to attend schools and universities. This enabled Jacob to complete a high-school education and train as a pharmacist in Vilnius.

Anti-Semitism appeared to be over — institutionalised anti-Semitism at least: the distinction between peoples as practised by the state. Like many of his contemporaries, Jacob Rothkowitz pursued full assimilation. He believed that major reforms were still needed in Russia, but that they had to happen from within. In his view, this could only succeed if the Jews became more Russian than the Russians.

From his student days, Jacob abandoned the Yiddish he had been brought up with, to say nothing of Hebrew, and spoke only Russian. His views were strongly influenced by the Haskala, a movement that sought to remove the contradictions between Enlightenment rationalism and Jewish religion and philosophy. The Haskala advocated the separation of church and state. Politically, Jacob sided with the Marxists, who in Vilnius decided to collaborate with Jewish radical groups and organise strikes.

The assassination of Alexander II in 1881 was the first bad omen. The May Laws introduced the following year deprived Jews of the most basic rights, but by then Jacob had completed his studies and was working as an assistant pharmacist in St Petersburg. His life was largely unaffected by the new measures.

At the age of twenty-seven, he married sixteen-year-old Anna Goldin, who came from a prosperous East Prussian Jewish family. She was in the fourth grade of high school when she met Jacob. Anna's first governess had been an Englishwoman, and she liked people to call her Kate. The young couple moved to the countryside and settled in Michalishek, the Lithuanian village where Jacob had grown up. Their first children, Sonia and Moise, were born there. In 1895, the family moved to Dvinsk, where the two youngest sons came into the world, Albert and Marcus. Marcus, born on 25 September 1903, was a late addition to the family: thirteen years younger than his sister and eight years younger than his nearest sibling.

Rothko may have described his parents as staunchly anti-religious, but this was overstating the case. That said, they were keenly aware of the predominance of the Orthodox Jews and the social control they exercised. The Rothkowitzes went to synagogue every Saturday and sometimes took their children with them, all except their youngest. Marcus's health was fragile.

Moise Rothkowitz, the eldest son, recalled that on Yom Kippur, his father soon tired of the prayers and chants, and took to reading political pamphlets, which he concealed in his prayer book. Politics and literature were subjects closer to Jacob's heart; at this stage in his life, the rabbi's preaching left him cold. The 300 books he had at home were treasured possessions. 'We were a reading family,' Sonia Rothkowitz remembered. 'Very interested in literature — all of us.' And for her father, literature meant Russian literature.

A progressive intellectual, Jacob encouraged his wife to read and made no distinction between his daughter and his three sons. All four were to receive a decent education so that one day they could contribute to the radical reform of Russian society. Their mother, Kate, did the laundry to save on the expense of a housemaid, at night so no one would see the pharmacist's wife toiling away at the wash tub. Sonia was put through high school in Dvinsk and then studied dentistry at Warsaw University. Moise followed in his father's footsteps and trained as a pharmacist at Vilnius University. Albert embarked on the same path.

Throughout his life, Marcus would speak of his father with respect. He revered him as a biblical patriarch, 'a man of great character, great intelligence'. Jacob Rothkowitz's early death, in 1914, must surely have contributed to the aura that surrounded him in the eyes of his youngest son. But older brother Moise also praised him as a quiet man and a dreamer, an idealist who was morally conscientious and passionate about his political persuasions. Despite a ban on gatherings, he invited Bund members to meet at his home. Until 1905, he shared their commitment to gradual change.

The brutal suppression of the 1905 uprising awakened a grim pessimism in Jacob. It was the point at which he realised that tsarist Russia could never be reformed from within. In Dvinsk, soldiers shot and killed nine protesters. More alarming still was the slogan adopted by Russian nationalists in the following months: 'Destroy the Jews and

The synagogue in Dvinsk (now Daugavpils) attended by Jacob, Kate,
Sonia, Moise, and Albert Rothkowitz, but not ailing Marcus.

save Russia.' After 1905, Jacob attended Zionist meetings and decided
that his youngest son should receive a strict religious upbringing.

Until the age of four, doctors believed young Marcus's chances of
survival were slim. He was constantly ill, the result of a calcium
deficiency as it turned out. His sister, Sonia, remembers him eating
the plaster off the walls at home in a kind of instinctive craving. To

improve his strength, he was sent to stay with a farming family in a village north of Dvinsk, where he was given a quart of milk a day.

He returned to the city with an insatiable appetite that would never leave him. Half a century later, Rothko would tell his daughter how he had skated to school across the frozen river. To a friend, he described the glorious Russian sunsets. He told another friend how he always wore his school bag on his back to protect him from the stones thrown by anti-Semitic boys. It's a story dismissed as nonsense in Daugavpils: in those days, all schoolchildren carried their bags on their backs.

Equally questionable is his account of the family's history: Cossacks took the Jews from a village into the woods and made them dig a mass grave. The impression of that big square pit was so vivid in his mind that he felt sure the massacre had taken place during his childhood. He went on to say that the image of the grave had always haunted him and that it was locked into his painting in some profound way. A few years later, he even claimed to have witnessed the digging of the mass grave and the massacre that followed.

I put this to Alexander Volodin, a history teacher in Daugavpils. He is adamant: no pogroms ever took place in Dvinsk. Pogroms were collective acts of physical violence often accompanied by arson. 'It's possible that Rothko heard about the pogroms in Lithuania from his father, but they did not end in mass executions. The Nazis made their Jewish victims dig graves before they were shot; that macabre practice was part of the Shoah. But Rothko could not have seen any of this with his own eyes; he had been living in the US almost thirty years by then. It is striking, however, that he identified so closely with the Shoah.'

Immediately after World War II, he painted his first abstract canvases, which were thick with menace. Red, grey, and black became his predominant shades.

Jacob Rothkowitz sent his youngest son to *cheder*, a school for boys starting as young as four or five. They were taught by a *melamed*, or teacher, in his own living room (*cheder* literally means 'room'). The children learned to read and write Hebrew and to recite prayers; the *melamed* translated the Pentateuch with them, the five books of Moses, as well as other biblical writings and liturgical texts. Marcus deeply resented his father's decision. His sister had attended Russian state schools; his brothers had received a non-religious Jewish education. He was the exception. His father may have thought of him as the chosen son, but he saw himself as being set apart in a class of deeply religious bigots.

Jacob went from being a left-wing liberal to a stern and unbending Orthodox Jew. This transformation was also difficult for his wife to accept. Kate was constantly at odds with her husband over her lack of strict adherence to religious rules and rituals. 'When I got married, I was sixteen years old,' she would tell her daughter. 'I didn't know anything. He taught me everything.' But from a mild, understanding, encouraging father, he turned into a biblical-times potentate.

If Jacob had not travelled ahead to the United States in 1910, he would have been at odds with his family for life. Not only did Kate refuse to run her household according to strict Orthodox precepts, but Marcus also came home from school at the age of nine insisting he never wanted to set foot in a synagogue again. During the school holidays, he had been made to attend synagogue more than a hundred times, and he was sick of it. He later claimed that he forgot the Hebrew he had learned within a matter of weeks. This was untrue: as an adolescent in America, he wrote a story, a play, and a few poems in Hebrew. It was only after Jacob's death that he distanced himself from the faith altogether, though at the time he resolved to visit the synagogue every day for a year in memory of his father. After a few months, he gave up and never saw the inside of a synagogue again. And in time, his knowledge of Hebrew did indeed fade.

I visit the churches of Daugavpils: Protestant, Catholic, and Russian Orthodox. I save the synagogue for last. The building is diagonally opposite the house where Mark Rothko was born. The rabbi shows me around. All of the city's synagogues were destroyed during World War II; this building was newly erected after the communist era, in the third year of Latvia's independence.

'The Rothkowitzes left just in time,' the rabbi tells me. 'In 1915, Dvinsk came under attack by German forces. There was an aerial bombardment, and the city was shelled by artillery from the hill across the river. Most of the factories were relocated to towns far behind the front, and the workers had to follow. Even if the family had lived to

Albert and Sonia Rothkowitz (left), a cousin (middle), Marcus and
Moise Rothkowitz (right).

tell the tale, they would have been wiped out in World War II.'

Hitler unilaterally ended his non-aggression pact with Stalin in
June 1941 and launched a three-million-strong offensive against the
Soviet Union. Germany's 56th Armoured Division reached Dvinsk
on 26 June, and its soldiers were greeted as liberators, with flowers
and singing. After six days of recuperation, the division pushed on
towards Leningrad. Even before German Gestapo and special-ops
units — *Einsatzkommandos* — took over control of the city from the
military, Latvian fascists got to work. On 29 June, they destroyed
every synagogue in Dvinsk and shot dead 1,100 men and boys against
the wall of the prison on Shosseynaya, a hundred metres from the
house where Rothko was born.

On 25 July, all of the city's Jews were herded into a camp at the
foot of the fortress on the far side of the river. No water, no food,
no sanitation. A heatwave hit in early August, and 1,500 of the sick
and the old were killed to create space in the camp. Days later, 8,000
Jews were murdered in the forests. Ten days passed and another 3,000
were killed, then 4,000, followed on 8 and 9 November by 11,000

more. Winter came, and the bitter cold claimed the lives of thousands of internees. On 15 May 1942, Latvia's national holiday, 400 of the 30,000 Jews of Dvinsk were still alive.

'Those 400 souls still had two more years of war to get through,' says the rabbi. 'Only a few made it. The Jews who live in the city and attend the synagogue nowadays came to Daugavpils from Belarus and Ukraine after the war.'

'The Jew spoke German,' Modris Eksteins wrote in his personal history of the Baltic states, 'and was on occasion more German than the German. The Jew spoke Russian and again could be a better spokesman for Russian culture than the Russian. The Jew was a town dweller, a cosmopolitan. The Jew was all things — but to many Latvians, caught up in a mood of growing paranoia and crude nationalism, he represented all things foreign, all things dangerous.'

When I start talking about the Bund, the rabbi smiles. 'Those were wonderful, hopeful times that brought out the best in Jewish people: their sense of community and solidarity with the poor.' But Nicholas II dismissed any notion of progress as a despicable plot hatched by Jews and freemasons. For him, there was but one church that preached the true faith: the Russian Orthodox Church.

After the Revolution, nothing much improved. 'Trotsky was supposed to succeed Lenin,' the rabbi says, 'but in the eyes of the communists, Trotsky combined two insurmountable disadvantages: he was a true intellectual, and he was a Jew.' Then came the Nazis. 'In these parts, they did not have to stir up anti-Semitism: it had been spreading among the population like scarlet fever for a good two centuries.'

The city's Historical Museum is located next to the synagogue. The photographs that hang there illustrate the rabbi's words. Bridges, stations, and buildings blown apart in World War I, more buildings and infrastructure reduced to rubble in World War II. Few photographs of the concentration camp at the foot of the fortress exist.

One room forms a sharp contrast to the walls of black-and-white photographs: it contains thirty paintings by Mark Rothko, reproductions on canvas, skilfully crafted in Vienna. I walk past these abstract works, and they make a much more sombre impression on me than when I first saw the real paintings, in 1988, at Museum Ludwig in Cologne. Lines from a poem Rothko wrote at sixteen come to mind:

Heaven is like a lamp in the fog
At the end of a long, dark road

Yet it was not anti-Semitism that made Jacob Rothkowitz decide
to emigrate to the United States. His two eldest sons were due to be
called up for military service, and the idea that they would soon wear
the same uniform as the tsarist troops who had crushed the 1905
uprising was something he could not bear.

An equally important factor was Jacob's dire financial situation.
Time after time, the philanthropist in him won over the businessman.
Every customer with a sob story left his pharmacy with free medicine,
but the suppliers had to be paid regardless. The bills were piling up,
and Jacob saw no way out, not in Dvinsk or anywhere else in the
north-east corner of Europe. Nor was emigration to Palestine an
option; who would be willing to finance the journey for him and his
family? His one hope was his younger brother Sam, who had emigrated to the United States in 1891 and founded a clothing business,
the New York Outfitting Company, in Portland, Oregon, in partner-
ship with Nate Weinstein. The Weinsteins came from Michalishek,
the same Lithuanian village as the Rothkowitzes. Before Jacob left for
America, three of Nate's brothers had already made the journey from
Michalishek to Portland. All of them worked for the firm.

In 1910, Jacob too travelled to Portland, in the western United
States. Moise and Albert followed their father two years later. Moise, a
qualified pharmacist, and Albert, a pharmacist in training, had to stow
away in freight wagons and cross Lithuania, Poland, and Germany
without passports, before finally boarding a ship in Bremen. They
were only granted entry to the US because members of the Weinstein
family were waiting for them at Ellis Island. Finally, Kate, Sonia, and
Marcus followed in the summer of 1913.

For Sonia, the departure was more the sad closing of a chapter
than the hopeful start of a new life. Below her parental home on
Shosseynaya, she had started her own dental practice. Not only
that, but she was courting and had to leave her sweetheart behind
in Dvinsk. Abandoning her language and her culture was as much
of a struggle. The most Russian of all the Rothkowitz children, she
had no illusions about the country for which she was bound. To her,
Americans were 'all mercenary, all money, and nothing else'. But her

father insisted she come to the United States. She refused at first, but in the end the prospect of staying on without her parents and brothers proved too daunting. Emigration brought her little happiness. Thirty years after leaving Dvinsk, she found herself a widowed mother of three who had taken in her elderly mother and was running a cof-feeshop by the name of Jack's.

Young Marcus embarked on the journey of a lifetime. He was allowed to give the ferryman the three kopecks for the river crossing. On the far side of the Daugava, then called the Dvina in Russian, he boarded a train with his mother and sister, and travelled across Latvia and Courland to the port of Libau (present-day Liepāja) on the Gulf of Riga. In a second-class cabin aboard the SS *Czar*, they crossed the Atlantic, arriving in Brooklyn on 17 August 1913. The journey across America to Portland took a further two weeks.

'An exhausting, unforgettable journey,' Rothko later recalled. At the time, he wondered 'whether they were ever going to get to the end of it'. On the train, he was ashamed of his Russian smock suit — standard attire for young boys in Dvinsk — and of not being able to speak a word of English. From the very beginning, he felt like an outcast in America, and would remain so all his life. Even three or four decades on, he was never able to 'forgive' having been relocated ('transplantation' was the word he used) to a country where he never felt fully at home.

One of his first paintings, *Street Scene* from 1937, depicts the closed front of a windowless building on the left and a static, isolated couple on a flight of steps. The woman has her arm around the man's shoulder; behind them stands the looming figure of a bearded Jewish elder. The painting is strongly reminiscent of the early works of Marc Chagall, another uprooted individual, who grew up 250 kilometres east of Dvinsk, in the Belarussian town of Vitebsk, also on the banks of the Dvina. In another early Rothko painting, *Family* (1936), a father bends over a mother and newborn baby. This almost biblical family group is rendered in sickly, green-tinged tones and surrounded by faded reds and greens.

One million foreigners were admitted to the US in 1913. Most were Eastern European, and of those Eastern Europeans, most were Jews.

In Portland, the Rothkowitz family moved into a two-storey wooden house in the Jewish quarter, then known as Little Russia. The end point of their wanderings had been reached; Lithuania and Latvia could be consigned to the photo album and life from then would consist of today and tomorrow, no more yesterdays. Seven months after the reunited family enjoyed their first copious meal under their own roof, Jacob died of colon cancer. He was fifty-five years old.

Jacob's death ushered in years of poverty for Kate and the children. After school, Marcus sold newspapers on a corner in downtown Portland: evening papers until nine and then the first edition of the morning papers, which hit the streets around 10.00 pm. He often came home with a black eye: every paperboy wanted his own street corner, and Mark, chubby and small of stature, was easy to bully out of a good spot.

For Marcus, the word 'transplantation' came to mean social regression. He became fixated on words beginning with 'trans' and used them constantly: 'transform', 'transcend', 'translate', 'transpose', 'transplant'. In his own mind, he was continually having to negotiate borders. The high marks he obtained at school and the opportunity to study at a distinguished institution such as Yale University did little to smooth away those boundaries. Yale had come within reach thanks to a scholarship that was supplemented by his uncle. But Marcus continued to feel like a pauper, an outsider.

Most of Rothko's abstract paintings include a separation at some point, marking the transition from one colour to another. It does not take the form of a line; he had no time for Mondrian's schematics. No, this was a fissure, a boundary, a twilight zone.

In 1988, when those paintings were exhibited at Museum Ludwig in Cologne, I spent a long time gazing at them. A coherent vision unfolded before my eyes, the sense of a recurring fracture. The experience led me to choose one of the paintings for the cover of the book I had just finished, *De moordenaar van Ouagadougou* (The Assassin of Ouagadougou), based on the diary I kept during a revolution in West Africa. At first, Rothko's heirs were reluctant to give permission. His daughter, Kate, named after his mother, wanted to know more about the book's contents. When I let her know that I had written about irreparable fractures and the cruelty of history, she granted her approval.

Marcus Rothkowitz came to painting late in life. At school, he devoted his attention to 'useful' subjects, and neglected drawing and sports. He was a keen reader, but not of novels; he immersed himself in the Greek tragedies. A precocious learner as a result of emigration, he heard a lecture by activist Emma Goldman in which she broached the themes of anarchism, free love, Nietzsche, and birth control. Marcus was twelve at the time. At fourteen, he followed the example of his sister and his brothers, and pored over newspaper reports about developments in the east. 'We followed and applauded the Russian Revolution.'

At Yale, he had a reputation for brilliance among his fellow students, primarily because he had the gift of the gab. He spoke and others fell silent. He saw his future in the unions, more as an organiser and strike leader than as a lawyer.

From Yale, he moved to New York to 'wander around, bum about, starve a bit'. One day, he dropped in on a friend who was sketching a life model in a studio at the Art Students League with a few other students. Looking on, Marcus decided on the spot that *this* was where his future lay. In 1925, he enrolled at the New School of Design in New York. Painting gave him a physical pleasure to which he became addicted. Just as his father had traded politics for faith, Marcus sidelined activism for art.

His first paintings lacked direction and were only really of interest to those who knew his personal history. Initial experiments with watercolours resulted in largely unoriginal landscapes. It took him twenty years to discover that his calling was abstract expressionism.

The few people who got to know him in the 1930s described him as the loneliest man they had ever met. He was alone, desperately alone. No art dealers, collectors, or critics were interested in his paintings. He lived on five dollars a week. On Saturday afternoons, he went to the Russian Bear, a hangout for Russian exiles.

His first wife, Edith Sachar, came from a Russian-Jewish family. Both her parents had been born in Kyiv. With the Sachars, Marcus felt like he was with his own family: they might not understand his desire to be an artist, but they spoke the same language. His marriage to Edith, who was nine years younger, did not last. He later complained that it had been like living with a stranger.

Marcus Rothkowitz obtained US citizenship in 1938 — a quarter of a century after his arrival — and in 1940 changed his name on the advice of a New York art dealer. 'Marcus, I have so many Jewish painters. Why don't you make your name Rothko?'

Nine months after his divorce, he married Mell Beistle, a blonde girl from a WASP background. She was nineteen years his junior and never called him by his first name. 'I was a foreigner,' he said, 'and she made an American out of me.'

To her and everyone else, he became Rothko.

During the war, Rothko taught at art schools. He left the fight against Nazism to others. Not for one moment did he consider enlisting in the army. As he commented to his first wife, 'The Rothkos are not heroes.' His poor eyesight would probably have led him to fail the medical in any case.

In 1947, 1948, and 1949, he surprised the art world with his abstract paintings, though from the start, he took issue with that label. 'I will say without reservations that from my point of view there can be no abstractions. Any shape or area which has not the pulsating concreteness of real flesh and bones, its vulnerability to pleasure or pain, is nothing at all. Any picture which does not provide the environment in which the breath of life can be drawn does not interest me.'

For Swiss art collector Ernst Beyeler, Rothko achieved something close to perfection in his painting. 'The canvases pose questions to the viewer and invite him to meditate. When you look at the shapes long enough, you soak up the colours and find the light in them.' A light that in Rothko's hands takes on a mythical or sacred dimension.

For his own part, Rothko scrupulously avoided interpretation. 'If people want sacred experiences, they will find them here. If they want profane experiences, they'll find them too. I take no sides.' He let the viewers decide what they did or did not want to see.

Yet his work gave almost every viewer the sensation of entering an unknown, unreal, shadowy world that could be either heaven or hell. It was an effect Rothko created by applying ten, twelve, fourteen, and sometimes as many as twenty layers of paint to the canvas, layers as thin and transparent as tissue paper. The colour of each layer differed slightly from the layer beneath, and so red or black began to consist of many different shades: the red of lava, the black of a mudslide, or some other substance in motion and constantly transforming. Rothko played with the elements and gave his canvases a cosmopolitan vitality.

Another twelve years would pass before his big breakthrough. Before he became, in the words of Stanley Kunitz, 'the last rabbi of Western art'. He gave lectures, taught classes. His pronouncements on art were so numerous that they would fill entire books. He received art critics at home. 'He enjoyed talking about art from 10.00 in the morning until 5.00 in the afternoon,' said Elaine de Kooning, writing for *Art News* magazine. Not about himself; about art. As she saw it, he played only one role, 'that of the Messiah — I have come, I have the word.' In this regard, he was even more driven than Elaine's husband, Willem de Kooning, another artist not exactly known for his modesty.

For Peter Selz, another art critic, Rothko was akin to a Jewish patriarch. 'He looked like it. He thought like it. He acted like it.' For Sonia Rothkowitz, it was simpler. 'He was — in everything — exactly my father.' The same voice, the same interests, the same powers of persuasion. The same depth. The same glasses and the same blurred vision: Mark Rothko was nearsighted.

Rothko had something else in common with his father: he grew more rigid in his thinking and turned his back on innovators. Rothko and Mell were among the official guests at John F. Kennedy's presidential inauguration, an honour that delighted him. But after a sister and brother-in-law of the president came to Rothko's studio and asked if they could take one or two works home on approval, he refused to have anything more to do with the Kennedys. Ordering a painting on approval, what were they thinking? As an artist, he had every right to be offended, but it was hardly a reason to wash your hands of the entire Kennedy clan.

His views on the latest developments in the art world were as hardline as his own radical break with figurative painting in the 1940s. Pop art? Far too commercial. Andy Warhol? A charlatan to whom he refused to be introduced. When Warhol and a few of his entourage turned up at a party Rothko was attending, he turned on the hostess and demanded, 'How could you let *them* in?'

He took an even harder line in the regime he imposed on his daughter, Kate. Going out? Dating? Dancing? Out of the question. She had to learn and study, become a doctor, or better still, a specialist, a surgeon. He demanded abstinence and discipline, also from his wife, Mell, who had started drinking heavily.

To make matters worse, he became a father for the second time. His son, Christopher, was born shortly before his 60th birthday. He told a friend, 'I'm too old. I can't take that anymore. I could have been his grandfather.' Life had begun to pall.

In an effort to overcome bouts of depression, he shut himself away in his studio. If someone took him to a restaurant, he complained that it was criminal to pay more than five dollars for a decent meal. For the series of paintings the Tate Gallery in London ordered from him, he used only two colours: grey and black. Canvases that appeared to mine the same darkness as the Rolling Stones hit 'Paint It Black'.

From the Rothkowitz family home on Shosseynaya, I walk to the river. It's three in the afternoon and already dusk is settling in. The water churns towards the city in a wide stream, before changing course and disappearing into the woods some 300 metres away. The city and the woodland are at close quarters; the trees rub shoulders with the houses.

Winters were long and dark in Dvinsk, and the houses in Rothko's time had no electricity, no running water, no bathroom or toilet. To bathe, you had to go to the public bathhouse; you emptied your bowels in a shack out in the yard. When the temperatures dropped below minus fifteen, you only left home when you had to.

June and July were at the other end of the spectrum: three hours of night-time at most, and evenings that offered an endless invitation to stay outdoors. The Rothkowitzes picnicked on the banks of the Dvina; the children swam in the river. In August and September, the picnics moved to the forest, where the children picked mushrooms.

Later, in New York, Rothko professed to hate nature, insisting that the great outdoors made him feel uncomfortable. As an American urbanite, he had no desire to be reminded of greenery and forest air. His life revolved around eating, smoking, drinking (he started at ten in the morning), sitting in his studio, lying down, thinking, reading and rereading (Nietzsche, *The Birth of Tragedy*), listening to music (Mozart), and painting. Nature belonged to the past.

I cross a wooden bridge. This same river crossing existed in 1905, though it must have been destroyed anew with every siege of the city. On the other side, I climb the hill that gave young Marcus Rothkowitz his first panoramic views. From the top, I look out over the city, the surrounding forests, the river winding through the darkest green.

In his biography of Mark Rothko, James Breslin features a telling quote from Simone Weil: 'To be rooted is perhaps the most important and least recognised need of the human soul.' Rothko was uprooted, as was Marc Chagall, as was Chaïm Soutine, as was Chaim Jacob Lipchitz. They stored the things they had lost in their visual memory and gave them a place in their paintings and sculptures.

It was Rothko who lost the most: after his homeland came the loss of his father, and after his father, his faith. He endured the greatest displacement and would become the most radical of the four Jewish artists from the Pale of Settlement, the Chertá. He had no need to break with tradition; he was already too detached from it. All that remained was to continue down the path of exile, and this he did consistently, with scant regard for vilification or disparagement. He defined his art as 'an unknown adventure in an unknown space'.

The unknown adventure began at Dvinsk's Libau station. Its high point came in New York in 1961, when Rothko was given a retrospective at MoMA, a rare honour for a living painter. During the exhibition, Rothko could be found in the museum's halls on a daily basis, and although he was an introvert, he struck up conversations with sceptical-looking visitors in an effort to convince them. He was still unsure of himself, still considered himself an outcast, more likely to see rejection than acceptance in someone else's eyes.

New York was also where the adventure ended. After two failed marriages and a tormented existence that had alienated him from almost everyone, Mark Rothko took his own life early on the morning of 25 February 1970. In both arms, just below the hollow at the elbow, he cut deep enough to almost sever the artery.

He was sixty-six, the age at which Romain Gary also ended his life. Both men came from the Chertá, both renounced religion, achieved fame in the West, married a blonde beauty, and fathered children late in life. Both suffered when their work and its deeper meaning were misunderstood. Both were hypochondriacs and ended their lives for fear of physical decline, of bodily and also mental impotence.

When James Breslin, Rothko's biographer, visited Daugavpils in March 1991, no one he spoke to there knew Mark Rothko —

not by name, nor by reputation. Breslin travelled to Daugavpils via
Leningrad, the shortest and simplest route at the time: an express
train took him to the city in a matter of hours. Eighteen years later,
Daugavpils is hermetically sealed off from Russia. If I had gone by the
same route, it would have taken me days to obtain a visa.

Breslin showed the curator of the local museum some reproductions of Rothko's paintings. She looked at them intently and murmured, 'kon-struk-tee-veest'. Rothko meant nothing to the students
of English Breslin lectured, abstract painting even less so. The notion
that anyone would pay thousands of dollars for such pictures amused
them no end. They had little tolerance for information on their city's
famous painter, impatient instead to find out more about Breslin's
hometown New York and 'the legendary land of "Ka-lee-forn-ya"'.

The authorities, local historians, and members of the Latvian
Jewish Cultural Committee were friendly and did their best to be
helpful, but they barely knew what to do with the biographer. Out of
desperation, they took him to the cemetery, where 120,000 victims of
Nazism were buried or had been reburied, most of them Jews. They
also showed him the place in the forest where the mass killings had
taken place. Fifty years on and still no grass would grow there.

I hear the same story when I visit the site. The following afternoon
around a dozen students gather around my table at the university cafeteria. I've brought along the catalogue of the major Rothko retrospective at the Tate Gallery and turn the pages slowly while the students
look over my shoulder. 'Incredible.' 'Magical.' 'A genius.' These are
their reactions. The catalogue's final pages are devoted to the grey-
and-black paintings from the late 1960s. 'That was Daugavpils under
communism,' one of the students says.

For today's students in Daugavpils, Mark Rothko is 'the greatest
painter Latvia has ever produced'. I can't help but smile, knowing that
Rothko himself never spoke of Latvia. The city of his childhood was
in Russia; he always spoke of his Russian past.

One of the students, a tall, slender girl, wants to know if Rothko
ever doubted his art. I nod. Yes, he had his doubts. He loved being
seen as a genius and treated as a genius, but there were many times
when he wondered whether his paintings were nothing more than
coloured facades: beautiful, decorative, and devoid of any human or
spiritual nourishment. Those paintings, he sometimes thought, were

like folding screens, behind which he hid his selfhood, his own history, his tragedy. 'That's exactly why they appeal to me,' the girl nods. 'The presumptive, invisible ... When you come from this country, you have a lot to hide.'

In 1963, over lunch in New York, art dealer Frank Lloyd asked Willem de Kooning and Mark Rothko what he could do for them.

The painters looked at each other and laughed. Could they ask the art dealer for *anything*? Yes, anything.

De Kooning: 'Okay, stop people from copying me.'

Lloyd nodded. He would take care of it.

And Rothko said, 'Will you give me a one-man show in Dvinsk?' That was his deepest wish.

12

Tabula Rasa

IN SEARCH OF ARVO PÄRT

Estonia, December 2009

I am standing on the square in Rakvere where Arvo Pärt used to ride round and round on his bicycle. In winter, the weeks before Christmas. It must have been 1947. Arvo was twelve, and not an evening went by when he wasn't glued to the radio. The Finnish station was his favourite; it came through loud and clear in Estonia's northern reaches, with barely a hiss or a crackle. Helsinki and the free world being less than seventy kilometres away as the crow flies was among the absurdities of a childhood in communist Estonia.

Radio Finland offered this lanky kid more listening pleasure than the Estonian or Russian stations, which bristled with Soviet propaganda. Arvo loved music of all kinds, and Finnish radio served up everything from jazz, swing, tango, and Glenn Miller to Bach, Mozart, Grieg, and, of course, Sibelius. In 1947, tuning in to a Western radio station was strictly off limits for all Estonians. Even sending a letter from Estonia to Helsinki or Stockholm was punishable by deportation to Siberia. Arvo's listening habits were not an act of protest; he was too young for that. He was simply in search of music he did not already know, especially symphonic music.

A symphony orchestra sounded tinny on his Soviet-made radio. For wider, wilder soundscapes, he had to venture outside. Loudspeakers hung from the lampposts on Turu plats, the town square. Most of the time, they blared speeches by party leaders or socialist marching songs, but in the dark weeks around Christmas, there was scope for something more festive, and with any luck Rimsky-Korsakov's *Sheherazade* or Tchaikovsky's *Pathétique*, *Little Russian*, or *Winter Daydreams* might lighten the sinister mood.

Rakvere was a hard-grafting town where most people earned a living in the meat-processing industry. In the 1940s and 1950s, there wasn't much entertainment on offer. Nor today, for that matter. There's a castle, a fortress with foundations that date back to 1253. In summer, this ruin serves as the backdrop for theatre performances, but in the off-season it's the province of schoolchildren being shown around against their will. The dramatic arts used to liven things up; for decades, Rakvere was the smallest town in Estonia — in all of the Soviet Union, in fact — to have its own professional theatre company. Those days appear to have gone; the town is still home to a huge theatre, but not a single performance is scheduled for December. The next show, in five weeks' time, is by a local band making a bid to reach the national final of the Eurovision Song Contest.

Looking down from the castle, an army of Soviet housing blocks seems to be advancing on the church. The blocks, practically identical and aligned in rows of four, fill the town centre. Workaday Soviet planning has edged the Lutheran Church of the Trinity onto the periphery.

The first Church of the Trinity was destroyed during the Livonian War (1558–1582). It was rebuilt, only to be burned down twice during the Great Northern War (1700–1721), a conflict in which the Swedes initially had the upper hand but were eventually defeated by the Russians. In 1852, the building took on its present form: white with a red roof and a slender red tower.

In the mid-eighteenth century, the citizens of Rakvere, then called Wesenberg, took up arms to oppose Russian annexation. All of the town's wooden houses went up in flames. The rebellion inspired novelist Jaan Kross to write his *Rakvere romaan*, which in most foreign editions was given a double title, in English *The Women of Wesenberg or the Citizens' Revolt*. Mention Rakvere to an Estonian and they will probably think of Kross's novel. Either that or sausages. The meat-processing plant still occupies the northern part of town, and its smells drift down to the southernmost streets.

The buildings on Turu plats were badly damaged during World War II. When Estonia gained its independence in 1991, the cheerless replacements from the Soviet era made way for sleek black blocks with a decidedly Western touch but just as little architectural imagination. They house branches of Nordea Bank and Svedbank, along with a bookshop, a travel agency, a pharmacy, a chocolate shop, and a bar-restaurant. The travel agency attracts the most customers, with its sunny posters for cheap holidays in Turkey.

Though the cold here cuts to the bone at this time of year, it's the darkness you really long to escape. Try as I might, I cannot get used to the fact that daylight doesn't appear until 10.30 am and dusk sets in at 2.30 pm. My biological clock has lost the plot, and I find myself craving a hot meal at four in the afternoon.

Pangahoone, the most striking structure on Turu plats, survived both the Nazis and the Soviets. Built to house a bank, it was completed in 1933. White walls soften its austere lines. Only two of the square's tsarist-era wooden houses have been preserved. One is on the verge of collapse; its smaller, sprightlier companion is now home to the seven-room Art Hotel, where I am staying. Every other day, the town's geriatric notables turn up in the dining room, take their places at a long, oval table, and lunch together without exchanging a word.

The centre of Turu plats is empty, as it must have been in 1947. No fountains, no birches or oaks, no illuminated signs: empty, completely empty. The place must have been crying out for music in those winter months when Arvo cycled round and round. He had lost his heart to the symphonies he heard and was determined not to miss a note. He could have stood and listened, but the biting cold would soon have got the better of him, here, so close to the Baltic coast. Cycling kept him warm.

The temperature is fourteen below zero. A spot by Svedbank offers me some respite from the wind. I stand there and picture him pedalling, fast or slow, depending on the tempo. It could be the opening of a Soviet coming-of-age drama, shot in black and white. A strange anomaly in the gloom, this lanky kid enraptured by a symphony. I can almost see the puffs of breath escaping from his nose and mouth, his legs working harder where the square slopes gently upwards, like the foot of a hill.

In later years, Pärt would dismiss this vision of the boy on the bike as apocryphal, or at least greatly exaggerated. But in Rakvere, they still like to tell it, to make the world-famous composer of spiritual music a little more human. Once, he was just a boy rattling around Turu plats on an old black bicycle, mastering orchestral melodies simply by cycling round and round.

Perhaps he biked over to the square to escape his home and his stepfather. Pärt has always been reticent about his childhood. Are clues to be found in *Symphony No. 2*, in which the squeaking and jangling of toys swell to a hellish roar? The final movement echoes the melody of *Sweet Dreams*, one of Tchaikovsky's piano pieces for children. But in Pärt's work, those dreams are preceded by the dark beating of timpani, the lovely tune blown apart by a shrill outburst from the orchestra.

He must have been an unusual kid. His mother had managed to get hold of an old Russian piano. The middle keys were done for; only the deepest tones and highest registers produced a decent sound — not a keyboard that invited the beginner to pick out *Für Elise*. Instead, Arvo indulged in improvisations, avoiding the faltering middle keys and experimenting with his own tunes, shifting from light and high to dark and deep. The dilapidated piano not only forced him to improvise but also steered him towards minimalist music.

Later, as a composer, he would continue to make the most of limited resources. One of his best-known works consists of one sustained low octave on the piano and a number of recurring, rarefied notes. He called it *Für Alina*.

Arvo Pärt was born on 11 September 1935 in Paide, a small town seventy kilometres south-east of Tallinn. His parents split up when he was three years old, and he moved with his mother to Rakvere, where one Estonia ends and another begins. The north-east holds no trace of the verdant western, central, and southern woodlands; nothing here recalls the friendly provincial towns of Paide, Pärnu, or Tartu. Shale oil is mined in the border region with Russia. To extract the schist, kilometres of tunnels have to be drilled through solid stone.

One town along from Rakvere, in Kohtla-Järve, you can visit one of these mines and its sixty kilometres of tunnels. The Kohtla mine was opened in 1937 and closed in 2001. Former miners now act as guides, and without exception they are Russian. In the 1940s and 1950s, they were shipped in by the thousand from elsewhere in the Soviet Union and housed in dormitory towns. The blackened blocks of flats still stand today, in a desolate landscape of puddles, mud, and car wrecks. Most of these Russians are now unemployed. Nothing could tempt them back to Russia, where the standard of living is far lower, but nor do they belong in Estonia, not even on paper. To obtain Estonian citizenship, they are required to pass an exam that tests their knowledge of the Estonian language, culture, and law. They do not speak Estonian, and a question on the exact proportions of the Estonian flag is sure to stump them. Needless to say, the vast majority of 'true Estonians' couldn't give you the answer either. None of the Russians would even consider taking the exam. They have gradually grown accustomed to the humiliations that came with independence, but refuse to submit to them voluntarily.

Estonia is home to roughly one million Estonians, a quarter of a million Russians, and 50,000 Ukrainians. Almost a third of the population is officially stateless, and their voting rights are severely restricted. For the former miners, factory workers, engineers, doctors, and soldiers among this group, this is barely palatable. Most of them live in the area between Tallinn and Narva, a border town where Russian speakers make up 96 per cent of the population. Many eke out a living doing odd jobs. The men drink, the women go to church. The only buildings that have been refurbished bear an onion-shaped dome and a Byzantine cross.

Russians have become Estonia's second-class citizens. Anyone who suggests to an Estonian that this is unfair will be given short shrift. In 1941 and 1949, tens of thousands of Estonians were deported to Siberia, among them almost all of the country's scholars, teachers, professors, writers, journalists, Lutheran pastors, judges, and lawyers. Only a few hundred ever made it back to Estonia. In the 1950s, the council of ministers of the Estonian Soviet Socialist Republic consisted of seventeen Russians and nine Estonians, most of whom had lived elsewhere in the Soviet Union for more than twenty years. To ensure sufficient labour for Estonian heavy industry, 200,000 Russians were drafted in between 1945 and 1953, and a further 300,000 between 1960 and 1989. Children were taught in Russian at primary and secondary schools; academic dissertations had to be written in Russian. At the University of Tartu, most degree courses did not go beyond two years; to complete their studies, students had to head for Moscow or Leningrad. In government departments, municipal offices, and the civil service, Russian became the only permissible language. It was the only language heard on buses and trams, not spoken softly but with an air of triumphalism. In 1983, over 80 per cent of television programs were in Russian. Estonians were not permitted to serve in the armed forces; all troops stationed in Estonia were Russian. Some

Estonians refer to this as 'cultural genocide', others as the 'beheading' of the Estonian-speaking population.

'We had what we had,' Arvo Pärt soberly observed as he recalled his youth. 'My parents and professors told me that the time before the Soviets was quite different. We listened wide-eyed, open-eared, but for us it was nothing.'

He was barely able to conceive of a time before the Soviets.

Does a landscape or an environment define music? It's hard to imagine Schubert without mountain streams, Sibelius without the endless Finnish forests, Saint-Saëns without Paris in all its worldly splendour. Yet Vienna inspired Haydn and Beethoven and, a century later, Strauss senior and junior, Mahler, Schönberg, Webern, and Berg. At most, you could say they each highlighted a particular aspect of the city: their differences are more striking than their similarities. Yet driving through north-eastern Estonia, it's hard to resist making a connection between Pärt's stark, sombre music and the gloom of the surroundings.

Aged ten, Arvo began attending Rakvere music school. It was there that he learned to play piano, often performing as an accompanist at school concerts. He played oboe in the school orchestra, sang bass in the school choir, and drummed in the school band, which performed in the town's only dance hall. An ordinary childhood, not boring exactly, but thrills were few and far between. Having a stepfather instead of a father was anything but exceptional in Soviet times. The church, the traditional defender of family values, had lost its hold on the populace. For Soviet citizens, both marriage and divorce were quick and easy: twenty minutes at the town hall and that was that.

I venture into the music school, a modern building just behind Turu plats. The lady behind the counter is so startled when I speak to her in English that she and her slippers beat a hasty retreat. A moment later she returns with director Rita Mets, a sturdy woman with an immensely capable air and loosely curled, mid-length blonde hair. She looks at me, eyes bright with expectation, and we shake hands. When I tell her I'm from Amsterdam and on the trail of significant places in the life of Arvo Pärt, she raises her hands to the ceiling and exclaims, 'What an honour!' I follow her into the largest of the piano studios, where she introduces me to artistic director Toivo Peäske, a distinguished piano teacher in his sixties who sports a grey goatee. He taps the grand piano — the make is 'Estonia' — and says, 'This is *not* what Pärt learned on. Back then, the school only had old Petrof pianos.' I ask his permission, run my fingers over the keys, and hear a warm, full, slightly free-floating tone. 'The one good thing Stalin did for us,' Toivo smiles.

Estonia, I learn, was home to a host of piano workshops in the nineteenth century, run by Baltic Germans who had learned the trade in Germany. In 1893, they were merged into a single manufacturer — Estonia — which only made upright pianos. In 1950, by way of exception, the factory produced a grand piano, which was given to Stalin as a gift. The dictator was so pleased with it, he decreed that from then on Estonia would produce grand pianos.

'That's how it was in those days.' Toivo shakes his head, as if he can't quite believe that the vagaries of the Soviet system are dead and gone. In any case, Estonia the piano company still exists, having been privatised immediately after the restoration of independence in 1991. The firm produces around 400 grand pianos a year. Four of them have found a home at Rakvere's music school, alongside a dozen Estonia upright pianos. Rita shows me every classroom in the school, each one freshly painted in pear-drop colours. 'Thank you, Brussels!' she beams. 'Thank you, European Union!' With equal pride, she shows me the school's most expensive instrument, a xylophone. 'A gift from Arvo Pärt!'

Four hours later, I have been introduced to the full complement of teachers, a staff of about twenty — not much for a school with 200 students. The next morning, I return to pore over the old school registers. Among the 1953 keyboard graduates, I find the name Arvo Pärt among those of Yevgenia Bogdanova, Leida Lullu, Virve Krusenberg, Vaike Toming, and Heljo Jõe. Of Pärt's contemporaries, only Yevgenia went on to have a musical career of any note: as an accompanist of ballet rehearsals and founder of Tallinn Street Ballet amid the euphoria of 1991. 'Street' rather than 'state' ballet: a nice touch.

The list of teachers shows that Pärt stayed on at the music school for another year to teach the youngest pupils. It was his first paid job.

Jaan Pakk, Arvo Pärt's first piano teacher, and director of the music
school in Rakvere.

In 1954, he said goodbye to Rakvere and to his piano teacher Jaan
Pakk.

In the school's concert hall, I spend a while gazing at the framed
photograph of Jaan Pakk. A man with a broad face, white hair combed
back off his high forehead, and real kindness in his eyes. Someone I
would have loved to have as my piano teacher, a man you would do
your best never to disappoint simply because he was so incredibly
nice. Pakk founded the music school in Rakvere immediately after
World War II and served as its director from 1945 to 1963. His portrait hangs alongside Pärt's, the only two pictures in the hall. 'For Pärt,
Pakk was a father,' explains Toivo. 'He gave every student confidence
in themselves.'

Arvo started composing at the age of fourteen. At seventeen, he entered a competition for young composers for the first time. His piano piece *Meloodia* did not win a prize, due to its 'lack of any overtly Estonian roots or influence'. It leaned noticeably towards Rachmaninoff and, Pärt would later recall, 'was not personal music'. However, Rachmaninoff continued to be an influence.

He also performed *Meloodia* at a school concert. 'Of course, that was at the old music school at Pikk tänav 59,' says Rita. We walk there together, past grand homes where Polish, Russian, Swedish, and Baltic German merchants lived in the nineteenth century. Famous actors and actresses lived there too: the imposing grey-white structure of Rakvere's theatre stands at the head of the street.

Pikk means 'long' in Estonian, and Pikk tänav goes on for miles. Beyond the mill, the houses become smaller and stand further apart, wooden houses painted mustard yellow or light green. It's easy to imagine that I'm out for a stroll in the Russian countryside. 'That makes all kinds of sense,' Rita says. 'We're only sixty kilometres from Lake Peipsi, and on the other side is Mikhailovskoye, Alexander Pushkin's parental estate and place of exile. Only logical that there's a distinctly Russian feel to the place.'

The music school has been turned into an attractive office, for which a tenant has yet to be found. 'We could easily have stayed here,' Rita observes, 'but commissioning a whole new building was cheaper than restoration, so that's what we did. On the plus side, we're right in the heart of town, but further removed from its history.'

On the way back, she points out a tumbledown mansion. 'It used to be the clubhouse of the volunteer fire brigade. In a densely forested country like Estonia, the fire brigade is an institution. The clubhouse was a kind of community centre. It even had a concert hall and was the town's main music venue from the 1920s and into the 1940s. People came to hear Beethoven but also Rudolf Tobias, Mart Saar, Heino Eller, Adolf Vedro, Eduard Oja, composers unknown outside Estonia but who made remarkably good music and laid the foundations for Estonia's immense musical culture.'

Immense? A bit of an exaggeration?

That evening, I am invited to attend the music school's Christmas concert. Two former students, Annalisa Pillak, mezzo-soprano, and Jaanika Rand-Sirp, piano, perform songs by Brahms and Mahler. All perfectly lovely, but my ears prick up when the language becomes

Rakvere's former music school at Pikk tänav 59.

Estonian, and I listen to Ester Mägi's boisterous, sometimes spoken and sometimes sung *Kolm setu muinasjutulaulu*.

'A young composer?' I ask Rita afterwards.

'Not so young these days.'

The twinkle in her eyes tells me I've got the wrong end of the stick. Later that evening, I learn that Ester Mägi was born in 1922, is alive and well, and hopes to celebrate her eighty-eighth birthday in a few weeks. She has phenomenal choral works to her name, several of the music teachers assure me, along with atmospheric miniatures for piano inspired by Lapland melodies.

In 1954, Arvo Pärt continued his studies at the Music Middle School in Tallinn. He was called up for military service and played oboe and drums in a military band for two years. Barracks life was tough on him. He came down with a kidney ailment that caused him pain and insomnia for ten years, an experience that may have helped him as a composer, he later reflected. In 1957, he was admitted to the Tallinn Conservatory of Music.

I take the express bus from Rakvere to Tallinn. Pärt would have taken the train. As a student, he could also have headed in the opposite

The street in Rakvere that Arvo Pärt walked almost daily on his way to
the music school. Wooden houses, a taste of the Russian countryside.

direction: Rakvere is the first stop on the Tallinn–Moscow Express.
In 1951, Ester Mägi chose to pursue her musical studies in Moscow,
but by 1957 hatred of all things Russian had grown so fierce that Pärt
would have chosen Tallinn over the Russian capital any day of the
week.

Taking the bus is something of a necessity. Modern Estonians shun
the railways, associating trains with the stink and drabness of Soviet
times. Only one train a day now runs between Rakvere and Tallinn.
Express buses depart every two hours.

Snow fell steadily overnight. For the first fifty kilometres, I dream
with my eyes open as a Christmas-card forest glides past. White-
trimmed birch, pine, and oak radiate a sculptural calm. Snow muffles
every sound. The sun pokes through the haze of clouds, so low I can
almost look it straight in the eye. It keeps us company for ten minutes
or so, then disappears for what might easily be ten days. Every passenger gazes out the window. No one speaks, no one is on their phone:
this is a landscape that demands contemplation. In my mind, I hear
Pärt's *Pilgrim Song*.

The bus stops twice: once at a hamlet consisting of a run-down

Lutheran church and three houses, and once to pick up four cross-country skiers shivering on the hard shoulder. They bring a blast of freezing air onto the bus with them but beam merrily at each other, grateful there's still room on board.

The road widens to a four-lane dual carriageway but remains deserted. After another fifty kilometres, the forests give way to railway lines and shunting yards. Diesel locomotives pull pitch-black tankers of Russian oil to the power plant. The high-rise flats of Lasnamäe are testimony to the immense misery that plunged the Soviet Socialist Republic of Estonia into permanent lethargy towards the end. Built between 1984 and 1986, Lasnamäe became a kind of suburb of Leningrad; workers freshly imported from Russia moved into three-room flats in twenty-storey towers. After independence, Lasnamäe remained a gloomy Russian enclave. To quote an Estonian pop song from the 1990s, the place left you with empty eyes.

Passing this place, it is hard to believe that Tallinn can lay claim to a well-preserved medieval Old Town complete with city walls, and wide avenues lined with imposing buildings constructed between 1890 and 1910: the National Opera, the Estonia Concert Hall, the Estonian and Russian theatres.

On arrival at the bus station, I take a taxi to the Von Stackelberg Hotel, situated on one of those avenues. Recently opened in a ren-ovated townhouse commissioned in 1874 by Baltic German baron Theophil von Stackelberg, it still smells of paint and newly fitted carpets. It's only a short walk to the music conservatory, or at least the building where Pärt completed his studies. The conservatory itself has long since relocated to the suburbs. In Pärt's time, it stood next to the Russian Theatre, overlooking Freedom Square.

Composing came easily to young Arvo. 'He just seemed to shake his sleeve and the notes would fall out,' recalled fellow student Avo Hirvesoo.

Pärt was also fortunate with his composition teacher, whose advanced age proved to be a distinct benefit. Heino Eller was getting on for seventy when he started teaching Pärt and had lived through the glory days of the Leningrad Conservatory. As Pärt later reflected, his teacher brought new standards to small Estonia thanks to his training in St Petersburg with its centuries-old musical tradition. As a violinist, Eller had studied under Leopold Auer, who taught Jascha Heifetz during the same period. In instrumentation and counter-point, he had been moulded by Alexander Glazunov, who taught composition to both Sergei Prokofiev and Dmitri Shostakovich. The young Prokofiev detested Glazunov (who always feared for his hear-ing when listening to Prokofiev's deafening orchestral works), while the young Shostakovich admired his teacher's exceptional erudition. Glazunov was familiar with the work of the great contrapuntists of the Dutch and Italian schools, and had a fondness for Josquin des Prez, Jacob Obrecht, Johannes Ockeghem, Orlando di Lasso, Giovanni da Palestrina, and Andrea Gabrieli, the very composers with whom Arvo Pärt later felt a kinship.

Back in Estonia, Eller developed into a sensitive, accomplished violinist and chamber musician, a composer who laid the founda-tions for twentieth-century Estonian music, and a pedagogue who devoted equal attention to the oldest and most modern music. Eller's exceptional qualities as a teacher may have been intimately connected with the many setbacks he suffered. During the first year of his violin studies in St Petersburg, he injured his arm so severely that he had to abandon his musical career. He went on to study law, a course he completed five years later, in 1912. In World War I, he served as a soldier in the army of Nicholas II. When the war was over, he tentatively resumed studying the violin, finally graduating from the conservatory in 1920, at the age of thirty-three.

Eller taught violin at the music school in the university city of Tartu. This was followed in 1940 by an appointment to the prestigious post of professor of composition at the Tallinn Conservatory, but again fate stepped in: shortly after the German occupation, his wife, Anna, was arrested and deported. Anna Kremer, a pianist Eller had met at the Leningrad Conservatory, died in a German concentration camp in 1942. In 1942 and 1943, the darkest years of his life, Eller composed his *Lyrical Suite*, which originally consisted of ten pieces for piano. In the version for string orchestra, Eller pared back the suite to six reveries with a rigorous form that means their profound sadness never tips into sentimentality. So much music is controlled grief; the fact that Eller, a violinist, composed four major piano sonatas and 180 more modest works for piano has everything to do with his Jewish wife's tragic and violent death.

Arvo Pärt at the home of his teacher Heino Eller. Tallinn, 1960.

Heino Eller taught no fewer than fifty composers, at least ten of whom made a name for themselves at home and abroad. His last student was Lepo Sumera, who would go on to play a prominent role in the struggle for independence and become culture minister in the transitional government from 1988 to 1992. A composer as culture minister — that tells you something profound about Estonia. Alongside Pärt, Eduard Tubin, and Erkki-Sven Tüür, Sumera was among Eller's most gifted students.

Musicians in Tallinn tell me Eller was an amiable man: experienced, wise, engaged, encouraging. Although he himself was a product of the late Romantic school, he raised no objections when Pärt began to struggle through the textbooks of Herbert Eimert and Ernst Krenek in his efforts to master the twelve-tone technique: each student had to make their own way.

'I find it difficult to say what impressed me more,' Pärt wrote about his teacher in 1999, 'his manner of teaching or his personal charisma.' He saw Eller as a generous and noble soul. 'He gave me a path, but this path was very broad. He didn't push in any direction, he supported you even if what you wrote wasn't exactly like his own credo. He was very human, and it was a vivid apprenticeship. There is only one central composition school in Estonia, and it's Eller's school.'

At the Pika Jala Muusikaäri, an olde-worlde shop near the city gate on Nunne that sells everything from instruments to sheet music and CDs, I ask about Eller's work. The saleswoman doesn't understand me at first — I pronounce his name 'Eller' instead of 'El-yer' — but once the penny drops, she plucks two CDs and a hefty photo book from the shelves and invites me to take a seat on the only chair by the cash register. Her command of both English and German is limited, but with a little of both and the help of the pictures in the book, she succeeds in convincing me that Eller is to Estonia what Sibelius is to Finland. Eller's *Kodumaine viis* (Homeland Song) has taken on the same symbolic significance for Estonians as *Finlandia* for the Finns. Leafing through the pages, I begin to realise the full extent of the isolation Estonia suffered throughout the twentieth century. Not one of the faces pictured looks familiar to me. I know none of the musicians, composers, politicians, patrons, or stars of the opera. To begin with, I don't even recognise Arvo Pärt in the 1960 photo taken at Heino Eller's home: beardless and with his hair slicked back, his young features look decidedly Slavic.

For the remainder of the afternoon, we listen to music by Eller, music as Estonian as the local dessert *tuuliku kama* (a mix of oatmeal porridge and blueberries), yet always extending across borders: north to Sibelius and Grieg, east to Tchaikovsky and Glazunov. Music that forms a prelude to Pärt's compositions in its tranquillity and splendour. 'I have come across a saying by Eller,' Pärt wrote in the liner notes to one of the CDs, 'one that I never heard him utter while he was teaching: "It is more difficult to find a single right note than to put a whole mass of them down on paper." Although he never talked about it, he obviously succeeded in anchoring the painful search for the one "right note" in my soul.'

In the final years of his studies, in 1962 and 1963, Pärt found a job with Estonian radio, working as a producer and sound engineer, or *Tonmeister* to use that most satisfying of German job titles. The former radio freak could not have wished for a better gig.

Arvo's love for the recording process would eventually bring him into contact with Manfred Eicher, the founder of ECM Records in Munich. Eicher, a former double-bass player with the Berliner Philharmoniker who liked to jam with jazz musicians in his spare time, was painstaking about his recordings. ECM — short for Edition of Contemporary Music — released Keith Jarrett's famous *Köln Concert* and sold three million copies. The label's second major success came in 1977 with Arvo Pärt's *Tabula Rasa*. The CD opens with the composition *Fratres* for piano and violin, and Eicher had the inspired idea of bringing in classically trained violinist Gidon Kremer to perform the piece with jazz pianist Keith Jarrett. It became Pärt's international breakthrough.

The road that led to *Tabula Rasa* was long, and paved with a succession of defeats, accusations, persecutions, and bans. In his earliest compositions, Pärt used the twelve-tone technique, an approach that rankled with the Soviet authorities almost instantly. *Nekrolog*, an orchestral work dedicated to the victims of fascism, premiered in Moscow in 1961. For the General Secretary of the Union of Soviet Composers, it possessed exactly the same characteristics as the evil against which it was directed: it expressed a state of fear, terror, despair, and despondency. That same official, Tichon Khrennikov, had already slated the music of Prokofiev and Shostakovich in 1948. At least Pärt was in good company.

The attack did nothing to alter Pärt's course. His *Symphony No. 1* and *Symphony No. 2* were every bit as forbidding and uncompromising, with a stirring middle movement in *No. 1* to rival the powerful, rhythmic passages from Shostakovich's war symphonies. Had he continued down that path, Pärt would still have become a composer of note; in that second movement of *Symphony No. 1*, he coaxes a

Arvo Pärt in Estonia.

whole range of subtleties, vulgarities, and ecstasies from the orchestra, bringing both strings and brass to an explosion. But after *Symphony No. 2* (1966), he hesitated. In *Pro et contra*, a work for cello and orchestra written at the request of Mstislav Rostropovich, he leans towards atonality one moment and Baroque concerto grosso the next. The third movement is a thrilling piece of music, with a tight rhythm and a climactic burst of triumphant chords that come straight from Handel. And still the docile members of the Composers' Union could hear nothing but chaos. Support or commissions from official quarters would clearly not be forthcoming.

Writing music for film and theatre enabled him to scrape a living. This was a route well travelled by Soviet composers: Shostakovich, Prokofiev, and Alfred Schnittke had taken it before him. Pärt provided music for some fifty films, work he later dismissed as conveyor-belt stuff. He fell into a spiritual and professional crisis, went in search of other paths, and began to study Gregorian music and the rise of polyphony in the Renaissance.

For five years, he filled sheet after sheet with notes without getting anywhere. He filled entire books, mechanically, day after day, like a monk copying texts. At times, he would picture a landscape and devise a melodic line that reflected its contours. Or he would try to weave melodies from the literature he read — Dante, for instance, or medieval Georgian poet Shota Rustaveli. These exercises were a search for his own tone, his own sound, his own style of notation, an approach that, slowly but surely, became second nature to him. During this long period of self-examination and purification, he shut himself off from other music. He avoided concerts, even steering clear of the scant performances of his own works. It was as if he were searching for a musical rebirth, groping towards the blankness of a child in the cradle, an unwritten page, a slate wiped clean, a tabula rasa. During that time, he developed an acute sensitivity to sounds, all kinds of sounds, and eventually gravitated towards bells.

Pärt was idiosyncratic and utterly unique in his choices. In 1968, he joined the Russian Orthodox Church, and composed *Credo* that same year. Another remarkable decision, given that Pärt was not a member of Estonia's Russian minority. As an Estonian, he had been baptised in the Lutheran faith. *Credo*, a work for piano, mixed choir, and orchestra, was an outright attack on the communist system. 'I believe in Jesus Christ,' the choir sings by way of introduction. And then follows the text of Matthew 5, verses 38 and 39: 'You have heard it said: "An eye for an eye and a tooth for a tooth." But I say unto you: do not resist evil.' After which the choir sings the creed in conclusion: 'I believe.'

Pärt could not have been clearer. He based the melody on the *Prelude in C* from Book One of Bach's *The Well-Tempered Clavier*, drawing on a host of other influences: serial, Gregorian, late-Romantic, cacophonic, and yes, even free jazz and pop percussion. *Credo* became an ecstatic piece that sets the listener's skin tingling, from the choir's first outburst to the final hushed note; it is short — thirteen minutes at the first performance, fifteen at the later one — powerful, and compelling, even for non-believers.

The Soviet authorities were horrified. How could such a work have escaped the vigilance of the censors? The chief censor, a party diehard, had been out of office when *Credo* landed on his desk, and despite a title designed to ring Soviet alarm bells, his deputies had paid it no heed. The premiere was part of a program that included Igor Stravinsky's *Symphony of Psalms*, which the authorities took as a double provocation.

Krista Varik was in the audience on 16 November 1968. The saleswoman at the music shop on Nunne put me in touch with her. In Tallinn's Concert Hall, Krista points out where she was sitting: twenty-second row, third seat on the right. The venue is not unlike Amsterdam's Concertgebouw before its renovation, a somewhat stuffy philharmonic hall from the late nineteenth century. The Sunday afternoon concert is over and the auditorium is all but empty, quiet but for a faint murmur from the cloakroom. I ask Krista to take the seat she sat in that night. She sits down, closes her eyes, and the memories come.

'Like all concerts in the city, then and now, it began at seven in the evening. There was no interval. The program began with Stravinsky's *Symphony of Psalms*, which already heightened the mood. Then came the first strains of *Credo*. Accompanied by the orchestra, the choir sang "Cre ... do ..." in hushed tones. This went on for twenty or thirty seconds, quiet as can be. Then came the eruption. A thousand decibels. The choir roared. "Credo in Jesum Christum". From that moment on, nothing in Tallinn was quite the same.

'I would say the average age in the room was twenty-two. Not a day older. When the choir burst out, something incredible happened. We looked at each other, some of us with hands clasped to our mouths, like children, both startled and excited. We stayed in our seats, yet we knew in an instant that this was the end of communism and materialism, a return to our own identity. The middle section of *Credo* was subdued, with that beautiful Bach motif on the piano. Then an unimaginable cacophony erupted. Honestly, it was deafening ... so loud, chaotic, insane. Everyone rose to their feet. It was impossible to stay seated, as if we had finally been given a way to vent our pent-up anger after all those years.

'After the shrieking trumpets and the choir chanting, almost shouting, "ha ... ha ... ha ... ha," a few thin notes on the piano brought calm. Then came that magnificent "But I say unto you: do not resist evil. I believe." We grabbed each other's hands, squeezed each other's hands. Everyone started rocking, crying. We had to wait another twenty-three years for our liberation, but that moment signalled the start of our Singing Revolution. And Arvo Pärt was our saviour. I say that without any exaggeration. That's how it was.'

The conductor that evening, Neeme Järvi, also remembers the premiere of *Credo* as a colossal historical event. 'Everything Pärt wrote was an event in Estonia, especially for young people. *Credo* outdid everything, the audience was delirious. But the next morning, we were in for a big scandal. It was not the music itself that caused problems, it was the ideology. It is, of course, a work with strong religious overtones.'

Pärt was called to account. What lay behind his composition? What were his political aims? The composer could answer in all honesty, 'None.' *Credo* said nothing more than that he had become religious, not out of protest but out of conviction. The authorities nevertheless concluded that Pärt had engaged in subversive activities, and *Credo* was added to the list of banned compositions. From their perspective, this was a wise move: 1968 was the year of the Prague Spring, a youthful protest movement that could only be contained by deploying 6,800 Warsaw Pact tanks. Unrest was simmering in the vassal states of the Soviet empire, coming to the boil. What had happened in Prague could easily spill over and onto the streets of Riga, Tallinn, Vilnius, Warsaw, or East Berlin. Any form of protest had to be nipped in the bud, including artistic, musical protest. A decade would pass before *Credo* was performed in Tallinn again.

After his interrogation, Pärt once again withdrew for a few years, devoting his energies to the study of medieval music. This came to fruition in the polyphonic structure of *Symphony No. 3*, which dates from 1971. He was only half-satisfied with the result. Following another retreat, Pärt radically changed direction. He started making music which he referred to as 'tintinnabular' (from *tintinnabuli*, Latin for 'small bells'), music with the resonance of bells ringing. This was sparse music, consisting of simple harmonies, triads, or a single note. 'I have discovered that it is enough when a single note is beautifully played,' he said of this type of music in 2005. 'This one note, or a silent beat, or a moment of silence, comforts me. I work with very few elements — with one voice, with two voices. I build with the most primitive materials — with the triad, with one specific tonality. The three notes of the triad are like bells.' It is a technique he applied in *Fratres, Summa, Cantus, Tabula Rasa*.

Most Estonian composers thought Pärt was courting madness during his years in retreat, but support came in the form of violinist Andres Mustonen, who had founded an early music ensemble, Hortus Musicus. Not only did Pärt regularly attend the group's rehearsals, but the musicians also performed his most recent works, and he discussed with Mustonen how and on which instruments they should be played. Hortus Musicus became his sounding board, or, as Pärt himself put it, 'a midwife for my new music'.

Founded in 1972, Hortus Musicus had a joint focus: playing music so new that the notes were still fresh on the page *and* work that predated Bach: early European polyphony *and* madrigals and dance suites from the Renaissance. These ten musicians, all from the Tallinn Conservatory of Music, donned medieval costume and performed in cellars beneath houses from the Hanseatic era. They moved into a house on a narrow street in Tallinn's Old Town, in the shadow of the medieval ramparts.

I visit the building, which is now full of old instruments: harpsichords, spinets, drums, and violas. Its walls are hung with prints of medieval Tallinn. Only then do I fully grasp how consciously Hortus Musicus sought to return to Estonia's primeval past, to its earliest beginnings, when the Danes were defeated at the Battle of Tallinn and the construction of the hill town by the Baltic began. In embracing this concept, Mustonen and the musicians of Hortus Musicus made an astute choice: without going up against the Soviet authorities directly, they could start writing a new history by harking back to the beginnings of the old one.

And then came a clean slate. When they first laid eyes on the score of *Tabula Rasa*, the musicians exclaimed, 'Where's the music?' Pärt's piece for two violins, prepared piano, and strings consists of just a few slow notes. The piano chimes like a bell. It took some getting used to. But as far back as 1977, the piece was performed in Bonn by Gidon Kremer, Tatjana Grindenko, Alfred Schnittke (yes, the composer), and the Lithuanian Chamber Orchestra, and ever since it has remained one of the most delightful works in modern music.

The same can be said of *Fratres*, *Summa*, and *Cantus*. Tranquil, spiritual, meditative music to some. Dull, esoteric murmurings to others. Profound and genuinely religious to the ears of admirers. Neo-medieval posturing, according to the naysayers.

One group has shown unbridled enthusiasm for Arvo Pärt: film directors. Dutch film critic Jan Pieter Ekker wondered how many films incorporated Pärt's music and came up with no fewer than fifty titles, not counting animation, feature-length documentaries, and docudramas. Just to be clear, this has nothing to do with the soundtracks Pärt had to compose to earn a living during the Soviet era, but focuses solely on the spiritual works from his post-*Credo* period. They can be found in American, British, and German productions, a host of French films, and others that span the globe from Mexico to Japan, taking in the Nordic countries and Israel along the way. These are films aimed at mainstream audiences (Paul Thomas Anderson's *There Will Be Blood*, Tom Tykwer's *Heaven*, Robert De Niro's *The Good Shepherd*, and Leos Carax's *Les Amants du Pont-Neuf*) and arthouse films (Andrei Zvyagintsev's *The Banishment*, François Ozon's *Le temps qui reste*, and Jean-Luc Godard's *Dans le noir du temps*). Looking down the list, you start to wonder if any interesting films at all have been made since 1995 without incorporating Pärt's music. *Für Alina*, *Cantus*, *Fratres*, and *Spiegel im Spiegel* are among the directors' absolute favourites, featuring in ten to twelve films each, but *Te Deum*, *Litany*, *Salve Regina*, *Annum per annum*, *Peace Upon You, Jerusalem*, and especially *Silouan's Song* are also well represented.

Not that Ekker is a fan of Pärt's music. Despite describing it as 'religious and hushed, minimalist and gentle, austere and hypnotic', he goes on to argue that it throws up a smokescreen. He calls Pärt's compositions 'avant-garde music for the millions' and 'one size fits all': infinitely deployable to add lustre to any contemplative, salutary, or tranquil scene, from soaring emotions to near-death experiences; ideal shorthand for intimacy, peace of mind, or a life out of balance.

Music that is 'simultaneously brimming with meaning and as empty as can be'. And which has now become as clichéd as 'underscoring a love scene with cloying strings'.

Having seen around thirty of the fifty films Ekker lists, I am left to conclude that Pärt's music hits the spot every time. It's a conclusion that Ekker himself ultimately reaches, albeit reluctantly: 'Yet somehow it works … and sounds nowhere near as cheap as those cloying strings.'

Ekker fails to mention that the works of John Adams and Philip Glass feature on just as many soundtracks, if not more. There's something about minimalist music in general that lends itself to evoking desires, expectations, and tensions. For decades, you could hardly watch a weighty TV documentary without being treated to a burst of Mahler. That doesn't make Mahler any less of a composer.

Pärt's music may be accessible, but it is far from simple. The thoughtfulness of his approach and the ingenuity of his compositions are evident from Paul Hillier's analysis of Pärt's scores. Hillier is the conductor of British vocal group Theatre of Voices and has worked with Pärt on many occasions. His recordings include *De Profundis*, for mixed choir, which Pärt wrote in 1980.

Hillier believes every conductor should embark on a rigorous study of the score before committing to the performance of a work. Taking this principle to heart, he ended up writing an entire book on Pärt, the lion's share of which consists of his meticulous readings of Pärt's scores. What do the notes tell us? Hillier's conclusion: they reveal a nigh-on mathematical approach, a dizzying variety of influences, enormous depth, and unimaginable subtlety. Hillier sees Pärt as one of that rare breed of composers who handle complex structures with apparent ease, an approach to rival that of Monteverdi, Mozart, or Satie.

Organist Christopher Bowers-Broadbent comes to the same conclusion. 'When I'm learning a new piece by Arvo, I often find myself thinking, "God, I need more notes." The simplest of music is the hardest to play, and with Arvo's music you need enormous poise. You simply cannot make a mistake.'

Is the music Arvo Pärt makes typically Estonian? When I put this question to musicologists and connoisseurs in Estonia, they nod vehemently at first. For them, Pärt has iconic status. His global fame coincided perfectly with the self-awareness and cultural momentum of the newly independent Baltic countries. They point out that Pärt's music is tonal, and that serialism never gained much traction in Estonia. Toivo Tulev, born in 1958, and Erkki-Sven Tüür, born in 1959, also write tonal music with drawn-out, elegiac motifs, very much in the same vein as Eller and Pärt. There is something readily recognisable in Estonian music. A young musicologist tells me with a chuckle, 'When you hear a sombre tune that you feel is way too slow, you can bet it's Estonian.'

Finger wagging earnestly, the same young musicologist tells me that Pärt's oeuvre is firmly rooted in the age-old traditions of Estonian song. Tartu, over 100 kilometres south-east of Tallinn, hosts a festival of song every five years, a tradition dating back to the nineteenth century. About 1,000 singers took part in the first festival in 1869, thirty times that number in 2009. The Singing Revolution continued to resound at the 1988 Tartu festival; the 300,000 Estonians who flocked to the event alternated patriotic songs with political slogans demanding independence and the end of Soviet dictatorship.

Another major event on Estonia's musical calendar is the Tallinn Choir Festival, held every four years. Hundreds of choirs participate. I don't know if there's any research to back me up, but I feel sure Estonia must lead the world in choir membership per capita, with Lithuania and Latvia a close second and third. The Chamber Choir of the Estonian Philharmonic, which Pärt often calls on to perform his work, is renowned the world over. Many a European opera house calls Estonia when they need a choir for crowd scenes.

'We don't know exactly why,' musicologist Vita Matiss tells me, 'but the combination of forest and sea air, and the months of dry cold must be exceptionally good for the throat and the vocal cords.' Jaak Johannsen, a bass in the Estonian National Male Choir, offers a more mundane theory: 'Military service has been abolished in Estonia. We only have a small professional army. Men use their vocal cords to assert their masculinity.' Could be, I suppose …

Choral works account for at least half of Pärt's oeuvre. He draws his inspiration as much from early Western European music as from the traditions of the Russian Orthodox Church. Pärt himself once remarked that his musical development is western and his spiritual development eastern. In that sense, he is a true Estonian: for centuries, his homeland was caught between eastern, Russian influences and western influences ranging from Germany and Denmark to Sweden and Finland. In terms of culture, religion, and the economy, the German influence was strongest. This shows in Pärt's music. He has written three collages on Bach: *Collage sur B-A-C-H*, *Wenn Bach Bienen gezüchtet hätte* (If Bach Had Been a Beekeeper), *Credo*, and a *St John Passion*. That said, he has also borrowed from Sibelius and Finnish traditional songs.

Pärt went his own way, delving into eight centuries of music and distilling spiritual elements that his contemporaries considered to be outdated or at odds with a modern, automated, individualistic society. He sensed that a new time was coming, one that would be as religious as the late Middle Ages.

On Sunday morning, I attend a service at the Alexander Nevsky Cathedral in Tallinn. It's cold inside. The patriarch, trembling and old as the hills, struggles to make himself heard. The cathedral is chock-full, not just with women, as I was used to in Russia, but men too. I am surrounded by the nouveau riche, the nouveau pauvre, and all other sections of the Russian community in the Estonian capital. The singing is so pure and on key that I assume it must be coming from a loudspeaker. Only then do I spot the choir in a niche above the entrance. A young priest with a long, tangled beard and fire in his eyes strides up to me and snatches the hat from my head. His fanaticism startles me. I know the Orthodox faith dictates that men should bare their heads and women cover theirs, but he could just as easily have pointed. He fixes me with a hostile stare. I turn on my heels and leave.

Alexander Nevsky Cathedral was built between 1894 and 1900 to crown the Russification that took place in the final decades of the nineteenth century. Not coincidentally, it was built directly opposite Toompea Castle, the seat of parliament, and a few hundred metres from Toomkirik, the city's largest Lutheran church. The name was also significant: Alexander Nevsky was the Russian hero who defeated the German knights in 1242. When independence dawned in 1919, there were those who wanted to place sticks of dynamite under the Alexander Nevsky Cathedral. The writer Friedebert Tuglas was among them: 'This egregious Russian samovar is crying out for an anarchist's bomb.' In the end, the plan foundered due to lack of funds.

Arvo Pärt unleashed a wave of spiritual music. In Estonia, the likes of Veljo Tormis, Galina Grigorjeva, and Toivo Tulev composed religious works. In Russia, Alfred Schnittke did the same. Italian Luigi Nono turned his back on politics and the Communist Party and drew inspiration from the early Russian mystics. English composer John Tavener converted to the Greek Orthodox faith. Americans Philip Glass and John Adams looked to India for spiritual nourishment. Dutchman Robert Zuidam, whose career as a composer began with punk rock, chose poems by sixteenth-century Spanish mystic John of the Cross for his *Canciones del alma*. In France, Olivier Messiaen completed his oratorio *La Transfiguration de Notre Seigneur Jésus-Christ* in 1969. In 1983, his opera *Saint-François d'Assise*, based on the life of Francis of Assisi, saw the light.

While the faithful abandoned their churches in droves and newspapers dropped the words 'Catholic' or 'Protestant' from their mastheads, it seemed that composers could not do without God. The same applied to poets, or at least those who had heard their language polluted by the deadening idiom of communism. Czesław Miłosz went on to learn Hebrew and Greek with the aim of reading the Bible in the original and translating it into Polish. As Gerard Rasch, an expert on Miłosz, observed, 'He experienced in modern, overly homogeneous Polish the lack of a style that could be called "high". A style that could express the higher, the sublime, that could carry biblical content, that preserved what should be preserved of older forms of Polish. Without a doubt, the realisation of this lack partly has to do with the degradation of language under communism.' Rasch argued that this resulted in a superior translation of the *Psalms*, *Job*, *The Gospel of Mark*, and John's *Book of Revelation*. Miłosz had long since renounced the Catholic faith when he started those translations. In the preface to his translation of *Job*, he likened his Bible translations to a cleansing ritual.

For Pärt, it was no different. Through spiritual music, he absolved himself from socialist realism and other communist influences. Yet it galls many an Estonian that Pärt turned so emphatically to the Russian Orthodox faith. Surely that was the religion of the oppressor? True, the Soviets had been fiercely atheistic and destroyed churches by the thousand, but those fifty years of Soviet domination in Estonia had been preceded by two centuries of Russian enslavement, and the faith Pärt espoused was the faith of the tsars. The Russians have always been the archetypal enemy, more so than the Danes, the Swedes, and even the Germans. For four or five centuries, the Russian threat was constantly looming and for over two and a half centuries they called the shots. For Estonians, Russia is an ongoing trauma.

There can be no doubting the sincerity of Pärt's conversion. In a kind of biblical parable, he once explained how he had arrived at that point. 'In the Soviet Union once, I spoke with a monk and asked him how, as a composer, one can improve oneself. He answered me by saying that he knew of no solution. I told him that I also wrote prayers, and set prayers and the texts of psalms to music, and that perhaps this would be of help to me as a composer. To this he said, "No, you are wrong. All the prayers have already been written. You don't need to write any more. Everything has been prepared. Now you have to prepare yourself."' In other words, he had to open himself up to the Bible's message.

Having become a believer, Pärt wrote dozens of choral works. In his instrumental works, he used *zvon*, or Russian bells. This too rankles with many an Estonian. A distinctive style of music for these bells was developed in the Russian Orthodox Church from the seventeenth to the late nineteenth century. The sound is profoundly Russian and something practically every Russian composer from Rimsky-Korsakov to Prokofiev incorporated into their work, most notably Rachmaninoff in his choral symphony *The Bells*. The bells are not tuned to a particular scale but simply ordered from higher to lower, each with its own tone. Nor do they follow fixed rhythmical patterns. Due to its religious associations, *zvon* fell out of favour under the Soviets, and in the 1930s and 1940s, thousands of bells were melted down to make cannon. But in the 1960s, the Soviet authorities fostered a love of folklore, and bells underwent something of a revival. Unwittingly, by seeking to emphasise the specific identities of the various peoples within the Soviet Union, the ideologues were playing with fire. For Pärt, it meant that a work like *Cantus*, based on chimes, was lauded by the Soviet authorities as Slavic and drawing on a long-standing folk tradition.

There were other influences too: Pärt's own teacher Heino Eller had been inspired by bells. In 1926, Eller composed the piano piece *Kellad* (The Bells). He was living near a church in Tartu at the time, and whenever he heard the bells, he was reminded of a friend who had died young. *Kellad* became a farewell song that, if you skip the turbulent middle section, could have been written by Pärt himself.

As long as Pärt took his inspiration from Bach, Estonians had no trouble following him: he was simply connecting with the long-established Lutheran tradition in the north of the Baltic region. But reconciling themselves to his Russian Orthodox and Slavic leanings is another matter. Not that they will openly admit this; Pärt, after all, remains the most famous artist Estonia has ever produced, more famous by far than writer Jaan Kross or those other eminent composers Lepo Sumera and Erkki-Sven Tüür. But a measure of hatred towards Russia still sits in the heart of every Estonian, and Pärt's eminence does nothing to extinguish the smouldering fires of revanchism. Writing music that drifts heavenward is one thing, but why does it have to drift in an easterly direction?

There is another way to view these tensions: Pärt's music shows the strength of Estonia's Russian connections to this day. Patriarch Alexy II, head of the Russian Orthodox Church from 1990 until his death in 2008, was born Aleksei Mikhailovich Ridiger in Tallinn. Both his father — a priest — and his mother belonged to the Russian minority. He studied at Leningrad Theological Seminary, returned to his hometown as a priest in 1950, rose to become bishop in Tallinn and metropolitan in Novgorod. His appointment as patriarch followed in 1990. As the first spiritual leader of the Orthodox Church in Russia following the collapse of the Soviet Union, he played a leading role in its revival. He was particularly successful under Vladimir Putin, lending a sacred glow to the president's regime. Alexy II brought back the gold leaf to the church domes.

The complexities of the Soviet regime are demonstrated by the fact that Leningrad Theological Seminary, where Aleksei Ridiger received his training, was also a bastion of the KGB. It was far from uncommon for clerics to act as informants for the security service. People confided in their priests, and those priests could only fulfil their pastoral duties if they occasionally operated hand-in-glove with the communist rulers. To defend one, you had to give ground on the other, Alexy II confessed after the collapse of the communist system: 'one' being faith, 'the other' integrity.

There was more to the Russian Orthodox Church than spirituality.

Pärt understood the need to distance himself from notions of power, notions to which the patriarchs were in no way immune. Politically, the focus of his opposition shifted from the Soviet authorities to the Russian oligarchy. In 2006 and 2007, he dedicated every performance of his music to journalist Anna Politkovskaya, the fiercest critic of the Russian political elite, who was murdered on 7 October 2006. Spiritually he may have belonged to the east, but in terms of social justice, he had no desire to be lumped in with Russia's new ruling class.

In 2009, he went one step further. On 10 January, the premiere of his *Symphony No. 4*, for strings, harp, and percussion, took place in Los Angeles. Pärt dedicated the work to oil tycoon and philanthropist Mikhail Khodorkovsky, who had recently been sentenced to eight years in prison, and to 'all those imprisoned without rights in Russia'. A slap in the face for Putin: Khodorkovsky was his sworn enemy.

Musically, Pärt continued to push further and further into Russia. In *Lamentate*, a forty-minute work for piano and orchestra that premiered in 2003, he tunes into Rachmaninoff, albeit in an entirely original way, with his own resources and sense of tonality. Even so, *Lamentate* fits squarely within the Russian musical tradition. The same goes for *Symphony No. 4*. It's a grand and challenging work that spans thirty-seven minutes, in which you can really hear how intensely he listened to Tchaikovsky's symphonies as a boy, cycling round and round on Rakvere square.

Pärt might counter that he has also composed *Arbos*, a piece in which different tempos (4:2:1) reflect the life cycle of a tree. The trunk growing from the roots, the branches from the trunk. Through this work, he connects with Germanic, Scandinavian, and Baltic forest mythology. Trees are practically sacred in Estonia, and *Arbos* is a sacred work.

In *Cantus* — to give it its full title, *Cantus in memoriam Benjamin Britten* — he draws on a different source altogether: the music of Benjamin Britten. Pärt had only come to fully appreciate Britten shortly before the English composer's death in 1976. Explaining the background to *Cantus*, Pärt wrote of the extraordinary purity he found in Britten's music, a purity he had only ever found in the ballads of Guillaume de Machaut.

As this array of influences demonstrates, Pärt has no desire to paint himself into a corner. Aware that his roots lie in a small country, he knows he must keep seeking inspiration beyond its borders to avoid atrophy. Pärt has a deep affinity with Estonia but little connection. After the scandal caused by *Credo*, the authorities made it almost impossible for him to work as a composer. He also ran into financial difficulties.

Pärt was anything but meek. A true dissident, he acquired a taste for provocation. In 1972, he caused another scandal, entering a competition organised by the Composers' Union with a work that was asking for trouble: a series of contrapuntal variations on the 'Internationale'. In a socialist republic, this was tantamount to sacrilege. The orchestral parts were not written out, and the work was never performed, but a copy of the score wound up on the desks of the party ideologues in Moscow. Once again, the machinery of intimidation sprang into motion. There were interrogations, threats, and a ban on travelling to Finland, where Pärt was due to present his instrumental works at a chamber music festival. Friends came to his aid and defended him in public, pointing out that Pärt was as precious to the Estonians as Shostakovich was to the Russians. This elicited a dry response from the party bosses: 'Shostakovich is not so precious to us.'

During the 1970s, the Soviet authorities were encouraging Jews to emigrate to Israel. In 1972, Pärt married for a second time. His wife Nora was Jewish. When he was targeted by a new measure — a ban on buying or selling his music — the couple decided to take advantage of the emigration scheme. On 18 January 1980, Arvo, Nora, and their two sons boarded a train to Vienna. From there, they were due to fly on to Israel. But two days later, they arrived in the Austrian capital to be greeted at the station by a representative of the music publisher Universal Edition and offered indefinite leave to remain. By the summer, the Pärt family were Austrian citizens.

The Pärts did not feel entirely at home in Vienna, and eighteen months later, they relocated to West Berlin. After the Wall came down, they continued to live there. When Estonia regained its independence, Pärt made regular trips to Tallinn for performances or recordings of his work. But the city stirred up too many bad memories for him to consider moving back.

Arvo Pärt shortly after leaving Estonia.

Pärt has become a European with the look of a Russian Old Believer. His bald head, full beard, and weary gaze echo Solzhenitsyn, another dissident who looked like he could have come straight from a Russian Orthodox monastery. Fashion seems to have passed the composer by completely; more often than not, a chunky-knit jumper and grey, baggy trousers are his outfit of choice. Though his beard has greyed, there is still an air of timelessness about him.

The last work Pärt composed while living in Estonia was *Spiegel im Spiegel.* If the music reflects his state of mind at the time, he must have been battle-weary: long, bowed notes on the violin, murmurings on the piano in a slow one-two-three tempo. A child could play it, though that child would have to be inconsolable.

Compared to *Spiegel im Spiegel*, Pärt's first work written in the West is bursting with optimism and zest for life. *Annum per annum* (Year by Year) is a solo work for organ that can fill a cathedral to its highest vaults. The piece was commissioned to celebrate the 900th anniversary of Speyer Cathedral. Though instrumental, the work adheres strictly to the liturgy of the Catholic mass: K(yrie), G(loria), C(redo), S(anctus), A(gnus Dei).

With *Annum per annum* and *Wallfahrtslied*, a breathtakingly beautiful pilgrim song for male choir and string orchestra composed in 1984, hopes were high: living in the free West, Pärt would at last realise his full potential. But perhaps this was too much to ask.

In the land of Bach, he set out to emulate the great master. His *St John Passion* — in full, *Passio Domini Nostri Jesu Christi secundum Joannem* — was completed in 1982 and begins as powerfully as *Annum per annum*. But once the swell of the choir subsides, the recitatives knit together in drawn-out chants. Above all, Pärt's *St John Passion* demonstrates just how intense, inventive, moving, poignant, and full of mystery Bach's Passion is. Through Bach, the suffering of Christ becomes palpable even to an agnostic; all Pärt has to offer is an undramatic and not very musical reading of the gospel.

For a while, it appeared that Pärt might share the fate of many dissidents who fell silent on settling in the free West. It's almost as if, without an all-encompassing antagonist, they lacked the incentive for bold action. His faith was strong, however, and he came back with four pure, spiritual works. In 1993, *Te Deum*, *Silouan's Song*, *Magnificat*, and *Berliner Messe* were released on a single album and made a deep impression. *Silouan's Song* even outdoes *Credo*, *Cantus*, or *Tabula Rasa* in its sublime evocation of the vast forests of the north, as if distance enabled Pärt to distil in music the atmosphere in which he grew up and came of age.

He did not forget Estonia and his Estonian friends. On 18 February 1990, Pärt attended the Dutch premiere of *Miserere* at Muziekcentrum Vredenburg in Utrecht. One person determined not to miss that performance was Indrek Hirv, an Estonian graphic designer, poet, and playwright who had fled to the West in the early 1980s. Hirv knew someone who worked at Vredenburg and asked if he could meet Pärt. A meeting was arranged. During the interval, Hirv stepped into the

Arvo Pärt at home in Berlin, 1990.

soloists' room. Before they could even shake hands, Pärt said, 'I still owe you money.'

In 1977, Pärt had been as poor as a church mouse. All performances of his work were banned, and he had no prospect of a commission. Yet, as a composer, he still had to generate his own income, and so he handed out business cards to musicians or publishers who, despite the censors, might be willing to take a chance on his music. Hirv designed a card for him in pastel shades and used an etching technique to make a hundred copies. Anything printed required official approval, while etchings were governed by more lenient rules for artistic reproduction. Pärt had no way to pay the designer, not that Hirv had expected otherwise. In those bleak and frugal years, people on the same side did each other favours and helped each other out where they could. Solidarity prevailed, which in practical terms meant that everyone was in debt to everyone else.

Pärt had not forgotten. Thirteen years later, in Utrecht, despite

Hirv's protests, he pulled out his wallet and paid what he owed: the sum of 100 German marks, though the designer had only come backstage to tell Pärt how deeply the music had moved him.

I attend a concert at Niguliste kirik, the Lutheran Church of St Nicholas in Tallinn's Old Town. As the setting for many recordings of Pärt's work, the name was familiar to me. The building was destroyed in the aerial bombardment of 1944 and rebuilt during the Soviet era. In 1984, with restoration almost complete, the tower burned down. Under Soviet rule, the church became the Museum of Atheism. After independence in 1991, Niguliste was turned into the Museum of Religious Art, housing the most important works from Tallinn's churches.

Niguliste's acoustics make it an ideal space for choral works and orchestral works by small ensembles. This particular concert has an added bonus: the opportunity to see Andres Mustonen in action. The man who was a driving force behind Pärt's early music will be performing selected works by Arvo Pärt and Helena Tulve with his Hortus Musicus and the chamber choir of the Estonian Philharmonic.

Again, I am struck by the dark consolation offered by Pärt's simple, compelling melodies. His use of silence is remarkable. He dares to insert one, two, even three bars of stillness, and the note that follows pierces your skin. With Pärt, you can almost hear music in the space between the notes.

The performance this night includes *Orient & Occident* and *Silouan's Song*. Outside, snow is falling; inside, the audience seems spellbound. Out of nowhere, I recall a long-forgotten incident from my childhood: waking up in tears one night because I had dreamed of music that did not exist here on earth. Music so beautiful that, long after that night, I kept wondering where I might hear it again. The opening bars of *Silouan's Song* in Tallinn's Niguliste kirik remind me of the music from my dream. Not sung by voices, but played on fourteen stringed instruments.

Religious faith left me long ago. Yet Pärt draws out precisely those elements from the Bible that still exert a hold. Of the fifteen pilgrim songs from the Book of Psalms, he selects the most moving, Psalm 121, for his *Wallfahrtslied*:

I will lift up my eyes unto the hills, from whence cometh my help.
My help cometh from the Lord, which made heaven and earth ...
The Lord is thy keeper: the Lord is thy shade upon thy right hand.
The sun shall not smite thee by day, nor the moon by night.

To *Te Deum*, he gives the motto: 'The wind blows wherever it pleases. You hear its sound, but cannot tell where it comes from, or where it is going.' John 3:8. It is poetry, perhaps even poetic philosophy.

For Pärt, the gospels came as a revelation. Everything he found wise, sincere, contemplative, and soothing in those pages, he poured into his music. A lapsed Protestant or Catholic could never have produced the works Pärt composed: for them, the Bible is old; for the former communist, it was new. At the conservatory in Tallinn, Pärt not only received a theoretical and practical education in music, but also had to attend lectures in political economy, the history of the Communist Party, and the 'science' of atheism. Like the rudiments of basic arithmetic, it was instilled in him that religion went hand in hand with exploitation and had spawned centuries of misery. Pärt was a little too curious to take this at face value. He wanted to decide for himself what was valuable and what was deplorable about religious belief.

Although Pärt joined the Russian Orthodox Church and used Church Slavonic for his *Kanon Pokajanen* (Canon of Repentance), in his *Berliner Messe* and *Missa Syllabica* he followed the Roman Catholic liturgy in Latin. For his later choral works, he used prayers, psalms, and Bible texts in English, French, Italian, and Spanish. He married a religious Jewish woman and immersed himself as much in the Psalms of David as in the New Testament gospels. For him, the dividing lines between languages, cultures, and religions are thin. As a composer, but also as a man of faith, he adheres to the postmodern view that you should cherish the good that the past has to offer and reject the bad.

Pärt was so far ahead of his time that he sensed as early as the mid-1960s that the coming century would be a religious one. But nothing is created in isolation: he had the support of his compatriots. The Soviet authorities may have been incensed by the premiere of *Credo* in Tallinn, but the Estonian audience rose from their seats as one and gave it such an overwhelming ovation that — as Krista Varik told me

— the entire piece had to be performed again. That night, Pärt must have realised he was on to something, that he was writing exactly the kind of music that spoke to audiences of a new era, a new state of mind, and a religious experience that could not be eradicated. In Pärt's *Credo*, the trumpets of those in power rip through the devoutly sung profession of faith.

Support had also been forthcoming in other ways. In Tallinn, Pärt lived in an apartment building set aside for musicians and composers. He had not constantly been at odds with the authorities; early in his career, two works he had written for the youth theatre earned him a prize from the Composers' Union, a prize that opened the door to certain benefits, not least the right to housing. His upstairs neighbour was Veljo Tormis, his former high-school music teacher, only five years his senior. Tormis went on to become one of Estonia's foremost composers, specialising in choral music. An admirer of Pärt's vocal works, he encouraged him to continue on his chosen path. Downstairs lived the young conductor Neeme Järvi, who also became a committed advocate of Pärt's music. Heimar Ilves, professor of music history at the Tallinn Conservatory, encouraged Pärt by sharing his open-minded views on spiritual matters. And Pärt enjoyed the backing of Andres Mustonen, Tallinn's great early-music specialist. He was not alone: many of his contemporaries and compatriots saw traditional, sacred music as the wellspring for groundbreaking contemporary compositions.

In 1968, shortly after the premiere of *Credo*, Pärt said in an interview for Estonian radio: 'I am not sure there could be progress in art. Progress as such is present in science. Everyone understands what progress means in the technique of military warfare. Art presents a more complex situation ... many art objects of the past appear to be more contemporary than our present art. How do we explain it? Not that genius was seeing 200 years ahead. I think the modernity of Bach's music will not vanish in another 200 years and perhaps never will ... the reason is not just that in absolute terms it could simply be better than contemporary music ... the secret to its contemporaneity resides in the question: how thoroughly has the author-composer perceived, not his own present, but the totality of life, its joys, worries, and mysteries?'

Pärt did not choose east or west; he turned his gaze upwards. He had a habit of taking the few journalists, writers, and musicologists who were fortunate enough to interview him to the nearest abbey or church. In that sacred setting, he invariably made the same three points: (1) anyone who wanted to understand him should listen to his music; (2) anyone who wanted to know his philosophy of life should read the writings of the church fathers; (3) anyone who wanted to know about his private life would leave empty-handed. He became harder — harder on himself and on those who attempted to fathom his motivations.

The people of Rakvere are less concerned about such matters. They celebrated the seventieth birthday of their illustrious son by giving him the freedom of the town and holding an Arvo Pärt chamber-music festival in his honour. A salute to the kid who once rode round and round the square on an old bicycle, absorbing a new line of melody with every lap.

In Rakvere, I was told something else about the man. I was told that Pärt left Estonia in 1980 and that his first piano teacher, Jaan Pakk, died four years later. How he managed it remains a mystery, they said, but Pärt was somehow able to enter the Estonian Soviet Socialist Republic illegally and head straight for Rakvere to attended the funeral of the man who taught him and who founded the town's music school. He made no attempt to conceal his presence; all Rakvere knew he was there. The party hardliners could easily have informed on him; the security service could have arrested him. But Pärt's tribute to his teacher made such an impression that they let it slide. Since that cold December day in 1984, no one in the town has had a bad word to say about Arvo Pärt.

Like many a moving story, perhaps even the story of the boy who cycled round Rakvere's square in the dead of winter, it is too good to be true. Jaan Pakk passed away in December 1979, before Pärt left Estonia. But the fact that it is told at all speaks volumes about the esteem in which the composer is held. A composer who stands for so much more than the extraordinary music he has made.

13

Exiled from Mõisamaa

THE FATE OF ANNA-LISELOTTE VON WRANGEL

Estonia, February 2010
In search of a past that has faded slowly into the shadows, I pick up
the trail surprisingly quickly. It's only a short drive from the centre of
Tallinn to the district of Nõmme. Both Metsa tänav and the house at
number 39 practically introduce themselves. This is a house built to
withstand harsh winters. The roof with its thick, ribbed tiles extends
to the plastered grey walls of the ground floor. The window panes
— outer, inner, upper, lower — are all on the small side. The overall
impression is distinctly German: not much in the way of charm, but
sturdy enough to brave biting Arctic winds and thick packs of snow.

I circle the property. Gardens here are bounded by the sketchiest
of partitions, low fences you can step over with ease. Anything higher
seems to be mouldering away. Already I feel like a trespasser in someone else's life.

Nõmme is Tallinn's oldest garden town. During the last years
of tsarist rule, the population of this Baltic port doubled and, to
manage the rapid influx, the government launched a competition.
It was won by Finnish urban planner Eliel Saarinen, whose proposal
threaded traffic arteries and linear green spaces through yet-to-be-
constructed suburban settlements. Driving south, you can still see his
concept in the patterns of the roads and parks, much as you recognise
Haussmann's austere hand in the sweeping boulevards of Paris.

Nõmme became home to members of the better-off, better-edu-
cated classes who made up the senior management of industrial firms
and trade offices. As one of the legal team at Saku Brewery, Lotti's
father was among them.

I circle the house one more time. Trees tower high above the roof,
Baltic pine powdered with freshly fallen snow. Dogs bark in the distance, a car engine growls closer by. But it's the cawing of crows I hear

The house on Metsa tänav in Tallinn's Nõmme district.

most, enough to convince me I'm in the countryside already.

Lotti, full name Anna-Liselotte Baroness von Wrangel, spent the first thirteen winters of her life in this house. I know Lotti only from photographs and stories, yet I can picture her stamping the snow off her shoes on the mat by the front door. Being here brings her close, despite the passage of time.

The cold soon gets the better of me and I head back to the car. I spread the road map on the empty passenger seat, drive out of the city, and make a blunder: instead of the trunk road to Kohila, I find myself on the dual carriageway to Pärnu.

Twenty years ago, as a foreigner here, there was no need to think for yourself: leaving the city without an escort was strictly forbidden. At the side of Tallinn's southern exit road, an abandoned Soviet police lookout post still stands sentry. A reminder of the days when exiting Tallinn was a privilege reserved for those with an official permit, in the company of an ever-vigilant Intourist guide.

By cutting through the village of Saku, I get onto the trunk road after all, and fourteen kilometres further on, Hageri looms out of the mist. I recognise the church from the photo I have with me, which dates from 1934. Same tower, same snow — well, an equally thick covering at any rate. The base of the tower is four-sided and the mid-section octagonal, white building blocks topped with a red cone. The church is flanked by four oak trees; not a house in sight, except for the rectory. I get out to the sound of another dog barking. The sexton approaches and asks if he can help me.

'I'm looking for Reverend Thomson's grave.'

He nods and leads the way, as if it's the most normal thing in the world for someone to turn up unannounced and ask to see the good man's final resting place. Reverend Thomson, he has been dead for seventy-two years. We walk to the cemetery, snow creaking under our shoes. The sexton takes off his woollen mitt respectfully before brushing the snow from the stone cross atop the tombstone. The inscription on the grey marker reads KONSTANTIN THOMSON 1855–1938.

Swedes are numerous in these western regions of Estonia. By Swedes, I mean people of Swedish origin. The first Swedish immigrants settled back in the days of the Vikings. A second wave followed in the sixteenth century. In their own circles, they continued to speak Swedish, to set themselves apart from the German barons.

The sexton opens the door to the church with a rusty key. Pointing at a side door, he strides up the aisle. With nothing much to go on, I feel sure he's about to show me a picture of Reverend Thomson hanging on the vestry wall.

I'm only half wrong. Instead, we slither over the path to the rectory, where the picture is hanging in the catechism classroom. The reverend has an impressive beer belly. His face reminds me of the professor from *Wild Strawberries*. A moustache so bushy, it's in danger of plugging his nostrils. Eyes wide as saucers.

'Annemarie,' I say.

Annemarie was Reverend Thomson's daughter. And Lotti's mother.

The sexton nods and clearly wants to say something, in Estonian, German, or Russian, but cannot find the words. I shake his hand, still cold from the snow.

And then it comes to him.

'Amchen.'

That's what everyone used to call Annemarie. Amchen. Or shorter still: Ami.

Hageri's church in the winter of 1934.

From Hageri, I drive about ten kilometres south-east. Another landmark I recognise, this time from an old postcard, is Kernu Manor: an imposing country residence along the E67 to Pärnu, boasting six chimneys and a facade with thirty windows. The neoclassical portico supported by four pillars on either side of the steps is still intact. Gone are the elongated conservatories to the left and right of the main building that once offered a panoramic view of the lake and gave the manor the grandeur of a royal residence.

The lake is frozen, and the reeds poking out of the ice at its centre suggest it can't be deep. The perfect setting for a local pastime: motor racing on ice. Three or four speeding cars skid and slide in erratic circuits around the reedy centrepiece. A century ago, it would have been horse-drawn sleighs competing for bragging rights. At least they would have made less noise. An Audi smacks into the side of an old Mercedes; engines shriek.

I pass through the main entrance. Before I can marvel at the chandelier, the smell of lukewarm soup and bodily functions hits my nostrils. A procession of men and women in nightclothes passes before me, slouching, dawdling, limping, skipping, and occasionally standing stock-still. No one pays me any heed. One is clutching a broom, others a newspaper, a cup, or a bedpan that has yet to be emptied. A

Kernu Manor on a postcard from the 1930s, with the brickworks on the left.

turd catches my eye and I have to swallow hard. Some of the women groan, others sob; the men snort or utter cries. Their cries are the least unsettling of the sounds that greet me.

The Kernu Estate — Kirna in German — came into the possession of the von Neukirchen and von Ulrich families in the seventeenth century. In 1784, Count Berend Heinrich von Tiesenhausen purchased the property and bequeathed the lands to the Ungern-Sternbergs. The neoclassical manor was built by Berend Baron von Ungern-Sternberg between 1810 and 1813. He did not live there himself and lent it to Count Alexei Bobrinsky, the illegitimate son of Catherine the Great. In 1863, the manor became the property of the Rosenthal family, followed by the Kotzebue family in 1880, the chief woodsman Edgar Schmidt in 1901, and then Nikolai Baron von Wrangell in 1911. He gifted it to his son Vladimir in 1917.

Vladimir, Lotti's father, was born in St Petersburg in 1898 and was given Kernu Manor and the estate as a nest egg. His father and grandfather had grown up on the Terpilitsy estate, halfway between Narva and St Petersburg, but with the tsarist empire on the brink of collapse, Terpilitsy was sure to fall prey to looting revolutionaries. Kernu offered a safer haven. Away from the main route to St Petersburg, it might — with a bit of luck — escape the vengeful wave of revolt.

The von Wrangell family came from south-east Estonia and had their roots in Germany. From the fifteenth century, the von Wrangells married into Baltic German noble families such as the von Felsens, the von Löwensterns, and the Rausch-von Traubenbergs. Some of these names could barely fit on a calling card: Schaffhausen-Schönberg-Eck-Schaufuss, for example. In the seventeenth and eighteenth centuries, the family's descendants bought and sold around twenty manors and estates in Estonia. Their name expanded along with their assets: von Wrangell was appended by zu Ludenhof or zu Lagena or the name of another distinguished residence, depending on the estate and the branch of the family tree.

In the nineteenth century, the von Wrangells swarmed across Russia. They became senators, governors, judges, and explorers (Ferdinand Petrovich Wrangel was one of the founders of the Russian Geographical Society and explored the north coast of Siberia between 1820 and 1835). They became admirals, naval ministers (the same Ferdinand Petrovich), or — in no fewer than twelve cases — generals in the tsarist army. To tone down their German-ness in Russian circles, they dropped one *l* in their name and sometimes even ditched the *von*.

In St Petersburg, Alexander Yegorovich Wrangel witnessed Dostoevsky's last-minute reprieve from execution. Five years later, he was appointed prosecutor in Semipalatinsk, the Siberian town to which Dostoevsky had been exiled. One of the writer's younger brothers asked Wrangel to take him a letter, some linen, a few books, and fifty roubles. Wrangel did as he was asked, and he and Dostoevsky became friends. From 1856, Dostoevsky would invariably begin his letters to Wrangel with 'My very best, irreplaceable friend Alexander Yegorovich!' The baron lived up to his billing, both as the irreplaceable lender of considerable sums of money and the man who kept Maria Dmitriyevna Isayeva's husband out of the way whenever Dostoevsky wanted to see her. It was thanks to Wrangel that Dostoevsky had been able to woo her without any of the townsfolk catching on. For the writer, who was sentenced to ten years in Siberia, Wrangel's house was open day and night. The prosecutor would often come home after a trial to find his friend in the living room. 'He would pace back and forth in the room,' Wrangel wrote in his self-published memoirs, which circulated among the family, 'with cloak wide open, smoking a pipe and talking aloud to himself; his head was always full of new ideas.'

After two and a half years, Alexander Yegorovich was recalled to St Petersburg, from where he travelled half the world representing Russia as an ambassador. In Copenhagen, he again fulfilled the role of match-maker, forging a union between future tsar Alexander III and Danish princess Dagmar. As thanks for this successful mediation, he came to possess another estate. But far more important to him was the chance to see Dostoevsky again, when the writer's exile was finally over.

Nikolai von Wrangel, Alexander's son, had three daughters and two sons, Georg and Vladimir. He refused to so much as look at his daughters again after he caught his wife committing adultery; he literally could not stand to see them. Nikolai led a tumultuous life, fighting in the White Army, fleeing to Dresden, becoming embroiled in the Balkan conflicts, and eventually winding up in Rome. Crossing paths with his daughter Vera at a Roman restaurant one day, he turned on his heels and made an abrupt exit. Weeks later, he picked up a gun and shot himself through the heart.

Son Vladimir had moved into the manor at Kernu, and much to his father's indignation, married an Estonian clergyman's daughter, Annemarie. He was one of the first von Wrangels not to marry a woman of nobility. The resulting scandal would undoubtedly have rocked the family, had Lenin not stepped into the limelight of history. The 1917 Revolution put an end to every nobleman's dreams. The land reform act of 1919 required Vladimir to give up his estate, and four years later his manor. In 1923, Kernu became an asylum for the mentally ill, a role it still fulfils eighty-seven years later.

The concierge kindly points out to me the one painting on the staircase and the single chandelier that are all that remain of the original contents. The painting has been scratched and spat at so many times that it's hard to say what it once depicted.

I return to my car and drive twenty kilometres south. Here the trail runs colder. It takes me a long time to find Mõisamaa, a hamlet south of provincial road No. 28. I am lucky enough to run into a postman, who explains that Mõisamaa is both the name of a hamlet and a country house that is somewhere else entirely: one kilometre north-east of Kernu. He draws the route on the back of an envelope and tells me I can keep it. 'It's only advertising,' he says.

Kernu Manor in the winter of 1938, Lotti's last winter in Estonia.

Kernu was a manor with forty rooms; Mõisamaa is a wooden house with ten. Vladimir and Annemarie von Wrangel moved there in 1921, the home where five years later their daughter, Lotti, was born. A farmhouse built by the labourers who worked in the fields of the estate.

After searching for hours, I see it tucked away behind a snow-covered field, half-hidden in the woods. There's no mistaking it: a wooden house with three stone chimneys. Three windows to the left of the front door, three windows to the right. A dormer with two windows above the front door, and plenty of space under the roof. A house you could easily fall in love with as a child, not stuffy but cosy, with an attic where the girls could dress up and play princess in ball gowns found among the mothballs, packed in chests that had made the move from Kernu Manor.

I have to leave the car at the side of the small road. Every step leaves me up to my knees in snow. A dog barks and an old woman comes out of the house. I wave, knowing her name and exactly who she is: Armilde.

Once Vladimir got his job with the brewery's legal department, Mõisamaa became his summer house. He and his family spent the winters in Tallinn, at the house on Metsa tänav in Nõmme district. The wooden house in the country was looked after by Alexander and Ida, who lived all year round in the two side rooms. They died many years ago. Ever since, the house has been home to Armilde, Ida's sister.

How old would she be? Eighty-five? Ninety-five? It's hard to tell. She beckons me inside, pours me a bowl of tea, and gestures that it will help against the cold. There was no letter or phone call announcing my arrival. I have not told her my name, she does not know where I am from, but she spreads a thick layer of butter on a slice of rye bread and offers it to me. Slowly but surely, I believe that I am discovering the ways of Estonia: quietly friendly, silently hospitable.

After drinking down my tea, I take a photo from my inside pocket. The child on the left is Lotti: a remarkably pretty girl with two long braids. She is smiling, petite, and slender. The boy on the right is Claus, her elder brother. Olaf, her younger brother by two years, is standing in the middle. The family all called him Oli. Their father, Vladimir, is standing behind Oli, hands on his son's shoulders. An amiable man in mid-length trousers and a hunter's coat, with a shotgun slung over his shoulder. He has just returned from shooting pheasant in the forest; the dog that accompanied him gives Oli a paw.

Does Armilde know the photograph?

She nods. Lotti, Liselotte, Anna-Liselotte, was born here in this wooden house, in Mõisamaa. Not Claus; he was a winter child, born in the city in late February. Though Olaf came into the world in the last week of July, he too was born in the city. Oh and by the way, she asks in halting German, where did I get this photograph?

'From Karin. Lotti's daughter.'

'Ah Karin, dear Karin. Are you her husband?'

'No, no.'

With a few ponderous sentences — I have to search for the words — I try to make it clear that we were close enough in age and association for that to have been a possibility. But … the rest becomes too difficult to explain.

'Karin and I studied together.'

'Ah …'

Now she understands. Though not entirely.

'Are you here to bring something?'

Mõisamaa in the winter of 1935.

'I bring greetings from Karin. But I have mainly come to see the place for myself. Karin wants me to describe the house.'

Before it collapses. Before it's gone for good.

Or, worse, before it's sold when Armilde passes on and the house undergoes a tacky restoration at the hands of a shady Russian businessman who wants to go hunting in the woods or race his Audi on the frozen lake at Kernu.

'Take your time, look around,' Armilde says. 'I haven't changed a thing. It's the same house that Lotti, her brothers, and her parents left in 1939. All the furniture is from that time. I told Karin she could take whatever she wanted — she was here a few years ago. After all, I said, it belongs to your family. She cried and cried. She took an oil lamp, and a signed photograph of Dostoevsky. That was all.'

I make a mental note to ask Karin about that photo. Signed by Dostoevsky!

'You have to understand: they were gone within days. Lotti, Olaf, Claus, the baron, the baroness ... They took only the bare essentials, some clothes, nothing else. It was all so strange. Ida and I saw it with our own eyes, but one year on we still couldn't believe that the baron and baroness had gone. They never let us call them that, by the way. Only *proua* and *härra*, sir and madam.'

The family at Mõisamaa: Anna-Liselotte (Lotti), Olaf (Oli), Claus,
and father Vladimir (Volodya). The picture was taken by mother
Annemarie (Amchen).

All her life, Lotti would think back on Mõisamaa as a peaceful place,
far from the harshness of the world. A place where she and her brothers
would fish in one of the dozens of streams that criss-crossed the forest,
where they built hideaways in the tallest trees, with no thought of
what tomorrow or the day after would bring. Those summer holidays

Playing in the sandpit at Mõisamaa in summer. Lotti is on the left.

lasted ten weeks, but in her mind, they were as endless as the June days when they did not go to bed until after midnight, when the light faded slowly from the sky.

Lotti was thirteen when she had to leave Estonia, a hurried departure in 1939. The last image that stayed with her was the city skyline seen from the boat, Tallinn's church towers and ramparts getting smaller and smaller until they disappeared on the horizon. It was an image that returned hundreds of times in her dreams, but not something she shared, not even with her daughter, Karin.

For sixty years, every impression from her childhood lay beneath a white sheet, lost to memory. Until a fellow golfer came along to write a piece on her for the club magazine.

'Where were you born?'

'In Estonia.'

'Where's that?'

It was a moment of bewilderment. Of intense loneliness.

From 1947, Lotti lived in Amsterdam, and from 1972 in a log cabin outside the city. The cabin was Finnish. She had it sent over from Helsinki as a flatpack, which was then assembled in a lovely lakeside spot among the birches and bushes at Vinkeveen. At first, she used it as a holiday home, but after five years or so she moved there permanently. It reminded her so much of Mõisamaa.

It was in this setting that the interview for the golf-club magazine took place. Lotti looked out the window over the man's shoulder as she spoke. A chill crept into her voice:

> For centuries, Estonia was a province of tsarist Russia. In 1919,
> it was in danger of being overrun by the Bolsheviks, who had
> seized power in the Revolution. The Estonians fought a war for
> their independence. The Baltic German nobility formed the Baltic
> Regiment to stand with the Estonians against the communists. The
> large landowners promised that the land would be divided among
> the farmers who fought for the cause if the communists were kept
> out. They won, and in the free state of Estonia that was proclaimed
> in 1920, the land was redistributed as promised. I was born in that
> free state of Estonia. My father fought in the war of liberation, and
> he too gave up much of his estate. Of course, this also meant that we
> became a lot poorer overnight. There were no more luxuries. My
> father went to law school to support his family. We gave up our big
> house with its forty rooms and moved into a simpler wooden house,
> where we lived until 1939. That year the Russians came, a result
> of the pact made by Molotov and von Ribbentrop. We and 30,000
> others thought it best to flee. If we had stayed, we would not have
> survived. When the Russians came, all the intellectuals were taken
> away and killed.

At a stroke, she had pulled the white sheet from her childhood and told her story, in words I suspect she had heard from her father and repeated verbatim. He had clearly kept things brief and simple for his little girl of thirteen. The reality was more complex, fraught with contradictions that were almost unfathomable to an outsider.

The downfall of the barons occurred in three stages.

The 1905 peasant uprising continued throughout the year. Around 160 properties were torched and razed to the ground. A further 140 were looted or severely damaged. At least 100 estate managers and landowners were lynched. A gang of heavies formed by the Baltic German nobles struck back, killing fifty-three farm workers.

The hatred that erupted in 1905 was directed almost exclusively at *mõisad* — the plural of *mõis*, a word that covers mansion, homestead, country house, or rural palace — the French *manoir* or English *manor* comes closest. There were over 1,000 *mõisad* in Estonia. In the eyes of the rural population these were symbols of oppression and had to be destroyed, preferably every last one of them, to put an end to what Baltic German historian Reinhard Wittram called 'the most purely aristocratic land on the planet'. Flipping through picture books that feature postcards of the old Estonia, it's hard not to see the whole country as an idyllic backwater.

Peasant farmers occupy an important place in Estonian history. Until 1816 they were serfs, and until 1919 humble tenant farmers on land owned by the Baltic German ruling classes. And yet, for four, five, six centuries they succeeded in preserving the Estonian language and Estonian songs, culture, and traditions. Estonia owes its very existence to its peasant farmers.

The 1917 revolution was an urban affair. Following the fall of the tsarist regime in February 1917, two revolutionary groups tried — and failed — to seize power in Tallinn. They failed due to the lack of support among Estonian farmers and nationalists, whose leader Konstantin Päts was wary of another period of Russian domination. It was precisely because he never failed to listen to the country's peasant population that Päts would become the great man of the first independent Republic of Estonia (1919–1939).

On 26 March 1917, 43,000 protesters took to the streets in Tallinn. In Petrograd on the same day, 13,000 Estonian soldiers from the tsar's army made their way to the Tauride Palace, where the provisional Russian government under the leadership of Prince Georgi Lvov was based. Lvov feared the worst and, within four days, accepted the reclassification of the Baltic provinces according to linguistic criteria. The measure took effect in May and heralded the independence of Estonia, Latvia, and Lithuania.

Under the Kerensky government, which succeeded the government headed by Lvov, the first free elections were held in Russia's Estonian province: rural areas voted in May, the cities in August and September. In Tallinn, the Bolsheviks won 31 per cent of the vote; in Narva, 47 per cent. In no Russian city could the Bolsheviks count on such strong support. It was a clear signal to the wealthy Baltic nobles that the threat to their power did not come from Russian quarters alone. Workers in both Estonia and Latvia were more radical and better organised than their Russian counterparts.

On 25 October 1917, the revolution began in Petrograd. Two days after the Bolshevik putsch, a revolutionary military committee attempted to seize power in Tallinn. Similar attempts were made in Narva and Tartu, but there the revolutionaries could not count on the support of the peasants, whose only aim was to deal a crushing blow to the Baltic German landowners and take a good chunk of land for themselves. For them, collective farming held no appeal whatsoever.

Meanwhile, World War I raged on. The Germans took Latvia in August 1917 and Estonia in January 1918. Until the collapse of the German empire in November 1918, German troops kept the Bolsheviks at bay.

In Estonia and Latvia, support for the Bolshevik cause dwindled after Lenin reneged on an earlier promise. Two days after the start of the October Revolution, eager to drum up the widest possible support, he issued a declaration that gave non-Russian peoples the right to secede from Russia and establish an independent state. But when the Finns, Lithuanians, Latvians, Estonians, and Poles did exactly that, he sent in troops.

By early January 1919, the Red Army had occupied large parts of eastern and southern Estonia and almost all of Latvia. Soviet forces advanced to within thirty kilometres of Tallinn. Along the way, they made thousands of arrests and killed 600 civilians. In Tartu, nine priests and the Orthodox bishop were murdered; clerics were driven out of every town and village, religious ceremonies banned, and church property confiscated. With this campaign, the Soviets turned the peasants against them once and for all.

An army of volunteers came together to fight the Red invasion under the command of Johan Laidoner, a former lieutenant colonel in the tsarist army. Laidoner faced the almost impossible task of going up against the Red Army with a ragtag fighting force that consisted of thousands of peasant farmers, farm labourers, students, schoolboys, and the members of assorted sports and hunting associations, along with thousands of soldiers who had served in the tsarist army, thousands of Latvian, Danish, Swedish, and Finnish volunteers, and — as Lotti told her interviewer — a Baltic German regiment less interested in Estonia's independence than in driving out the Bolsheviks at any cost. A British naval squadron supplied arms and ammunition, sealing off the port of Tallinn to ward off a Red attack from the sea.

In January 1919, Estonian troops succeeded in driving the Bolsheviks back across the border; in February, the Reds launched a counteroffensive and recaptured the entire south-east. The outcome hung in the balance until May 1919, but a cunning move by the Estonians proved decisive: they crossed the border and sought contact with Russia's anti-communist White forces led by General Nikolai Yudenich, who were operating from a base at Pskov. The White movement wanted nothing to do with Estonian, Latvian, and Lithuanian nationalists; their cause was the restoration of the tsarist regime throughout Russia, including the Baltic countries and Poland. Nevertheless, with the help of the Estonians, Yudenich's troops were able to deal a heavy blow to the Red Army. The Reds retreated far enough for the Estonians to reach the Daugava river. There, a new enemy awaited, one that presented the members of the Baltic German regiment with a pressing moral dilemma.

After the defeat of the German army, demobilised soldiers in Courland had formed Freikorps, volunteer paramilitary units that had taken up arms against both Bolsheviks and nationalists. Facing defeat by the Red Army, Latvia's provisional government led by Kārlis Ulmanis called on their help. The Freikorps united thousands of disillusioned men who, unable to see a way out of the situation in which they found themselves, took the law into their own hands. From 19 to 23 June 1919, under the command of Count Rüdiger von der Goltz, they faced the Estonian army at the Latvian town of Cēsis. For the Germans of the Baltic Regiment, this was a battle of brothers: they had to shoot down men clad in long black cloaks with whom they shared a language and a thwarted destiny, men who had also come to the aid of the Baltic Germans in Courland. The Estonian army won the battle on 23 June and was in a position to advance on Riga, but a hastily concluded agreement with the Latvians prevented this. Under the terms of that same agreement, Rüdiger von der Goltz and the members of the Freikorps were dispatched to Germany.

As a young man of twenty, Lotti's father served on the front line throughout these battles and half-battles, an experience that shaped his character. A cousin described him as 'a reserved man who, after 1919–1920, always sought to avoid conflict. I never heard him raise his voice. Under all circumstances, he remained a Baltic gentleman.'

In the autumn of 1919, he lost his best friend and brother in arms. In a bid to come to terms with his grief, he turned to poetry. He handled words less ably than he did his rifle, but that does not detract from his sincerity. In the shape of his friend, he held death in his arms, and it is as if, for the first time, he realised what bullets were designed to do.

The army retreated into Estonian territory and engaged in one last offensive: in October, it joined forces with Yudenich's White Army to launch an attack on Petrograd. By this time, the Estonians were battle weary and had lost some 3,500 men. They only took part at the behest of the British and lent their support to the White Army's north-west flank without much conviction. The siege of Petrograd — where father and son Mikhail and Sergei Eisenstein had fought on opposite sides — ended in failure for Yudenich, but it was enough to convince Lenin that he could not wage a long, hard war against the Whites in the south while simultaneously fighting off the Estonians, Latvians, and Lithuanians in the west. In December 1919, the Bolsheviks agreed an armistice with the Estonians, and on 2 February 1920, they signed the Treaty of Tartu, which recognised Estonia's borders and independence.

Three months earlier, before the independence struggle had been settled, Estonia's 'parliament in waiting' had already passed a land-reform law. The lands owned by the church and the tsarist crown — 55 per cent of the country — and the estates of the Baltic German nobility were confiscated. The nobles did not mourn this loss as much as you might expect; their estates and mansions were already beginning to cost more than they brought in.

By the early twentieth century, the German landed gentry had rapidly transitioned into city dwellers whose main aim was to secure a solid future in trade and industry rather than to maintain a backward-looking position of power in the country. Lotti's father was a case in point: instead of moping about the loss of his Kernu estate, he opted for a legal career in Tallinn. By the late 1920s, 84 per cent of Baltic Germans lived in the city, where they soon established a new position of power: five out of ten engineers were of Baltic German descent, as were four out of ten doctors and three out of ten lawyers. Tallinn's largest private bank, G. Scheel & Co., had Baltic German roots.

In June 1919, Hermann von Keyserling, Professor of Philosophy at the University of Tartu and cousin of writer Eduard von Keyserling, proposed the formation of a 'Baltikum', a federal, multilingual state based on the Swiss model in which Estonians, Jews, and speakers of German, Russian, and Swedish would have proportional parliamentary representation. This idea overlooked the fact that Estonia's population was fairly uniform: in 1919, a little over 88 per cent was Estonian, with German speakers accounting for 2 per cent, Russian speakers 8 per cent, and Swedish speakers 0.6 per cent. Jews made up only 0.5 per cent of the population. Moreover, among the German-speakers, there was a strong tendency towards assimilation. Many Baltic Germans had married into Estonian society and spoke Estonian at home. Between 1935 and 1940, 200,000 Estonians changed their names, following the example of Prime Minister Karl Einbund, who became Kaarel Eenpalu.

Most Baltic Germans accepted the new reality of independence. In the 1930s, only a minority sympathised with the Estonian National Socialist Party, which sought an alliance with Nazi Germany. The only major resentment was to be found among a group known as the *Kleindeutsche*, mostly made up of Germans who had come to Estonia in the nineteenth century to serve the nobility. Their sons became errand boys, masons, carpenters, or shopkeepers; many of their daughters were housemaids. Much of this group lived in dire poverty. The *Kleindeutsche* hated the barons with a vengeance but were equally ill-disposed towards Russian Bolsheviks, Estonian nationalists, and Jews. Tallinn-born Alfred Rosenberg came from these circles. Adolf Hitler invited him to come to Munich, where in 1923 he became editor-in-chief of the *Völkischer Beobachter*, the newspaper of the Nazi Party. In his daily editorials, Rosenberg shaped Nazi ideology. Until the very end of the war, he fulfilled the role of party ideologue with Hilter's blessing.

Shortly after she arrived in the Netherlands, someone asked Lotti where she was from.

'Estonia.'

'Oh, they were on the wrong side in the war.'

From that moment, she resolved to speak Dutch so well that it would never occur to anyone to ask her that question again. For two months, all she did was listen, absorbing the pronunciation of the *t*, the *r*, the long and short *a*. She later said of that time, 'I wanted to feel at home, to belong somewhere. I set aside my past and listened so intensely that I couldn't speak another word of Russian or Estonian.' When those two months were over, she began to speak her first sentences in Dutch, without the slightest hint of an accent. Like her father before her, she took on another state of being.

From 1920, Vladimir von Wrangel dropped the *von* from his signature and never allowed himself to be addressed as baron again. To him, Germany was a foreign land: born in St Petersburg, he had come to Estonia at the age of ten and went on to marry an Estonian woman whose distant ancestors came from Sweden. He wanted nothing more than to spend all his summers in Mõisamaa, and all his winters and springs in Tallinn. His eldest son, Claus, attended a German grammar school, and in 1938, he sent Lotti to a German all-girls school, the *Deutsches Progymnasium für Mädchen* in Tallinn. Her school reports give Estonian as her main subject, German as her second.

Surrounded by his three children, Vladimir looks every inch the contented father in photographs. During the early years of the economic crisis, he managed to hang onto his job at Saku Brewery, and by the mid-1930s, he had been promoted to chief financial officer.

For Vladimir, the Molotov-Ribbentrop Pact was a bolt from the blue. Two signatures scribbled in Moscow — one German, one Russian — put an end to his freedom and the wellbeing of his family. The non-aggression treaty of 23 August 1939 consigned his Estonia to the Soviet Union from then on, together with Latvia, Lithuania, Finland, and a section of Poland. The lion's share of Poland would fall to Nazi Germany. From one day to the next, that was where his future lay.

Despite his Baltic German roots, Vladimir von Wrangel had never been to Warsaw or Berlin, much less Hamburg and Munich. His wife and his friends called him Volodya, the pet name of all Russian Vladimirs. Out of nowhere, Volodya had been branded a German, and worse, the puppet of an inhuman regime. His Estonian passport and Russian vocabulary had become worthless. To those who knew nothing of his background, he would simply be a kraut.

In a speech at the Reichstag in October 1939, Hitler proclaimed

Lotti and Claus in Tallinn.

the *Heimholung ins Reich*. He needed the Baltic Germans to colonise Poland and make it part of the German empire. His deep dislike of the nobility and the pleasure he took in seeing the Baltic counts and barons humbled were factors he kept to himself. In his speech, he asked the *Volksdeutsche* or ethnic Germans elsewhere in Europe to

Lotti in Tallinn.

uproot themselves and sacrifice their home for the sake of being German.

Few Baltic Germans were willing to make that sacrifice. But, as Lotti pointed out, what choice did they have? 'If we had stayed, we would have been killed by the Soviets.' There was no choice. Their fate had been sealed. On 18 October, the Soviet army marched into Estonia. Between October 1939 and May 1940, 13,000 Baltic Germans left Estonia for the Reich, most of them heading for Poland. A similar exodus of 52,000 left Latvia. A further 7,000 followed from Estonia in January 1941. In total, 72,000 Baltic Germans abandoned their homes.

In January 1941, the Red Terror began. Six thousand Estonians were arrested in the months that followed. From 14 June, another 9,156 people were deported to Siberia in a single week; among them were the last Baltic Germans who had refused to leave Estonia. Not one of them survived.

And what about the war? The man from the golf club magazine continued his inquiries.

Lotti began to speak more slowly, with greater difficulty. 'The Germans transported us to the newly occupied part of Poland. Beyond that, I don't really want to talk about those five years. It was so dreadful. I lost so much.'

'But ...'

A shake of the head was enough to silence him. She could say no more about it.

Years of silence would follow.

Lotti's younger brother has the clearest memories of the family's departure. In October 1939, Olaf was eleven years and three months old. Half a century later, he would write:

> The hammer blow that came down on us was painful. We were already in bed when my parents called my brother, my sister, and me into my father's study. They explained to us that within six weeks we would be moving to Germany. We were ordered to say nothing about our impending departure for ten days. My brother let out a cry of joy, while I felt just the opposite. My sister said nothing, not a word. We were still in Estonia when it was occupied by Russian troops, supposedly marching into the country for its own protection and taking control of several military bases. A round of farewells followed. I will never forget the Estonian troop captain who gave us military instruction, the tears rolling down his cheeks as we said

goodbye. When we sailed on 30 October 1939, the first snow was already falling. The best part of my childhood had come to an end.

The Wrangels were assigned to the first transports. For a family that had brought forth twelve tsarist generals, the risk of reprisals from the Red Army was too high.

It was only in later life that Lotti felt able to divulge the details of this forced departure and the war years to her daughter, Karin. Aboard a crowded passenger ship, she sailed with her brothers and her parents from Tallinn to Stettin (Szczecin). From there, the family was directed to Reichsgau Wartheland, the region halfway between Warsaw and Berlin that Poles called Wielkopolska (Great Poland). Wartheland had been part of the German Empire until 1918, when the Treaty of Versailles decreed it part of the independent state of Poland. That newfound status lasted exactly twenty years; under Nazi expansionism, German rule was reasserted.

Thousands of Baltic Germans were ordered to travel to Wartheland. In trains, they were taken to Posen, present-day Poznań. They slept in the gymnasiums of the indoor sports stadium, awaiting a medical examination. The families had to appear naked before a panel of examiners, the men and boys first, followed by the women and girls. They were checked for infectious diseases, and in this state of undress, it was easy to spot any man or boy who was circumcised. The Germans only half-trusted the Baltic Germans; there could easily be Jews among them. Vladimir, Amchen, and Lotti felt degraded by the examination; the boys did their best to shrug it off.

The Wrangels were assigned an apartment that still contained the belongings of its former residents, Poles who had been arrested by the Germans. Vladimir was so unsettled by this that he couldn't eat for days, but was somewhat consoled by the fact that the German authorities did not force him to join the National Socialist Party. However, he was urged to change his first name to Woldemar and restore his surname to its former glory. From that time on, he was once again Freiherr von Wrangell, not with one *l* but two.

Lotti barely slept a wink during their two months in Posen. 'I am in someone else's bed,' she said to herself, 'under someone else's covers. And meanwhile a strange boy or girl is sleeping in my bed in Nõmme or my attic room in Mõisamaa.' She was convinced her

Annemarie (Amchen).

pillow smelled of the previous occupant.

The family's move to Schwarzau (present-day Chaławy) coincided with Christmas. Freiherr Woldemar von Wrangell was offered any number of country houses — huge, ridiculously huge, more modest — he could take his pick. Now that the Polish nobility had been driven out, real estate was in plentiful supply. In consultation with Amchen, he chose the smallest option available: a nondescript property barely bigger than their home back in Tallinn. Their hope was that this might limit any friction with the locals to mild chafing. That said, the house in Schwarzau, thirty-five kilometres south of Posen, came with a generous plot of land, and Vladimir knew good, dark soil when he saw it.

These 287 hectares made a farmer of Vladimir: he grew crops (beets) and bred livestock (pigs). A gentleman farmer with twenty labourers in his employ. 'It was not my choice to come here,' he told the Poles on the first day. 'If I'd had my way, I would have lived out my days in Estonia. We will just have to make the best of it together. I am no farmer — I need your help. I will do everything I can to take care of you and your families.'

It was a promise he would keep.

What won the Poles over more than anything was his proposal to protect the holy statues that stood at the side of the country roads. The Nazi storm troopers systematically destroyed any shrines and statues of Christ and Our Lady they came across. Vladimir suggested storing them in a barn behind the manor house for safe keeping until the war was over. From that moment on, the Polish locals greeted him in passing.

Lotti was sent away to a girls' school, the *Oberschule für Mädchen* in Wreschen (Września), some forty kilometres east of Posen. It proved to be a grim experience. In Tallinn, the schools she'd attended had been within the walls of the Old Town, a pleasant stroll from home through narrow streets and steep cobbled lanes. Wreschen was a muddy town on a desolate plain. Lotti missed the Hanseatic houses and Baltic vistas. She knew Poland would never feel like home. The region around Posen was deprived, and as a Baltic German, there were areas and city districts that she was not permitted to enter; to use a coarse German term of the time, these were places to which the Poles had been *verschleppt* (carted off).

At the start of the school holidays or the holiday weekends at Ascension or All Souls' Day, she took the train home to Schwarzau via Posen. The journey could take anything up to four-and-a-half hours, as the train regularly had to make way for troop transports. The highlight of her Polish schooldays was a diphtheria epidemic, during which she was allowed to stay at home for weeks on end.

For the first year, she was barely able to keep up with the curriculum. After resitting exams in maths and English, she was allowed to move up a year, but returned in the autumn to find the threat of expulsion hanging over her head. From 1941, things gradually improved, and she began to make friends. There were class outings: to the operas *Fidelio* and *Die Entführung aus dem Serail*, and the theatre, to see *Tasso*. 'Goethe!' she wrote in a letter home, complete with exclamation mark.

Olaf fared little better in the first year at his new school in the town of Schrimm (now Śrem). Overwhelmed by the transition from Estonia to Poland, he failed his exams. At home, he gave a short speech to his parents. 'I am among the 20 per cent who failed. But of that 20 per cent, I am the best.' Most of his time was taken up with the Hitler Youth, where he and his younger cousin Wolf were encouraged to sing and roar to their hearts' content.

Shocked by the slogans his son had begun spouting, Vladimir intervened. He took Olaf out of the school and sent him to board at *Baltenschule Misdroy* (in present-day Międzyzdroje), two hundred kilometres north, on the West Pomeranian peninsula of Wolin on the Baltic Sea. There, Olaf's classmates included Claus von Amsberg, the son of a German planter from Africa who would go on to become Prince Consort to Queen Beatrix of the Netherlands.

The *Baltenschule Misdroy*'s mission was to drill young men to be exemplary members of the Baltic and Prussian nobility. The regime was conservative and strict: order, discipline, and manners were at least as important as a sound education. Like all pupils at the boarding school, Olaf automatically became a member of the National Socialist youth organisations, starting with *Deutsches Jungvolk* and progressing to the Hitler Youth. In Schrimm, he had thrown himself into the singing, shouting, and marching in uniform: topped off with a click of the heels and a Hitler salute, it had felt like a souped-up version of playing soldiers. But in Misdroy, he began to resent the unbridled dominance of Nazism.

Lotti's elder brother, Claus, volunteered for military service. A few days after passing his final exams in Posen, he signed up for the Wehrmacht, without consulting his parents. He wanted to fight the

Russian communists and told his father in a letter dated 15 October 1942 that he felt duty bound by personal conviction and family honour. Claus was eighteen years old.

Vladimir firmly believed that Hitler was no good. At the start of the war and within the confines of the family, he expressed this view on a daily basis, to Lotti, to Claus, and even to Olaf when he was home during the holidays. From the moment Claus volunteered for active service, he said nothing more, so as not to undermine his eldest son's decision. In private, he continued to despise Hitler as a power-hungry maniac who sacrificed entire countries and entire peoples to a sickening ideology.

On 20 July 1944, Vladimir disappeared. No one, not even his wife, Amchen, knew where he was. He did not reappear on the Schwarzau estate until later the following day. On 20 July, Count Schenk von Stauffenberg had made an attempt on Hitler's life at the Führer's headquarters in East Prussia. Baron von Wrangell had nothing to do with the attack itself (or he would no doubt have been arrested and executed like everyone else involved), but it is likely that he was standing by to play his part in the events that were supposed to have followed. Having removed Hitler from the equation, Stauffenberg's resistance group's plan was to seize control of the relevant military and administrative bodies in order to sign a peace treaty with the Western Allies while continuing the fight against the Soviets. This plan was entirely consistent with Vladimir's views. He later hinted to his wife that, on 20 July, he had been at an undisclosed location helping to prepare for its implementation in Poland.

As a young soldier, Claus von Wrangell wrote twenty letters home. Not one of them makes any mention of Hitler. Never does he use the words '*der Führer*' or '*unser Führer*', nor does he praise the National Socialist cause. He even avoids the word 'German', as if it is somehow tainted. He and his 'comrades' — a word he uses dozens of times — are fighting the Soviets. Moscow must fall so that Papa, Mutti, Lotti, and Oli can go back to Estonia. The cause for which he is fighting is an honourable return to Mõisamaa, the wooden house where the family spent their summers. In the mud and cold, 'to which we Balts are a little better suited than the other comrades', he does not lose sight of his goal for a second. What is good for his family is good for

Claus in his Wehrmacht uniform, with sister, Lotti, in Schwarzau
(present-day Chaławy).

Europe. His personal crusade coincides with a battle that will decide
the fate of the continent. For every step he advances, the communists
have to take a step back.

It sounds heroic. Yet the war, the front, and the heat of battle
remain distant in his letters. After a few weeks' training, he receives his
orders and is dispatched to the north-east. Before 1942 is at an end,
he has reached Riga. His progress is apparently effortless; nowhere
does he mention resistance. Another few hundred kilometres and he
will have reached Mõisamaa. But then he is called back to Warsaw
and sent to the eastern front.

He rises quickly through the ranks, so quickly you begin to suspect that the men around him are dropping like flies. He becomes
sergeant, officer candidate, lieutenant. His only complaints concern

hardships you might encounter on a poorly organised camping expedition. 'Terrible trouble with the lice, unpleasant creatures.' Morale is much more important and 'among our lot it couldn't be higher'.

He asks his parents to pack as many candles as they can into the kilo parcels they are permitted to send him twice a month. Like the other NCOs, he spends every evening writing to his mother, father, and other family members by candlelight. At field post number 15009, he receives anything up to nineteen letters a day. To answer them all, he has to sit late into the night at the little table assigned to him in the bunker. The soldiers' rations only allow for one candle a week; any extra have to be arranged through their personal provisions. *Kerzen (sehr wichtig)*, he asks repeatedly: Candles (very important)! Magazines too — when the supply lines to the front falter and there are no letters to answer, reading is one surefire way to get through the long evenings. Knäckebröd is another special request for his kilo parcel, along with marmalade ('in a tin please'), bacon, and also some butter. And biscuits or other confectionery. 'You know me and my sweet tooth, Mutti.' He is still a boy writing to his mother.

As Christmas approaches, the letters focus almost exclusively on the food parcels, which can weigh anything up to two kilos for the festive season. The whole family pitches in; Lotti bakes biscuits for her brother. Claus asks his mother to put together two additional parcels, one for a comrade who has no family and another for a soldier who receives nothing from home. He also asks for two marks for Private First Class Hans Ratayczak, two marks for Private First Class Arthur Hermann, and one mark for Corporal Ernst Schmeller, all of whom are considerably worse off than their fellow soldiers.

In his letters to his father, Claus takes a manlier tone, though he still begins tenderly with 'Dear Papa'. Copious amounts of alcohol are consumed to celebrate his promotion to sergeant, and Claus discovers he can hold his drink: 'looks like I've inherited your capacity for staying sober, Papa'. Not that this is all good news, as it means he doesn't 'get merry as quickly as the others'. He asks his father for stories from his hunting expeditions. How many hares has he bagged? How many pheasants?

He does his best to reassure his mother. Her letters are desperately effusive, starting with 'My dear, dear boy' and ending with 'May God watch over you, I love you so much, tomorrow I will write to you again, all my love and a great big kiss'. When word comes that he is lying injured in a Riga field hospital, she wants to drop everything and go to him. He is under orders to take three weeks' bedrest, and is burning up with fever at night, though 'the wound itself is giving me no trouble and my knee is also much better'. He provides no details of what happened to him. He might be talking about a bad case of blisters.

At Christmas, the letters from both sides turn into a determined denial of the war. His parents only have the smallest of trees to decorate (less than a metre tall, not a patch on the ones that used to fill the entire hall back in Tallinn). Claus writes of missing Lotti and Oli and exchanging gifts.

In the new year, postal deliveries grind to a halt. Parents and son are deprived of news for months on end. In his letter of 22 June 1943, Claus apologises for not sending word sooner: he recently became an acting officer and was recalled to Berlin, possibly due to illness or injury. His boils are getting better, he writes, and he also mentions 'courses of instruction', which suggests that he spent the previous months undergoing officer training.

He's given a few weeks' leave in July, which he spends with his parents in Schwarzau.

On 20 August 1943, he is in Warsaw for the second time. 'It remains,' he writes, 'a curious combination of Western European civilisation, luxury, and urban enterprise, with Eastern European, Polish squalor and coarseness.' He complains about the prices as if he were a tourist: paying 11 złoty (almost five marks) for an ice cream that would have cost him five cents on the street in Estonia.

Not a word about the destruction of the Warsaw ghetto — the last buildings had been flattened in July. All correspondence from the front line was censored; the men were forbidden to pass on information about towns, cities, and territories, or the progress of battle. Even so, fulminating about the price of an ice cream in Warsaw on 20 August 1943 demonstrates a bafflingly blinkered world view.

Ten days later, Claus is in Russia and dispatched to the front. Things are starting to look bad for the Nazis. After six gruelling months, the Battle of Stalingrad has turned in Russia's favour, and from February onwards, the German army is being pushed back mile by mile. Even so, Claus remains chipper and writes to his parents: 'Early tomorrow, my journey continues. Where to, I don't yet know myself.'

He describes Russia as a land with tremendous potential and an unprecedented future. However, 'living in this devastated, derelict country doesn't bear thinking about. I don't think anything could lift my spirits here among the rubble and the dirt.' What he sees leaves him feeling disheartened. 'Who knows how long it will take for a measure of order and cleanliness to return to this place, before the cities no longer look so ravaged and the people so neglected?! A huge task awaits us in this land.'

He boards trains that take him ever closer to the front. Sometimes he travels in the opposite direction, though he never makes it clear why. His war still reads very much like a travelogue, with days spent in train compartments or at rural railway stations. Encouraged that his knowledge of Russian is 'considerably greater than I thought', he sometimes sits for hours talking to some Russian gent or other and is seldom lost for words.

Back in the company of his comrades, piano chords rise up. Everyone around him is 'starved of music'. You would almost be forgiven for thinking that the Führer's name is Beethoven and the swastika an exercise in musical notation. The following day, he heads another 150 kilometres west, by road this time. He makes a painful admission to his mother and frets that she will be angry and unhappy with him: he has lost the fountain pen she gave him for his birthday.

Early October finds him in the emergency room of the field hospital, but his fever subsides as quickly as it came. He tells his parents they will have to wait until the holidays for a full report on progress at the front, but wants them to know that the Russians have taken a drubbing and that the last few weeks have cost the enemy dearly. Their divisions are severely depleted, and he has seen for himself how miserable their men look.

One week later, he is back with his unit. On 22 October, he writes in true soldierly fashion: 'Yesterday, we finally got back at the Russians and inflicted substantial losses. Today is much quieter. After yesterday, "Ivan" seems to have had enough.' In the evening, the piano sounds again.

That same day, 22 October 1943, he writes a second letter to his parents. His last.

The letter his father sends him on 3 November is returned

unopened. His mother's letter of 18 November comes back too. This time the envelope bears a stamp: *Zurück. Empfänger gefallen für Großdeutschland*. Return to sender. Recipient killed in action for the Greater Germanic Reich.

A few weeks later, a card arrives from the front, signed by Kurt Wolfsdorf. In four sentences, he tells the von Wrangell family that on the way to the field hospital he learned from a comrade that Claus had died a hero's death. Their son, he adds, was a good comrade. The injuries or illness that caused his death go unmentioned.

Officially, he was listed as missing until 1966, when a Hamburg court declared him dead.

I read Claus's war correspondence in a Tallinn hotel room. Perhaps that's why I see him in a different light: as an exiled Estonian who donned a uniform to win back his country. There were swastikas on his sleeve and on his cap. But if his letters are anything to go by, Claus barely seems to have noticed them.

It was Karin, Lotti's daughter, who gave me the letters. She came across them while clearing out a storage unit after her mother's death. Lotti had kept them hidden, mainly from herself, to avoid confrontation with the past. Karin typed them up, photocopied them, and attached a photo of Claus to the twenty A4 sheets.

Not a boy in uniform, but a boy in a smart black jacket and a white shirt with a wide, open collar. Straight dark-blond hair, side parting, ears that stick out, lips pressed in a smile as intelligent as it is mischievous.

'Is that your son?' the chambermaid asks when she has finished cleaning my room.

Before I can answer, she exclaims in English, 'What a fine young man!'

I nearly say, 'A volunteer in Hitler's army.' Instead, I mutter, 'He's far too young for you.'

For the whole of 1944, Amchen, devastated by the death of her eldest son, barely left the house. Summer came and went, and Lotti returned to school in Wreschen. In the autumn of 1944, the schools were closed. Girls and boys were put to work, along with all the women and men. Some had to work in the fields; others were assigned to

Volodya and Amchen's last letter to Claus — the letter that came back.

jobs in the city. Lotti was given *Bahnhofsdienst*, tasked with keeping the station clean and looking after children travelling without parents.

At Christmas, Lotti was back in Schwarzau. Covered in snow, the grounds surrounding the house looked like something from a fairy tale. But the beauty was deceptive. On 1 January 1945, the family celebrated New Year's Eve there for the last time, and a cousin by the name of Wolf Thomson came to visit.

On 11 March 2010, Thomson emailed me from Canada. At the age of eighty-two, his anger remained undiminished:

> Three weeks later, our world in that part and all of eastern Europe came to a terrible and bloody end when the Soviet hordes stormed across the plains of Poland and eastern Germany, causing the frantic flight and brutal death of millions. The three of us, Lotti, Oli and I, separated from one another, miraculously survived a wave of destruction that can be classified as the second Holocaust.

The second Holocaust? It was hell, that's for sure. Soviet troops had already crossed the Russian-Polish border and were advancing at a rate of ten, eleven, twelve kilometres a day. The Nazis ordered all

Claus in his final year of high school, weeks before he volunteered to
serve in the Wehrmacht.

Germans to stay put. Anyone who attempted to flee was a traitor to
the belief in ultimate victory and unfit to be called German. Refugees
were shot without mercy. Yet on 20 January 1945, Baltic Germans
were suddenly ordered to leave their homes. Those in rural areas were
to travel by horse-and-carriage, the city dwellers by train.

Vladimir harnessed two horses to a covered wagon and instructed two coachmen to take his wife and her relatives as far west as possible. He promised to follow within a day, after he got the children from the village primary school to safety.

Amchen left along with her mother, mother-in-law, and sister. Vladimir was never heard from again. No one has ever discovered what happened to him, or what befell the schoolchildren. Twenty years passed before a witness came forward. 'We left deep in the night, three men on horseback. One of them was Vladimir. At one point, I turned left, the other two turned right.' End of story.

Huddled in a blanket, Amchen braced herself for what was to come. The horses fought their way through blizzards, the wagon swaying and slipping behind them. Twice, it overturned. The coachmen begged Amchen to be allowed to return to their wife and children. Understanding that it was inhuman to cut off the Poles from their kin, she agreed and took over the reins.

Lotti was working at the station when news reached her that she had to flee immediately. She ran to the house where Arist, her first boyfriend, lived. In letters to her mother, she had sung his praises and even confessed that she wanted to marry him. He too was from Estonia, having moved with his parents to a suburb of Posen. Lotti arrived to find the house empty. She was stunned. Pulling open doors, she found the wardrobes had been stripped bare: not a stitch of clothing remained. Though eighteen, she felt like an abandoned seven-year-old.

In panic, she jumped on the first train heading west. An over-crowded train that picked up speed for a few kilometres, then ground to a halt for hours. It was full speed ahead or a terrifying wait: every-one on board knew that Red Army planes could skim low and strafe the wagons with machine-gun fire.

The train stopped at every little station to pick up more refugees. In one town, it only slowed, passing the platform at walking pace. The door of a carriage was thrown open, a woman was bundled aboard by soldiers, and the train steamed away. Immediately, the woman began screaming and banging on the door that had closed behind her. Her three small children had been left on the platform. Hours passed and still she screamed. Her voice would haunt Lotti's nightmares for the rest of her life.

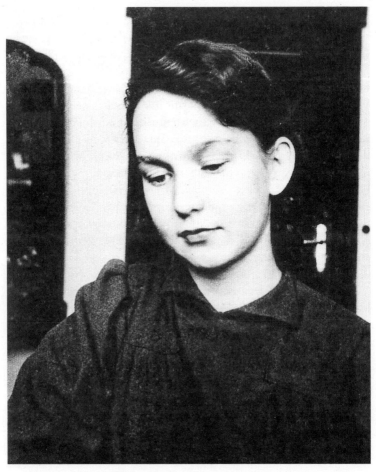

Lotti in Poland, shortly before her flight to the West.

The train continued westward. Brief bursts of speed, then a long, agonising crawl. At last, they came to another station, where they were ordered off and the train started back to pick up more refugees in Poland.

The big map of Poland and Germany that Lotti had taken with her came in useful. A few weeks earlier, Amchen had told Lotti and Oli that they should try to reach Kröchlendorf, a village in northern Brandenburg where the von Bernuth family had a country residence. The von Wrangells had struck up a friendship with the von Bernuths in the 1940s. They owned the estate that bordered on Schwarzau and had shown Vladimir and Amchen the ropes when they arrived in Poland.

Lotti's mother had marked a few more crosses on the map: these were villages or towns where relatives lived. On foot, Lotti was able to reach the home of an aunt and uncle. They had managed to get hold of a truck and were just about to hit the road when their niece arrived. Though it was a tight squeeze, there was room for one more in the cabin.

They set off with some hope, but on roads clogged with carts and fellow refugees, the going was slow. By the end of the first day, they had barely travelled thirty kilometres. On the second day, Lotti's aunt and uncle sent her packing. Provisions were running low and buying food along the way was too costly: Lotti would have to fend for herself. These were not distant relatives — her uncle was Vladimir's brother.

Lotti continued on foot. Karin still has the map her mother took with her. Torn along the edges and folds, stained by rain and mud. A red dotted line shows the route she took, with crosses where she stopped along the way. Some days she was lucky to travel five kilometres, and often she had to skirt around combat zones. Roads or entire areas could be blocked off, leaving her no choice but to retrace her steps for miles in the hope of finding an alternative route. She was on the road for weeks.

Amchen's route was even longer. Beyond a wide circle around Berlin, every railway line had been bombed. Her horses pulled them on through Saxony and Brandenburg, plodding towards Kröchlendorf. There was danger on all sides. The horses or the wagon might be stolen at any moment. And in those weeks and months, every woman lived in fear of rape.

Lotti slept by the side of the road, in barns or in the woods. She never spoke about what happened to her on her journey, not even to her mother. On rare occasions, she tried. Playing as a child, Karin would hear her mother and her grandmother talking in the front room. But Amchen always brushed aside any veiled references with a phrase like, 'Oh child, those were strange times …'

Olaf fought among the ruins of Berlin. At Misdroy, they had rushed him through his final exams — 'war exams' as they were known — so that he could be packed off to Berlin with his classmates. Dressed in their Hitler Youth uniforms, these boys of sixteen and seventeen were drafted in to defend the Nazis' last remaining bunkers and strongholds. This fate had not been forced on the Misdroy boys; Olaf had initially refused to go but later relented. Seeing the others getting ready to leave, he did not want to abandon his friends.

These boy soldiers were so terrified that they resorted to Dutch courage. In April, drunk on cheap wine, Olaf was wounded. For the next month, he lay in a basement sick bay; in June, he was able to slip away among the Soviet troops and head west on foot. Eventually, he reached the displaced-persons camp at Trebel, where he was able to embrace his mother and sister again. Like Amchen and Lotti, he owned nothing but the clothes on his back. Somehow, he had managed to hang on to his watch.

For a time, Olaf worked as a labourer on Lüneburg Heath, earning a few marks a week. Since Germany's capitulation, his wartime school diploma from Misdroy had become a worthless scrap of paper.

Amchen moved into the von Bernuth family's manor at Förste in the Harz region. She scrubbed, ironed, cooked, tended the vegetable garden, and fed the chickens. For years she stayed, profoundly grateful to the von Bernuths for the roof over her head. If nothing else, the hard work was a way of keeping her thoughts at bay. Though she knew better, there was always the hope that Vladimir had been captured by the Red Army and that one day he would return.

Two hundred and fifty kilometres further north, in the city of Hamburg, Lotti was pinning a note to a tree: *English teacher offers her services*. At the girls' school in Wreschen, her lowest marks had been for maths and English, but now bluffing was her only option. Some of her first students had a better command of the language than she did.

Through these private lessons, she met a journalist, who wangled her a job with broadcaster Nordwestdeutscher Rundfunk: it was typing mostly, and it paid a pittance, but if you asked sweetly, the British soldiers on guard at the gate would slip you cigarettes. From her monthly salary of 150 marks, she sent fifty back home to help put Olaf through school. He had stopped working and was cramming for the final exams that would earn him a proper school diploma. In May 1946, Lotti sold the jewellery she had stuffed in her coat pocket as they fled Estonia. Her silver charm bracelet and turquoise brooch — 'which I never wear anyway' — fetched enough for her to set aside a thousand marks for her brother's studies. She never once stopped to consider her own education. Any cash she and her mother could spare was invested in the boy.

Amchen, Lotti, and Oli spent Christmas 1946 apart: Lotti in Hamburg, Oli at a boarding school near Hamburg, and Amchen in Förste. The letter Lotti sent to her mother on 17 December was the most heart-rending she had ever written. Until then, she had always urged her mother 'not to dwell on any sadness in her letters': she would always battle on. But in the days leading up to the traditional family holiday, her feelings got the better of her. 'You cannot begin to imagine how endlessly I love you,' she wrote to her mother. 'I am so dependent on you that it frightens me sometimes. You are everything to me, and yet it's you I must be without at this time of year. The one thing that can help us through is thinking back on all the Christmases we celebrated together; you, me, Papa, Claus, and Oli. Though it will make us sad, it will also give us an eternal sense of connection.'

In turn, Olaf wrote to Lotti. 'What a Christmas. Such darkness. But I will hold you. Always. No matter where we are.'

The following year brought reason for hope. Amchen, whose health had been poor throughout 1945 and 1946, began to find her feet again. Olaf passed his final exams and was admitted to Nordwestdeutscher Rundfunk's class of aspiring journalists. And in Hamburg, Lotti met a Dutch soldier who served with UNRRA, the United Nations postwar relief agency.

Jan Beernink and his fiancée were at a party thrown by allied soldiers when he first laid eyes on Lotti. He was enough of a gentleman to escort his fiancée home first, but then immediately jumped on his bike and raced back to the party to woo Lotti. Her slender, boyish charms had bowled him over.

Before the year was out, he had returned to his homeland with Lotti in tow. Lotti had no papers. Since leaving Estonia, she had been a displaced person, a stateless citizen without a passport. Jan went ahead, entering the country legally and then bribing a local farmer north of Oldenzaal in order to sneak Lotti across the border. She had to crawl into the Netherlands under cover of darkness.

Jan and Lotti had married in Germany, and in Amsterdam he

applied for a passport for the newly wed Mrs Beernink. The immigration officer looked kindly on them, and the only document he required Lotti to produce was her Estonian birth certificate, which her mother had brought with her in her handbag. Though not enough for full citizenship, it earned Lotti a passport with the handwritten addendum 'shall be treated as Dutch in practice'.

The lights of Amsterdam thrilled her more than anything. Not the lit-up windows of the canalside houses, which might have been vaguely reminiscent of Tallinn. No, after the dark ruins of postwar Hamburg and the evening blackouts in Wreschen, it was the streetlights she fell in love with.

Karin was born in June 1948.

Like many a former soldier, Jan Beernink struggled to adjust to life in peacetime. He drifted from one job to another. At the first trading office, his salary enabled them to rent an apartment on the fashionable Apollolaan; two jobs later, they had to make do with a smaller flat on the far less salubrious Biesboschstraat. Jan's idea of fun was to go fishing with friends. He wasn't much of a family man.

Before long, Lotti confided to Amchen in a letter that her marriage was not a happy one. The answer that came by return of post was a clarion call: in that case, you need to learn a trade and stand on your own two feet.

In 1953, Karin was sent to live with her grandmother in Germany. By this time, Lotti had already done some modelling. With her slender neck, short hair, sparkling eyes, and petite, athletic figure, she bore more than a passing resemblance to Audrey Hepburn. Perhaps it was this connection that led her to study design at the fashion school.

Day in, day out, Karin listened to Grandma Amchen's stories until she was convinced that she had been born in Estonia herself. Every other day, Uncle Olaf came to visit. In the world of broadcasting, his star had risen swiftly, and he had gone from reporter to political editor. Although she had no idea what he was on about half the time, Karin understood one thing: that voice on the radio belonged to Uncle Oli.

When Karin returned to the Netherlands six months later, she couldn't help but notice how good her mother's Dutch had become. No one could tell that she was from Germany, let alone that she'd been born in Estonia and had spent her high-school years in Poland. Even more admirably, her written Dutch was flawless and completely

Lotti around 1954.

natural. In 1956, she was hired as a fashion editor, and by 1958, she was editor-in-chief at *Marion*, a magazine that mainly featured sewing patterns.

Lotti came up with half of the patterns herself; the other half she purchased from foreign magazines. She also wrote all of the accompanying copy. Times were still tough and off-the-peg fashion still unaffordable for many families, so most women made their own clothes. In its heyday, *Marion* had 465,000 subscribers; the editorial team doubled year on year, hitting a peak of sixteen staff. Lotti became a household name on the Dutch fashion scene, with all the attendant perks. If she needed a picture taken, the country's leading portrait photographer, Paul Huf, did the honours. Through his lens, she seemed to embody the spirit of the 1960s. She was the last person you would associate with a traumatic past or an aristocratic background. Being a baroness by birth was something she concealed as if it were a congenital defect.

Professionally, she and Oli flourished. He became a leading political pundit on radio and television. In 1965, he entered the political arena himself and was elected to the Bundestag for the CDU. As a member of the parliamentary party, he helped shape the Christian

Democrats' policy on Eastern Europe. By the phone on the desk of his Bonn office stood a framed picture of his brother, Claus.

For seventeen years, Olaf Baron von Wrangel served in the Bundestag. On being appointed program director of the Norddeutscher Rundfunk, he gave up his parliamentary seat but remained active behind the scenes as a key advisor to Helmut Kohl, especially during the critical period when glasnost gathered momentum and the Wall fell. When the Soviet Union collapsed, East and West Germany were reunified within a matter of months.

In his memoirs, published in 1995, he nevertheless described himself as a 'problem child'. If anyone deserved credit, he wrote, it was his sister, who had always given him the impression that she could 'solve any difficulty with ease'.

Karin seldom saw her mother angry. One notable exception was election day 1970, the first time she was old enough to vote. In all innocence, she returned from the polling station and announced to her mother, 'I voted CPN, Mum.'

The colour drained from Lotti's face, and her lip began to tremble. 'How could you?' she blurted out.

It would never have occurred to Karin to vote communist to spite her mother. She felt as much love for Lotti as Lotti did for Amchen. She was incredibly proud of Lotti, of her willpower, of everything she had achieved. Lotti was a mother to be reckoned with: always well dressed, always positive and cheerful. But Karin, her only child, had no idea how traumatic her mother's past had been.

In appearance, Karin was more like her father: Jan had been a tall man, with a broad face and a far-away look in his eyes. They had never really had much contact. He died in 1966, shortly before her eighteenth birthday. A year later, her mother remarried, to Sjef Hafkamp, a friend of the family. Karin had known him since she was a toddler; he was a warm man, and she felt sure he would take good care of her mother and make her happy.

From the age of fifteen, Karin went away to boarding school. The choice had been her own: Amsterdam in the 1960s was a welter of distractions, and she had struggled to keep her schoolwork on track. Her marks had been so poor that she had to repeat a year.

Things improved, and in 1968 she passed the entrance exam for

Lotti in the Netherlands, editor-in-chief of *Marion*.

the School of Journalism in Utrecht. Student life came as a liberation. She spent every evening at the student union, drinking and smoking weed until the words 'cool, man' were constantly on her lips.

A year earlier, I had been admitted to the School of Journalism myself. I got to know Karin as an exuberant young woman, a bit of a rebel, in touch with the times: rangy, defiant, larger than life. She was the drummer in a rock band.

The Mantoux test — a mere scratch on the arm — brought the first year of her studies screeching to a halt. She was diagnosed with TB and had to spend the next year recovering at a woodland sanatorium near Soest, with nothing to do all day but rest. Fellow student Willem Kloppert came to visit, the last person she had expected to turn up at her bedside: with his wild hair and Frank Zappa moustache, he had always struck her as aloof. By the time she resumed her studies, the two were inseparable. But when Willem got a job in Arnhem, they saw each other less and less, and eventually decided to call it a day.

Karin continued to play drums, so obsessively that she almost damaged her hearing. Looking back, she saw it as a dogged effort to shake off the torpor of those endless, listless, bedridden months at the sanatorium, where her only connection with student life had been *GRrroM*, the school's fortnightly magazine, which she read from cover to cover. The sixth issue of 1969 was entirely devoted to a visit by Prince Claus — Olaf's former schoolmate Claus von Amsberg — who had agreed to be interviewed by four of the school's budding journalists, despite protests by a number of their teachers. It had been three years since Claus married Princess Beatrix of the Netherlands, but the controversy surrounding her marriage to a German so soon after the war was still raging.

Karin read the interviews and felt a needle pierce her soul. Her Uncle Olaf had been reunited with Claus von Amsberg at the home of a shared acquaintance. They spent an entire evening talking about their Misdroy schooldays and those desperate weeks defending the outskirts of Berlin. Uncle Olaf had told Karin about their conversation when he visited her at the sanatorium. At the time, she only had the sketchiest notion of the von Wrangels' past, but she could already sense the depth of the family's pain.

Half a lifetime later, Karin heard from a friend that I was writing a book about the Baltic countries. That same day, she got in touch with me.

'You interviewed Claus,' was the first thing she said when we met

Karin, Lotti's daughter, in her student years.

up a few weeks later. She was still living in Utrecht; I hadn't seen her in forty years.

It was true: I had been among the fresh-faced reporters selected by the editors of *GRrroM* to give the prince a polite grilling. I was astounded that this of all things had stuck with her all those years. As a student, Karin had never said a word about her family's Baltic past.

'Not that I was ashamed. It just wasn't something I thought about back then.'

That day would arrive.

In 1982, Karin joined the staff of Muziekcentrum Vredenburg, Utrecht's main venue for live music, as an editor. Five years into her career there, she welcomed the musicians of the Estonian ensemble Hortus Musicus, who had flown in from behind the Iron Curtain to perform works by Arvo Pärt, Lepo Sumera, and Galina Grigorjeva. Karin was at the back of the hall when the coffee-time concert started. It was the first Estonian music she had ever heard. In no time, tears were streaming down her cheeks.

Afterwards, the musicians were kept on a tight leash by minders from the Estonian Ministry of Culture, but during a visit to Café 't Hoogt their vigilance let up long enough for her to have a brief conversation with violinist Mail Sildos.

'My mother used to live in the Nõmme district of Tallinn,' she began hesitantly.

'What a coincidence. That's my district too,' Mail said.

'I really want to visit the house, I want to see it so much.'

'The political climate is still very tense. If things improve, I'll send word.'

The following year, Hortus Musicus gave another concert, this time in Bruges. Mail sent Karin a postcard from Belgium: 'You can come now.'

Intourist, the Soviet state tourism organisation, refused to allow Karin to leave Tallinn and travel south on her own. If it hadn't been for Mail, she would never have seen Kernu, or Hageri, or Mõisamaa. Every kilometre she covered had to be in the company of a guide.

For Hageri, she even needed a special pass.

'What do you want to do there?'

'Go to church. I'm religious.'

The guide shook his head. If she was that intent on prayer, there were plenty of churches in Tallinn.

One Saturday, Mail sneaked her out of town. Illegally.

In the rectory at Hageri, she encountered a large group of people celebrating the eightieth birthday of one of the parishioners. The old woman sat beneath the portrait of Pastor Konstantin Thomson, and the celebrants sang for her.

'Who are you?' the sexton asked.

'Annemarie Thomson's granddaughter.'

'In that case, we'll sing for you too! A song of welcome!'

Karin was beginning to understand how much in Estonia was expressed in song. This particular song had four verses; three too many. By the end of the first, she was sobbing like a child.

Her visits to Kernu and Mõisamaa were brief; they had to be back in Tallinn by nightfall. She filmed and photographed as much as she could. Lotti hadn't dared to go with her; this was before the Singing Revolution, the Wall had yet to come down. But she had asked her daughter to record as much of her visit as possible. On seeing those images, Lotti's homesickness began in earnest: by the look of things, not one door, not one shelf at Mõisamaa had changed.

It would be another five years before Lotti set foot in her home-land. In the meantime, Karin had married a TV journalist, Gerard de Lange, who worked for a current-affairs show called *Reporter*. It was Gerard who suggested that his mother-in-law should revisit the places from her childhood, and take a camera crew with her.

Lotti, now retired, hesitated for a long time. She had always kept her past to herself and suddenly here she was, facing the prospect of putting it into words — on camera to boot. Eventually, she agreed but not wholeheartedly. Husband Sjef and daughter Karin travelled with her. The party flew to Helsinki and took the ferry to Tallinn. This was a cinematic choice: it would make for a cleaner narrative arc if Lotti returned to Tallinn as she had left it fifty-two years before, across the sea.

In front of the camera, Lotti clammed up. In Nõmme, Hageri, and Mõisamaa, she stared at window frames and doorposts with the air of an insurance adjuster who can spot no obvious signs of damage. All emotion was barricaded behind the icy smile of someone who wanted to appear beyond reproach. Only once, on the ferry, as the skyline of Tallinn drew closer, did her feelings show. Her eyes filled with tears, but her voice remained calm.

When the film was broadcast, it prompted two angry letters from Estonians living in the Netherlands. Lotti had no right to speak for anyone, the writers complained, especially not on national television. This woman lamenting her eviction from Mõisamaa and maligning the Soviet regime wasn't even Estonian, she was German. One of those filthy-rich aristocrats who used to rule the roost in our Estonia.

Those letters made Lotti sadder than she had ever been. 'Is there no end to it?' she wondered. Karin tried to raise her spirits, but

Lotti replied with a reference to Nabokov, her own bitter twist on a sentence from his memoir *Speak, Memory*. The book had taken up residence on her bedside cabinet, and she practically knew it by heart: 'The hatred for the Soviet dictatorship I have been cherishing all these years is a hypertrophied sense of lost childhood, not sorrow for lost banknotes.'

There was nothing else for it, Karin concluded: the reunion had to be redone. Better organised, better prepared, and this time as a family, complete with Uncle Olaf. No flights; they would make their own way north by car. And above all, they would take their time.

First it was Lotti who prevaricated, then it was Olaf. His health was not good enough to make the trip. Nonsense, Karin insisted, he simply couldn't summon the courage. Next year, he promised. But one year became two, became three. Grandma Amchen passed away, aged ninety-five. A new century dawned. There was always a reason to delay.

In 2004, they set off at last. It was June, the weather was clement. Outside the house in Nõmme and at the church in Hageri, Lotti maintained the reserve of a woman who sees emotions as the preserve of young girls too foolish to know better. Olaf remained a stiff old man. Though he walked with head up and shoulders back, there was effort and pain in every step. At Kernu, his only comment was, 'The brickworks is gone. It used to be left of the house.'

The turning point came at Mõisamaa. Lotti and Olaf were deeply moved to meet Armilde again and to see the house unchanged: not only was the furniture the same, it was arranged exactly as they had left it. The wallpaper above the sideboard consisted of newspapers stuck to the wall. Newspapers from 1939. Olaf leaned closer, took off his glasses, and read, *Von Ribbentrop and Molotov Make Pact*. He began to tremble so violently that his glasses fell to the floor.

The moment Karin will always remember occurred in the evening. It was about eight o'clock and still light, the sky tinged with pink. Lotti and Olaf were in front of the house, on the spot where as children they had played in the sandpit every summer. Standing some thirty paces away, Karin noticed a sprightliness in Olaf's movements and even thought she heard Lotti laughing. She edged closer, careful not to intrude but also curious. What were they talking about? Why did they suddenly look so happy?

Close enough to hear, she realised that Lotti and Olaf were speaking Estonian together. From one moment to the next, the words had been restored to their memories, words they were no longer sure how to pronounce, that tripped awkwardly from the tongue. Laughing, they corrected each other, wondering whether the *a* in this word or that was short or long.

In this reunion, the language of their childhood had returned, a language they might have never have spoken or allowed themselves to speak for the rest of their lives.

One word was repeated again and again. It turned out to mean 'many happy returns'. In all the emotion, everyone but Olaf had forgotten that it was June the 29th, Lotti's birthday. A day she had celebrated in Mõisamaa for the first thirteen years of her life.

Lotti died in 2007, Olaf two years later.

With both of them gone, Karin gathered hundreds of letters, documents, and photos belonging to her family, the von Wrangel zu Ludenhofs.

On a winter's afternoon, she brought them to my door, including the deed of sale for Kernu Manor. One month later, I set out on my journey from Nõmme to Mõisamaa.

14

From the Drainpipe to the National Archives

A WALK THROUGH TALLINN WITH ILYA SUNDELEVICH

Estonia, December 2009

Ilya Sundelevich is a little wary. What exactly is it I want?

'A walk through the city.'

'Just a walk?'

'Walking, looking, listening.'

'What for?'

He shakes his head and blows his nose. It's a freezing afternoon, the temperature hovering around minus eight. Ilya tugs his tweed cap over his forehead, worried he might be coming down with the flu.

'To see the places that are part of your personal history. I've heard you're well worth listening to.'

'Who from?'

I mention a name.

'Ah, I see ...'

He gives me a cautious smile and murmurs an apology.

'I was born in 1949. That is to say, I grew up with the KGB. I hear a question and a red light clicks on in the back of my mind. Some things never leave you.'

Speaking your mind meant punishment or, perhaps even more crippling, the fear of punishment.

'Estonians were afraid. Those of a certain generation still are. Afraid, always afraid.' Ilya points to a wide street with blackened concrete buildings on the right. 'That's where the fear began.'

We turn our backs on the biting wind that swirls around the open expanse of Freedom Square and walk along Harju tänav, a street destroyed by the Russian bombardment of 9 March 1944.

'Ten per cent of the Old Town was reduced to rubble, 30 per cent of the whole city, bombed by 300 Red Army planes. Look up and try to picture them, flying five to a formation. That means sixty formations came over. Survive that and you'll never sleep soundly again.'

The bombs killed 634 people; another 659 were seriously injured. Almost 20,000 were left homeless, and much of Harju was reduced to rubble. The street ran past Niguliste kirik, the Church of St Nicholas. Only the lower section of the tower remained standing.

'The communists were in no hurry: it took them forty years to rebuild the church, and when it was finished, they turned it into a museum of atheism. Not so the houses that were destroyed. They were too stark a reminder of the callous nature of the bombing and the hundreds who had died. Harju was rebuilt in no time, with the ugliest Soviet housing imaginable.'

Ilya quickens his pace, as if to shake off the shadow of the Stalinist-era blocks as soon as possible. We turn left onto Niguliste tänav.

'In this entire area, three houses were spared. Three! The finest and most elegant — that yellow one over there with the Gustavian-era windows — was my grandfather's house.'

He stops and takes a little bow.

'My grandfather's former house, I should say. By the summer of 1940, he had been kicked out. The Soviets expropriated all private homes larger than 130 square metres.'

A cheery little waltz pipes up, accompanying Ilya's words. The stretch of Harju in front of the church remained undeveloped, and an ice rink has been brought in to liven up the flat expanse. Girls on skates are pirouetting to ballet music by Tchaikovsky.

The reason behind the bombardment remains murky. According to Ilya, it served no military-strategic purpose. Later, it was said to be Russia's retribution for Estonian collaboration with the Nazis, but Ilya dismisses this as post-hoc justification. Three days before the attack on Tallinn, Russian planes flattened Narva, a Russian-speaking city on the Russian border where the number of Nazi collaborators could be counted on the fingers of one hand. Ilya puts the bombardments of Narva, Tallinn, and the centre of Tartu squarely at the door of Stalin and his seemingly random acts of destruction, designed to instil fear and reinforce his reputation as a strong man. These acts signalled the start of Soviet tyranny. From the very beginning, the hatred among Estonians ran deep.

'Your name sounds Russian: Sundelevich.'

'Polish.'

'And Ilya?'

'My parents, grandparents, and great-grandparents were born in Tallinn. My family has lived in this city for at least two centuries. My father's side hails from Lithuania, when the country was still Polish, my mother's side from Poland itself. They migrated north in the late eighteenth or early nineteenth century. Almost all Tallinn's Jewish families come from Lithuania, Poland, Belarus, or Ukraine. Under the influence of Swedish and Finnish protestants, there was little anti-Semitism here in the last century, far less than in Vilnius, Warsaw, or Riga in any case.'

The yellow house opposite Niguliste is the very picture of comfort and prosperity. Ilya's grandfather wove Gobelin-style tapestries of wool and silk there; like most of Tallinn's Jews, he was an educated, highly skilled artisan. The workshop took up the entire lower floor of the four-storey building, the office occupied the first. A beautiful Hanseatic house with Swedish influences.

'Its beauty consoled my mother in her final years. She suffered from Alzheimer's, lived in a state of utter confusion. But when I brought her here, to this house, memories began to surface and for a while she knew who she was. Towards the end, we came here almost every day. She looked up at the facade and talked to me as if she was a little girl.'

We enter a narrow alley, climb to the upper town, and then head back downhill for twenty metres or so on a narrow street with a gentle curve. There we halt outside café-restaurant Du Nord.

'This was the place to come if you wanted to rub shoulders with Tallinn's writers, painters, and musicians in the Soviet years. It's not far from a historic building once reserved by the writers' union to house their members. Jaan Kross was a regular at Du Nord. I often dropped by myself. The artists would tell me about all the things they weren't allowed to paint, the photographers showed me pictures that had fallen foul of the censor. It was a strange time — we shared an aversion to the regime, and that strengthened the ties between us.'

Du Nord stands empty; it went bankrupt shortly after the restoration of independence. A time when mutual solidarity gave way

The restored houses in Tallinn's Old Town.

to 'every man for himself', mutual support to thirst for individual success.

'There are days when I walk down this street and feel a pang of nostalgia. But by the time I reach Du Nord, it's passed.'

We reach Pikk tänav and stop in front of another building.

'The former KGB headquarters. See those bricked–up windows in the basement? That was so passers-by wouldn't hear the moans, the screams, and the dry pop of gunshots. In the late 1940s, the cellars were used for executions. In the '50s and '60s, it was more interroga-tion and torture.'

'People you knew?'

'Family members, distant relatives, friends. I remember a pal from school being picked up across the street from me one day. I honestly couldn't tell you what he'd done wrong. Perhaps they were just out to make an arrest. If I'd been walking there on the other side, it might have been me. The worst thing about the dictatorship was how arbi-trary it all was.'

The inscrutable building on the corner of Pikk and Pagari, still part of the Ministry of Interior, is an unappetising shade of brown. Three-quarters of the facades in the Old Town have been painstak-ingly restored to their former glory, repainted in fresh colours. Only Pikk is still cast in sombre hues, as if to remind anyone passing through of the darkest period in Estonian history.

'The KGB chose this location because of that church there — Oleviste, the Church of St Olaf. As far back as 1500 it had a 159-metre tower, the tallest structure in Europe until the nineteenth century. The KGB used it as a radio mast. All the information they gathered here was transmitted straight to Moscow.'

We turn right onto a narrow street and arrive at the slightly wider Sulevimägi. Ilya stops in front of an impressive townhouse.

'This is where my paternal grandparents lived when my father returned from Germany in 1939. But first, an amusing parable. My grandfather told my father, "Son, you must learn to be fluent in German because this city will always be German." He was wrong, the language became Russian. My father told me, "Son, you must learn to be fluent in Russian, because this city will always be Russian." Wrong again, the language became Estonian. I told my boy, "Son, you must learn Estonian, because Estonians will never give up their independence."'

'And?'

'He's currently learning English for all he's worth.'

Ilya's father attended German-speaking schools in Tallinn, primary and secondary, and studied German at the University of Dorpat (now Tartu). He left for Germany and became a journalist at *Kölner*

The bricked-up basement windows of the former KGB building in
Tallinn.

Tageblatt. In the summer of 1939, he returned to Tallinn to visit his
parents. The Molotov–Ribbentrop Pact prevented him from leaving.
Two months later, Soviet troops marched into Estonia; three months
later, he was arrested and sent to a forced labour camp in Siberia.

'Thank God. If he had stayed in Cologne, there was a 90 per
cent chance that his life would have ended in the gas chambers of
Auschwitz. For some, Siberia was a gift from on high. Only in Estonia
can history be that idiotic. Well, it was no picnic — my father came
back a wreck of a man. But at least he lived to tell the tale.'

We cross Raekoja plats, home to the town hall, and head for Suur-
Karja, passing dozens of restaurants on our way. No city in the north
boasts as many eateries per head of population as Tallinn, packed from
noon to midnight at this time of year. In the weeks before Christmas,
the number of Finns and Swedes triples. They come to Tallinn to eat,
drink, and shop. The city's restaurants and department stores make
them feel so much wealthier, with prices half what they would expect
to pay at home.

In front of Barons Hotel, we stop for a moment.

'In Tallinn, there's a saying that every bank becomes a hotel. That's

true of Barons, at any rate. It was built in 1903 as the head office of
G. Scheel & Co., a Baltic German bank.'

Directly opposite Scheel stood the house where Ilya's maternal
grandparents lived.

'My grandmother was a renowned pianist. After training in St
Petersburg under Anton Rubinstein, she returned to Tallinn, the
city of her birth. On the top floor, she often gave recitals. In the
1920s, when Estonia's national consciousness underwent a revival, the
character of those gatherings changed. They became salons where
writers, poets, painters, musicians, and academics came to debate
major political, social, and cultural issues. In the 1930s, the top floor
of her home was given over to a full-blown artists' society. And now
look what's become of it!'

Across the top floor windows, STRIPTEASE is writ large in red neon.

'A nightclub for Russians, Finns, Swedes, and Estonians. If my
grandmother had seen this coming, she would have joined the communist party in a heartbeat. I'm pretty sure I inherited my artistic
leanings from her, though I came to photography and the visual arts
relatively late. Life as an artist under Soviet rule was not much of a
prospect.'

Instead, Ilya studied economics and management, specialising in
logistics and the organisation of healthcare institutions. He gained his
first work experience at a Tallinn hospital.

'In 1977, they chucked me out. I'll show you where it happened.'

At a brisk pace, we cross Vene — Estonian for 'Russian' — and
arrive at the Russian Orthodox Church of St Nicholas.

'The Soviet Union wanted rid of the Jews, at the whim of yet
another half-crazed party leader. Brezhnev got it into his head that
all Jews had to emigrate to Israel. In 1977, I was given to understand
that it would be better if I left the country. If not, I was likely to face
"considerable difficulties". I decided to leave, along with my mother,
wife, and son. Not that they made it easy for us: obtaining an exit
visa was pricey, and money had been tight for a long time. In the late
1940s, my father returned from Siberia a broken man. During the
final years of his life, we were living in what you would call poverty.
When he died, all we had to our name was the Russian silver my
grandfather had collected and my father had managed to hang on to.
We decided to donate half the silverware to the Tallinn City Museum,

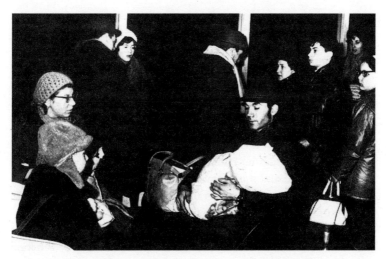

A Jewish family leaving the Soviet Union under duress in 1977.

but even that didn't get us our visas. I realised I had to be bolder with the other half and enlisted the help of an old schoolfriend, a priest at the Russian Orthodox Church of St Nicholas, this very church.'

The building's twin, square-topped towers and the round dome over the nave give it the air of a Catholic church from the neo-classical period. The cross atop the dome is the only obvious Byzantine feature. There's not an onion dome in sight.

'My priest friend had a thick beard and the puffy face of a heavy drinker. I knew him as a man you could trust, but he was also a shrewd operator with useful contacts in all sections of Russian society. We started by knocking back three bottles of cognac to steady our nerves. Then he called the police. The headquarters of the Soviet state and security police were right over there.'

He points to a building on the corner of Vene and Munga. 'Within two minutes, a police van pulled up. The officers demanded to see the silver, and it was thrown into the van. Then they came back in, pulled me off my chair, and dragged me out onto the steps. I tried to get back on my feet. Three sheets to the wind, I reached out with both hands and grabbed the zinc drainpipe that ran from the gutter. The cops began tugging at me, and the three of us ended up rolling down the steps. A section of the pipe had come off in my hand. I have no idea what happened next. Maybe they threw me into a holding cell for being drunk and disorderly. Whatever happened, I woke up at home the next day. In my jacket pocket were the exit visas for myself and my family.'

'Surreal.'

'I could hardly believe it myself. I had a cold shower to sober up and then took a walk down to the church. The drainpipe was good as new.'

Ilya lived in Israel for twenty years. He made a career for himself, eventually becoming the business director of Jerusalem's largest hospital. Work-wise and money-wise, all was well. He learned to plan, develop, manage, adapt, and streamline, skills that in his personal life proved to be of little use.

'Our marriage was on the rocks. My wife just couldn't adjust to life in Israel. The divorce dragged on for years: a failing of the legal system, no fault of hers or mine. She left for the US, and I remarried, this time to a Jewish woman born and raised in Russia. I became a father again, to a baby boy. Yet still there was this longing inside me. Without even realising, I was waiting for the moment when I could resume my former life.'

In 1996, Ilya returned to Estonia with his wife, his young son, and his mother to lay claim to his family's property. The Estonian government had promised to return to all rightful claimants the houses and other property confiscated during the Soviet occupation. In cases where property had been destroyed, the government offered financial reparation.

'My plan was to stay for three years and settle all the claims. I foresaw all kinds of difficulties and an interminable legal battle. The Lithuanian government had announced a similar scheme but went back on its promises time and again. To my surprise, things in Tallinn went smoothly. Almost as a matter of routine, I was granted ownership of the houses that had belonged to my paternal and maternal grandparents. Selling them took a little longer — I wanted to sell because I had my mind set on returning to Israel — but within four or five months, everything was settled. By then, I was so pleased with how things were going and the mentality in the new Estonia that I decided to stay on, much to the delight of my mother, wife, and son. My mother's entire past was here in Tallinn, and my wife had no problem leaving behind the strife in Jerusalem. And to my son,

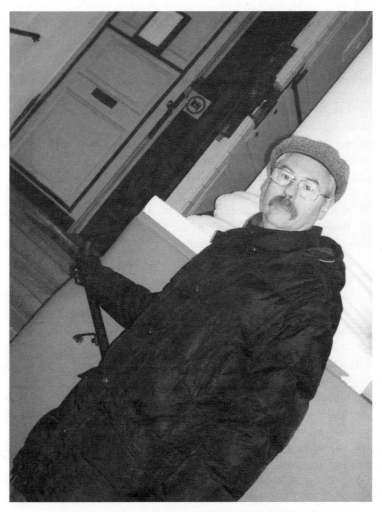

Ilya Sundelevich on the steps of the Church of St Nicholas in Tallinn,
where his life took a surreal turn.

Europe seemed like one big adventure.'

We cover another kilometre and come to a deserted part of the
Old Town, stopping in front of an old building with closed shutters.

'This place means nothing to any visitor to Tallinn. But it's where
the foundation of my existence lies. And that of many other Estonians.
It's home to the National Archives.'

Once Ilya had decided to stay in Estonia, he wanted Estonian citizenship. But this required proof that one of his parents had been a resident in 1940. He stepped into the archive building with trepidation. Would the Soviets even have kept the records of a Jewish father and a Jewish mother?

'I pictured myself walking into a scene from Kafka. One where a short-sighted chap in a grey overall shakes his head, shuffles from one filing cabinet to another, and makes me come back four or five times without ever finding a document. Until finally he says, "Please don't take this the wrong way, sir, but I'm afraid you don't exist."'

The reality was different. A woman in her early forties took care of the entire business in under three hours. Among his mother's papers, she found a 1939 tax return paid in 1940, when Ilya's mother had been working in a garment workshop.

Ilya told her, 'You know more about my family than I do. I had no idea my mother even had a job before the war.'

When he stepped onto the square outside, he literally jumped for joy. He can still point to the exact spot where he hit the ground. It was the happiest fall of his life.

The Tallinn street Ilya loves the most runs along the north-west flank of the city wall. On Kooli tänav, he insists, you can still taste, smell, see, and feel the Middle Ages. The street is not paved with smooth, grey slabs of Finnish stone like the avenues of the city centre, but with rounded local cobbles edged by pale seams of snow in winter and rainwater in summer. It's not hard to imagine why the city was afflicted by regular outbreaks of the plague, an indiscriminate killer.

A tall, elongated residential complex leans against the rampart. It dates from the late sixteenth or early seventeenth century and is in deplorable condition.

'I know the owner. He has no plans to sell, renovate, or even demolish the place. It houses the same tenants as before the restoration of independence. A rare exception. With the advent of capitalism, most of the Old Town's residents were forced to leave.'

Could it be that the owner doesn't want to get on the wrong side of the Russian mafia? Ilya shakes his head.

'All that played out ten or fifteen years ago, around the time I was selling off the family homes. I was keen to get rid of them as soon as possible, especially the property opposite Barons Hotel: an ideal location. I was proven right, and it was converted into a nightclub. In 1997, the entire real-estate sector was a shady, if not criminal enterprise. From 2000, the authorities began reining things in. Nowadays, organised crime controls drug trafficking, prostitution, and arms smuggling. But unless you're in need of a gun, a line of coke, or a girl for the night, you will only encounter the mafia in the newspapers. Tallinn has become a normal city, that is to say as normal as Stockholm, Helsinki, Copenhagen, Hamburg, or Amsterdam. But it will always be a port on the doorstep of Russia, Finland, and Sweden, strategically placed for smuggling just about anything.'

As we stand there, two black Mercedes, limousines with tinted bulletproof glass, pull up in front of a stall that sells Christmas presents. Three burly bodyguards jump out of the first car, the contours of firearms clearly visible under their grey jackets. They take up position in the middle of Kooli and bring the street to a standstill; no car, not even a pedestrian is allowed to pass. Then a fourth bodyguard emerges from the second Mercedes and opens the rear door: a small, plump man in a long, black fur coat appears and buys a few trinkets from the little old lady at the stall. When he hands her three banknotes (no doubt three times the actual price), she makes a sign of the cross and kisses his hand. The man gets back into the car, the bodyguards follow, and the limousines race off, tyres screeching.

'From Russia with love,' I mutter.

It is a bit of a caricature, Ilya agrees.

'We've learned to laugh about it. The chap in the fur coat is not to be envied. Each minute could be his last. You're better off dying in astrakhan than in rags. But dead is still dead.'

Kooli leads on to Gümnaasiumi. The high school there, one of the oldest in Europe, runs the entire length of the street. Its founder, Sweden's King Gustav II Adolf, also founded the University of Tartu. He appointed Johan Skytte as chancellor, who argued in his inaugural address that the university should seek to educate as many noble as peasant children. A rare slice of modernity in 1632.

'Education,' Ilya says, 'has always been particularly good in Estonia. Even in Soviet times, it made Estonia the most modern and Western of the Soviet republics. Of the three independent Baltic countries, Estonia has taken the lead economically, socially, and culturally. Tallinn is home to KUMU, a brand-new museum of modern art designed by Finnish architect Pekka Vapaavuori. Estonia is not afraid, willing to throw open its borders and award a contract to one of Europe's top architects. It's the outlook of a country that believes in itself. Self-confidence stems from a solid education.'

We traverse the Old Town and return to our starting point. The cold has reached a point where tiny icicles are forming on Ilya's moustache. The streetlights come on. Night is already falling and the clock has yet to strike four.

At Harju tänav 13, we enter Tallinna Linnagalerii, Tallinn City Gallery. The photos on the wall are Ilya's. Every last one is a shot of the city. I recognise the buildings he has pointed out to me.

'It's my story, yes. My story in pictures.'

Two video installations are hung among the photos. The images on screen repeat: same streets, same buildings, but the commentary alternates between Estonian and Russian.

'Two entirely different commentaries on the same locations. Just as you would have heard a completely different story today if you'd toured the town with a Baltic German or an Estonian whose roots lie in Ukraine. Every group has its own history, its own sources of pride and frustration, its own suffering. I like art that has an idea behind it, a point of departure.'

Ilya extends his arm for a farewell handshake.

'Where do you live nowadays?'

The question takes him by surprise, especially when I suggest walking him to his front door.

Our route takes us through a different city. First comes early-twentieth-century Tallinn: the Russian Theatre and the Estonian Drama Theatre (which began life as the German Theatre), then the Estonia Concert Hall and Estonian National Opera, sitting cosily side by side. Almost immediately, this is followed by late-twentieth-century Tallinn: the prime real estate of a district dubbed Little Wall Street, complete with a thirty-storey Swissôtel, a swish Finnish department store, Viru Keskus shopping mall, and an underground bus station.

'After the 1944 bombardment, this part of town remained a wasteland for a long time,' Ilya says. 'The neighbourhood around Viru tänav was among the hardest hit. I grew up in the one corner left standing.

The architecture was far from remarkable, but I've always had a fond-ness for the prewar feel of those streets and apartment blocks. When I returned to Tallinn in 1996, I went looking for a home there. It even became a condition for staying in Estonia: I simply had to find a flat in the neighbourhood where I grew up. A stone's throw from the house where I used to wake to the sound of my father whistling Yiddish tunes, I found myself somewhere nice and affordable, with a bit of character. And then, like all Estonians, I had to have a little place in the country. It's a quirk we share with the Scandinavians: we can't be content without a rustic hideaway. Once I had found myself a wooden farmhouse not far from Rakvere, I knew I could live out my days here in my homeland.'

Passing Viru Keskus shopping mall, I stop and point out a splurge of graffiti on an expanse of wall.

STOP FU/TURISM.

Not exactly controversial. Except that above the i, someone has scrawled a Star of David.

On it goes — even here! Even now!

Ilya shrugs. Walk around any city and you'll find anti-Semitic slogans on some wall or other. It's the work of an isolated few.

'The far-right nationalists are not that interested. If only because there are too few of us. Two thousand Jews, give or take a few hundred; you can't scare a population with that. Tallinn has never been fertile ground for that strain of populist deception. Estonia has never been home to more than 5,000 Jews. Compare that to 500,000 Russians. There's your target for Estonia's far-right nationalists. You'll find a lot worse about the Russians scrawled on Tallinn's walls.'

Snow starts to fall. I ask Ilya if he's worried about the future of the Baltic countries.

'If we're talking about the next ten to twenty years, I'm pessimistic. But looking thirty or forty years down the line, I'm an optimist. Half of Tallinn's population is Russian; in Riga, it's higher. You can't consis-tently keep a group that size out of government. The divisions couldn't be clearer. Russian stands for poor, unemployed, disenfranchised. The political parties of the Russian speakers are left-wing, from communist to social democratic to green. The nationalist parties are predominantly right-wing. Which means we're on a collision course. In Riga, the Russians won the local elections in June 2009. They are no longer

prepared to suffer in silence; they want recognition. The coming years
will be crucial. But if the minorities issue can be resolved twenty
years or so from now, the generations that follow will come together
and make things happen. I still speak Russian at home. I understand
Russians, I know what's on their minds. Treat them as fully fledged citizens and they will wholeheartedly commit to Estonia and Latvia. They
have lived here for decades after all, and have little left in common with
the Russians of Irkutsk or Vladivostok. Russians are vodka-swilling
layabouts unless you give them something to work for; do that and
they'll work till they drop. With them, there's no middle ground.'

Ilya has reached home. Our ways part outside his front door.

But not for long.

The very next evening, we meet again. Ilya has invited me to the
sixth edition of the Juudi Süvakultuuri Festival Ariel, of which he is
the founder and organiser. It is a Jewish festival of song held annually
at the Nuku Theatre.

Wherever songs are sung in Estonia, the venue is full. The star of
the evening is Sephardic singer Savína Yannátou from Thessaloniki.
It's a wonderful show, but more memorable still is a scene that preceded it.

Concerts and stage performances start at seven in Estonia. From six
o'clock, the Nuku Theatre began to fill up. To honour the brotherly
links between the Russian Orthodox and Greek Orthodox churches,
Ilya had invited the Russian patriarch to attend. He turned up in
full regalia, gilded staff in hand. A bearded priest in a black habit
went before him, shoving people aside to permit the church leader to
stride forth in a dignified manner. His objective was a corner table:
the patriarch was peckish. Since the Nuku is a children's theatre with
daily matinees, there was a tempting selection of cakes and pastries in
the foyer. The patriarch sent his priest to do the honours. One wodge
of cream cake was clearly out of the question; in no time, the priest
had returned with four.

I took in all of this from an adjacent table. Never have I seen a
religious elder and a priest feast on earthly delights with such abandon. I sat there wondering who would have taken a devilish delight in
describing such a scene. I plumped for Gogol, and realised how close
Tallinn is to Russia after all.

15

Simm

THE MAN WHO CAVED

Estonia, January 2010

Perhaps it was his name that sparked my interest. From the very first news story, it was lodged in my brain.

Simm.

For his early detective novels, George Simenon shortened his name to Sim. A name you can take in at a glance. Even at the height of his success with Maigret, the book covers never bore his full name. Simenon sufficed. Powerful. Succinct.

Add an *m* and Simm still sticks in the mind. An ideal codename. Designed to cut through radio static. Simple to tap out in Morse. S. I. M. M.

Simm could so easily be the stuff of fiction, a crime novel or thriller. But he is not the creation of Simenon, Le Carré, or Mankell. Until he hit the headlines, the only book to feature his name was the telephone directory.

Herman Simm owed his career to a head wound, a bloodied face that transformed him into a hero of the independence struggle.

On 15 May 1990, several hundred Interfront supporters attacked Estonia's parliament. These were precarious times. Estonia was balanced on a knife-edge between two contrasting fates. To one side lay the prospect of Western democracy, and membership of the European Union and NATO. To the other, a future as a vassal state of Russia, in thrall to the Soviet Union, which, although in its death throes, was still capable of lashing out.

Interfront — the International Front for the Preservation of the Soviet Union — was the most fanatical, most dangerous, and most violent of the pro-Russian groups. It enjoyed the support of soldiers and veterans alike, backed by communist trade-union executives and the old party faithful who had never skipped a May Day parade. Interfront was bent on cutting the Estonian, Latvian, and Lithuanian independence movements off at the pass.

When democratisation in Estonia began to seem unstoppable, Interfront decided to act. Intent on replacing the Estonian flag with the red of the Soviet republic, a few hundred supporters of the paramilitary group planned to storm parliament, housed in the former palace of the Russian governor on Toompea, a hill on the southern edge of Tallinn's Old Town. Once the red flag was flying high for every resident to see, the men of the hammer and sickle believed they could start retaking the positions they had so recently lost.

Their mission failed. The leaders of the independence movement had been smart enough to set up a militia of their own to protect and defend government buildings. In an earlier operation, Interfront had tried to seize control of the national television station, the 314-metre-high Teletorn. This time, the independence movement knew what it was up against, and a cordon had been put in place around the parliament. The pro-independence militia led by Colonel Herman Simm charged, charged again, and managed to break through Interfront's ranks.

On the front line of these counterattacks, Simm was dealt a few well-aimed blows, and pictures of his bloodied face were splashed across the next morning's front pages. Captions celebrated his role in preventing the Soviet faithful from seizing control of parliament. From one day to the next, Simm became a national hero.

The blood on his cheeks had an impact far beyond the headlines. In 1994, the fledgling state of Estonia was in search of a redoubtable police chief. One name in particular stuck in the minds of the ministers of the interior, justice, and defence: Simm, the former militia commander.

Herman Simm was born in 1947 in a town called Suure-Jaani, in the heart of Estonia. Herman with one *n* not two, an important distinction for Estonians. It suggested no German or Russian ancestry, at least as far as anyone knew. Herman had been born out of wedlock.

His mother, in any case, was Estonian. She abandoned Herman when he was two years old. Months after narrowly escaping deportation to Siberia in the ethnic cleansing of 1949, she married a man

Herman Simm, chief of police in Tallinn, 1994.

she thought might offer her protection — a match born of fear rather than fondness. Young Herman was sent to live with his grandmother, and when she died, an aunt took care of him. When Herman was twelve, she was officially registered as his foster mother.

These facts only emerged later. At the time of his appointment, Simm's security screening had been hasty, if not sloppy. In 1994, those responsible set greater store by his familiarity with the inner workings of the civil service, him having been employed at the Home Office for several years. It also helped that Simm looked the part: a sturdy chap with broad shoulders and thick sandy hair. He invariably wore a beige mackintosh, even in winter. In short, he had the appearance of a detective long before he had anything to do with the police force.

In his new position, Simm seemed determined to maintain as low a profile as possible. It was almost as if he wanted to erase himself from the picture. He rarely attended staff parties or ministerial receptions. If his inspectors and brigadiers had something to celebrate, Simm would opt for the great outdoors and take them on woodland excursions. His idea of entertaining the staff was a game of tug-of-war.

His leadership qualities were notable by their absence. As police chief, Simm only deepened the chaos Estonia experienced in the immediate aftermath of the Soviet era. His achievements in the fight against smuggling, corruption, human trafficking, and other forms of crime were negligible. On his watch, the newly formed mafia had every opportunity to organise and expand their operations. Eight of the ten crime syndicates that emerged were Russian-dominated.

That said, life at police headquarters wasn't all bad. Simm became romantically involved with a high-ranking police lawyer. Heete was her name, and she headed up the legal department. She was in her late forties, two years younger than Herman, and had an unusual hobby: she was a board member of the Association of Radio Amateurs. Under Soviet rule, Heete had been a Tallinn police officer and, like many senior public servants, had made a seamless transition from communism to liberalism.

While they were both working at police headquarters, Herman and Heete kept their relationship under wraps. They didn't have to dissemble for long. Herman was kicked upstairs in 1996, leaving them free to see each other openly. They went shopping together (they both loved shopping), took holidays together, and bought a house together, followed soon after by a place in the country, a farmhouse not far from the Baltic coast. In July 2001, they got married.

Simm's promotion followed the 1995 election of a new government on a pledge to tackle crime and corruption. Amid accusations of incompetence, he couldn't hold on to his position as chief of police, but Heete would continue to head the legal department until 2008, keeping him abreast of all judicial investigations for years to come. Simm had married the right woman.

As ignominious exits go, it could have been a lot worse. Simm was sidelined rather than sacked. The former police chief had been a patriot since the first stirrings of the independence movement after all. His only real crime was being bad at his job.

At the time, the Ministry of Defence was looking for someone to head its newly established Internal Security Service, a job to which no one aspired. In the wake of the KGB's forty-two-year reign of terror, the position was widely viewed as inferior, if not tainted. Yet Simm raised no objection to trading the bustle of police headquarters for a side wing at the Ministry of Defence, without so much as a nameplate on the door. His new post restored his anonymity.

He turned out to be a conscientious and diligent security officer. He set up dossiers, organised a network of informants. By his standards, he became remarkably sociable. Every few weeks, he invited his former police colleagues for a drink at a bar down by the port. The chat often turned towards developments in major cases, especially those involving the mafia. The rest of the information came courtesy of his wife.

For over ten years, Simm worked steadily to build the Estonian security service. His sandy hair turned grey. He went from sturdy to overweight, hardly surprising for a man who could be found at his desk from early morning until late in the evening. He deliberately kept his team small, preferring to work a little harder rather than delegate. This enabled him to see the bigger picture, he argued, and public money could be better spent on expanding the service's network of informants. Besides, with a population of one and a half million, Estonia was essentially a dwarf state. Just how important was its national security in the grand scheme of things?

Dwarf state or not, Estonia gained membership of NATO in 2004. From that moment on, Simm went from ant to spider, from a dark corner to the centre of a vast web — all day, every day. The insignificant but already overzealous public servant became a glutton for paperwork.

All files relating to national security landed on his desk, including analyses of the chinks in Estonia's lines of defence and the shortcomings of the young Estonian army. His remit didn't stop there: he had access to all NATO reports on the security of northern, western, and central Europe, and every key document from nations with which Estonia had agreed to exchange information: Germany, Poland, Latvia, Lithuania, Finland, Norway, and France. This meant access to data on terrorist organisations, on arms procurement and sales, on individuals or institutions under surveillance. Simm was in a position to gather as much intelligence as his high-powered counterparts in Helsinki or Berlin. He also held a diplomatic passport. No border guard could order him to open his attaché case, a case that was always packed to the brim.

In 2005, Jürgen Ligi became Estonia's new minister of defence. Ligi had it in for Simm, believing that, even during his stint as police chief, the man had shown a marked tendency towards paranoia and other personality disorders. Simm would turn up at friends' birthday parties wearing a bulletproof vest. When this prompted sniggers, he insisted that someone was out to kill him. He publicly humiliated subordinates for being untrustworthy or corrupt; every petty thief was a hardened criminal, every high-ranking official a potential spy. By his account, Tallinn was a den of espionage and iniquity.

Ligi saw Herman Simm as far too unstable for the post of security chief and hatched a plan to unseat him. Simm was given an honorary position as a security consultant, which effectively spelled the end of his career. Even so, it was three full years before he vacated his office and took his darling Heete to Tallinn's annual boat show to pick out a motor cruiser on which they could enjoy a well-earned retirement sailing among the islands of the Baltic. Their choice of vessel exhibited good taste and deep pockets, a conspicuously extravagant purchase for a public official who had just been hung out to dry.

The Simms didn't get to make many trips on their cruiser. Late in the summer of 2008, they flew to Madrid. This was four months after Herman had finally cleared his desk and closed his office door behind him, and five months after his proud moment at the presidential palace, where Estonia's highest honour, the Order of the White Star, had been conferred upon him. Travelling to Spain together, Herman and Heete looked like any other tourist couple, but they were travelling incognito. Herman checked them in at the hotel under an alias.

On the concourse of one of Madrid's busiest railway stations, Simm was seen exchanging words with a thin dark-haired man. Unfortunately for him, this agent — operating under the name Antonio de Jesús Amorett Graf — was being tailed by a NATO counterintelligence team. Amorett Graf travelled on a Portuguese passport, was registered as a resident of Madrid, and was thought to be on the payroll of the Russian security service. Cameras clicked.

It took NATO's secret agents a while to discover the true identity of Antonio de Jesús Amorett Graf. This flowery, far-fetched alias belonged to Sergei Yakovlev, who was indeed a Russian spy. Prior to Madrid, his area of operations had been the Middle East.

Heete and Herman Simm at the boat show in Tallinn, 2007.

Nor were they immediately able to identify the man with the sandy-grey curls who handed Yakovlev a bag that almost certainly contained documents. When the penny dropped, it set off all the alarm bells at NATO headquarters in Brussels. Herman Simm? Holy shit! Our man in Tallinn!

The Estonian government was alerted, as were the justice ministry and security service. Lavly Lepp was assigned to the case, a young prosecutor with a reputation as a go-getter. She did not wait long. On 19 September 2008, Herman Simm and his wife were arrested. Two days later, they were indicted on suspicion of high treason.

The evidence was overwhelming. Since 1996, Herman, allegedly with Heete's assistance, had been working for the SVR, Russia's secret service, the successor to the KGB. For twelve years he had passed on all Estonia's secrets to Moscow, and for four years all of NATO's secrets too. For these activities, he had been paid the sum of seven million crowns (over 400,000 euros), enough to buy seven plots of land totalling 100 hectares, a white townhouse outside Tallinn, a farmhouse by the Baltic, and a motor cruiser. Most of the money had no doubt been transferred to a secret bank account in Switzerland or an even more accommodating tax haven. Except for his moment of indulgence at the boat show, the prosecutor noted, Simm had been

anything but ostentatious. On paper, the plots of land he had purchased were owned by the sons of his foster sister — the daughter of
the aunt who had raised him.

Simm had been on his way to visit his aunt when he was arrested.
Once his cover had been blown in Madrid, prosecutor Lavly Lepp
resisted the temptation to apprehend him immediately. Instead, she
had him shadowed for a while, tapping his phone calls to gauge
the extent of his spying activities. Back in Estonia, Simm arranged
another meeting with Sergei Yakovlev. On 16 September, Yakovlev
cancelled suddenly. Not by coded message but with the briefest of
calls to Simm's mobile phone, in which he said little more than, 'I'm
ill.' It was the last anyone heard from him. Yakovlev disappeared without trace, and has never surfaced since.

Lepp feared that Simm too might vanish. On 19 September,
Herman and Heete got in their car and drove east. To the border
town of Narva? To Russia? It was a risk Lepp was not prepared to
take. She decided to make an immediate arrest, as soon as the couple
made a stop.

Simm drove at a snail's pace to a suburb of Tallinn, parked at Keila
shopping centre, and went in to buy a treat for his aunt. A police team
encircled the mall. Suspecting nothing, Simm strolled back to his car
with his purchase. By this time, an ambulance was stationed around
the corner; the prosecutor was fully prepared for the possibility that
Simm was armed and dangerous, and that a shoot-out was imminent.
As it turned out, Herman's only worry was dropping his fruit flan. He
offered no resistance, nor did Heete, who was waiting in the car.

When Lavly Lepp first spoke to Simm, she sensed relief more than
anything. 'Thank God,' he mumbled, almost inaudibly. At last, it was
over — a sentiment she came to understand during the next phase of
the investigation.

Abundant evidence was found at Simm's home: a compact radio
transmitter, two pistols, two shotguns, and a considerable amount in
cash. Yet financial gain does not appear to have been Simm's main
motive. Nor was he driven by ideology. Simm was not a man on a
mission, just a man in a tight corner.

In the late 1960s, Simm had been a student at Tallinn Polytechnic
Institute. Having completed his two preparatory years, he opted to

major in chemistry. Herman's acuity and appetite for hard work made him an outstanding student, and he was given the chance to continue his studies at the academy of the Interior Ministry in Moscow.

Before long, he joined the ranks of the KGB. Not of his own volition: the security services had branded him a black marketeer. His offence was probably nowhere near as serious as it sounds. Buying a pair of jeans from a Western tourist and selling them on to a friend at a ten-rouble profit was enough to get you convicted. Simm was offered the chance to avoid a court case and a criminal record by working for the security service.

He proved to be an exemplary recruit. This would have come as no surprise to his schoolteachers, who had always been impressed by his work ethic and unfailing eagerness to learn. Within the ranks of the KGB, Simm showed the same ambition as he had at the Polytechnic. In Moscow, he had also been quick to join the Communist Party. God forbid that his new bosses might think ill of him.

Simm's runners must have patted themselves on the back. The Estonian looked set to be a huge asset. After only a few months, they trusted him to accompany delegations of athletes, scientists, politicians, and artists on trips abroad. 'Accompany' was a euphemism for round-the-clock surveillance — constant following, constant monitoring. Simm did not do this single-handed: up to eight agents — male and female — could travel with a single delegation and were also tasked with keeping an eye on each other. With one of the female agents, Simm fathered a child. Herman Simm's daughter was born in 1974. He recognised the child as his but refused to marry her mother. One more indiscretion that the KGB could use to pressure and manipulate him.

Back in Tallinn, Simm chose not to reveal any of this to the aunt who had raised him as her own. From the sweeping political and ethnic purges of 1949 until Stalin's death in 1953, she had been forced into hiding. Like his biological mother, she detested the Soviets and thought no death too slow or painful for their Estonian stooges. Simm knew he risked incurring her lifelong contempt by telling her anything about the bind he had got himself into.

He kept something else from his foster mother too. Back in Estonia, he made his profession of faith in the Lutheran church. In addition to being a Soviet spy, Simm became a man of religion, a staunch protestant. The latter was at odds with the former, but by this stage, everything in his life had come to revolve around fear.

In Tallinn, Simm became a key KGB informant, a status he retained until the collapse of the Soviet Union. After 1991, the Russians let him be for five years. But no sooner had he been appointed head of the Estonian Internal Security Service than the strategists in Moscow presented him with another impossible choice. Either he started working for the SVR or the file on his KGB history would find its way to the right people in the Estonian media.

It was blackmail, pure and simple. And Simm caved. The Russians went on to control him for another twelve years.

In a bid to prevent exactly this kind of extortion, Estonia's parliament had passed a law in 1995 that granted amnesty to KGB informants and secret agents. Anyone who came forward would avoid prosecution and imprisonment, and their name would be put on a secret list accessible to only the most senior judicial bodies in the land. Anyone who failed to come forward risked being named publicly and pilloried as a result.

One thousand former agents and informants took the confidential option. Five hundred other names appeared on a public list. Neither list contained the name Herman Simm.

Nor is his name to be found anywhere in the confiscated KGB archives. Not that anyone really expected it to be there. Shortly before Estonia gained its independence, the KGB transferred much of its Estonian archive from Tallinn to Moscow. By 1995, all files on key informants, infiltrators, snitches, and spies were long gone.

The arrest of Herman Simm sent shock waves through Estonian society, more intense than the resignation of any minister or the fall of an entire government. Indignation turned to fury, contempt to despair.

'The sky has come crashing down on us,' wrote Ainar Ruussaar, editor-in-chief of Baltic News Service, in the first report he devoted to the arrest. 'Thanks to one of our own, Russia, our enemy, obtained copies of all our military secrets, and has been doing so since we gained independence.' The response from public prosecutor Lavly Lepp was equally dismayed: 'What a humiliation. We had just become part of the Atlantic family, and now one of our own has betrayed us.'

The most sanguine reaction came from the ranks of officialdom. No surprise, given that for years Simm had been able to go about his clandestine business under the supposedly watchful eye of politicians, senior officials, policymakers, and the military. Ministry of Defence spokesperson Aari Lemmik put in a word for the officials with egg on their faces. 'We are far from proud of what has occurred,' her statement began. 'However, no country can rule out this kind of treason. There will always be a human factor at play.' *The Human Factor.* Estonia had entered the world of Graham Greene.

Ostensibly, Simm had only briefly exploited the national-hero status thrust upon him for his role in defending the parliament building, the status that ultimately earned him the job of police chief. The time about which his foster mother would later say, 'Back then, I was really proud of him.' Simm led the good life and became a regular at Tallinn's trendy bars and restaurants, with a girlfriend twenty years younger at his side. In 1994, she ended their relationship. Simm drowned his sorrows a while, but swiftly concluded that it was time to get off the road to ruin.

Heete was not a woman who turned heads, but you could tell a mile off that she had the strength of character to weather almost any storm. This was the woman Herman wanted to grow old with. No luxury yacht, sports car, or gold Rolex required. True, Herman began cherishing the modest dream of owning a motor cruiser on which he and Heete could sail off into the sunset. Forget the casinos and nightclubs, the 007 lifestyle. If he longed for anything, it was for a quiet life with a woman his own age, a woman he could count on. Not a leather-clad model who made his head spin, but a wife with a well-stocked picnic basket. Perhaps Simm was the stuff of fiction after all. If only Graham Greene had been around to pen *The Quiet Estonian.*

Simm became a spy because he caved in to blackmail. As time went on, he did seem content to profit from the situation, in the hope of giving Heete a comfortable old age. It is hard to imagine that he kept the woman he married in the dark about his activities. Her arrest suggests that radio amateur Heete had worked with her husband to come up with a way of passing his information to the enemy. Simm's

approach did not stretch to computers, microfilm, or even photocop-
ies. He relayed his stolen secrets to Moscow in classic Cold War style.

Both man and wife were cut out for espionage. An inconspicuous
couple in their fifties, they had few peccadilloes. A fondness for art
was one, and even then the paintings were modest in size, the kind
people of a certain age like to hang on the wall above the sofa: misty
landscapes bathed in sunlight, maples reflected in still waters, a coastline with an island in the distance. In the end, they owned around
fifteen of these Arcadian vistas.

And yes, they had a penchant for sailing. There is a snapshot of
them together, eyeing up the vessel of their dreams at the Tallinn boat
show.

Though it's possible that Simm kept one extravagance a secret,
even from his wife: as a man of faith, he donated a chandelier to the
Lutheran Church in Suure-Jaani.

Of course, Simm should have sailed off into the sunset in 2005 when
he was sidelined as head of Estonia's Internal Security Service. But
the SVR continued to exert its hold over him. He had made himself
indispensable. What other secret agent in the Western world was so
ideally placed to pass on a stream of NATO secrets? Simm became a
victim of his own success, and his own weakness. A man who caves in
to blackmail once will be haunted by threats and insinuation all his life.

After his arrest, tongues started wagging. Former colleagues at
police headquarters recalled Simm's obsession with subterfuge. In two
out of every three cases, he expressed doubts as to whether the suspect
might be harbouring far darker secrets than the offence they were
being charged with. Simm was always digging for more, a lot more
(even though the Russians were not using his services at the time).
His subordinates claimed he constantly wanted to be the centre of
attention, and cited his posturing with the bulletproof vest at parties
as an example. But tales like these only began circulating after his
arrest. Simm's conduct as an agent tends to show the opposite: he
proceeded cautiously and deliberately.

In 2004, he passed classified documents about the Russian mafia
and Russian secret agents to Germany's counterintelligence service.
Documents intended to inform or mislead? A selection of the former
perhaps, in an effort to appear above suspicion, accompanied by more

of the latter, to put Western counter-espionage operations off the scent.

On balance, perhaps his volubility about the threat of spies was more cunning than clueless. Simm cannot even be blamed for his own arrest. His fateful meeting with Amorett Graf in Madrid had been at the behest of the Russian security service. If anyone had blundered, it was the SVR, not Simm. It was their job to be aware that Amorett Graf had been under surveillance for over a year, his every assignation recorded on camera.

Seven days after Simm's arrest, a solemn gathering was held at Tallinn's National Library to commemorate the victims of the MS *Estonia* disaster, the ferry that was lost in the Baltic fourteen years earlier in a raging storm on the night of 27–28 September 1994. The speaker was Jutta Rabe, an investigative journalist from Germany. She was there to shed some light on the disaster, about which much remains unclear.

The vessel, en route from Tallinn to Stockholm at the time, was said to be robust and powerful. Built in a German shipyard, it was neither old nor in need of repair. Weeks before the disaster, it had been inspected and found seaworthy. Conditions when the *Estonia* set sail on 27 September were bad, with gale force winds and high seas, but for the time of year this was the rule rather than the exception. Nor was the ferry overloaded. There were 989 people on board a ship built to take 2,000 passengers and 377 crew. The maximum number of cars, 460, was nowhere close to being exceeded. There was one strange detail, however: a number of trucks on the vehicle decks had not been secured and started sliding when the ship began to take on water. Within half an hour, the ferry capsized and sank beneath the waves.

'Underwater cameras revealed that the ship's bow doors had been knocked open,' Willem Ellenbroek and Henk Raaff write in their book *Oostzee-journaal* (Baltic Sea Journal). 'We will probably never know why the crew failed to get more passengers onto the lifeboats and rafts. Perhaps everything went so fast that it simply wasn't possible; perhaps the crew panicked.'

A total of 852 lives were lost.

At the memorial gathering fourteen years later, Jutta Rabe spoke of a link between the *Estonia*'s demise and Herman Simm. This was an explosive claim, but in the days that followed not a word of what she said appeared in the Estonian press. Finnish daily *Turun Sanomat* was alone in printing the news, on 2 October 2008.

According to Rabe, Simm was involved in secret arms deliveries from Russia to Israel. The weapons were transported to Sweden via Estonia in trucks aboard the ferry service between the two countries. For seven crossings, up to and including the night the ship sank, the *Estonia* was carrying high-tech weapons and possibly even plutonium. It is possible that the trucks on the vehicle decks were not secured because the crew were under orders not to go near them.

The investigation into the disaster started almost as soon as the storm had abated. Simm was present on the diving platform during the first attempt to locate the wreck, reportedly having taken the place of another official at the last minute. He allegedly ordered the divers to search the captain's cabin for a small metal box registered in the name of Alexander Voronin.

For many months, Voronin had been suspected of smuggling high-tech weaponry. The dive reports mention the discovery of the box in question, not in the captain's cabin, but in cabin 6230, where VIPs were usually accommodated on the captain's orders. Alexander Voronin had been on board the ship, travelling with his fifteen-year-old son and his father-in-law. All three survived the disaster. They told journalists that they had been on a business trip to Denmark. The box was handed over to the Swedish authorities only to disappear shortly afterwards, an indication that the Swedes were in on the plan and colluding to cover it up.

Ten years after the disaster, a Swedish customs official admitted that they were under orders not to check certain trucks as they drove off the ferry in Sweden. Another bizarre aspect of the case: the captain and ten crew members who survived the *Estonia* disaster were removed from hospital by a commando unit in an intervention Rabe referred to as a kidnapping.

Alexander Voronin's business operations were based in Kohtla-Järve, an Estonian town close to the military zone where uranium was enriched during Soviet times. The company Kosmos Association, which Voronin ran with his father-in-law, had dealings with the Kurchatov Institute in Moscow, a research and development body in the field of nuclear energy. Voronin died of a heart attack in 2002, two weeks after German newspaper *Süddeutsche Zeitung* revealed details of secret arms shipments aboard the *Estonia*.

Simm, Jutta Rabe argued before her open-mouthed audience, had been a protégé of Mart Laar, Estonia's first prime minister following the restoration of independence (1992–1994). Laar supplied fifty million US dollars' worth of Russian weapons to Israel; only, much to the consternation of the receiving party, the weapons turned out to be faulty. The prime minister also became involved in a dubious rouble transaction and was forced to step down in 1994. In 1999, he returned as prime minister, again for a relatively short time: until January 2002. Laar enjoys a reputation as a man who got things done. In no time at all, he regulated the privatisation of the business sector in Estonia. Many still associate him with the Baltic Tiger period, when the country's economy grew by leaps and bounds.

Whenever Laar was in power, Simm came in for a promotion. According to Rabe, he was Laar's key agent.

Several Estonian websites ran with the results of Rabe's painstaking investigation. Laar, the former prime minister, was well-disposed towards Israel, as was Alexander Voronin, who came from a Russian Jewish family and expressed the conviction that he had only survived the *Estonia* disaster because his wife had lit thirty-three candles for him on the night in question on a candleholder she had bought in Jerusalem.

Behind the Simm scandal, the websites saw a vast Zionist conspiracy. Boris Yeltsin, Russia's president at the time, had supposedly favoured Jewish entrepreneurs when he opened up state-owned companies to private shareholders and created a new oligarchy with a power base that Putin would have to work hard to crush. These conspiracy theories were mostly the work of men with Russian surnames, men who had never been able to stomach the dismantling of the Soviet empire. They despised Yeltsin as much as they despised Laar and Simm, and had no qualms about resorting to the kind of language used back in the 1970s, during the Soviet Union's last major anti-Semitic campaign. The fact that Russia readily supplied arms to Iraq, Iran, and Hamas during the chaotic 1990s is something they conveniently overlooked.

Simm's trial had been scheduled for April 2009, but to everyone's surprise, court proceedings got under way in the second week of February. The Estonians seemed determined to push ahead as quickly as possible to minimise any further damage to their international reputation.

In anticipation of the need to handle a wide range of defence secrets, the trial was held behind closed doors. Only the bare bones of the case entered the public domain. Simm, it was revealed, had passed on a total of 2,000 documents to Russian intelligence. He had done so in fourteen locations across Europe, avoiding three countries in particular: Britain ('too many cameras'), Norway ('too expensive'), and Germany ('too many police'). For his espionage activities, he faced a minimum of three and a maximum of fifteen years in prison.

On 26 February 2009, Herman Simm was sentenced to a jail term of twelve and a half years. This made it likely that he would spend the rest of his life behind bars.

The extent of Heete's participation in her husband's activities remains unclear. Her cooperation with the investigation was described as exemplary and the case against her was eventually closed.

Simm also lost most of the small fortune he had amassed. Ordered to pay the equivalent of 1.3 million euros in damages, it was the only part of the sentence he appealed against. Though seemingly resigned to his conviction for high treason, he was keen to point out that betraying his country had not made him a wealthy man.

Sadly for him, this was not far from the truth. I went in search of the white townhouse owned by Mr and Mrs Simm. It turned out to be a plain but roomy semi-detached house in a nondescript neighbourhood. Following the trial, Heete moved to an undisclosed address.

In 2006, a NATO meeting had been held at the Dutch military base at Brunssum, attended by the top security officers of all the member states. Each delegation was given a CD containing the names of all individuals either known to be or strongly suspected of spying for Russia in the NATO countries. This information was supplemented by a list of known and possible double agents. Courtesy of Simm, that CD was on Vladimir Putin's desk within a week.

You'd be forgiven for thinking that an Estonian master spy could pocket in excess of a million for supplying such valuable intelligence: a single disc that, at a stroke, rendered a lengthy, laborious, and prohibitively expensive campaign of infiltration surplus to requirements. Putin informed Simm's contact Sergei Yakovlev that he was 'very impressed', but apparently it was worth little more than a pat on the back to the Russians. For this mine of information, Simm was rewarded with a 5,000-euro bonus.

In his KGB days, Simm could count on a fixed monthly stipend, a sum equivalent to 1,000 euros. Extra payments were made for important documents, but never much in excess of 2,000. A 141-page NATO report later identified Simm as the 'most damaging spy in Alliance history'. But the money was not exactly pouring in.

This was a reality that Estonia's appeals court also had to face. Simm filed for bankruptcy. The court examined his income and assets, taking into account the 1.3 million euros in damages and the cost of his legal defence. Their calculations confirmed Simm's claim: he was declared bankrupt.

Since his conviction, Herman Simm has been spending his days reading the Bible in Tartu prison. He seems at peace with his fate, a peace that few of his fellow Estonians share.

The espionage case unsettled young and old alike. Having achieved membership of both the European Union and NATO, Estonians believed they had finally reached calmer, safer waters. This was a clear break with the past, the dawn of a stable, peaceful future. Simm's betrayal shook them out that carefree reverie.

Eighteen, nineteen, twenty years after Estonia, Latvia, and Lithuania gained their independence, Russia still has its eye on the Baltic countries. Two decades and counting of freedom are no guarantee; the danger comes from the east, as it always has. The eternal enemy lies in wait and — as in the eighteenth, nineteenth, and twentieth centuries — that enemy is Russia. Simm ushered in a new Cold War era.

'The case of Simm is indicative of the current state of the world,' the chairman of Estonia's parliamentary committee on security affairs Jaanus Rahumägi reflects. 'While everyone in Western Europe was focused on the Middle East and Asia, Russia was building an efficient intelligence system in Europe.'

Thanks to Herman Simm, many an Estonian finds it difficult to sleep soundly. The country's own language, culture, and way of life are thriving as never before. Jaan Kross's novels grace the shelves of every bookshop, Arvo Pärt's music can be heard in any concert hall, yet Estonians are left wondering how many Simms might still be at large, in Tallinn, Tartu, or Pärnu. Or Riga and Vilnius for that matter. And how much damage such traitors might do.

'Treading air' is how Jaan Kross described Estonians' attempts to live in a free and independent country. It became the title of his penultimate novel. Having endured eight years of imprisonment in Siberia, from 1946 to 1954, Kross knew what he was talking about. He died in 2007, aged eighty-seven.

Since Simm's arrest, Estonians have become reacquainted with the art of treading air. And they must wonder if Jaan Kross had a crystal ball. His novel ends with the lines: 'But thank God I know I no longer have to square these things away using a set of pharmacist's scales. That's your job now. But then which court — if any — has absolved us of this responsibility?'

Herman Simm was convicted, yet most of the burning questions remain unanswered. Which secrets were the Russians most interested in? Was Simm involved in secret arms deals? Did he interfere in the investigation into the *Estonia* disaster? And make sure that key evidence never saw the light of day?

Some tread air until they merge with the clouds and never come back down to earth.

A journalist from an Estonian daily newspaper agrees to tell me what he knows about Simm, but is only willing to talk if I guarantee his anonymity. We arrange to meet in Pirita, a seaside town not far from Tallinn.

At Viru Keskus, I hop aboard a number eight bus, and within minutes we are speeding along a coastal road. Dilapidated wooden villas among the stunted dunes mourn their tsarist past. Further on lies a stretch of parkland, the setting for Kadriorg Palace, which Peter the Great had built for his wife, Catherine. The Baltic shimmers in the winter sun. The dull black shapes I take for seals turn out to be shelves of granite in the shallows just offshore.

A city by the sea is already halfway to happiness. A city where you can smell the salt breeze whenever you fill your lungs. An open city, bustling, vibrant. Tallinn's Old Town often reminds me of Antwerp, but it's Antwerp by the sea. A wonderful city, despite the long winters.

Ten minutes later, I get off in Pirita and walk about fifty metres through the pines to the beachfront restaurant where I have arranged to meet my contact. He's already waiting at a small table by the window. I recognise him by the sign we agreed: a folded newspaper sticking out of his left jacket pocket.

The journalist — let's call him Jack — orders sushi. Japanese cuisine spells cutting-edge dining in Tallinn. The couple at the next table are quaffing champagne. He is an older gent; she's wearing a flame-red miniskirt and can't be a day over twenty. A procession of emaciated Estonian models clad in Milan's spring fashions strut their way across a TV screen two-metres wide. The wood fire crackles; the temperature outside hovers around minus twenty. Everything about the place is sleek and polished, though the restaurant and nearby motel date from 1980, when Moscow hosted the Olympics and Pirita was the venue for the sailing events.

Through tinted glass, I have a captivating view of Tallinn: the Old Town on the hill, the glass and concrete beyond, the modern apartments overlooking the port. Ferries come and go, arriving from Helsinki or setting sail for Stockholm and St Petersburg. Forty ferries call at Tallinn daily. Jack reckons there would be a hundred-kilometre tailback if the cargo on all those vessels had to be checked on a daily basis.

Tallinn, he tells me, was always an outlier in the Soviet Union. For twenty years it remained hermetically sealed off from the West, but in the mid-1960s the first chink in the Iron Curtain appeared with the resumption of ferry services between Tallinn and Helsinki. The motive was purely economic: the Soviets were short of foreign currency. In 1965, the first Finns embarked for Tallinn, 9,000 of them; by 1989, that number had grown to 100,000.

For Russians, Estonia was the land of pretty girls, whose long, bare legs were already tanned in May. The first sex club opened in 1974, and its regular patrons included a startling number of card-carrying party members. The club was completely illegal, but embodied a brand of subversiveness to which the authorities were prepared to turn a blind eye.

Tallinn's Old Town, with the ferry terminal and the Baltic Sea in the background.

Jack stresses that he is not out to condone any aspect of Simm's subterfuge, but points out that the man was able to thrive in a climate that at best could be described as latently corrupt. Estonian attitudes towards the Russians have been ambiguous for centuries. Russia was the absolute enemy, more so than Germany, but dealing with the enemy can be a lucrative proposition. It's an attitude that runs deep within Estonians.

'You'd be better off not incorporating what I'm about to tell you in your book, unless you want to be dismissed as a troublemaker, an enemy of the Estonian cause. Don't get me wrong, I love Estonia like I love my own mother, but I refuse to be blinkered by mindless nationalism. I'm sure you have reservations about certain aspects of your homeland; I'm no different. Two books, one by Martti Turtola and one by Toomas Karjahärm, were published here in 2002 and take a close look at the dealings of Konstantin Päts. For Estonians, Päts is the father in fatherland: he's the great man of the interwar period and the First Independent Republic of Estonia. He was seen as a conservative and a champion of the peasant cause — anti-urban, anti-Russian, anti-communist. But his mother was Russian, and he grew up speaking Russian, imbibed the Russian Orthodox faith and the Russian mindset. Turtola and Karjahärm show that he had a financial interest in the Estonian-Russian Chamber of Commerce and that from 1929 to 1933 he was on the Soviet payroll as an 'influential agent'. These findings pale in comparison to the poor man's arrest by the Soviets in 1940 and his death in a psychiatric ward in 1956, locked away in a madhouse near the city of Tver for insisting that he was Estonia's rightful president. Like all independent Estonian politicians, he was treated ruthlessly. I don't blame Päts for anything. My parents still have his portrait on their wall, and I have never asked them to take it down. In terms of courage, the man was up there with Churchill. But for Estonia, independence has never meant full independence. We've always had to play a game of give and take, and that's true to this day. Not every Estonian becomes a Simm, but there's a little bit of Simm in all of us. Which is why his case left us so traumatised.'

And what about arms smuggling? I ask. Is that what was behind the *Estonia* disaster?

Jack takes a long look out the window before he answers.

'There's only one way to dispel the persistent stream of rumours: a no-holds-barred investigation. And nobody wants that: not the Swedes, not the Estonians, not the Russians. No wonder suspicions keep piling up on the doorstep. The wreck has never been raised. For fear of what? It's the same with Simm: a speedy trial, a heavy sentence, but no real attempt to get to the bottom of things. A small country is like a village: when a scandal breaks, everyone is involved, directly or indirectly. Fifty years of dictatorship can't be wiped out just like that. I think we still shy away from openness. You never know what might surface. We have a saying: "Only old men still have a taste for vodka." But the Soviet lives on in us. We'd rather look the other way, cross the road at the first sign of injustice or unfairness. When there's a stink, we hold our noses instead of finding out where it's coming from. We mastered the intricacies of the free-market economy in the space of a few years. In budgetary terms, we're in better shape than Italy, Spain, Portugal, and France. The one thing we still can't get to grips with is openness. Even a national disaster — and that's what the sinking of the *Estonia* was — can't compel us to hold a parliamentary inquiry. If you ask me, our country is still so young that deep down we live in fear of someone or something coming along and wrecking our national pride.'

I took my first trip to Estonia aboard a coaster. Shortly after passing Gotland, the captain changed course. A seasoned mariner and a man of principle, he took one look at a cross on the chart and steered around it. If we had stuck to our route, we would have sailed right over the wreck of the MS *Estonia*.

Sailing over a grave is something a seaman does not do. Let alone a mass grave. The drowned are due as much respect as those who are dead and buried.

'We don't have flowers,' the captain said to Huig, his lumbering bosun, 'but can you tie a knot?'

'Which one?' the tattooed bear asked.

'Turk's head.'

Huig grumbled but did as he was asked. He took a length of white rope and tied a Turk's head, the most intricate knot of all. Just south of the site of the wreck, he cast it overboard. The white knot rose to the surface and lay bobbing on the waves.

Acknowledgements

My special thanks go to Emile Brugman (this book marks the twenty-fifth year of our collaboration), Ellen Schalker, Anita Roeland (who edited the text, dotted the i's — and the ė's — and once again allowed me to share in her vast knowledge of Russia), Lesley van Venrooy (for compiling the bibliography), Merel Poldervaart (for the illustrations), Willemijn Lindhout and Sjoerd de Jong (for the corrections), Hester Schaap (for the map), Karin Beernink (who read the manuscript many times and saved me from glaring errors), Marre van Dantzig (who kept an unwavering eye on the big picture), librarian Bert Verbeek (who tracked down every book I was looking for except one, and it still bugs him), Robbert Wagenborg (the Groningen shipowner from the first chapter; had he not been kind enough to let me board one of his ships, I may never have set foot in Pärnu), Bart Ruyterman (head of crew and fleet management at Wagenborg Shipping in Delfzijl), captain Jaap Stengs, the crew of MS *Grachtborg*, Ainars Roze in Riga, Jānis Roze Jr in Riga, Ināra Beļinkaja in Riga, Ari Doeser (director of the Royal Dutch Booksellers Association and initiator of my first trip to Riga), Maria Heiden, Maarten Asscher, Sandra Kalniete in Riga, Solveiga Rush, Gidon Kremer, Eline Flipse, Dovid Katz in Vilnius, Maria Krupoves-Berg in Vilnius, the Yiddish students at the University of Vilnius, Irena Veisaitė in Vilnius, Simonas Gurevičius in Vilnius, Algirdas Šukys in Kaunas, Saulė Gaižauskaitė (who after our conversations even sent me photos of the pavement in Vilnius to prevent me from overlooking any detail), the Gaižauskas family in Vilnius, Darja Sviridova in Kaliningrad, the staff of Hotel Grotthuss in Vilnius (apologies once again to Edith von Grotthuss), Ilmārs Berg in Aizpute, Alexander Volodin in Daugavpils, the students of the Humanitārā fakultāte in Daugavpils, Rita Mets in Rakvere, Toivo Peäske in Rakvere, Pika Jala Muusikaäri in Tallinn, Krista Varik in

Tallinn, Indrek Hirv in Tartu, and the von Wrangel family (for all the family secrets they confided in me), Wolf Thomson in Toronto, Marcel Worms (who put me in touch with Ilya Sundelevich), Ilya Sundelevich in Tallinn. And, first and foremost, Marie-Claude Hamonic, for four years of help, support, advice, and encouragement.

Photo Credits

Abromovitch, R. (ed.), *The Vanished World*, New York, 1947: 261
AKG/ANP: 190
Beernink, Karin; the von Wrangel family: 316, 320, 322, 323, 324, 332, 333, 336, 340, 345, 346, 348, 353
Beļinkaja, Ināra: 29
Bosch, Ellie: 357
Brokken, Jan: 3, 5, 6, 7, 15, 39, 48, 57, 100, 108, 109, 113, 285, 286, 314, 365, 367, 371, 396
Burmeistars, H. / Jan Brokken: 34
Čajčyc, Alexander: 191
Gaižauskaítė, Saulė: 146, 148, 149, 156, 158, 165, 167
Kayaert, Robert; Queen Elisabeth Competition: 85
Kröller-Müller Museum: 184
Lundqvist, Mats: 292
Olniansky, Ida: 90
Rabin, Kenneth: 264
Rooväli, Küllike: 383
Jāņa Rozes apgāds, Riga: 11, 13, 18, 20, 21, 24
Rush, Solveiga, *Mikhail Eisenstein: themes and symbols in Art Nouveau architecture of Riga 1901–1906*. Riga: Neputns, 2003: 42, 59
Vermeeren, Gerard: 136

Sources

Ajar, Émile, *La vie devant soi*, Paris, 1975

Ajar, Émile, *Pseudo*, Paris, 1976

Ajar, Émile, *L'angoisse du roi Salomon*, Paris, 1979

Amis, Moshe, *The Jews of Latvia*, Tel Aviv, 1971

Anfam, David, 'The World in a Frame', in *Rothko: the late series*, London, 2008

Anissimov, Myriam, *Romain Gary, le caméléon*, Paris, 2006 (revised paperback edition), first published: 2004

Arendt, Hannah, *The Human Condition*, Chicago, 1958

Arendt, Hannah, *The Origins of Totalitarianism*, London, 1958 (revised edition), first published: New York, 1951

Arendt, Hannah, *The Jewish Writings*, edited by Kohn, Jerome, and Feldman, Ron H., Amsterdam, 2008

Arendt, Hannah, *Eichmann in Jerusalem: a report on the banality of evil*, London, 1963

Arendt, Hannah, and Heidegger, Martin, *Briefe 1925 bis 1975: und andere Zeugnisse*, Frankfurt am Main, 1998

Arendt, Hannah, and Jaspers, Karl, *Briefwechsel: 1926–1969*, Munich/Zürich, 1985

Baensch, Henry von, *Geschichte der Familie Von Wrangel vom Jahrezwölfhundertfünfzig bis auf die Gegenwart*, Dresden, 1887

Barañano, Kosme de (ed.), *Jacques Lipchitz Rétrospective*, catalogue of the exhibition at Le Bellevue, Biarritz, 2009

Barons, Krišjānis, *Latvju dainas*, six volumes, Riga, 1894–1915

Barry, Ellen, 'Estonia Spy Case Rattles Nerves at NATO', *The New York Times*, 25 December 2008

Beyeler, Ernst, *Leidenschaftlich für die Kunst: Gespräche mit Christophe Mory*, Zürich, 2005

Bezemer, J.W., and Jansen, Marc, *Een geschiedenis van Rusland: van Rurik tot Poetin,* Amsterdam, 2008 (revised and enlarged edition); first published as Bezemer, J.W., *Een geschiedenis van Rusland: van Rurik tot Brezjnev,* Amsterdam, 1988

Blanch, Lesley, *Romain: un regard particulier,* Arles, 1998

Borgnäs, Lars, 'War Materials Smuggled on Estonia', *Estonia Litigation Association,* 12 February 2004

Bork, Bert van, *Jacques Lipchitz: the artist at work,* New York, 1966

Bregstein, Philo, *Terug naar Litouwen: sporen van een Joodse familie,* Amsterdam, 1995

Breslin, James E.B., *Mark Rothko: a biography,* Chicago, 1993

Briedis, Laimonas, *Vilnius: city of strangers,* Budapest, 2009

Brocke, Edna, '"Big Hannah" — My Aunt', afterword in Arendt, Hannah, *The Jewish Writings,* 2008

Brouwers, Arnout, 'Aleksej II, Restaurator van de orthodoxie', *de Volkskrant,* 6 December 2008

Cogniat, Raymond, *Soutine,* Paris, 1973

Cohen, Israel, *Vilna,* Philadelphia, 1992

Compton, Michael, *Mark Rothko: die Themen des Künstlers,* introduction to the catalogue of the exhibition *Mark Rothko 1903–1970 Retrospektive der Gemälde,* Museum Ludwig, Cologne, 1988

Dagen, Philippe, 'Fluxus: l'art courant Dada', *Le Monde,* 19 July 2009

Dawidowicz, Lucy S., *The Golden Tradition: Jewish life and thought in Eastern Europe,* New York, 1984, first published: 1967

Döblin, Alfred, *Reise in Polen,* Berlin, 1926, reissue: Munich, 1987

Dohrn, Verena, *Baltische reizen,* Amsterdam, 1995

Eisenstein, Sergei, *Autobiography,* translated and edited by Marshall, Herbert, London, 1975

Eisenstein, Sergei, *Film Form: essays in film theory,* New York, 1949

Ekker, Jan Pieter, 'Bespiegelmuziek: de aantrekkingskracht van componist Arvo Pärt op filmmakers', *de Volkskrant,* 27 March 2008

Eksteins, Modris, *Walking since Daybreak: a story of Eastern Europe, World War II, and the heart of our century,* New York, 1999

Ellenbroek, Willem, 'Wereldgeschiedenis tot heil van de mensheid', *de Volkskrant*, 29 March 1996

Ellenbroek, Willem, and Raaff, Henk, *Oostzee-journaal: een reis door Scandinavië, de Baltische republieken, Kaliningrad, Polen en Noord-Duitsland*, Amsterdam, 1995

Embrechts, Annette, 'Mikhaïl Baryshnikov: een ster die geen ster wil zijn', *de Volkskrant*, 29 May 2009

Ettinger, Elżbieta, *Hannah Arendt — Martin Heidegger*, New Haven, 1995

Figes, Orlando, *Natasha's Dance: a cultural history of Russia*, London, 2002

Figes, Orlando, *A People's Tragedy: the Russian Revolution 1891–1924*, London, 1996

Flior, Yudel, *Dvinsk: the rise and decline of a town*, translated from the Yiddish by Sachs, Bernard, Johannesburg, 1965

Gary, Romain, *Education européenne*, Paris, 1961 (revised edition), first published: 1945

Gary, Romain, *La promesse de l'aube*, Paris, 1980 (revised edition), first published: 1960

Gary, Romain, *La danse de Gengis Cohn*, Paris, 1967

Gary, Romain, *La nuit sera calme*, Paris, 1974

Gary, Romain, *Vie et mort d'Émile Ajar*, Paris, 1981

Gaus, Günter, *Zur Person*, Munich, 1964, including the interview with Hannah Arendt 'Was bleibt? Es bleibt die Muttersprache'

Grotthuss, Sophie von, *Briefwechsel mit Goethe, Erzählungen und Essays*, with a preface by Hahn, Barbara, Würzburg, 1994

Hammacher, Abraham M., *Jacques Lipchitz: his sculpture*, New York, 1961

Hangouët, Jean-François, *Romain Gary*, Paris, 2007

Hanley, Monika, 'Legionnaires Day Tensions on the Rise', *The Baltic Times*, 12 March 2009

Hein, Ants, *Eesti mõisad, Herrenhäuser in Estland, Estonian Manor Houses: 250 photos from 1860–1939*, Tallinn, 2004

Hillier, Paul, *Arvo Pärt*, Oxford, 1997, Oxford Studies of Composers, Oxford, from 1965

Hong, Jin Ho, *Das naturalisch-szientische Literaturkonzept und die Schlossgeschichten Eduard von Keyserlings*, Würzburg, 2006

Hope, Henry R., *The Sculpture of Jacques Lipchitz*, catalogue of the exhibition at the Museum of Modern Art, New York, 1954

Jacobs, Hans, Nooteboom, Cees, Plomp, Hans, and Visser, Carolijn, *Baltische reizen*, Amsterdam, 1993

Jauvert, Vincent, 'Opération Jésus: le pire traître que l'Alliance atlantique ait nourri en son sein', *le Nouvel Observateur*, 18 December 2008

Kalniete, Sandra, *With Dance Shoes in Siberian Snows*, translated from the Latvian by Margita Gailitis, Champaign/London, 2006

Katz, Dovid, *Kingdoms of the 7 Litvaks*, Vilnius, 2009

Katz, Dovid, *Lithuanian Jewish Culture*, Vilnius, 2004

Katz, Dovid, 'The Sounds of Silence of Jewish Lithuania' preface to *Sounds of Silence: traces of Jewish life in Lithuania*. See also: Zibutz, Isaac, Vilnius, 2009

Kauffmann, Jean-Paul, *Courlande*, Paris, 2009

Keyserling, Eduard von, *Abendliche Häuser*, Göttingen, 2004, first published: 1914

Keyserling, Eduard von, *Am Südhang*, with an afterword by Brinkmann, Richard, Stuttgart, 1998, first published: 1914–1916

Keyserling, Eduard von, *Beate und Mareile. Eine Schlossgeschichte*, Munich, 1998, first published: 1903

Keyserling, Eduard von, *Die dritte Stiege*, Göttingen, 1999, first published: 1892

Keyserling, Eduard von, *Feiertagskinder*, Zürich, 2006, first published: 1919

Keyserling, Eduard von, *Fräulein Rosa Herz: eine Kleinstadtliebe*, Göttingen, 2000, first published: 1887

Keyserling, Eduard von, *Fürstinnen*, Munich, 2005, first published: 1917

Keyserling, Eduard von, *Harmonie: Romane und Erzählungen*, Munich, 1998, first published: 1905

Keyserling, Eduard von, *Im stillen Winkel: Erzählungen*, Zürich, 2006, first published: 1914

Keyserling, Eduard von, *Schwüle Tage*, with an afterword by Taube, Otto von, Zürich, 1954, first published: Berlin, 1904

Keyserling, Eduard von, *Wellen*, Berlin, 1911

Kimberley, Nick, 'Arvo Pärt: a musical journey', liner notes with the double CD *Arvo Pärt: a portrait*, Naxos, 2005

Koc, Richard A., *The German Gesellschaftsroman at the Turn of the Century; a comparison of the works of Theodor Fontane and Eduard von Keyserling*, Bern, 1982

Kohn, Jerome, 'A Jewish Life: 1906–1975', preface to Arendt, Hannah, *The Jewish Writings*, New York: Schocken, 2007

Krastiņš, Jānis, *Jugendstil in der Rigaer Baukunst*, Michelstadt-Neuther, 1992

Krastiņš, Jānis, *The Art Nouveau Architecture of Riga*, Riga, 1998

Krastiņš, Jānis, *Mihails Eizenšteins, Zwaigne* nr. 10, Riga, 1989

Krause, Tilman, 'Der Fontane in Moll: ein Plädoyer für den zu Unrecht vergessenen Erzähler Eduard von Keyserling', *Die Welt*, 9 January 1999

Kremer, Gidon, *Une enfance balte*, Arles, 1999

Krielaars, Michel, 'Aleksej II, Kerkvorst die tegen de macht leunde', *NRC Handelsblad*, 6 December 2008

Kross, Jaan, *Keisri hull*, Tallinn, 1978

Kross, Jaan, *Professor Martensi ärasõit*, Tallinn, 1984

Kross, Jaan, *Mesmeri ring*, Tallinn, 1995

Kross, Jaan, *Paigallend*, Tallinn, 1998

Kruk, Herman, *The Last Days of the Jerusalem of Lithuania: chronicles from the Vilna ghetto and the camps: 1939–1944*, New Haven, 2002

Landsbergis, Vytautas, *Vainikas Čiurlioniui*, Vilnius, 1980

Landsbergis, Vytautas, *M.K. Čiurlionis Complete Works for Piano: a critical edition*, Kaunas, 2004

Levin, Dov, *The Litvaks: a short history of the Jews in Lithuania*, Jerusalem, 2000

Lévy, Bernard-Henri, 'Gary, triste comme un vieux lion …', *Le Magazine Littéraire*, March 2004

Lieven, Anatol, *The Baltic Revolution: Estonia, Latvia, Lithuania and the path to independence*, New Haven, 1993

Löffler, Fritz, *Das epische Schaffen Eduard v. Keyserlings*, Munich, 1928

Mak, Geert, *In Europa: reizen door de twintigste eeuw*, Amsterdam, 2004

Manteuffel, Karl Freiherr von, *Meine Siedlungsarbeit in Kurland*, Leipzig, 1942

Marsden, Philip, *The Bronski House: a return to the borderlands*, London, 1995

Mertelsmann, Olaf, *The Sovietization of the Baltic States: 1940–1956*, Tartu, 2003

Miłosz, Czesław, *Rodzinna Europa*, Paris, 1959

Miłosz, Czesław, *Gedichten*, poems selected and translated from the Polish into Dutch by Gerard Rasch, Amsterdam, 2003

Miłosz, Czesław, *Beginning with My Streets: essays and recollections*, translated by Madeline G. Levine, New York, 1991

Minaudier, Jean-Pierre, *Histoire de l'Estonie et de la nation estonienne*, Paris, 2007

Morachevskii, A.G., 'Theodor Grotthuss (to 220th Anniversary of His Birthday)', *Russian Journal of Applied Chemistry*, January 2005

Mullett, Adam, 'Lithuania to pay Jewish Community', *The Baltic Times*, 11 March 2009

Pärt, Arvo, 'Erinnerungen an Heino Eller', liner notes to the CD *Neenia*, Munich, 2001

Patai, Irene, *Encounters: the life of Jacques Lipchitz*, New York, 1961

Plioplys, Audrius V., 'The Influence of M.K. Čiurlionis upon His Contemporaries', *Lituanus Lithuanian Quarterly Journal of Arts and Sciences*, 30:2, 1984

Rothko, Mark, *Äusserungen, Interviews, Texte von 1943–1961*, from the catalogue of the exhibition *Mark Rothko 1903–1970 Retrospektive der Gemälde*, Museum Ludwig, Cologne, 1988

Roze, Aina, 'Letter to My Father', in *We Sang Through Tears: stories of survival in Siberia*, Riga, 1999

Rush, Solveiga, *Mikhail Eisenstein: Themes and Symbols in Art Nouveau Architecture of Riga: 1901–1906*, Riga, 2003

Rutkis, Jānis, *Latvia, Country and People*, Stockholm, 1967

Sacotte, Mireille, *La Promesse de l'aube de Romain Gary*, Paris, 2006

Safranski, Rüdiger, *Ein Meister aus Deutschland: Heidegger und seine Zeit*, Munich, 1994

Safranski, Rüdiger, *Romantik: eine deutsche Affäre*, Munich, 2007

Savigneau, Josyane, *Marguerite Yourcenar, l'invention d'une vie*, Paris, 1990

Schlögel, Karl, *Städte lesen*, Munich, 2008, Dutch translation: Hauth-Grubben, Goverdien, *Steden lezen*, Amsterdam, 2008

Schmid, Fidelius, and Ulrich, Andreas, 'New Documents Reveal Truth on NATO's "Most Damaging" Spy', *Spiegel International*, 30 April 2010

Seton, Marie, *Sergei M. Eisenstein: a biography*, London, 1952

Smeets, Hubert, 'Ik beloof je dat we zullen vechten', interview with Eduard Limonov, *NRC Handelsblad*, 2 July 1993

Sohn, David, 'The Pogrom against the Jews', in *The Bialystoker Memorial Book*, New York, 1982

Stülpnagel, Ulrich von, *Graf Eduard von Keyserling und sein episches Werk*, Rostock, 1926

Swallow, Norman, *Eisenstein: a documentary portrait*, London, 1976

Tammsaare, A.H., *Tõde ja õigus I*, Tartu, 1926

Tammsaare, A.H., *Tõde ja õigus II*, Tartu, 1929

Taube, Otto Freiherr von, *Im alten Estland*, Stuttgart, 1944

Thomas, Morgan, 'Rothko and the Cinematic Imagination', in *Rothko: the late series*, London, 2008

Tomasi di Lampedusa, Giuseppe, *Il gattopardo*, Milan, 1960

Tomasi di Lampedusa, Giuseppe, *Viaggio in Europa: epistolario 1925–1930*, Milan, 2006

Truc, Olivier, 'Herman Simm, l'espion estonien qui a berné l'OTAN et l'UE', *Le Monde*, 3 January 2009

Turtola, Martti, *President Konstantin Päts*, Tallinn, 2002

Valiulina, Sana, *Het kruis*, Amsterdam, 2000

Venclova, Tomas, *Vilnius: a guide to its names and people*, Vilnius, 2008

Visser, Carolijn, *Uit het moeras*, Amsterdam, 2000

Volkov, Solomon (ed.), *Testimony: the memoirs of Dmitri Shostakovich as related to and edited by Solomon Volkov*, translated from the Russian by Antonina W. Bouis, New York, 1979

Weber, Richard A., *Color and Light in the Writings of Eduard von Keyserling*, New York, 1990

Williams, Emmett, *Mr. Fluxus: a collective portrait of George Maciunas 1931–1978*, New York, 1998

Wilson, Jonathan, *Marc Chagall*, New York, 2007

Wrangel, A.E., *Vospominaniya o F.M. Dostoeyskom v Siberii*, St Petersburg, 1912

Wrangel, Olaf Baron von, *Abgeordnete des Deutschen Bundestages, Aufzeichnungen und Erinnerungen*, Vol. 14, Boppard am Rhein, 1995

Young-Bruehl, Elisabeth, *Hannah Arendt: for love of the world*, New Haven, 2004

Young-Bruehl, Elisabeth, *Why Arendt Matters*, New Haven, 2006

Yourcenar, Marguerite, *Alexis ou le traité du vain combat*, Paris, 1929

Yourcenar, Marguerite, *Le coup de grâce*, Paris, 1971 (revised edition with a foreword by the author), first published: 1939

Yourcenar, Marguerite, *Quoi? L'éternité*, Paris, 1988

Zaklikowski, Dovid, 'How Jacques Lipchitz Found G-d, The Rabbi and the Sculptor', www.chabad.org

Zibutz, Isaac, *Sounds of Silence: traces of Jewish Life in Lithuania*, Vilnius, 2009

Zweig, Stefan, *Die Welt von Gestern: Erinnerungen eines Europäers*, Zug, 1944

Translation Credits

Quotes not credited below were translated from the Dutch.

Beach, John Markham (Gary): 93–4, 111
Carson, Peter (Turgenev): v
Colquhoun, Archibald (Tomasi di Lampedusa): 250–1
Crow, Robert (Pärt): 290, 290–1
Dunn, Greg (Tuglas, Rahumägi, Kross): 300, 393, 394
Frick, Grace (Yourcenar): 228
Gary, Romain with Camilla Sykes (Gary): 127, 128–9
Gregor, Mary J. (Kant): 190
Howard, Joan E. (Savigneau/Yourcenar): 231
Kimber, Robert and Rita (Arendt, Jaspers): 192, 211
Leach, Catherine S. (Miłosz): v, 102, 106, 113–4, 256–8
Malone, Tony (Keyserling): 233, 237, 238
Marshall, Herbert (S. Eisenstein): 53, 54
Miller, Gary (Keyserling): 237
Morgan, Bayard Quincy (Keyserling): 234
Neugroschel, Joachim (Döblin): 103–4
Osers, Ewald (Safranski): 207
Seton, Marie (S. Eisenstein): 64, 66, 70, 72
Young-Bruehl, Elisabeth (Arendt, Jaspers): 192, 194, 195, 207, 210, 212, 213

Secondary sources
Bergan, Ronald, *Eisenstein: a life in conflict*: 50, 51, 58, 60
Figes, Orlando, *Natasha's Dance: a cultural history of Russia*: 63, 66
Rush, Solveiga, *Mikhail Eisenstein: themes and symbols in Art Nouveau architecture of Riga 1901–1906*: 50

Acknowledgements

The translator would like to thank David Golding for his many improvements to the text, and Greg Dunn and Leino Mandre for their invaluable contributions on matters Estonian and beyond. A special word of thanks to David Bellos for taking the time and trouble to help out a random translator in need of an accurate quote.